CRIME, MADNESS, & POLITICS
IN MODERN FRANCE

CRIME, MADNESS, & POLITICS IN MODERN FRANCE

The Medical Concept of National Decline

ROBERT A. NYE

PRINCETON UNIVERSITY PRESS | PRINCETON, N.J.

HN
440
.P8
N94
1984

for Mary Jo and Lesley

CONTENTS

ACKNOWLEDGMENTS

A Junior Humanist Fellowship from the National Endowment for the Humanities, which financed a trip to France, enabled me to begin this study in 1972. Subsequent grants from the College of Arts and Sciences and the Research Council of the University of Oklahoma, and from the American Philosophical Society supported later trips to France. The Research Council was also generous with last-minute help for illustrations and copying.

I am indebted to the staffs of several libraries for help, in particular those of the Archives nationales and the Bibliothèque nationale in Paris, the municipal libraries of Lyon, Toulouse, and Nancy, and the university library at Lausanne, Switzerland. In this country I used the collections at the University of Oklahoma, the University of California at San Diego and at Berkeley, Princeton University, and the Institute for Advanced Study.

I have profited considerably from having spent the academic year 1981-1982 at the Institute for Advanced Study, not as a member, but as the grateful spouse of one. Much of the writing of this book was done in the incomparable scholarly environment the Institute provides for its guests. Mary Jo's industry and talent made it possible. A partial sabbatical leave from the University of Oklahoma played no small role in making this year such a fruitful one.

Other persons over the years have provided splendid settings for work. I am especially thankful to Vikki and Michael Lockwood, Jeanne-Marie and Tom Barnes, and Ingrid and Jim Scobie, who is greatly missed.

Many friends and colleagues have read or criticized portions or drafts of this book. I owe thanks to John Biro, Gary Cohen, John Gillis, Pat Hutton, Dave Levy, Guido Ruggiero, Bob Shalhope, Henry Tobias, and Sabetai Unguru. I feel a special obligation to Charles Rosenberg, who read the whole manuscript. Kris and Guido Ruggiero and Franz Moehn helped keep the man inside the scholar of sound mind for an entire year. Lee Congdon knows how much our conversations meant to me.

Martha Penisten heroically transformed disorderly batches of manuscript sent through the mail into the finished typescript. She has made

ACKNOWLEDGMENTS

the whole process of writing and revision more pleasant for me, and I am thankful for her help. I would also like to express my appreciation to Christine Williams for her indispensable assistance at certain stages of this study. Miriam Brokaw and Ed Tenner at Princeton University Press have given patient aid and advice in editorial matters, as has my colleague, Gary Cohen. Barbara Westergaard performed a careful and thorough copyediting.

As my friends and family have learned, some of the more exotic terms of *fin-de-siècle* medical pathology have crept into my daily speech as pejoratives. Though this process has helped persuade me of the ease with which such transitions are made, I apologize to all the "idiots of the will" and "moral imbeciles" of my acquaintance, and to my daughter Lesley, who risked the label "degenerate" if her homework was not done by 9:30 P.M.

I cannot set limits on my debt to Mary Jo. She has provided to me some portion of all those elements required to write a book: inspiration, criticism, sympathy, and time. She has so enriched my work and my life that I can no longer untangle what is hers and what is mine.

INTRODUCTION

When I began this study, my principal interest was in crime, most particularly in the emergence of a discipline of scientific criminology out of an amorphous body of anthropological, sociological, and ethical thinking. The book that has finally resulted is a general survey of social deviance in France from the mid-nineteenth century to the eve of World War I. There are various reasons that account for the expansion of the subject beyond its original scope.

First, it was soon evident to me, as it has been to everyone else who has looked through the older criminological literature, that crime was seldom treated as an isolated phenomenon, even by those who were most eager to establish scientific criminology as an autonomous discipline. Criminality was invariably regarded as part of a spectrum of social pathologies and other forms of deviance, of which crime was sometimes the cause, sometimes the expression. It seemed impossible for contemporaries to address homicide or shoplifting without speculating on the degree of insanity in killers, hereditary perversity in thieves, or alcoholic degeneracy in both. Other forms of social deviance—prostitution, suicide, and sexual perversion—were treated in much the same manner. It became clear that contemporaries thought these different variations of deviance were linked together more profoundly than we believe today.

There can be little doubt that the dominant concepts that related one form of deviance to another, and explained their origin and their nature, were biological ones. This was so, I discovered, not only for the specialists who studied these phenomena, but also for politicians and intellectuals, and for the journalists who helped shape popular culture. The purveyors of these biological concepts were not academic laboratory scientists; these were few in number, and as a group poorly equipped to apply and popularize an ideology of deviance. The most powerful spokesmen for this unified way of viewing social deviance were doctors. Medical men had enough training in basic science to be credible as scientific mediators between the mysteries of the clinic and the vexing problems of everyday life. Doctors were also well organized, thoroughly secular and political in their outlook, and fierce defenders of their professional and social prerogatives. In the late nineteenth century, with a glut of medically trained professionals in the market-place, it made excellent sense for doctors to expand their domain by claiming special expertise in formerly nonmedical fields. Thus, in the course of the 1880s and 1890s, crime, alcoholism, prostitution, suicide, and other social pathologies gradually joined insanity as subjects on the agenda of French medicine. It was in this era that the theoretical foundations were laid for the intrusive medicalization of the twentieth-century welfare state.

However, it was also clear that a medical model of deviance was not thrust on the French by a conspiracy of medical experts who hid behind a screen of technical language. Doctors and psychiatric specialists did attempt to expand their domain, but they were often invited to do so by politicians and administrators, by jurists, and by those who guided popular culture. Medical knowledge seems to have grown in public esteem in the course of the nineteenth century, but there seems little doubt that this advance was a product of the reciprocal requirements of both organized medicine and society itself.

What appears to cry out for explanation are the historical reasons for the extraordinary valuation of medical knowledge in late nine-teenth-century French life, and for the widespread application of that knowledge to problems of deviance. Michel Foucault and his acolytes have written some extremely suggestive accounts of aspects of this process of medicalization, but in his own work Foucault has eschewed traditional causal explanations of historical change and has mocked the efforts of social historians to explain changes in medical ideology by reference to social events. Yet, if one examines the history of the period following the Franco-Prussian War of 1870, and the preoccu-pations of educated Frenchmen and Frenchwomen in that era, the reasons for the popularity of a medical model of deviance emerge with some clarity. These reasons, as I argue in some detail, were rooted in the altered geopolitical situation of the defeated and divided nation and in the bleak ruminations that followed on the possible fall of La Grande Nation from great power status.

Of particular concern to the French were the health and well-being of a population that had been, in Napoleon's day, the largest in con-tinental Europe outside European Russia. Close attention to these mat-ters revealed rapidly falling birthrates and a host of social pathologies that appeared to call into question both the quantity and the quality of the French population. Ironically, these concerns were entrusted to a new Republican leadership, which was in the process of fulfilling the foiled political fantasies of a century of Republican militants. The thor-oughly secular outlook of the new Republican leadership was unusually compatible with a scientific and medical mode of social analysis; under the spur of the internal and external events of the era, a medical model of cultural crisis developed that exercised a linguistic and conceptual imperialism over all other ways of viewing the nation's plight. If this model of crisis was *medical* in nature, it served the thoroughly *cultural* aim of explaining to the French the origins of national decadence and the weaknesses of their population. Through this model the French perceived and labeled social deviance, and through this model they sought the means to cure it. The essentially biological nature of this model meant that deviance was perceived and analyzed in unusually deterministic terms, with definite consequences, as I hope to show, for the treatment of deviants.

I wish to emphasize, however, that this book is not so much a study of deviance in France during this period, as it is a study of the cultural perceptions of deviance, and of the relations between those perceptions and general trends in politics and French intellectual life. It is, as a consequence, a survey of the foundations and growth of a medical model in the nineteenth and early twentieth centuries, but will also stimulate, I hope, more detailed investigations of the role played by a medical model in particular areas of interest. I have tried to consider much of the recent analytical and historical literature on this general topic, so that my account will also serve as a methodological and bibliographical introduction to the historical study of deviance, with special reference to France.

Though my original aim to study crime alone has grown into a larger project, the emphasis in the book is still on what contemporaries regarded as criminal activity. The point I wish to stress is the obvious one that, since it is a social phenomenon, crime changes, sometimes radically, over time. But perceptions of those changes are not invariably isomorphic with the reality—so far as we can determine what that is—of crime itself. The discrepancies between patterns of crime and the social responses they provoke are therefore grist for historical explanation and the unifying principle for some of the test cases in this study.

In tracing the growth of a medical model of deviance, I have followed a chronological progression. But I have frequently departed from the narrative to devote detailed attention to issues of particular importance. Among the subjects to which I have given special attention are: the passage of the Relegation Law of 1885, which transported vagrants and other so-called habitual criminals to French Guyana for life; the debate in France and Europe over Cesare Lombroso's "born criminal"; the inclusion of prostitutes, alcoholics, anarchists, "apaches," and other socially marginal types in the medical model; the crisis in expert medical testimony and the proposal of a new asylum law in 1906-1907; and the great 1908 debate on the abolition of capital punishment, the last debate of its kind in France before its definitive abolition by the new Socialist regime on September 18, 1981. I conclude by attempting to relate the medical model of deviance to a strategy of physical and moral regeneration that took the form of sportive nationalism after 1900, thereby contributing to a French nationalist revival.

As is befitting an investigation of a cultural phenomenon, this study is largely about ideas and language: the language of stereotyping and labeling, concepts of individual and social responsibility for deviant and antisocial actions, and ideas devised to explain the causes of crime and madness and to demarcate the changing boundaries between them. This is also a study of the logic by which these explanations were constructed and by which either treatment or punishment was justified. There will be occasions when some of these logical operations will seem uncommonly familiar to the reader. This is because the formulas we have devised in our own era to justify this or that course of action in the treatment of deviants often repeat those of the last century, thus mocking the claims made for the novelty of present approaches to these age-old problems. One might also conclude that the contemporary arguments used to prove the utility of capital punishment, the innate perversity of certain criminals, or the notion that criminals are *both* insane *and* responsible for their crimes are as intellectually bankrupt and ad hoc now as they were nearly one hundred years ago.

No doubt we believe ourselves more dispassionate in matters of deviance policy than nineteenth-century Frenchmen. Think, after all, of the mountains of social science and psychiatric literature we have accumulated, of the advantages of experience and the observation of past mistakes. But even supposing specialists could find some way to allow us to study the deviant more objectively and to treat him more humanely than we have done before, how can we escape the powerful social and cultural anxieties provoked by deviance that threaten to sweep it into the realm of emotion and prejudice? The example of French society in the *belle époque* reveals the power of these anxieties in modern life and the extraordinary ability they have to colonize huge portions of our consciousness.

In sum, my general aim in this book is to try to demonstrate the *historical* nature of both "scientific" and popular thinking about deviance. I discuss the dialectical process in which theories were devised by "experts" to account for the perceptions of contemporaries, then reintroduced to the general public in a variety of modes that helped shape the ways people viewed and thought about deviants. The reciprocal influences connecting political, medical, and scientific elites with the larger society are important subjects I hope this book will illuminate. Finally, I attempt to explain the particular forms that theories of deviance took in France during the half-century before the war by appealing to the historical situation of the country during the Third Republic. It was not by chance that these theories took the medical and biological turn they did; it was the result of a series of developments in the industrial West that influenced France first and most deeply, but has ended with these theories becoming an integral part of our modern outlook on deviance.

CRIME, MADNESS, & POLITICS
IN MODERN FRANCE

CHAPTER I

The Historical Study of Deviance

Until quite recently, deviance has been terra incognita for historians of post-1815 European society. Historians have been studying the "underclasses," socially marginal individuals, and deviants in the early modern period for many years. For France, the work of the English historian Richard Cobb on bandits, criminals, prostitutes, and vagrants at the end of the eighteenth century would weigh respectably in the balance against the work done on the subsequent hundred years. Despite the great volume of writing on factory workers, poverty, and the poor, we still know relatively little about deviants in modern Europe or what contemporaries thought about them. Few archival monographs of the sort that abound for the early modern era have yet appeared; it is a sign of the relative immaturity of this field that modern historians still spend a disproportionate amount of time—even as this introduction does—writing and talking about the proper methods to use in exploring this new terrain. Though it seems strange to say so, the very abundance of materials available on modern deviance has provoked some of this emphasis on method. Guided in part by social science literature, historians have gradually discovered some of the pitfalls and complexities the sources conceal.

The scholar who sets out to study the history of deviance nowadays has a rich array of methodological alternatives readily at hand. Many of these new methodologies are the offspring of academic social scientists buttressed by extensive fieldwork in contemporary settings, though some practitioners have also studied aspects of deviance in historical societies. On a more theoretical plane, the study of historical deviance has also benefited from the revitalization of Marxian theory in the last few decades. Following the appearance of Rusche and Kirchheimer's *Punishment and Social Structures* in 1939, very little work appeared that attempted to relate changes in modes of punishment directly to economic and social evolution. However, the recent development of "critical criminology," particularly in Britain and the United States, has certainly done much to enrich Marxian social theory without necessarily making Marxists of all its adherents. Also on a largely theoretical level, the work of Michel Foucault and his collaborators and disciples has had a powerful influence on thinking about the history of deviance and social marginality on both sides of the Atlantic.

The attractiveness of these new—and renewed—theoretical perspectives seems to be a consequence of a crisis in the theoretical perspective that had until recently dominated studies of crime and deviance. This perspective, which we might call, for want of a better word, the criminological perspective, has taken as its point of departure the notion that deviance must be defined as the violation of social norms of conduct, of which mental illness is simply the most serious manifestation. This "criminological" theory of deviance grew out of a systematic effort by legal reformers in the last half of the nineteenth century to find a more reliable and empirically based conception of deviance than could be found in the "classical" law codes then in place throughout Europe. These reformers rejected the legal norms of the codes and concentrated on studying the social and biological origins of deviant behavior. In the long run, this concentration on etiology had the effect of convincing contemporaries that there was indeed a thing called deviance, which could be located, investigated, and treated. The origins of this optimistic variety of epistemological positivism in criminology are traced in later chapters of this book. Thus, it was the reluctance of the legal reformers of the 1880s—and their sociological and medical allies—to accept legal norms as the basis of definitions of deviance that led to their preference for the norms of society itself.

It is important to understand that, however much they argued about the proper method for identifying and scientifically studying deviant behavior, the reformers of the classical legal codes agreed that their efforts must be directed toward distinguishing the normal man from the deviant one. They ignored the legal criteria of the formal violation of laws by criminal offenders and the official commitment of the insane to asylum care, and preferred, moreover, to disregard the traditional distinction between the criminal and the lunatic and to shape a single, synthetic method for identifying both. Their methodological eclecticism, and their universal tendency to mix legal and medical categories, are apparent in the following remarks delivered by the great Belgian legal reformer Adolphe Prins at the Third Criminal Anthropology Congress in 1892:

> One ought to be wary about generalizing. The psychiatrist has a tendency to see the insane everywhere; the physiologist has tried to explain everything as the consequence of actions of the nervous

centers. The pure sociologist is disposed in favor of social causes; the jurist sees only a guilty man who must be punished; a religious individual sees only the possibility of amelioration. There is some truth in each of the sciences but none of them can dominate or be generalized. There are normal, degenerate, and obsessive individuals both in and outside of prisons. We must learn to distinguish the delinquent from the [normal] man.[1]

Another effect of regarding deviance as antisocial behavior was the implication that the aim of social intervention should be to return the deviant to the behavioral norms of society itself. In their efforts to achieve legitimacy and to make themselves as useful as possible to the courts and administrative authorities, the new experts on deviance concentrated on the practical penal strategies or the medical therapies that might promote normalization. Nor was the defining of normality itself simply left to other experts; deviance experts were intensely interested in locating the boundary between the normal and the pathological. But they could never manage to do this abstractly, or in the absence of some crisis requiring their direct intervention. They felt most secure when pronouncing on this boundary within their own fields of technical expertise, and their conclusions were usually quite practical and nicely adapted to what they believed was required of them by the public authorities and by informed opinion.

The chief consequence of this pragmatic attitude of deviance experts has been to make the theoretical matrix they constructed analytically useless for comprehending how definitions of normality gain acceptance, or how they change over time. Since the 1880s, deviance experts have resorted to general social or medical theory for concepts that might aid them in their correctional or therapeutic work, but they have displayed a singular lack of curiosity about seeking a better understanding of the profound social and historical forces that have shaped these concepts within the larger setting of their own societies. As a result, mainstream theorists of deviant and criminal behavior have been notoriously uncritical of their own activities and unreflective about the roles deviance experts play in social control. In criminology, for example, Clarence Ray Jeffrey has argued that criminologists fail to understand that "the term 'crime' refers to the act of judging or labelling the behavior, rather than to the behavior itself. Why people behave as

[1] Adolphe Prins, *Actes du troisième congrès d'anthropologie criminelle* (Brussels, 1893), p. 268.

they do and why the behavior is regarded as criminal are two separate problems requiring different types of explanation."[2]

The renewal of thinking about deviance and social marginality that has occurred since the 1960s has promoted assaults on these blind spots, stimulating lively debates within the medical, academic, and criminological communities throughout Europe and North America. The general orientation of the criticism has inclined toward a leftist or libertarian political point of view and has favored methodologies that analyze deviance as part of larger social or historical processes. The militant political tone is in part a reaction to the fact that asylum directors and psychiatrists, penologists and criminologists, and other members of the "helping professions" have often played pliant roles as functionaries in the modern social welfare state. Deviance experts and the "total" institutions they maintain have been subjected to withering criticism on the grounds that they have failed to respect the rights and dignity of the individuals in their charge and have uncritically abetted the extension and strengthening of mechanisms for controlling marginal social types.

The well-known work of Thomas Szasz has been in the forefront of the attack on the moral and political bankruptcy of the modern asylum and institutional psychiatry.[3] Michel Foucault has also written extensively on the modern asylum as a new historical form of social control.[4] Criminology and penology have been attacked by the new school of critical criminology, many of whose adherents are outspokenly leftist in their orientation. One of the best known of these texts, Taylor, Walton, and Young's *The New Criminology: For a social Theory of Deviance* (1973) has analyzed criminology as an ideology that has traditionally reflected the political aims of the dominant classes and served the function of social repression.[5]

[2] Clarence Ray Jeffrey, "The Historical Development of Criminology," in Hermann Mannheim, ed., *Pioneers in Criminology*, 2d ed. (Montclair, N.J.: Patterson Smith, 1972), p. 464.

[3] Thomas Szasz, *The Manufacture of Madness* (New York: Dell, 1970); *The Myth of Mental Illness* (New York: Harper, 1961). On the political dimensions of this debate in recent Anglo-American historiography, see Andrew Scull, "Humanitarianism or Control? Some Observations on the Historiography of Anglo-American Psychiatry," *Rice University Studies* 67 (Winter 1981), pp. 21-41.

[4] Michel Foucault, *Madness and Civilization: A History of Insanity in the Age of Reason*, trans. Richard Howard (New York: Vintage, 1973); *Mental Illness and Psychology*, trans. Alan Sheridan (New York: Harper & Row, 1976).

[5] Ian Taylor, Jack Young, and Paul Walton, *The New Criminology: For a Social Theory of Deviance* (London: Routledge and Kegan Paul, 1973), Chapters 1-7. See also the works of Richard Quinney, especially *The Social Reality of Crime* (Boston:

It would be a mistake, however, to dismiss these attacks on the theories and institutions of traditional deviance control as simple political axe grinding. Many of these apparently politically motivated writings have been extremely fruitful methodologically. Moreover, the criticism of the traditional theories of deviance and its management is not simply the product of a militant political program; philosophers, academic social scientists, and historians have also contributed to this criticism without raising charges of political bias. It is probably impossible, and perhaps undesirable, to eliminate all ideological and politically charged concepts from any historical account of deviance; for historians, it makes sense simply to identify what is methodologically productive in recent work and distill from it insights that may benefit their own studies.

Within academic sociology, labeling theory has provided the best-known example of the effort to escape the theoretical bind of the correctional orientation of mainstream deviance theory. The work of Howard Becker, J. I. Kitsuse, Kai Erikson, Edwin Schur, and others in the early sixties attempted to describe the processes whereby individuals were labeled as deviants by agents of police, legal, or welfare authorities. Many of these theorists, employing an interactionist perspective, also postulated a kind of secondary deviance to explain how individuals labeled as deviants accepted their deviant identities and were accordingly reinforced in their deviant behavior.[6] By the late sixties a considerable opposition to labeling had appeared, and a debate was engaged that continues to the present time. Though far from settled, this debate has produced a few instructive lessons for the historian of deviance.

In the first place, critics have challenged the notion of secondary deviance as merely another failed effort to explain the etiology of deviant behavior. How, they have asked, does one explain the *initial* action of the individual who receives a deviant label, even if one can explain his subsequent behavior? It is not the label, in other words, that creates deviance in the first instance.[7] In the face of these and

---

Little, Brown, 1970). A useful review of the early literature is Gresham M. Sykes, "The Rise of Critical Criminology," *Journal of Criminal Law and Criminology* 65 (June 1974), pp. 209-213.

[6] A good review of this early period can be found in Richard V. Ericson, *Criminal Reactions: The Labelling Perspective* (Lexington, Mass.: Saxon House, 1975), pp. 1-90.

[7] This point is made in Fred Montanino's review of these issues: "Directions in the Study of Deviance: A Bibliographic Essay, 1960-1977" in Edward Sagarin, ed., *Deviance and Social Change* (London and Beverly Hills: Sage, 1977), pp. 279-286.

other criticisms, labeling theorists have retreated from some of their initial positions.[8] Some have suggested that labeling may be salvaged by incorporating the research methods of ethnomethodology and small group research. Historians cannot easily follow social scientists onto that terrain; they can, however, learn from the theorists' retreat from specific theoretical claims and their movement toward a consideration of labeling as "a perspective whose value will appear, if at all, in increased understanding of things formerly obscure."[9] The "more modest aims," in Becker's words, of this perspective are simply "to enlarge the area taken into consideration in the study of deviant phenomena by including in it activities of others than the allegedly deviant actor."[10] Taken as a simple heuristic prescription, labeling theory may be useful for historical investigation.

Another criticism of labeling deserves mention. By concentrating closely on the social agencies and processes that engaged in labeling, theorists have often ignored the broader context of values from which those labels were shaped. They have also, one critic has asserted, overlooked "the ways in which such labels changed, and especially the political processes underlying the development and imposition of labels."[11] Conceptions of what constitutes deviant behavior are not created *ex nihil* to meet the practical requirements of the agents in institutions of social control. These conceptions of deviance are constructed out of the social and intellectual elements of the culture itself, of which the political process and its ideational components are important parts. A related development has been the recent "rebirth" of the sociology of law as a method for analyzing social control and deviance.[12] We shall have the opportunity to return to this point about the renewed importance of politics for the study of deviance.

After one has acknowledged the principal criticisms made of its shortcomings, the labeling perspective appears to offer some useful insights to historians. A few social scientists have applied some of these

[8] Criticisms of the labeling perspective may be found in Walter R. Gove, *The Labelling of Deviance: Evaluating a Perspective* (London and Beverly Hills: Sage, 1975); Robert A. Scott and Jack D. Douglas, eds., *Theoretical Perspectives on Deviance* (New York: Basic Books, 1972).

[9] Howard S. Becker, *Outsiders: Studies in the Sociology of Deviance* (New York: Free Press, 1973), p. 181.

[10] Ibid., p. 179.

[11] Pat Lauderdale and James Inverarity, "From Apolitical to Political Analysis of Deviance (Minneapolis: University of Minnesota Press, 1980), p. 18.

[12] Ibid., pp. 18-19; Montanino, "Directions in the Study of Deviance," pp. 290-291; D. Black, *The Behavior of Law* (New York: Academic Press, 1976). This point has been made by Jeffrey, "The Historical Development of Criminology," p. 465.

methods to historical subjects with interesting results. George Becker, for instance, has revealed the considerable ironies in the growth of a deviant label of "mad genius" out of the self-advertising eccentricities of the "Romantic genius" of an earlier era.[13] Without adhering directly to labeling mechanisms, a few historians have studied deviant stereotyping in ways that suggest the heuristic value inherent in the general labeling perspective.[14]

The resuscitation of Marxist and conflict-oriented theories of deviance has also generated a considerable amount of controversy and has raised interest in a few quarters about their application to historical investigation. The work of Richard Quinney and Austin Turk, and the collaborative volume by Taylor, Young, and Walton have probably been the most influential in this field.[15] The adherents of this approach have attempted to show that power and its uses are crucial to any complete understanding of how certain social elements receive deviant status and attract the attention of the forces of social order. By focusing on the elite groups that make law and enforce it, and by attempting to explain the variations in the policies they formulate on the basis of the social and economic interests of these elites, conflict theorists, like labeling theorists, have reversed the traditional concentration on the criminal and his act. They have effectively introduced into the study of deviance the genuinely historical problem of the relationship of political change to underlying social and economic change.

But conflict theory, and the Marxian echoes in much of critical criminology, suffer from the usual problem with economic determinist theories of political action, namely reducing the exercise of power to a conflict of interest groups. This emphasis undervalues the obvious aspects of autonomy and continuity in the modern state, but it also risks the accusation of resembling a conspiracy theory of policy making that cannot effectively explain issues about which there is evident public

[13] George Becker, *The Mad Genius Controversy: A Study in The Sociology of Deviance* (London and Beverly Hills: Sage, 1978). See the "Foreword" by Lewis A. Coser urging other such "bridging" studies, pp. 9-11. Becker discusses the labeling "paradigm" on pp. 125-133. An older historical study using labeling concepts is Kai Erikson, *Wayward Puritans: A Study in the Sociology of Deviance* (New York: Wiley, 1966).

[14] Louis Chevalier, *Laboring Classes and Dangerous Classes in Paris during the First Half of the Nineteenth Century*, trans. Frank Jellinek (New York: Fertig, 1973); L. Perry Curtis, Jr., *Apes and Angels: The Irishman in Victorian Caricature* (Washington, D.C.: Smithsonian Institution, 1971).

[15] These include, in addition to the works cited in note 5, Richard Quinney, *Critique of Legal Order* (Boston: Little, Brown, 1973); Austin Turk, *Criminality and Legal Order* (Skokie, Ill.: Rand-McNally, 1969).

consensus. This latter weakness is particularly manifest when conflict theorists leave the realm of property crime, where their class-based explanation works fairly well, to address the questions of violent crime, capital punishment, or definitions of insanity.[16] No doubt, as this book endeavors to show, public consensus on issues of deviance is often highly influenced by the information about deviant behavior presented by elites, but one would be hard pressed to explain all episodes of general public anxiety about deviance as a product of the interests of those who dominate state power.

E. P. Thompson has argued brilliantly against the proposition that we should regard law as the direct "instrument of class power *tout court*":

> If the law is evidently partial and unjust, then it will mask nothing, legitimize nothing, contribute nothing to any class's hegemony. The essential precondition for the effectiveness of law, in its function as ideology, is that it shall display an independence from gross manipulation and shall seem to be just. It cannot seem to be so without upholding its own logic and criterion of equity; indeed, on occasion, by actually *being* just. And furthermore it is not often the case that a ruling ideology can be dismissed as a mere hypocrisy; even rulers find a need to legitimize their power, to moralize their functions, to feel themselves to be useful and just.[17]

What is clearly required is what one critic has called "more specific and historically grounded theory that can deal with the emergence and establishment of particular ideologies and institutions of justice and link these to the wider question of the evolution of specific patterns of class and power—and of responses on the part of the powerless in modern societies."[18] One recent major effort to test conflict theories as explanations of crime and disorder in nineteenth- and twentieth-century cities has concluded that these "political explanations" cannot account for "the eruption of mass protest in the last quarter-century or, more important, the long-term trends in common crime."[19] By

[16] See, in this connection, the comments of James Inverarity in "Theories of the Creation of Deviance," in Lauderdale, ed., *A Political Analysis of Deviance*, pp. 183-186, and of Pat Lauderdale and James Inverarity in "Suggestions for the Study of the Political Dimensions of Deviance Definition," in ibid., pp. 226-231.

[17] Edward P. Thompson, *Whigs and Hunters: The Origin of the Black Act* (New York: Random House, 1975), p. 263.

[18] Elliot Currie in a review of *The Social Reality of Crime* by Richard Quinney, *American Journal of Sociology* 78 (May 1973), pp. 1570-1571.

[19] Ted Robert Gurr, *Rogues, Rebels, and Reformers: A Political History of Urban Crime and Conflict* (London and Beverly Hills: Sage, 1976), p. 6. This book is the meth-

concentrating wholly on the policies formulated by elite leaderships to protect their interests, conflict theorists have slighted the clear evidence amassed by sociologists and social historians that real changes in forms of deviance occur which are the product of social and economic change.[20]

The relative proverty of narrowly political explanations of changes in the identification and repression of deviance is also a major theme in the work of Michel Foucault. Foucault is something of a mystery to historians. Though his books are on "historical" topics, they are highly stylized and are infused with a kind of moral and aesthetic intensity that is more common in literature or philosophy than in historical writing.[21] His characterization of his work as "philosophical fragments in historical workshops" does not particularly help to classify him.[22] Nor does it encourage the social historian to learn that Foucault's methodological obsession is with the charting of "discontinuities," "ruptures," and "epistemological breaks," rather than with the usual practice of revealing how continuous and unsurprising the past really is.

As Patrick Hutton has recently pointed out, however, Foucault does not object to continuity per se, but to a *continuity of meaning*, which serves as the basis for his attack on the idea of progress.[23] It makes no sense, Foucault argues, to search for "hidden continuities" if what is continued across an epistemological rupture—say, prisons—means something different to people on either side. Though he has not yet embraced the positivist notion that there are causes in history that can be invoked to explain change, he seems to be more interested now in examining the conditions under which these sudden ruptures occur than in merely describing the systems of discourse on either side, as he did, for instance, in *The Birth of the Clinic*. Thus, he concluded

odological preface to the larger comparative study by Gurr, Peter N. Grabosky, and Richard C. Hula, *The Politics of Crime and Conflict: A Comparative History of Four Cities* (London and Beverly Hills: Sage, 1977).

[20] The volume *Deviance and Social Change*, edited by Edward Sagarin, addresses several instances of this kind. An essay that uses conflict theory but that approaches this issue in a nuanced fashion is Steven Spitzer and Andrew T. Scull, "Social Control in Historical Perspective: From Private to Public Responses to Crime," pp. 265-268 in David F. Greenberg, ed., *Corrections and Punishment*, Sage Criminal Justice System Annuals, vol. 8 (London and Beverly Hills: Sage, 1977).

[21] See Alan Megill's excellent review of Foucault as historian, in "Foucault, Structuralism, and the Ends of History," *Journal of Modern History* 91 (September 1979), pp. 451-503.

[22] This phrase appears in "Débat avec Michel Foucault," in Michelle Perrot, ed. *L'impossible prison: Recherches sur le système pénitentiaire au XIX* siècle (Paris: Seuil, 1980), p. 41.

[23] Patrick H. Hutton, "The History of Mentalities: The New Map of Cultural History," *History and Theory* 20 (October 1981), p. 254.

playfully in a recent interview, "You know very well that there is no greater advocate of continuity than me: the location of a discontinuity is only the affidavit of a problem that requires resolution."[24]

For the historians who can rise above Foucault's jibes about their deification of "la société," there are rich insights in his work for the history of deviance. Foucault has been interested in the problem of deviance in many of his "historical" works because he wants to discover the ways in which power is distributed in society to effectively discipline and control those who violate social norms. Foucault does not think, any more than do the critical criminologists, that there is a thing called a "deviant" on whose objective behavior we can base a science of deviancy. He regards the question of deviance in modern societies as embedded in the discourse, that is, in the language, that members of these societies use to distinguish between normal and abnormal behavior. For Foucault, the right to make this distinction does not lie with those who appear to have the greater share of authority in society simply because they control the political apparatus or dispose of the most personal wealth; this right is inherent in the discourse that everyone must resort to when he uses language. Power is not an entity that one possesses, to use in some arbitrary way; it is instead a byproduct of the successful application of discourse throughout the whole "social body." Thus, "power must be analyzed as something which circulates, or rather as something which only functions in the form of a chain. It is never localized here or there, never in anybody's hands, never appropriated as a commodity or piece of wealth. Power is employed and exercised through a net-like organization. And not only do individuals circulate between its threads; they are always in the position of simultaneously undergoing and exercising this power."[25]

It is the virtue of this analysis for the historian of deviance that the power to locate the deviant, to punish or treat him, to segregate or reintegrate him, is not an arbitrary function exercised by a ruling elite, but a product of the willingness to employ, or to undergo, discourse. Foucault tellingly rebuts the legal positivism that regards power as an extension of the sovereign power, "which was traced out by the theoreticians of right and the monarchic institution. It is this image that we must break free of, that is, of the theoretical privilege of law and

[24] Foucault has responded here at length to a question about continuity in the institution of the prison. "Débat avec Michel Foucault," in Perrot, ed., L'impossible prison, pp. 42-43.

[25] Michel Foucault, Power/Knowledge: Selected Interviews and Other Writings, 1972-1977, ed. Colin Gordon, trans. Colin Gordon, Leo Marshall, John Mepham, and Kate Soper (New York: Pantheon, 1980), p. 98.

sovereignty, if we wish to analyze power within the concrete and historical framework of its operation."[26] Once we have "cut off the head of the king" we can see how power, in modern societies, concentrates in "micro-techniques" or in "disciplines" that are widely scattered in the social fabric.

In *Discipline and Punish: The Birth of The Prison*, Foucault tells us that these "disciplines" appeared in the late eighteenth century following the "rupture" of the French Revolution, which gave birth to modern society and dealt the death blow to the old regime. We learn that these "techniques of power" are exercised by experts who oversee "scientifico-disciplinary" mechanisms; around these mechanisms there gradually emerge the factories, prisons, schools, hospitals, asylums, and other institutions that organize these domains of discourse.[27] The social and moral force of these "disciplines," among which we can recognize the infant sciences of psychiatry, penology, and criminology, derives from what Foucault calls "the effects of truth," namely the capacity of these disciplines to implement a strategic discourse of "truth and falsity" (*vrai-faux*). This "economy" of discourse operates as a "correlative formation of domains, and of the verifiable and falsifiable discourses that accrue to them."[28] It is the capacity of these technical discourses to organize the objects within their domains into acceptable categories of truth and falsehood that earns them their legitimacy.[29]

There is one characteristic all these "disciplines" have in common, which Foucault holds to be unique to modern societies: "The discourse of discipline has nothing in common with that of law, rule, or sovereign will. The disciplines may well be the carriers of a discourse that speaks of a rule, but that is not the juridical rule deriving from sovereignty, but a natural rule, a norm. The code they come to define is not that of law but that of normalization."[30] The "society of normalization" that

[26] Michel Foucault, *The History of Sexuality*, vol. 1, trans. Robert Hurley (New York: Vintage, 1980), p. 90.

[27] Michel Foucault, *Discipline and Punish: The Birth of the Prison*, trans. Alan Sheridan (New York: Pantheon, 1977), pp. 170-194.

[28] Foucault, "Débat avec Michel Foucault," in Perrot, ed., *L'impossible prison*, pp. 54-55.

[29] Foucault, *Power/Knowledge*, p. 93.

[30] Ibid., p. 106; see also *Discipline and Punish*, pp. 182-184. It must be clear that the process by which a "discourse" receives the sanction of veridicality (veridiction) is for Foucault a pragmatic one that by no means meets the epistemological requirements of a realist philosophy of science. From time to time he will suggest that there is a distinction between the veridical standards of these "discourses" and "science." *The History of Sexuality*, vol. 1, p. 54. In general, however, he seems to adhere to the notion of "rationality" favored by Bachelard and Canguilhem as the

is the product of the systematic application of these norms is the zero point against which all deviations are measured; it is the experts within the "disciplines" who are responsible for implementing these measurements.

A principal theme of this book is the way in which a wholly medical standard of normality achieved an overwhelming influence within the human and medical sciences. In the historical reconstruction of this development, it is most useful to do as Foucault has done and regard the changes in discourse employed in these disciplines as strategic in nature; reorientations of discourses occur because there are continuous battles within their boundaries between competing epistemological, political, and cultural positions. Foucault has retreated from the portrait of monolithic "epistemes" that he provides in his early work; he is now willing to acknowledge the existence of periods of "shambles" within discursive systems, and of periods of conflict between them, though this is still an underdeveloped theme.[31]

Foucault has been criticized by historians for ignoring the qualities of the human actors within his linguistic grids. How, asks Jacques Léonard, can one write the history of strategy without generals or of machinery without operators? And can one conclude from the existence of a discourse of normalization that nineteenth-century society actually underwent some sort of massive normalization?[32] Foucault's

---

basis for measuring knowledge claims in the sciences. Though there is not space to discuss this interesting question at length, there are two chief consequences of this position for Foucault's work. First, the "truth" of a scientific discourse is established on the strength of a certain internal coherence that is essentially logical and linguistic and which does not rely directly on experimental procedures. When a scientific "discourse" is abandoned in favor of a new one, as happened in psychiatry in the 1860s and 1870s, it is not because the old one failed to account for certain anomalous facts on a purely empirical level, but because of certain "strategic" considerations adopted by the "discourse" (not the psychiatrists themselves) at the prompting of a kind of cultural logic. The second consequence of this essentially pragmatic epistemology is the tendency for Foucault to treat science as an instrumental if not an ideological entity: what he has called the "disciplinary police of knowledge." The most troubling feature of this stance is the obvious one of relativism. By his own epistemological standards, his critique of the "disciplines" is itself a "discourse" whose worthiness must be judged by the same pragmatic measurements he has applied to others. Of course, it is possible that Foucault would not find this as grave a problem as most. If he is primarily interested in promoting a cultural crisis, as many have alleged, then this sort of epistemology is a good place to start.

[31] Foucault, *Power/Knowledge*, pp. 208-209.

[32] Jacques Léonard, "L'historien et le philosophe," in Perrot, ed., *L'impossible prison*, pp. 13-15; see Megill, "Foucault, Structuralism, and the Ends of History"; also my "Crime in Modern Societies: Some Research Strategies for Historians," *Journal of Social History* 11 (1978), pp. 499-504.

response is that to query him from the standpoint of historical detail is to misleadingly pit "little true facts against big vague ideas."[33] But that, of course, is exactly what the historian must do if there is to be any more precise understanding of the way societies have responded to their deviants than Foucault is able to provide—the case of Pierre Rivière being the notable exception[34]—in his rather general studies. One must test his theories, as Léonard has written, in the "disorder, the indifference, the jungle" of history.[35]

One of the first things one finds upon entering this jungle from the Olympian heights of theory is politics. Without forgetting the exaggerations of Marxian conflict theory about the primacy of state authority in defining and repressing deviance, one must recognize the crucial role politicians play in formulating laws that address the division between the normal and the pathological. If one considers politics in nineteenth-century France as possessing a discourse of its own, one discovers that it could be regularly influenced by the discourses of the medical and social sciences and could influence their language and their "strategies" in turn. Indeed, much of this book is about the dialectical relationship between politics and law on the one hand, and the political aspirations of the experts in the deviance professions on the other.

It is the great merit of the theoretical perspectives I have discussed here, whatever weaknesses they may possess, to have indicated the perils of regarding social deviance of all varieties as a property of the deviants themselves. One cannot, as the traditional criminological perspective would have it, study the behavior of deviants and conclude that one thereby understands the meaning of deviance. All these recent perspectives treat deviance as a *process* in which societies confer a social meaning on certain acts they consider deviant. This process is far from being an arbitrary one; it reflects the values, the anxieties, and the cultural norms of any society. What is more, the context of values and anxieties out of which standards of normal and pathological are shaped changes over time, sometimes radically so. As I have tried to indicate in this survey of these perspectives and the criticisms that have been mounted against them, the ways in which attitudes toward deviance are shaped and legitimized are highly complex. The historian who ignores this complexity risks misrepresenting a society's conception not

[33] Foucault, "Débat avec Michel Foucault," in Perrot, ed., *L'impossible prison*, p. 29.

[34] Michel Foucault, ed., *I, Pierre Rivière, Having Slaughtered My Mother, My Sister and My Brother . . . A Case of Parricide in the Nineteenth Century*, trans. Frank Jellinek (New York: Pantheon, 1975).

[35] Léonard, "L'historien et le philosophe," p. 12.

15

only of the pathological, but of the limits of the normal and acceptable as well.

If we turn now to an examination of recent historical work on deviance, we find that some of the distortions inherent in the traditional criminological approach have been perpetuated. This problem is especially grave for historians of modern eras who often have at their disposal reams of official statistics that can be subjected to quantitative analysis. The era of modern criminal statistics began in the 1820s in France, and most industrial societies had begun the regular collection of data on crime, suicide, mental illness, and other sources of official anxiety by the 1850s. These figures were not gathered or analyzed by contemporaries so that late twentieth-century social scientists and cliometricians could write learned treatises on the history of social pathologies. They were gathered by public officials who often had very concrete uses for them already in mind or who hoped to discover some clue that would help in the practical formulation of policy. Indeed, the history of statistical theory clearly reveals the extent to which the collection of data and their mathematical analysis are social constructions.[36]

The history of deviance in prestatistical eras has escaped the tyranny of official statistics, if not the tyranny of numbers, because researchers who dip into medical and criminal archives gain a vivid impression of the complex forces that underlie the judgments in asylum committals and criminal convictions. The political and social bias in these judgments is often clearly apparent, and the historical interpretations based on them must make allowance for it.[37]

By the same token, historians who have written on forms of deviance for which official statistics are less variegated than criminal statistics, more obviously opaque, or simply incomplete, have been forced to situate their subjects in specific institutional, social, or cultural domains. This certainly has been the case for the history of madness, sexuality,

[36] For the history of British statistics, see Donald A. MacKenzie, *Statistics in Britain, 1865-1930: The Social Construction of Scientific Knowledge* (Edinburgh: Edinburgh University Press, 1981). See also Ted Porter, "The Calculus of Liberalism: The Development of Statistical Thinking in the Social and Natural Sciences of the Nineteenth Century," Ph.D. dissertation, Princeton University, 1981.

[37] Some examples of this sort of research are Guido Ruggiero, *Violence in Early Renaissance Venice* (New Brunswick, N.J.: Rutgers University Press, 1980); Barbara Hanawalt, *Crime and Conflict in English Communities, 1300-1348* (Cambridge, Mass.: Harvard University Press, 1979); Joel Samaha, *Law and Order in Historical Perspective; The Case of Elizabethan Essex* (New York: Academic Press, 1973); A. Abbatiateci, et al., *Crimes et criminalité en France sous l'ancien régime* (Paris: Colin, 1971).

prostitution, alcoholism, and suicide.[38] Historians of modern crime, however, have regularly had resort to official statistics, because, as with those who risk life and limb to climb mountains, they were there.

Most historians who use official statistics at all make the ritual genuflections about their defects, though this has not deterred many from counting even so. There is disagreement about how unreliable official statistics are: at one extreme is J. J. Tobias, who thinks them useless;[39] at the other are V.A.C. Gattrell and T. R. Hadden, who find it quite possible to use them for most purposes.[40] Most commentators fall somewhere in between. The chief problem with official statistics is that they measure only *legal* crime, that is, actual trials in the courts, or the *apparent* crime that is reported to police but for which no criminal indictment is delivered—for lack of evidence, or other reasons.[41] The statistics are mute on so-called *real* crime, some of which never reaches the attention of the police at all. On the absence of the "dark numbers," Leon Radzinowicz has written, "Who can say what our attitude towards the criminal—in emotional terms as well as in terms of practical policy— would be if the whole, or at least a large segment, of the dark figures were brought to light?"[42]

Radzinowicz's comment raises another issue for the historian of crime who wishes to have the fullest possible account of the social perceptions

[38] It is impossible in a brief space to do justice to the richness of the historical literature in these areas. The conclusions from some of these works are incorporated into my text at appropriate points. Among the most outstanding are Andrew T. Scull, *Museums of Madness: The Social Organization of Insanity in Nineteenth-Century England* (London: Allen Lane, 1979); Andrew T. Scull, ed., *Madhouses, Mad-Doctors, and Madmen: The Social History of Psychiatry in the Victorian Era* (Philadelphia: University of Pennsylvania Press, 1981); Robert Castel, *L'ordre psychiatrique: L'âge d'or d'aliénisme* (Paris: Editions de Minuit, 1976); Alain Corbin, *Les Filles de noce: Misère sexuelle et prostitution aux 19ᵉ et 20ᵉ siècles* (Paris: Aubier, 1978); Brian Harrison, *Drink and the Victorians: The Temperance Question in England, 1815-1872* (Pittsburgh: University of Pittsburgh Press, 1971); Susanna Barrows, "After the Commune: Alcoholism, Temperance, and Literature in the Early Third Republic," in John Merriman, ed., *Consciousness and Class Experience in Nineteenth-Century Europe* (New York: Holmes and Meier, 1979), pp. 205-218.

[39] John Jacob Tobias, *Crime and Industrial Society in the Nineteenth Century* (London: Penguin, 1972), pp. 18-25, pp. 256-308.

[40] V.A.C. Gattrell and T. B. Hadden, "Criminal Statistics and Their Interpretation," in E. A. Wrigley, ed., *Nineteenth-Century Society: Essays in the Use of Quantitative Methods for the Study of Social Data* (Cambridge: Cambridge University Press, 1972), pp. 336-396.

[41] The distinction between crimes brought to trial and those not tried is recognized by most Western law codes.

[42] Leon Radzinowicz, *Ideology and Crime* (New York: Columbia University Press, 1966), p. 64.

of crime trends by contemporaries. Though the public is certainly coached by officials using statistics to support their arguments, most public consciousness of crime comes from a myriad of other sources: news accounts, literature, theater, popular culture, personal experience, and word of mouth. Aggregations of "cold and impersonal numbers," Robert Merton has argued, even for "pervasive social problems . . . are apt to arouse small public attention [compared to] problems, less serious even when judged by the beholder's own values, which erupt in the spotlight of public drama."[43] We need not go so far as Tobias, who suggests that the opinions of most contemporaries about crime are more accurate than statistics, but we must bear in mind that crime figures cannot in themselves reconstruct for us the degree of anxiety people felt about crime or the emotional climate provoked by dramatic episodes.

An important related issue is the possibility that episodes of public collective violence, not in themselves "criminal," might heighten public anxiety about crime and therefore provide a better index of anxiety about it than official statistics. Without explaining why, Lodhi and Tilly indicate that the close relationship of crime and disorder must be something that "people simply want to believe."[44] T. R. Gurr has observed the same relationship in his massive study of nineteenth-century urban crime. He offers the explanation that though they are phenomena of a different order, crime and collective disorder "are often treated as if they were similar. Both threaten some people's sense of well-being, and both lead to concerted demands for the reestablishment of order."[45] Neither Gurr nor Lodhi and Tilly could find evidence in the crime statistics alone to explain the surges of public concern about crime control that occurred so often in the nineteenth century.

There are other flaws in the official legal statistics that prevent us from simply regarding them as lower approximate totals for "real" crime. Noting the remarkable stability of crime rates in France from 1850 to 1950, Jacques Léauté has returned to the suggestion initially proposed by Enrico Ferri that police and legal institutions became "saturated" with criminals around mid-century and were prevented, for fiscal considerations, from expanding any further, thus keeping

[43] Robert Merton, "Social Problems and Sociological Theory," in Robert Merton and Robert A. Nisbet, eds., *Contemporary Social Problems* (New York: Harcourt, Brace, 1966), p. 713.

[44] Abdul Lodhi and Charles Tilly, "Urbanization, Crime, and Collective Violence in Nineteenth-Century France," *American Journal of Sociology* 79 (September 1973), p. 296.

[45] Gurr, *Rogues, Rebels, and Reformers*, p. 10.

legal crime rates at a level of artificial equilibrium.[46] Obviously, as Gattrell and Hadley have noted, the effects of any changes in policing must be carefully anticipated, but so must the creation or abolition of jurisdictional authority, such as occurred for juvenile criminals (together with changes in the age of majority) everywhere in Western Europe in the modern period. Shifts in the nomenclature of crimes or the creation of new categories of criminality also present difficulties. Public drunkenness was made a crime in France in 1873, bringing 4,000 new charges a year in the correctional courts, thus complicating, it would appear, the interpretation of long-term aggregate figures. Michelle Perrot has also suggested that a growing official reluctance to prosecute certain archaic "crimes," such as forest offenses and poaching activities, led to a diminution of the legal rates that preceded any decline in actual crime.[47]

Most of the recent historical work that relies largely or wholly on the court records of "legal" crime has sought to correlate the relationship of crime with social phenomena such as urbanity, urbanization, population growth, and industrialization.[48] But, as Perrot has indicated, the figures may also be used to chart changing rates of acquittal and conviction or the application of extenuating circumstances. These rates must also be used with some care since the nature of evidence used in court against crimes of violence and crimes of theft made the granting of extenuating circumstances and criminal non-responsibility in the former cases much more likely. One cannot, as has been done recently, conclude that French juries (and, by extension, the French) were less concerned about violence than theft because of the higher proportion of convictions in property crimes.[49]

In the end, the limitations of official criminal statistics are such that

[46] Jacques Léauté, *Criminologie et science pénitentiaire* (Paris: Presses Universitaires de France, 1972), pp. 224-225; André Davidovitch has made a similar point about the stability of these figures compared to the steady growth of *apparent* (unprosecuted) crime. "Criminalité et répression en France depuis un siècle (1851-1952)," *Revue française de sociologie* 2 (1961), pp. 39-40.

[47] Michelle Perrot, "Délinquance et système pénitentiaire en France au XIXᵉ siècle," *Annales. Economies, sociétés, civilisations* 30 (1975), pp. 72-74.

[48] In addition to Lodhi and Tilly, "Urbanization, Crime and Collective Violence," and Gurr, *Rogues, Rebels, and Reformers*, see Vincent E. McHale and Eric A. Johnson, "Urbanization, Industrialization, and Crime in Imperial Germany," *Social Science History* (Fall 1976), pp. 45-78, and (Winter 1977), pp. 210-247; also Howard Zehr, *Crime and the Development of Modern Society: Patterns of Criminality in Nineteenth-Century Germany and France* (London: Croom Helm, 1976).

[49] James M. Donovan, "Justice Unblind: The Juries and the Criminal Classes in France, 1825-1914," *Journal of Social History* 19 (Fall 1981), pp. 89-108.

one may use them to describe patterns of criminal behavior only at great risk. The statistics on crime are not "facts" as they were made out to be by penologists and criminologists until fairly recently. They are likely to tell us more, Pierre Deyon has written, about the "fears and obsessions" of society, than about "the transgressions of delinquents."[50] Michelle Perrot has expressed this strategy toward statistics with great clarity, bringing it directly into the perspective that I have been at pains to elaborate in this introduction: "There are no 'criminal facts' as such, only judgments about crime that create criminal acts and actors. In other words, there is a criminal discourse that expresses the obsessions of a society. The whole question is in knowing how this discourse functions and changes, to what extent it expresses reality, and how it is shaped by various mediating factors."[51]

There have been some interesting efforts to put this general strategy into operation by studying criminal trials in detail: "Murder trials," Richard Cobb has written, "light up the years and give a more precise sense of period than the reigns of monarchs or the terms of office of presidents."[52] Roger Williams has used various murder trials to highlight the social and political history of the Second Empire,[53] and Mary Hartman's fine comparative study of French and English murderesses between the 1840s and the turn of the century nicely illustrates the way in which trials open a window into the social history of the era.[54]

More central to this study are historical studies of trials in which issues of criminal responsibility and punishment were debated between doctors and lawyers using different forms of discourse. The classic example of this approach, Charles Rosenberg's *The Trial of the Assassin Guiteau: Psychiatry and Law in the Gilded Age* (1968), uses the occasion of a presidential assassination to explore the tensions within the psychiatric community between rival therapeutic strategies. For French history, Foucault's collaborative work on a parricide case of the 1830s (*I, Pierre Rivière*) deserves wider attention from historians than it has received. Not only does Rivière's confessional tract provide a striking account of French peasant life from within, but the historical essays

[50] Pierre Deyon, *Le temps des prisons: Essai sur l'histoire de la délinquance et les origines du système pénitentiaire* (Lille: Editions universitaires, 1975), p. 112.

[51] Perrot, "Délinquance et système pénitentiaire," p. 72.

[52] Richard Cobb, "The Memoires of Marie Besnard," *A Second Identity: Essays on France and French History* (London: Oxford University Press, 1969), p. 287.

[53] Roger L. Williams, *Manners and Murders in the World of Louis-Napoleon* (Seattle: University of Washington Press, 1976).

[54] Mary Hartman, *Victorian Murderesses: A True History of Thirteen Respectable French and English Women Accused of Unspeakable Crimes* (New York: Schocken, 1977).

from Foucault's collaborators illuminate admirably the scientific, political, and social currents that converged in Rivière's humble Normandy courtroom.[55] Roger Smith has recently applied this sort of contextual analysis to a series of murder trials in Victorian Britain. In Smith's view, the close examination of the boundary line between medical and legal discourse in trials signifies far more than a simple dispute between the rival voluntarist and determinist points of view of competing professional communities. The medico-legal dispute is important because "the existence of determinist and voluntarist discourses was endemic, as it still is, in the culture as a whole." Thus "medical evidence of insanity advanced in status only with the social phenomenon of the increasing acceptability of the determinist discourse."[56]

It has been my intention in this brief methodological introduction to discuss some of the approaches I have found most useful in studying the history of deviance in France during the Third Republic, and to identify some of the historian's most dangerous pitfalls. I have attempted to show that there is a variety of strategies that may be employed which reveal deviance to be an aspect of social, political, and cultural history and not simply a phenomenon that can be studied in isolation from these processes. Ideas about deviance are a genuine component of the history of mentalities and therefore a key to a fuller understanding of what French men and women believed were the limits of tolerable behavior during this period. It is a particular object of this study to show how a largely medical matrix provided the conceptual unity that encouraged the French to link together various forms of deviance. This procedure allowed many to see in each deviant act the promise of others to come, creating a climate of anxiety about pathology that amounted to a national obsession.

[55] Foucault, ed. *I, Pierre Rivière.*

[56] Roger Smith, "The Boundary between Insanity and Criminal Responsibility in Nineteenth-Century England," in Scull, ed., *Madhouses, Mad-Doctors, and Madmen,* pp. 373, 375. See, in general, Roger Smith, *Trial by Medicine: Insanity and Responsibility in Victorian Trials* (Edinburgh: Edinburgh University Press, 1981).

CHAPTER II

Criminal Law, Medicine, and Justice in the Nineteenth Century

The purpose of this chapter is to provide a brief introduction to the legal and institutional settings that governed questions of deviance in nineteenth-century France. There is a long prehistory to the medicalization of deviance that gained momentum during the Third Republic. An important part of this prehistory is the evolution of the criminal law from Napoleonic times to 1871, including the historic relations of political and legal authority that were perpetuated in the enabling legislation of 1875. French penal law and penal procedures are different enough in several important respects from the Anglo-Saxon legal tradition that I believe a short presentation of these differences would be useful.

A closely associated matter is the development of the legal framework for the certification and commission of individuals to asylum care in the nineteenth century. Since the passage of the 1838 law that set these procedures in place, there has been no substantial revision until the present day; there were, however, several efforts to modify or repeal the 1838 law in the course of the century, culminating in the efforts of 1907-1913, which I examine in detail. Moreover, there was a notable growth in the number of public asylums after 1838 and important changes in the theory and structure of psychiatry that must be discussed.

As the number of asylums grew after 1838, so did the number of penitentiaries, a reflection of the political influence of the powerful penitentiary movement during the July Monarchy. Though it appeared the penitentiary movement might suffer an early death, owing to Louis Napoleon's preference for other forms of punishment, support for cellular imprisonment enjoyed a vigorous revival after the fall of the Second Empire, and the legislative work that the reformers of 1846-1851 had been unable to bring to fruition was finally completed. To understand the full meaning of the 1885 legislation, we must follow the course of the penitentiary movement right up to the passage of the so-called relegation law that repudiated it.

Finally, I wish to review the historical situation of general medicine in France from the end of the eighteenth century until the founding of the Third Republic. As I hope to demonstrate, the attitudes and value orientations that encouraged doctors to apply medical criteria to the whole of social life at the end of the nineteenth century were already present, in embryo, at the end of the eighteenth century. The encroachment of an essentially medical outlook on traditional legal, philosophical, and moral domains was well underway by 1870; doctors had succeeded in making their technical knowledge indispensable to public health officials and the courts, and the medical avant-garde had made excellent progress toward the goal of situating medicine in the mainstream of modern scientific materialism. Later, when a series of demographic, social, and economic problems threatened to capsize the political equilibrium of the Republic, French medicine was prepared to guide the nation through the treacherous waters of pathology to the safe harbor of the normal.

The criminal law of the old regime was made, on the whole, to serve the interests of monarchical despotism. Criminal procedure, by the Ordinance of 1670, was inquisitional in nature; it left little in the way of effective defense to the accused, save a cumbersome process of establishing the evidence for a crime that occasionally defeated the prosecution's most heroic efforts. As is well known, punishment was fierce and generally physical. Torture to extract confessions was customary, and death, which could be brought about in a variety of horrible ways, was the penalty for a large number of crimes that would qualify today as minor offenses.[1] As Foucault has dramatically shown, punishment was not simply a judicial ritual, but a political one, designed to punish the body of a criminal who had offended the person of the monarch.[2] The forms that punishment took and the procedures for establishing the guilt and innocence of the accused were thus an expression of the principle of monarchical sovereignty that formed the basis of Bourbon absolutism.

It is not surprising that among the first acts of the revolutionary assemblies was the creation of a penal code that overturned the in-

[1] See Foucault, *Discipline and Punish*, pp. 32-46. For a fine recent account of the criminal law and criminal procedure of the old regime, see André Laingui and Arlette Lebigre, *Histoire du droit pénal* (Paris: Cujas, 1979).

[2] Foucault, *Discipline and Punish*, pp. 47-48.

quisitional judicial procedures of the old regime and replaced them with an accusatory system patterned on the English system, whereby an individual was allowed an adequate legal defense and was guaranteed a trial by a jury of his peers. As a reaction against the judicial despotism that had prevailed under the absolute monarchy, judges under the new system were allowed virtually no discretion whatsoever. To guarantee the equality of justice before the law, punishments were fixed in advance by the code for each crime, with an ascending hierarchy of punishment that corresponded to the increasing seriousness of the crime. These codes, and the Napoleonic Code that replaced them in 1810, placed far greater emphasis on the offense than on the offender in determining punishment.[3] This was a characteristic of all the "classical" codes formulated in Europe during this era; they sought to equalize punishment by having all crimes punished alike, banishing forever the capricious treatment of individual suspects by all-powerful royal magistrates.

For the legislators of the 1790s, law was the guarantor, par excellence, of the liberties of individual citizens. It is easier to understand the great contemporary prestige of Rousseau's "general will" if one regards the task of the lawmakers of that era as the remaking of a society from which all the traditional institutions had disappeared. Their principal weapon in this work was the law, which, to achieve the degree of legitimacy necessary for its function, had to be universally regarded as the expression of the will of the people. In the care of the legislative powers that gave it life, the law was the most effective dike that could be built against the return of despotism. The underlying principle that guided this essentially backward-looking posture was the doctrine of law as minimum constraint; article five of the Declaration of the Rights of Man held that any act not expressly prohibited by the law could not be restrained or punished. And the list of prohibitive laws, moreover, "should only provide punishments strictly and obviously needed."

The negative manner in which this principle was expressed made it dependent, not on certain rights specified as positive and universal (bill of rights), but on the continued willingness of the state to respect the ideal of minimum constraint and to interfere as little as possible

---

[3] See the discussion of the comparative aspects of the code by Marc Ancel, "Introduction," in Gerhard O. W. Mueller, ed., *The French Penal Code*, trans. Gerhard O. W. Mueller and Jean F. Moreau (London: Sweet and Maxwell, 1960), pp. 10-13.

with the private activities of citizens.[4] The suspicion with which the legislators of the 1790s regarded the judiciary, which might, after all, modify the law in applying it, led them to exalt codified law and statute, and to limit the autonomy of the magistracy in every way possible. A major effect of this outlook was to inhibit the development of a case-law jurisprudence in France and to make the legislature and the judicial administration the unique guardians of public liberties.[5] In the words of Robespierre, the tribune of the "general will," "if the law may be interpreted, augmented, or applied according to the will of an individual, man is no more under the safeguard of the law, but in the power of the one who interprets or augments it."[6]

Napoleon, for reasons different from those of the Republican parliamentarians who preceded him, also wished to limit the independence of the judiciary. Article 127 of the penal code of 1810 made it a breach of duty with loss of civil rights for any judicial official to interfere "with the exercise of the legislative powers either by making rules involving legislative dispositions, or by preventing or impeding the enforcement of one or several laws, or by questioning whether a law should be promulgated or executed." This stricture also applied to the judicial officer "who acts beyond the scope of his powers by encroaching upon matters which are subject to the jurisdiction of administrative authorities, either by issuing rules in such matters, or by enjoining the execution of orders issued by the administration."[7] If one adds to these restrictions the fact that magistrates were never in practice regarded as irremovable for purely political reasons, and were dependent on the minister of justice both for their appointments and their promotions, it is clear that the nineteenth-century magistrate was ill equipped to resist the will of the political powers.[8]

In the hierarchy of courts set up during the Napoleonic era, the function of determining the constitutionality of law lay not with a court, however dependent it might be, but with the upper parliamentary assembly, a practice willingly perpetuated by all successive regimes.

[4] Jean-Pierre Machelon, *La République contre les libertés? Les restrictions aux libertés publiques de 1879 à 1914* (Paris: Presses de la fondation nationale des sciences politiques, 1976), pp. 17-18.

[5] René David, *French Law: Its Structure, Sources, and Methodology*, trans. Michael Kindred (Baton Rouge: Louisiana State University Press, 1972), pp. xii-xiii.

[6] Quoted in Jean-Pierre Royer, *La société judiciaire depuis le XVIIIᵉ siècle* (Paris: Presses Universitaires de France, 1979), p. 183.

[7] Mueller, ed., *The French Penal Code*, p. 59.

[8] On the willingness of the administration to enforce article 127, see Machelon, *La République contre les libertés*, pp. 46-54; see also Royer, *La société judiciaire*, pp. 175-189, 247-250, 304-316.

Still, the worst effects of the absence of any "supra legislative norm" for protecting individual liberties might have been successfully vitiated had the revolutionary Declaration of the Rights of Man achieved the status of positive law during the course of the century. Certainly each successive regime after 1814 vowed to uphold these rights, but after the Constitutions of 1791 and 1793 they did not appear as enumerated and positive rights in any later constitutional structures. Ironically, when the enabling legislation that created the Third Republic in 1875 was passed, it did not mention the Rights of Man at all. As Machelon has explained this omission, "why proclaim again in the preamble of the constitution, or in the text itself, principles that had been largely recognized by earlier, less liberal regimes?"[9] The Republican leaders of that period repeatedly swore to uphold the Declaration in their public pronouncements, but they did so as the confident heirs of the legislative apparatus of the new Republic, from which vantage point they would be the final arbiters of issues relating to the abridgment of individual rights.

Throughout the period with which this study is concerned, therefore, the protection of the liberties of private citizens was only as strong as the willingness of legislative assemblies to recognize and ensure them. Throughout the Third Republic, justice ministers interfered in various ways with the administration of justice; assemblies suspended judicial nonremovability at their pleasure; magistrates and public prosecutors were suddenly removed from cases that threatened to turn in embarrassing directions; and there were numerous instances of "special" legislation contrived to limit the rights of certain individuals or groups "in the public interest." For all the above reasons, and for others I mention later, it seems absurd to deny, as Foucault has done, that the political elite in France had the power to impose its views on deviance upon the rest of society. There is simply no advantage to be gained in ignoring the role political power played in the Third Republic in helping to shape the views of deviance held by specialists and the general public alike.

If the judicial hierarchy suffered at the hands of its political masters in the nineteenth century, it did enjoy, by compensation, a considerable degree of latitude in dealing with suspects in criminal cases. The liberal system of criminal procedure adopted in 1791 had employed several measures—including indictment before a grand jury—that safeguarded the rights of the accused and ensured an orderly trial. The rise in brigandage and other forms of internal disorder during the

9 Machelon, *La République contre les libertés*, p. 30.

Empire, not to mention Bonaparte's own authoritarian instincts, led to the reappearance of some of the older inquisitional techniques in the Code of Criminal Procedure of 1810, in force in France until the late 1950s.[10] The grand jury was replaced by the *juge d'instruction*, whose task it was to gather evidence in support of a criminal indictment. The judge was allowed to do his work in camera, could detain the suspect at his pleasure, and was not obliged to inform the suspect of the charges against him or the nature of the evidence in their support. The examining magistrate was encouraged to obtain evidence or confession by duplicity and manipulation; he was aided in his efforts by the denial of legal counsel to the suspect until a reform of 1897.[11]

The assizes courts, where felonies and more serious crimes were tried, provided legal defense and a jury trial for an indicted criminal. However, the three presiding judges were not enjoined from taking sides in the legal battle; as the obedient "servants of the law" they readily engaged in the prosecution, the presiding magistrate often usurping the interrogation from the prosecutor. Until 1881, the chief assizes magistrate traditionally made a "summary" of the evidence against the accused, which amounted to a second presentation by the prosecution.[12] The same procedures existed in the network of correctional courts, which tried misdemeanors, except that the guilt or innocence of the accused was not decided by a jury at that level, but by the same magistrates who had conducted the interrogation. Reforms in the course of the nineteenth century only partly mitigated the inquisitional nature of criminal trials. There was constant pressure from judicial liberals during the Third Republic to restrain the especially extensive powers of the *juge d'instruction*; but one suspects that successive ministers of justice found it useful to have such procedures available when they wished an indictment for their own political reasons, for they limited their intervention in behalf of the suspect to an occasional ministerial circular.[13]

Unlike its more rigid sister code of procedure, the penal code itself underwent a considerable liberalization during the nineteenth century. Much of this process consisted of the final elimination of some ferocious

[10] For a discussion of these changes see Gordon Wright, *Between the Guillotine and Liberty: Two Centuries of the Crime Problem in France* New York: Oxford University Press, 1983), pp. 32-37.

[11] See the sections on the examining magistrate in A. Esmein, *A History of Continental Criminal Procedure: With Special Reference to France*, trans. John Simpson (Boston: Little, Brown, 1913), pp. 437-443, 505-507, 550.

[12] Ibid., pp. 556-562.

[13] Machelon, *La République contre les libertés*, pp. 144-145.

punishments that had been retained in the 1810 code (mutilation, the pillory, death for some crimes against property), but the most important factor in reducing the harshness of the code was the introduction of a greater measure of judicial discretion. The 1810 code had provided discretion to the judge in determinations of the sanity of the accused, there being no criminal responsibility for one in a "demented state" (*état de démence*) at the time the crime was committed (article 64). But in 1832 a general measure of "extenuating circumstances" was admitted to the code, permitting judges and juries the opportunity to impose a lesser sentence (within limits) than the one decreed in the code for a particular crime. This measure was the first in the general trend toward the individualization of punishment in modern criminal law that has now entirely transformed the binding legalism of the classical code into an instrument allowing the judge to fit the punishment to the criminal.[14]

Article 64 and the allowance for extenuating circumstances provided the opening wedge for the entrance of the medical expert into the judicial process. In view of the political and legal infringements on their autonomy, magistrates were initially jealous of the few discretionary rights they did enjoy, but they gradually permitted the appearance of more experts into the courtroom to assist in the deliberations on insanity and mitigating circumstances. In the course of the century, more and more discretionary authority was accorded to judges, including pronouncement of a suspended sentence in 1891 and a number of special provisions for juveniles, culminating in a reform of 1912 that in effect transformed the trial as a deliberation on evidence for crime into a hearing for determining the proper mode of rehabilitative "correction."[15] The Parole Law of 1885 even extended discretion about punishment beyond the courtroom. It put the authority to determine the proper length of a sentence (at least within a stipulated maximum and minimum) in the hands of the penitentiary administration and changed the criterion for length of incarceration from the nature of the crime committed to the potential for rehabilitation in its author.

The provisions for discretion in selecting the length and even the

[14] Ancel, "Introduction," in Mueller, ed., *The French Penal Code*, pp. 10-13. On article 64 and its predecessors in the codes of the old regime, see Jean Imbert and Georges Levasseur, *Le pouvoir, les juges, et les bourreaux* (Paris: Hachette, 1972), pp. 206-211.

[15] On this general evolution in relation to juveniles see Imbert and Levasseur, *Le pouvoir, les juges, et les bourreaux*, pp. 332-334; Henri Gaillac, *Les maisons de correction, 1830-1945* (Paris: Cujas, 1971), pp. 225-258; Jacques Donzelot, *The Policing of Families*, trans. Robert Hurley (New York: Pantheon, 1979), pp. 96-168.

nature of punishment in nineteenth- and twentieth-century criminal justice cannot be fully understood until they are connected with the parallel growth of claims by medical experts for greater influence on the system. The question whether to treat or to punish, and how much, is one that a judge of 1810, for whom punishments were decreed by law, would never have asked. By the end of the nineteenth century these questions were being asked regularly by judges, medical experts, and juries. Judges did not graciously yield this terrain to doctors; nor did medicine seize it by fiat. The process was gradual, marked by compromise and persuasion, and has proven to be more or less permanent in its effects.

As was the case with the criminal justice system, the state closely supervised the asylum system and the admissions procedure in the nineteenth century. But while the administration of justice was originally a collaborative effort of the state and the magistracy, the administration of madness was the result of a bargain struck between the state and French medicine. As we shall see again in the following section on the prisons, the state's right to punish and intern was essentially a political privilege based on the philosophical assumptions of Enlightenment rationalism and liberalism. First implemented within the revolutionary assemblies of the 1790s, this right was a derivation of the contract theory of sovereignty. Since the state was formed as a contract between free and rational individuals, the state disposed of the legal right to punish individuals who willfully violated the collective arrangements governing social activity. However, both the civil and the penal code excused from the normal sanction of the law those who were not responsible for their actions, on account of either insanity or *force majeure*. The freedom to act and contract was forfeited by an individual afflicted with "mental alienation." Such an individual received a civil *interdiction*, and the responsibility for his actions passed to a *tuteur* or *curateur* who became the guarantor of his actions under the social contract. In the expression of Lamarche-Vadel and Preli, "marked by the penal and civil code with irresponsibility, the mentally ill individual is a subject permanently or temporarily in breach of contract."[16]

The birth of the modern asylum was in part an effort by the French state to provide a *tuteur* for an insane individual who had none or whose relations were unable or unwilling to assume the responsibility. The *tutelle* or legal guardianship, could be passed to the director of

[16] Gaëtane Lamarche-Vadel and Georges Preli, *L'asile, Recherches*, no. 31 (February 1978), p. 19.

the asylum, usually a doctor, who would then become legally liable for the actions of his charges.[17] There is some irony in the notion that modern "total institutions," prisons and asylums, were created by a generation for whom liberal individualism and rationalism were cherished values. As Robert Castel has succinctly argued, "the identification of criminality and madness as requiring a specific treatment stands out against the background of a liberal regime: to the extent that the contractual structure of society is generalized, it rejects those who cannot play its games. Liberal society and the total institution function smoothly as a dialectical couple."[18]

Prior to 1838 there was no formal or legal basis on which *tutelle* could be transferred and individuals committed to medical care in public institutions. Private care for the insane had existed well before 1789, but public provision for them was haphazard at best, consisting after the mid-seventeenth century of the "general hospital," which was the "homeland to the poor, to the unemployed, to prisoners, and to the insane."[19] These institutions, which endured until the Revolution, were essentially catchall welfare institutions with a quasi-juridical status. Apart from simple poverty, the most common reason for the internment of a lunatic was the threat he posed to public order. The conception of dangerous lunacy was not a subtle one; the wild and raving behavior of a hallucinating individual was commonly accepted as the touchstone of danger in the old regime.

For the lunatics who happened to be accused of crimes, the authors of article 64 of the penal code very likely had a simple criterion of that sort of mind, since they defined insanity only as "dementia" and provided no other guidelines for the magistrate to follow. By the same token, the law of 1832 on mitigating circumstances for crimes, unlike many other penal codes, did not specify the "mental states" that qualified as mitigating ones, nor has case law since 1810 done much to qualify or displace the term favored by the authors of the Napoleonic Code.[20] In the absence of more precise criteria for deciding questions

---

[17] Ibid., pp. 20-23.

[18] Castel, *L'ordre psychiatrique*, p. 80.

[19] Foucault, *Madness and Civilization*, p. 39.

[20] The first major jurisprudential qualifications of "state of *démence*" did not come about until after the First World War. Even then, on the crucial question of "un simple égarement passager, du à émotivité," Levasseur and Doucet comment laconically, "La jurisprudence ne l'a pas admis." Moreover, drunkenness has never been admitted as a factor, in principle, of *force majeure*. French law is practically unique in not specifying the nature of extenuating circumstances. Some law codes are quite precise about which mental states subject a lawbreaker under their influ-

of penal irresponsibility, judges readily asked specialists in mental illness, though the code made no specific provision for their doing so. It was the very generality of the code that called forth the expert medical witness and made him a partner in the judicial process. But the magistrate did not have any clear legal guidance on what he should do with the lunatic once he was found penally irresponsible, with or without the assistance of a medical expert. To sentence a lunatic to prison or hard labor must have been unthinkable to many judges, but there was no clearly defined course of action before 1838, and, lacking relations or private means, the lunatic was often released. Judges, hamstrung by the treatment of insanity in the codes, were forced to give way in the matter of the lunatic ("redoubtable and innocent at the same time")[21] to the psychiatrists.

By the 1830s, thanks to the pioneering efforts of Philippe Pinel and his great pupil Etienne Esquirol, psychiatry was well established as medicine's first area of specialization. Pinel and Esquirol, whose work at the great Parisian asylums had suggested the effectiveness of treating insanity as a form of illness, had agitated vigorously for a system of state-supported asylums where the long-term benefits of their "moral" therapy could be fully demonstrated. In pressing for institutional and legal reform the founders of French psychiatry were as much motivated by humane and philanthropic sentiments as they were by the desire to medicalize the care and treatment of insanity.[22] The celebrated "moral treatment" they employed was remarkably similar to the therapy used by their great nonmedical contemporary Samuel Tuke, whose Quaker retreat near York claimed rates of cure well above those of traditional houses of lunacy.[23]

Pinel and Esquirol aimed to cure their patients by engaging them in a paternal dialogue. The object of this dialogue was to engage the rational element remaining in the otherwise alienated mind of the

---

ence to the full application of the law. See Georges Levasseur and Jean-Paul Doucet, *Le droit pénal appliqué* (Paris: Cujas, n.d.), pp. 231-233, 304-310.

[21] Castel's phrase in *L'ordre psychiatrique*, p. 48.

[22] This is the view of Castel, ibid., pp. 23-58, 85-103; on Pinel and his philanthropic motivations in particular see Gladys Swain, *Le sujet de la folie: Naissance de la psychiatrie* (Toulouse: Privat, 1977). Jacques Petit prefers the formula "humanitarian intentions, repressive aims" to describe the sentiments of psychiatry in this period. "Folie, langage, pouvoirs en Maine-et-Loire," *Revue d'histoire moderne et contemporaine* 27 (1980), p. 559.

[23] On Tuke's method and its origins see Foucault, *Madness and Civilization*, pp. 241-278; also Andrew Scull, "Moral Treatment Reconsidered: Some Sociological Comments on an Episode in the History of British Psychiatry," in Scull, ed., *Madhouses, Mad-Doctors, and Madmen*, pp. 105-118.

madman "in order to mobilize it against his madness."[24] By dealing in this way with only the rational core of the patient's mind, and generally treating him in a firm yet dignified manner, the founders of psychiatry hoped to help the patient reconquer the terrain of his mind lost to unreason. Though this mode of treatment required an amount of time and human resources that were never available in the nineteenth-century asylum, it is important to emphasize the essentially optimistic and curative outlook of this first generation. Their nosological system and their therapeutic methods were all of a piece: cures were possible, mental illness was not an inevitable life sentence in detention, and psychiatry was not yet so much in league with the police and the cause of public security as it was with the social philanthropy of the period.

The therapeutic and scientific claims of psychiatry, and the apparent helplessness of the courts in the face of madness, helped make of the law of 1838 on the *régime des aliénés* "an alliance between psychiatry and the government, excluding justice from any right to look upon madness."[25] The courts played no role whatsoever in either of the two main forms of internment, and their power to intervene in behalf of someone unjustly committed was in practice limited to initiatives by the madman's legal guardian or by the madman himself. The courts gained the right to recommend the transfer of the *tutelle* of nonresponsible individuals to asylum care, but in the end that decision did not rest with the judge, but with the prefect and the doctor. No court could order the release of an interned individual until the medical authorities deemed him cured and the prefect or responsible local officials no longer regarded him as a threat to public security.[26]

The new law met the needs of the state by outlining a process whereby individuals who were regarded as a threat to public order could be certified and committed to a network of public asylums provided by the law. A prefect, mayor, or police official could have an individual committed as a danger to public security under the auspices of a *placement d'office*; if the asylum doctor concurred, and a later medical examination confirmed that diagnosis, the commitment was final. By using a *placement volontaire*, families and private citizens without means could have a family member committed with the least possible inconvenience. The law required of them a doctor's cosignature, and a subsequent confirmation by the asylum psychiatrist. By making medical opinion a requirement for both internment and release, the 1838 law

---

[24] Swain, *Le sujet de la folie*, p. 97.

[25] Lamarche-Vadel and Preli, *L'asile*, p. 25.

[26] Castel, *L'ordre psychiatrique*, pp. 218-222. The full text of the law may be found in Castel, pp. 316-324 and in Lamarche-Vadel and Preli, *L'asile*, pp. 33-42.

probably did more to legitimize an autonomous medical psychiatry than any other single event.

The deficiencies of the law with respect to the rights of individuals labeled as insane are obvious enough. Though there is no way of judging how often it might have occurred, the private *placement volontaire*, requiring only the compliant attestation of a family physician, was a potential source of disaster for many an unloved rich or eccentric family member. In practice, the law was invoked much more often by local officials, who often had their personal grudges as well, than by private individuals.[27] Before the law had been in place twenty-five years, it had become pro forma for liberals and Republicans to denounce its inadequacies as an instrument for defending the civil liberties and financial assets of the insane.[28] Under the Second Empire, Republicans made of the "scandals" of arbitrary internment a grand public cause that compensated them in part for the controls placed on criticisms of the political regime itself. Moreover, owing to the resistance of departmental councils, only a slight majority of French departments actually built asylums at all, and these were often badly run and overcrowded, making therapeutic activity practically impossible.[29] Jacques Petit found only rare instances of cures in the asylums of Maine-et-Loire in 1840, and, according to Claude Quetel, by 1900 "one no longer cures the mentally ill: one keeps them and waits for them to die."[30] As we shall see, the therapeutic failures of the Pinelian asylum

[27] Castel gives the figures for 1853 of 6,473 *placements d'office* and 2,609 *placements volontaires*. *L'ordre psychiatrique*, p. 239. One probable cause for this disproportion seems to have been a collusion between local officials and family members to have individuals committed by *placement d'office* so the family could be spared the expense of a subsidy for the patient's care under *placement volontaire*. In the public asylums of the more tightly run departments, such as the Yonne under Haussmann's direction, there was every effort to stop this practice and increase the number of patients whose relations paid a subsidy. See Gerard Bléandonu and Guy Le Gaufey, "The Creation of the Insane Asylums of Auxerre and Paris," in Robert Forster and Orest Ranum, eds., *Deviants and the Abandoned in French Society*, trans. Elborg Forster and Patricia Ranum (Baltimore: Johns Hopkins University Press, 1978), pp. 200-204.

[28] Machelon notes these protests, but comments that the nineteenth-century legislator "did not give much priority to the question of the individual rights of the insane." *La République contre les libertés*, pp. 191-192.

[29] Exceptions to this rule were the Seine and Yonne departments for which Haussmann was the energetic prefect in the 1840s and 1850s. Even he, however, was forced to use considerable manipulation in obtaining full funding for the departmental asylum. See, in general, Bléandonu and Le Gaufey, "The Creation of the Insane Asylums of Auxerre and Paris," pp. 180-212.

[30] Petit, "Folie, langage, pouvoirs en Maine-et-Loire," p. 554; Claude Quetel,

provoked some new responses from French psychiatrists at the end of the century, though these were still presented under the ambiguous banner "humanitarian intentions, repressive aims."

As was true of the asylum system, the network of penitentiaries envisioned by the early nineteenth-century reformers was never completed. Financial considerations were certainly important reasons for this failure; the state was reluctant to assume the whole cost of construction and maintenance, and departmental notables resisted making up the shortfall to construct prisons, much as they had done with the proposal to finance insane asylums. We shall have the chance to examine in detail the *coup de grâce* that was given the penitentiary ideal in 1885, but the reasons for the failure to build prisons in adequate numbers are not simply financial ones; the ideal had begun to collapse much earlier from a combination of causes. Unlike its companion total institution for the insane, the prison was not assimilated into the domain of medicine before 1914. The utilitarian calculus of pleasure and pain, and the religious notion of punishment as a moralizing expiation were the root ideas of the model penitentiary, and they helped the prison to resist the process of medicalization that invaded institutions for the insane. Nonetheless, there was some infiltration of medical and other experts into the prison system in the earliest experiments, which has continued to the present day. The "model" prison of the end of the twentieth century looks very little like the huge disciplinary fortresses of the 1800s, but it is fully equipped with psychiatrists and other experts on behavior modification. It is not my point in this book to trace the progress of the infiltration of medicine into prisons, which, in any event, had made little impact by 1914, but to show the influence that medical ideas had on limiting the concept of punishment itself. Medical evaluations of crime and criminals helped create a climate in which support for penal reform was suspect and in which other alternatives enjoyed a great measure of sympathy.

The origins of the European penitentiary movement were roughly contemporary with the first efforts to reform the criminal codes of the old regime. Cesare Beccaria's *Dei delitti e delle pene*, the classic argument for the proportionality of crime and punishment, appeared in 1764, and the English reformer John Howard's book *The State of the Prisons*

"L'asile d'aliénés en 1900," *L'histoire* 7 (December 1978), p. 26. In his *Museums of Madness*, Andrew Scull discusses the rise in the numbers of incurables in the British asylum system after the 1840s, the reaction of the psychiatric community, and the gradual abandonment of "moral treatment." See his explanation for these phenomena and his discussion of the rising numbers of the insane, pp. 188-194, 222-253.

was published in 1777. The whole logic of the reform of law was to make punishment a deterrent by increasing it in regular measures to just offset the potential criminal's willingness to risk his criminal act. The ferocious and arbitrary punishments of the old regime had to be abolished because they could not be accommodated in a system in which these calculations were the rule. If the threat of punishment should fail to deter, however, the punishment itself ought to be of the sort that would moralize and rehabilitate the criminal, rather than break him physically and spiritually as was the practice at the time. Prisons, though assuredly much reformed versions of the keeps and jails of eighteenth-century Europe, could accomplish these ends admirably. Proportionality could be managed by adjusting the length of the sentence; equality was assured by the uniform nature of each cell in every prison; and humanity was served by the great decrease of violence in the "gentle way of punishment."

Penitentiary reform nourished practically utopian expectations in many progressive thinkers and politicians during the era of its greatest appeal, 1780-1840. Philosophers invented model prisons by the score, of which the most famous was Jeremy Bentham's design for a panopticon (1791). Reformers like Alexis de Tocqueville and Gustave Beaumont went to America to study the relative merits of the famous Pennsylvania and Auburn prison regimes. Legislators all over Europe debated the advantages of employing this or that system, and nearly all societies ended by making a commitment to prison building on a wide scale. The aim of the reformers was to give punishment a greater burden and a more important task than it had in the eighteenth century. In Foucault's words the objective was "to make of the punishment and repression of illegalities a regular function, coextensive with society; not to punish less, but to punish better; to punish with an attenuated severity perhaps, but in order to punish with more universality and necessity; to insert the power to punish more deeply into the social body."[31] The prison was to be a "universal school" that would educate prisoners and citizens alike.[32] Sites were chosen to inspire awe, and tours were conducted in the hope that the order and efficiency of the prison might be an inspiration to the society at large.[33]

[31] Foucault, *Discipline and Punish*, p. 82. For the hopes of the English penitentiary reformers see Michael Ignatieff, *A Just Measure of Pain: The Penitentiary in the Industrial Revolution, 1750-1850* (New York: Pantheon, 1978), pp. 44-79.

[32] Catherine Duprat, "Punir et guérir: En 1819, la prison des philanthropes," in Perrot, ed., *L'impossible prison*, p. 91.

[33] These were the hopes of the reformers at Geneva, who built a prison in 1825 partly after Bentham's specifications. Robert Roth, *Pratiques pénitentiaires et théorie*

Fashions in penitentiary design waxed and waned. The one feature they all shared was cellular imprisonment, which was the way reformers hoped to end the promiscuity and demoralization of collective incarceration. In France, after an early interest in the Auburn system, which stipulated collective work in silence during the day and cellular isolation at night, interest grew in the competing Pennsylvania system, especially after the publication in 1833 of Tocqueville and Beaumont's report on American prisons. This regime favored nearly complete individual isolation, in the conviction that this provided the best environment for reflection on past crimes and thus for the moralization of the wrongdoer. The Auburn system had the powerful support of the influential reformer Charles Lucas, but in the course of debates during the 1840s, the stricter Pennsylvania system gained in favor.[34] A bill supporting a system of isolation by day and night was on the point of being approved in 1848 when revolution broke out. Efforts to have the measure reintroduced during the Second Republic repeatedly failed. However, on account of an Interior Ministry circular of 1841, work on cellular prisons had been taking place on a small scale throughout the 1840s. When the "prince-president" took command in France, forty-six modern prisons had been completed in the central prison system.[35]

Louis Napoleon abruptly terminated this quasi-legal experiment in cellular imprisonment shortly after assuming the presidency. He preferred, as he announced in a speech in November 1850, the financial, hygienic, and colonizational benefits of criminal transportation to the penitentiary regime of the liberals.[36] Bonaparte lost little time implementing this program. A law of 1854 made all serious felonies punishable by forced labor—the second highest degree of punishment in the code—to be served in penal colonies outside metropolitan France. It was this measure, rather than any humanitarian sentiments, that led to the final disappearance of the notorious penal colonies (*bagnes*) for

---

sociale: L'exemple de la prison de Genève (1825-1862) (Geneva: Droz, 1981), pp. 162-164.

[34] For the debates and Lucas's role in them, see André Normandeau, "Charles Lucas," in Mannheim, ed., *Pioneers in Criminology*, esp. pp. 144-149. See also Wright, *Between the Guillotine and Liberty*, pp. 57-69; and Patricia O'Brien, *The Promise of Punishment: Prisons in Nineteenth-Century France* (Princeton, N.J.: Princeton University Press, 1981), pp. 13-51. On the changing fashions in prisons see Roth, *Pratiques pénitentiaires*, pp. 25-45; Ignatieff, *A Just Measure of Pain*, pp. 193-204.

[35] Deyon, *Le temps des prisons*, p. 130, Normandeau gives the number as forty-seven, with fifteen in construction. "Charles Lucas," in Mannheim, ed., *Pioneers in Criminology*, p. 148.

[36] André Zysberg, "Politiques du bagne, 1820-1850," in Perrot, ed., *L'impossible prison*, p. 199.

convicts sentenced to forced labor (*forçats*). The *bagne* at Rochefort was closed in 1852, the one in Brest in 1858; the oldest in service, Toulon (founded in 1748), was finally closed in 1873.[37] But these colonies closed so that Cayenne and New Caledonia might live. The 1854 law was adopted in an atmosphere of repression and social fear that gives the lie to reformist pretenses or the expressed wish to spread the mantle of French culture abroad. The British, who had employed transportation for serious offenders in some form since the early eighteenth century, had reduced the flow of prisoners abroad to a trickle by 1854, and were on the verge of abolishing the system altogether.

In a decisive manner, the principle of rehabilitation was abandoned altogether between 1850 and 1870. Cellular isolation was wholly abandoned in favor of the collective incarceration so despised by the liberals. Whatever progressive merits he might have had in other domains, Bonaparte's instincts about criminals were of an old-fashioned authoritarian type. Together with exiling serious felons to the insalubrious regions of the South American jungle, he instituted a system of surveillance of ex-convicts and an elaborate code of *interdiction de séjour*, which prohibited former convicts from entering Paris, Lyon, Marseille, and other large cities.[38] It is clear enough that all these measures had a distinctly political utility to a nervous dictator for whom the line between political and common crime was indistinct; but this did not prevent them, all the same, from profoundly influencing penal policy long after the end of the Second Empire.

The Orleanists and liberals who had been so close to their goal in 1848 gained a second opportunity to implement their ideal of cellular imprisonment in 1872. A commission, dominated by the philanthropic liberals of the July Monarchy, met from 1872 to 1875 to study the penal system and recommend a new policy. It found the prisons and policies of the Empire without merit, and proposed the passage of a law that would mandate a regime of cellular isolation for most of the time for most prisoners. A law was passed on June 5, 1875, that implemented these recommendations, but the legislature revealed the weakness of its conviction by financing the construction of new prisons out of departmental levies. Rehabilitation and moral improvement were once again in style, but by 1881 only 10 of the 437 departmental

[37] See, in general, ibid., pp. 165-205, and Jacques Valette, "Le bagne de Rochefort, 1815-1852," in Perrot, ed., *L'impossible prison*, pp. 206-235.

[38] Deyon, *Le temps des prisons*, pp. 128-130. Also, O'Brien, *The Promise of Punishment*, pp. 226-235.

institutions had been converted to a cellular design.[39] A law of 1893 mandated state administration of the most scandalous regional prisons, and promised subventions and financial incentives, but this effort was largely a failure.

The relative failure of prison reform in France is not simply another example of the French taxpayer wearing his pocketbook on the right. By the 1870s, as we shall see, convictions about rehabilitation were about to flag. This was not simply a French phenomenon. The last great burst of prison building in Europe took place in the 1860s, but this was followed by a dramatic decline of interest in the "separate system" as a cure-all for crime.[40] The reasons for this European-wide decline are complex. In part they are the practical consequence of a leveling off, in some cases a drop, in crime rates. But there was an important rise in concern in the 1870s about recidivism, a shift in interest away from the number of crimes committed and toward the nature of the individuals who were responsible for most of them.

Habitual criminals were made of sterner stuff than the usual offender. They could not be deterred by short periods of cellular imprisonment—or so their records suggested—and there was no effective legal device that could be used to single out a recidivist from other offenders and reserve for him a special punishment. Several efforts were made between 1870 and 1914 in Europe to deal with this matter. Leon Radzinowicz and Roger Hood have dealt with the English case, and judged it largely a failure.[41] The French Relegation Law of 1885 is another example of this species of penal policy.

But, as Radzinowicz and Hood have pointed out, the chief obstacle to writing a good law on recidivism that would satisfy both liberals and penal experts was the definition of, and explanation for, the habitual criminal. In England, the effort to create such a definition encouraged a search for expert opinion and technical advice. By the 1870s and 1880s there were many such experts available, and they were not stinting of their opinions.[42] The congresses of the International Union of Penal Law also clearly reveal the rise in interest at this time in knowl-

[39] Charles Bertheau gave the figure of 2,500 individual cells in all of France in 1882, of which only 1,300 had been built since 1875. *De la transportation des récidivistes incorrigibles* (Paris, 1882), p. 48.

[40] On the decline see Roth, *Pratiques pénitentiaires*, pp. 38-43; H. R. Henriques, "The Rise and Decline of the Separate System of Prison Discipline," *Past and Present* 54 (1972), pp. 61-93.

[41] Leon Radzinowicz and Roger Hood, "Incapacitating the Habitual Criminal: The English Experience," *Michigan Law Review* 78 (August 1980), pp. 1305-1389.

[42] See ibid., pp. 1313-1317.

edge about criminals that could be obtained from medicine and the social sciences. Leaving aside for the moment the role that "experts" may have played in raising the issue of recidivism in the first place, there is no doubt that medical practitioners and other specialists were prepared to accept a role as consultants in criminal matters. They had been preparing for such a role, in France at any rate, for a long while.

French medicine, Jacques Léonard tells us, only managed to free itself from the "tradition Molièresque" in which it had been historically embedded around the middle of the nineteenth century.[43] It is probably fruitless to try and identify a precise point at which the prestige and influence of the medical profession began to grow noticeably, but doctors, who had to compete with charlatans and folk healers for the attention (and fees) of the populace in the early part of the century, had achieved by 1900 a thorough monopoly of all matters pertaining to health. In the course of their rise to a position of dominance, French doctors pursued several strategies, with varying degress of success, which they hoped would raise their professional status, their income, and their social and political influence. Of course these aims are all interdependent, so that in pursuing one goal, a doctor necessarily contributed to the realization of the others. In practice, however, this did not always seem to be the case in the nineteenth century: doctors organizing to limit access to the profession were often in conflict with those seeking a wider public and political role for medical hygiene; and those seeking to make medicine more "scientific" differed from those who preferred a more traditional clinical mission for the profession. In the end most of these conflicts were harmonized to the satisfaction of all segments of the profession, and to the general benefit of the profession at large.

Despite great reforms in the standardization of medical education and licensing at the time of the French Revolution, doctors who held a degree in medicine from one of the official faculties did not advance much in income or status during the first half of the century. A law of 1803 had created two grades of doctors, those who held the *doctorat d'état* from Paris, Strasbourg, or Montpellier, and a lesser *officier de santé*. The possessor of the latter title followed a less rigorous course of study in various regional medical schools and was licensed by departmental examining committees. In reality, *officiers de santé* probably did not harbor the kinds of medical ambitions imagined by Emma

[43] Jacques Léonard, *La vie quotidienne du médecin de province au XIXᵉ siècle* (Paris: Hachette, 1977), p. 216.

Bovary's pathetic husband Charles, but as medical practitioners they were effective competitors to *docteurs* for clients, especially in rural areas.[44] Around 1848, the number of medical practitioners reached the highest level per capita of the entire century, bringing on anxiety about a "glut" of doctors and provoking intense debates about solutions to this "problem."[45] One strategy, fulfilled by a law of 1854, raised the standards for the *officier de santé*, thereby diminishing the technical gap between the two grades, while another voluntarily limited the number of doctorates in medicine, a kind of medical neo-Malthusianism aimed at producing more favorable doctor to patient ratios. The numbers of *docteurs* leveled off after 1847, moving from 10,643 in that year to only 11,995 in 1886. Meanwhile, the number of *officiers de santé* fell abruptly, declining from 7,456 in 1847, to 3,633 in 1876, and 2,794 in 1886. The overall number of practitioners fell between 1847 and 1886 from the century high of 18,099 to only 14,789.[46]

Meanwhile, doctors aggressively pursued the goal of a medical monopoly by uniting themselves in professional organizations, beginning with the Association générale de prévoyance et de secours mutuels des médecins de France (A.G.M.F.) in 1858. By the 1880s local practitioners began to form Unions des syndicats médicals to lobby for the abolition of the *officiers de santé*, though they failed to achieve legal recognition for these activities.[47] Despite internal division within the profession about the appropriateness of this goal, a law of 1893 permanently ended the junior grade of practitioner. A law of the previous year governing state medical assistance to the poor was also drafted in a form that satisfied local practitioners, who were interested in more paying clients without accompanying restrictions on their medical independence.[48] Through these strategies alone, doctors managed to

[44] Charlatans and folk healers were also viable competitors for a surprising length of time. See Matthew Ramsey, "Medical Power and Popular Medicine: Illegal Healers in Nineteenth-Century France," *Journal of Social History* 10 (1977), pp. 560-587.

[45] On the "glut" of doctors see George D. Sussman, "The Glut of Doctors in Nineteenth-Century France," *Comparative Studies in Society and History* 19 (July 1977), pp. 287-304; on the debates around mid-century, see George Weisz, "The Politics of Medical Professionalization in France, 1845-1848," *Journal of Social History* 12 (1978), pp. 1-30.

[46] These figures may be found in Jacques Léonard, *La France médicale: Médecins et malades au XIXe siècle* (Paris: Gallimard/Julliard, 1978), p. 88; on the 1854 law see Léonard, *La vie quotidienne du médecin de province*, pp. 168-169. Léonard also discusses these issues in his recent *La médecine entre les savoirs et les pouvoirs: Histoire intellectuelle et politique de la médecine française au XIXe siècle* (Paris: Aubier, 1982), pp. 201-219.

[47] On the "esprit d'association" after 1850 see Léonard, *La vie quotidienne du médecin de province*, pp. 177-189; also *La médecine entre les savoirs et les pouvoirs*, pp. 219-240.

[48] Martha Hildreth has convincingly described these organizational efforts and this legislation in "The Foundations of the Modern Medical System in France:

raise their standard of living and extract from the state a recognition of their exclusive right to treat patients in private health care.[49]

There were other strategies, however, that French doctors employed to raise the level of their corporate prestige and influence. These essentially ideological strategies much predate those based on organization or licensing; they first appeared at the dawn of modern medicine, even before the great reforms of the revolutionary period. No doubt doctors were attracted to science and materialism in the eighteenth century because, as Jacques Léonard has suggested, they believed that the intellectual outlook of the rival clergy gave aid and comfort to superstition and charlatanry.[50] But modern science also gave the eighteenth-century doctor a way of breaking down natural influences on the organism into constituent parts, each of which (climate, nutrition, air) might be understood and subjected to some degree of rational, and therefore therapeutic, control.[51]

The gradual emergence of a practical and "scientific" medicine from the academic and bookish discipline of the Renaissance tradition was not lost upon the state. The mercantile views that dominated policy making at the highest levels encouraged the bureaucrats of the monarchy to regard population as merely another physical factor, with industry and agricultural productivity, that contributed to the wealth and strength of the kingdom. The state took the initiative, therefore, in the founding of a Société royale de médecine that might coordinate medical knowledge and promote the health and well-being of the population. Foucault has argued that the willingness of doctors to engage in this sort of "noso-politics" meant that in the last quarter of the eighteenth century, doctors derived more of their prestige from their functions as public hygienists than from their functions as individual therapists. Health became an "objective of political power," and "at once the duty of each and the objective of all."[52]

After 1775 doctors regularly did surveys for the Société on diseases and epidemics that were endemic to France's predominantly rural population. In the execution of these surveys, they revealed certain attitudes and analytical dispositions that seemed to spring directly out of

Physicians, Public Health Advocates, and the Medical Legislation of 1892 and 1893," Department of History, University of California, Riverside, 1980.

[49] Léonard has discussed the rise in revenue for private practitioners in *La vie quotidienne du médecin de province*, pp. 103-107.

[50] Ibid., pp. 234-235.

[51] William Coleman, "Health and Hygiene in the Encyclopédie: A Medical Doctrine for the Bourgeoisie," *Journal of the History of Medicine and Allied Sciences* 29 (1974), pp. 399-421.

[52] Foucault, "The Politics of Health in the Eighteenth Century," in *Power/Knowledge*, pp. 169-170, 177.

their contacts with the peasantry. First, as Harvey Mitchell has shown in his review of these surveys, doctors tended to "view disease as operating within a total system and to devise therapy structures intended to nullify the morbid forces attacking it, rather than others predicated on the need to deal with specific malfunction."[53] In explaining the onset of disease, doctors favored placing the individual case in the broadest possible context, considering influences ranging from climate, geography, and soil to social life and individual character. In a manner that was typical of late eighteenth-century medicine, doctors put great weight on the "moral" factors that they supposed had a causal effect on "physical" symptoms and organic structures.[54] For doctors observing rural society, these "moral" characteristics were a compound of their observations and prejudices regarding the peasantry. On the one hand, doctors complained about the widespread moral obtuseness and superstitiousness of peasant life that made certain disorders endemic in the countryside; their profound ignorance made it difficult for the peasants to relate the symptoms from which they suffered, or to cooperate effectively with doctors in putting a "rational" therapy into operation. On the other hand, the peasant's tough and simple nature dictated that his diseases would also be simple, and that he would be able to resist many of the disorders that laid waste his more delicate countrymen in the cities. The physician explained this phenomenon by alleging that, in Donzelot's words, "instead of submitting to the artifices of dress and confinement, they enjoyed the beneficial effects of regular exercise; instead of surrendering to the passions, they were compelled by their labor to lead a regular existence."[55] The legislation of 1803 endorsed this belief by making the educational requirements for the rural *officier de santé* much less strict: "Rural people, having habits more pure than those who live in towns, have much simpler illnesses."[56]

[53] Harvey Mitchell, "Rationality and Control in French Eighteenth-Century Medical Views of the Peasantry," *Comparative Studies in Society and History* 21 (January 1979), p. 87. See also J.-P. Peter, "Une enquête de la société royale de médecine (1774-1794): Malades et maladies à la fin du XVIIIᵉ siècle," *Annales. Economies, sociétés, civilisations* 22 (1967), pp. 711-751.

[54] H. Mitchell, "Rationality and Control," pp. 87-88, 103-110; for the work of Cabanis, the chief medical theoretician of the connection between mind and body in the medicine of this era see Martin S. Staum, *Cabanis: Enlightenment and Medical Philosphy in the French Revolution* (Princeton, N. J.: Princeton University Press, 1980).

[55] Donzelot, *The Policing of Families*, p. 15; H. Mitchell, "Rationality and Control," pp. 108-109.

[56] Quoted in Charles Coury, *L'enseignement de la médecine en France* (Paris: Expansion scientifique française, 1968), p. 117.

The landmarks in the nineteenth-century history of public hygiene are numerous. Among the most important is the founding of the *Annales d'hygiène publique et de médecine légale* in 1829. The prospectus announced that "medicine does not have as its sole object the study and cure of illness, it also has a close rapport with social organization; it may aid the legislator in the preparation of laws, it often enlightens the magistrate in their application, and it invariably looks after, along with the administration, the maintenance of public health."[57] In 1848 a Comité consultatif d'hygiène publique was set up to advise the government on public health, but it met considerable resistance from department councils and from physicians who were wary of new taxes or the loss of local prerogatives.[58] It was not until the growth of a widespread anxiety about depopulation and national health in the 1880s that the Comité consultatif came into its own as a widely heeded influence on public policy; even then the chief influence was wielded by a coterie of medical professors and practitioners in the capital, and in the face of the suspicion of regional practitioners. Still, the case can be made that the medical elite, composed of medical educators and researchers, had never abandoned the goals implanted in the medical corps during its formative years. In performing a hygiene function for the state at the end of the old regime, and receiving its first public legitimation in the performance of this service, French medicine achieved a *political* sanction of its utility before it earned a social or economic one. Personal wealth and social status came in due time, as we have seen, but not until the medical community had gotten used to thinking about health and illness from a national perspective and in terms of the viability of whole populations. The habit of thinking in this manner became a more or less permanent part of the medical cosmology, despite the ebb and flow of state interest in medical knowledge.

Meanwhile, the strong intellectual ties between scientific ideology and the leaders of the new Third Republic provided the environment in which the public hygiene component of medicine could finally expand. During the 1860s and 1870s French academic medicine made a concerted effort to adopt a new "scientific" ideal of medical education, modeled in part on German higher education. This effort to capitalize on the growing prestige of science coincided with a particularly fertile period in medical research, led by the discoveries of Pasteur and Bernard, so that there was a particularly high degree of optimism about

---

[57] "Prospectus," *Annales d'hygiène publique et de médecine légale* 1 (1829), p. v.

[58] See Hildreth's discussion of this resistance in "The Foundations of the Modern Medical System in France," pp. 1, 21, n. 4.

revolutionary breakthroughs in the cure of disease both inside and outside the medical profession.[59] The new teaching corps was instructed by Jules Ferry and his heirs to teach and promote personal hygiene in the schools. Doctors and *instituteurs* were collaborators in the promotion of hygiene in local education commissions, temperance associations, and gymnastic societies. Under the Third Republic "practical hygiene became a pillar of laic morality," and politicians busied themselves with a steady flow of measures regulating foodstuffs, working conditions, and drinking water.[60] "Gentlemen, hygiene has a moralizing influence," said Martin Nadaud to his fellow legislators in 1888. "I have always remarked that men who keep themselves clean, like those who devote themselves to their work, are nearly all good citizens and heads of households."[61] This secular outlook was bluntly expressed by Doctor Jules Rochard in the *Annales d'hygiène publique* in 1885. "Hygiene," he averred, has "conquered public opinion. Its language is intelligible to everyone, and its results are evident, concrete, mathematical. It has these two advantages over therapeutics. Finally, it responds to the most deeply felt need of our era. In societies in which the level of wealth is rising and that of religious belief is going down, concern for the future and even for money itself becomes less important; the desire to feel good and die as late as possible replaces them; but only hygiene can satisfy these aims."[62]

Doctors heeded Rochard's plea to become "government men" in increasing numbers in the early Third Republic. Benefiting from their improved status as local notables, the number of doctors in the Chamber of Deputies rose from thirty-three in the legislature of 1871-1876 to sixty-two in the Chamber of 1881-1885. These were overwhelmingly Opportunist and Radical in their political sympathies, as were the eighty-one doctor-senators who sat in the upper house between 1876 and 1900.[63] These are unusual figures for modern parliamentary assemblies. No doubt they betoken in part the anticlerical zeal of many rural

[59] George Weisz has discussed this period in "Reform and Conflict in French Medical Education, 1870-1914," in George Weisz and Robert Fox, eds., *The Organization of Science and Technology in France, 1808-1914* (Cambridge: Cambridge University Press, 1980), pp. 62-66. For the developments in medical science and hygiene in this era see Léonard, *La médecine entre les savoirs et les pouvoirs*, pp. 131-185.

[60] Léonard, *La vie quotidienne du médecin de province*, pp. 209-211.

[61] Remarks made in the Chamber of Deputies on January 25, 1888, quoted in Léonard, *La France médicale*, pp. 204-205.

[62] Jules Rochard, "De l'influence de l'hygiène publique et de médecine légale 56 (1885), p. 20.

[63] These figures are in Léonard, *La vie quotidienne du médecin de province*, pp. 230-231.

practitioners, which was certainly an influence on local Republican electoral committees. But they also reflect the rise in the local economic and social status of doctors, as well as, I would argue, a growth in the authoritativeness of medical culture. There were, in any case, always plenty of doctors on hand for expert opinions on medical matters in the assemblies of the Republic.

In the end, the ideology of French medicine remained heavily informed by the public hygiene perspective throughout the nineteenth century. This perspective required doctors to consider health in the broadest possible terms as a matter for the entire population, not just a few individuals within it. But the breadth of this function also encouraged medicine to explore the population historically as well as descriptively, to examine the beliefs, the behavior, and the family histories of those who were suspected of weakening the fabric of society. It is in this sense that doctors were originally expected to fulfill the role of a "medical police," in Donzelot's words, "not understood in the limiting, repressive sense we give the term today, but according to a much broader meaning that encompassed all the methods for developing the quality of the population and the strength of the nation."[64]

The constitutive elements that were present in the ideology of the eighteenth-century "medical police" were still in existence at the dawn of the twentieth century. There was still, in 1900, the disapproval of immorality and vice that had prompted bourgeois doctors in the eighteenth century to complain of the "indecencies" of their patients. And, like their medical ancestors, *fin-de-siècle* doctors conflated moral and medical judgments in regarding character as having a formative influence on the human organism. Doctors in the late nineteenth century, as had doctors in the late eighteenth, viewed individual illness in the context of a "total system" of pathology; therapy was accordingly designed to treat the whole system, of which the illness was regarded as an expression. By the late nineteenth century, however, a dominant diagnostic model existed that provided a consensual "total system" into which medical practitioners could fit a bewildering variety of symptoms. This model, based on the bio-medical concept of degeneration, lent a nosological unity to the medicine of this period that eighteenth-century medicine had not attained. Degeneration was the perfect expression of a hygienic medicine whose primary concern was the health and moral well-being of a whole population. Though they were concerned about the effects of disease on all the French, the over-

[64] Donzelot, *The Policing of Families*, pp. 6-7.

whelming preoccupation of public health doctors by the 1880s was the health of the great towns, which they regarded as the sources of most contemporary pathologies. This distinction between urban and rural illness is yet another quality shared by late eighteenth- and early nineteenth-century medicine. The belief that the provinces nourished a Frenchman who was healthier and more vigorous than the urbanite was so widespread that it must surely be seen as a mediating factor in the universal scorn Theodore Zeldin's Parisians felt for provincials.[65]

The most important legacy of late eighteenth-century medicine to that of the nineteenth is unquestionably the emergence of the new binary term, normal-pathological during the revolution in medical perception that took place between 1790 and 1815. As Foucault has written, before the development of this new standard for measuring organic viability, eighteenth-century doctors used health as the measure of man's proper condition. When "vigour, suppleness, or fluidity," essentially mechanical and functional qualities, were lost through illness, it became the task of medicine to restore the organism to its natural state.[66] This minimalist therapeutic ideal was the result of centuries of medical empiricism and informed self-treatment, and is perfectly consistent with the harsh and restricted biological horizons of the old regime. But the elevation of medicine to the rank of first servant of public health at the end of the old regime, the transformation of its pedagogy during the Revolution, and its indispensability during the wars of Napoleon, conspired to give medicine a new social utility and a trenchantly ambitious outlook. Thus, as Foucault has stated,

> [after the French Revolution] medicine must no longer be confined to a body of techniques for curing ills and of the knowledge that they require; it will also embrace a knowledge of healthy man, that is, a study of non-sick man and a definition of the model man. In the ordering of human existence it assumes a normative posture, which authorizes it not only to distribute advice as to healthy life, but also to dictate standards for physical and moral relations of the individual and of the society in which he lives. It takes its place on that borderline, but for modern man paramount, area where a certain organic, unruffled, sensory happiness communicates by right

[65] For a summary of Parisian attitudes toward provincials in the nineteenth century, see Theodore Zeldin, *France, 1848-1945*, vol. 2 (London: Oxford University Press, 1977), pp. 29-85.

[66] Michel Foucault, *The Birth of the Clinic: An Archaeology of Medical Perception*, trans. A. M. Sheridan Smith (New York: Random House, 1975), p. 35.

with the order of a nation, the vigour of its armies, the fertility of its people, and the patient advance of its labours.[67]

Medicine after 1815 adjusted its standards more to normality than to health. Georges Canguilhem has shown how, in order to make their work scientific and value free, medical scientists attempted to locate biological norms objectively through quantitative measurements. They imagined that they could measure normal and pathological states by the "intensity" or the rates of certain vital functions. "Normal" states were, accordingly, a kind of statistical average; "pathological" ones were characterized by "extreme" rates of function. The former states received, Canguilhem notes, "the normative character of the state called normal,"[68] while the latter state was described as morbid or abnormal, or, in the equilibrium imagery of Claude Bernard in the 1850s and 1860s, as "inharmonious" and "disproportionate."[69]

Foucault has speculated on the broad implications of this new way of dividing up the world of life:

Furthermore, the prestige of the sciences of life in the nineteenth century, their role as model, especially in the human sciences, is linked originally not with the comprehensive, transferable character of biological concepts, but, rather, with the fact that these concepts were arranged in a space whose profound structure responded to the healthy/morbid opposition. When one spoke of the life of groups and societies, of the life of the race, or even of the "psychological life," one did not think first of the internal structure of *the organized being*, but of the *medical bipolarity of the normal and the pathological*. Consciousness lives because it can be altered, maimed, diverted from its course, paralyzed; societies live because there are sick, declining societies and healthy, expanding ones; the race is a living being that one can see degenerating; and civilizations, whose deaths have so often been remarked on, are also, therefore, living beings. If the science of man appeared as an extension of the science of life, it is because it was *medically*, as well as *biologically*, based; by transference, importation, and, often, metaphor, the science of man no doubt used concepts formed by biologists; but the very subjects that it devoted itself to (man, his behaviour, his individual and social re-

[67] Ibid., pp. 34-35.
[68] Georges Canguilhem, *Le normal et le pathologique*, 3d ed. (Paris: Presses Universitaires de France, 1975), p. 25.
[69] Ibid., pp. 34-40.

47

alizations) therefore opened up a field that was divided up according to the principles of the normal and pathological.[70]

Nineteenth-century doctors did not shrink from applying these principles widely, or from justifying their intervention in social or political affairs on the basis of their specialized knowledge. This was not the scientific arrogance of Flaubert's Monsieur Homais, or the grandiloquent positivism that Martin du Gard ridicules in Jean Barois and his friends; it was a basis for judging all living matter that had as profound a relationship to common sense as it did to philosophy. The binary term normal-pathological could be used to sanction social norms and social fears deeply felt by the masses with the approval of medical science. The terminology could also be used effectively to enlighten or persuade a nonscientific public because it is conceptually isomorphic with so many other binary terms that regulate the perception of social life: moral-immoral, criminal-honest, sane-insane, violent-passive. The power to pronounce on the nature of the norm and its pathologies gave nineteenth-century medicine a social authority out of all proportion with the numbers or the status of doctors. This power gave to medicine and its ancillary sciences the right to mediate between the general public and deviance, to pronounce on its causes, and to devise its cures. Medicine gained its social power because experts shaped a medical discourse that spoke to all those problems in comprehensible language, which appeared to many contemporaries to be an accurate portrayal of the world. The widespread influence of medical discourse about deviance had, as we shall see, profound consequences not only for the "pathological" part of the population, but also, as with any binary relation, for the "normal" one as well.

[70] Foucault, *The Birth of the Clinic*, pp. 35-36.

CHAPTER III

Between MacMahon and Boulanger: Crime and the "Moral Order" of the Opportunist Republic

As I have already suggested, no truly accurate account of the medicalization of deviance can overlook how medical ideas interacted with political, intellectual, and social forces within a detailed historical context. For the era 1870-1885, such a contextual strategy will reveal the extraordinary extent to which the advance of medicalization was dependent on factors external to medicine itself. If medicine supplied the language for this development, it cannot be said that doctors themselves had a large role in promoting the application of medical ideas to social problems in this relatively early period. The principal subject of this chapter is the Relegation Law of 1885, which transported "habitual" criminals—even for misdemeanors—to the colonies for life. The draconian nature of this legislation demands some explanation, not least because the most liberal piece of criminal legislation of the entire era, the Parole Law of 1885, was passed only a few days after this harsh measure. Both pieces of legislation were produced by an apparently comfortable Republican parliamentary majority which had, by that date, decisively defeated its Monarchist rivals.

In general, Foucault's portrait of the great era of prison reform between 1790 and 1848 does not prepare us at all for this turn of events. It is true that the effort to define the habitual criminal was a process in which the "disciplinary experts"—criminologists and psychiatrists—willingly participated. But the actual implementation of the legislation of 1885 owed perhaps more to political and legal concepts than it did to medical ones, and to developments that arose out of the social and economic history of the period. Recidivism and vagrancy—the issues of chief concern in this era—were not thoroughly medicalized by criminologists and psychiatrists until the 1890s. In the early 1880s a conception of the habitual criminal was fashioned piecemeal out of legal doctrine, a "Republican" theory of punishment, and some outmoded medical terminology. This development is important enough that its story deserves to be told in some detail.

The history of the founding of the Third Republic has been often and well told, but a brief introduction to the social basis and political dynamics of the new regime will serve to clarify the origins of relegation. The political class that took power from the coalition of local notables and *haut bourgeois* that had ruled France since Napoleonic times was the heir of a political tradition that had known mostly opposition, seldom power, throughout its history. Many of the Republican leaders of the 1870s had been in Napoleonic prisons, and had their newspapers censored and their public movements watched. Yet the men who took power in the late seventies were not revolutionaries, but sober and cautious spokesmen for what Léon Gambetta called the "nouvelles couches sociales." The new regime that replaced the *République des ducs* relied on peasant proprietors, tradesmen, shopkeepers and merchants, and the numerous cadres of the liberal professions. The Third Republic was founded on a social base composed primarily of property-owning farmers or individuals who were otherwise self-employed, the "producing classes" of Saint-Simon's great utopia: "Those who think, those who work, those who accumulate wealth, and those who knew how to make a judicious use of it, liberal and profitable to the country."[1] Included in this coalition were many of the Republic's *grands industriels*, who, in their own intraclass struggle with the Orleanist financial bourgeoisie, were seeking powerful political allies.[2] It is enough to say that the common denominators of this new alliance were property, order, and democracy, "defined, certainly, not as the equality of fortunes, but as the equality of opportunity."[3]

In building their electoral majorities in the seventies, Republican campaigners endlessly stressed the defense of order, social conservatism, and a thorough disapproval of the class antagonisms that had led to the Commune of 1871. Indeed, Gambetta's use of the phrase "nouvelles couches sociales" in the Grenoble speech of 1872 provoked a sharply unfavorable reaction among Republicans, who hoped to sep-

[1] Speech of Gambetta in Abbeville, June 10, 1877, cited in Pierre Barral, *Les fondateurs de la IIIᵉ République* (Paris: A. Colin, 1968), p. 235. See also Robert D. Anderson, *France 1870-1914: Politics and Society* (London: Routledge and Kegan Paul, 1977), pp. 35-38.

[2] See in general for the discussion of this theme Sanford Elwitt, *The Making of the Third Republic: Class and Politics in France, 1868-1884* (Baton Rouge: Louisiana State University Press, 1975), especially Chapters 3 and 4.

[3] Jean-Marie Mayeur, *Les débuts de la IIIᵉ République, 1871-1898* (Paris: Seuil, 1973), p. 49.

arate themselves from insurrectionary politics.[4] Gambetta later felt himself forced to remind his friends that "I said *couches* [strata] not *classes*. That is a distasteful word I never use."[5]

Gambetta's Belleville manifesto of 1869, which remained for several years the program of Radicalism, and for a longer time of Gambettism, heavily stressed the need for political reforms such as universal suffrage and individual liberties. The separation of church and state and lay education were other items on his agenda that later consumed the attention of loyal Republicans. However, Gambetta limited his treatment of social and economic reforms to vague demands for changes in tax structures, a Saint-Simonian attack on "idleness," and "economic reforms, which touch on the social problem, whose solution, *although subordinate to political reform*, must be constantly studied and researched in the name of the principle of justice and social equality."[6]

It was, of course, only a matter of time before the lack of an ambitious social program became a disadvantage to Republicans campaigning in urban working-class districts. The relative absence of labor activity after the debacle of 1871 was gradually replaced by strike activity and political regrouping after 1878. Meanwhile, Republicans who had limited themselves to the realization of political victories found themselves suddenly without immediate objectives after the gains made at the end of the decade. In Elwitt's words, "to the extent that the *seize maisards* were turned back, the foe became more difficult to locate. The time was approaching when he would have to be invented."[7]

The elections of 1881 were the first legislative elections in which the success or failure of the Republic was not the principal issue. The programs of the Republican contingent showed, therefore, far more diversity than ever before, the most notable example being the appearance of a Radical cohort centered around Georges Clemenceau. Clemenceau's 1881 platform for the eighteenth *arrondissement* of Paris included several specific social programs intended to appeal to his artisan and working-class constituency. He argued for taxes on inheritance, reduction of the workday, child labor legislation, and old age and job-injury insurance. Not content with announcing his own program, he attacked the "scandalous" behavior of the Ferry ministry that had presided over the elections, thus announcing his open break with

[4] J. P. T. Bury, *Gambetta and the Making of the Third Republic* (London: Longman, 1973), pp. 115-117.

[5] Cited in Elwitt, *The Making of the Third Republic*, p. 55.

[6] Cited in Appendix 3 in Jacques Kayser, *Les grandes batailles du radicalisme, 1820-1901* (Paris: Rivière, 1962), pp. 318-319. My emphasis.

[7] Elwitt, *The Making of the Third Republic*, p. 159.

the mainstream Republicans. The moderate Ferry did not hesitate, for his part, to identify the new enemy. In a speech in Le Havre in October 1883 he announced that "the peril of monarchy no longer exists"; the "greatest, the only peril of the moment" is the left.[8]

In the 1881 Chamber the political alignments broke down in the following manner. Royalists and Bonapartists had 45 seats apiece. The "center-left," Republicans with liberal tendencies and Orleanists with Republican ones, had 39 places. Ferry's Gauche républicaine had 168 seats and Gambetta's Union républicaine had 204. The "extreme left" was composed of two groups. One, "ministerial," which kept its options open to the right, had as its major figures Floquet, Allain-Targé, and Lockroy, and called itself the "Gauche radicale." It divided the 46 places of the extreme left about evenly with the radical group led by Clemenceau and Camille Pelletan.[9] The cabinets of this legislature were made up nearly entirely of Gambettists and Ferryists, who had adopted the name "Opportunists" (a title much regretted by the time the next election rolled around) as the best way of expressing their mutual belief that reforms should not be forced, but should occur only at the "opportune" moment. This was, of course, a euphemism for their shared conviction that reforms should be exclusively political and anticlerical and pose no threat to the social order. Still, within these limits Opportunist ministries passed legislation defending freedom of the press and public meetings, took the first steps toward a free, lay, obligatory education, reestablished divorce in France, and legalized trade unions. However, the 1881-1885 legislature is best known for having presided over the expansion of French colonial activity in Indochina and Tunisia under Ferry's tutelage. Though a minor setback in Tonkin led to the fall of Ferry's longest-lived ministry (February 1883-March 1885), the colonial acquisitions of these years were permanent, delighting an anxious Bismarck and the French colonial lobby, and infuriating patriots and révanchists who regarded colonialism as a poor substitute for a stronger European France.

A considerable amount of work has been done on the Opportunist-dominated assemblies of the early Republic, contributing to our knowledge of the social origins, financial connections, ideology, and political behavior of the generation that secured France's longest-lived modern regime. But the accomplishments of the Opportunists were not merely

[8] Quoted by Kayser, *Les grandes batailles du radicalisme*, p. 125.

[9] This breakdown is taken from R. D. Anderson's very judicious *France 1870-1914*, p. 166.

limited to the great issues of colonies, education, and clericalism, over which so much political blood was spilled in the eighties. What the Opportunists did (and did not do) about crime and deviance are as revealing of the essential traits of the Opportunists and their political enemies as any of these great issues. In certain ways, as I wish to argue, a detailed look at the politics of crime and punishment cleaves as close to the bone of Republicanism in the eighties as any other subject of legislative concern. The debate over the transportation of recidivists provoked discussion over a range of issues that touched every major political flashpoint in the era: colonialism, clericalism, the "social problem," personal liberties and public order, and the Republican tradition itself.

The politics of crime and deviance also provides us with insights into aspects of the careers and personalities of the main political figures of the epoch that have seldom been discussed or squared with the Radical, Opportunist, or Conservative mainstreams from which they drew their nourishment. We know much about Georges Clemenceau's hatred of Ferry, his opposition to colonialism, his courageous support of social legislation, but his struggle with the Ferryists took other forms as well. We know in exhaustive detail the ideological origins of Ferry's optimistic and laic educational philosophy, but how does that fit with his views on the rehabilitation of criminals? And what of Gambetta, whose political aspirations and patriotism are extensively documented, but whose views on social matters were either vague or (some say) willfully concealed? The law on recidivism was, in effect, Gambetta's legislative offspring, and, despite his death in December 1882, was a powerful testimony to the nature (and limitations) of his republicanism. René Waldeck-Rousseau, whose organization of the Republican defense against anti-Dreyfusism in 1899 was the glory of his later career, received his political baptism in these debates as the minister of the interior. It was his job to push through a deeply flawed piece of criminal legislation that was at odds with the more generous aspects of Republican social philosophy. Finally, the debate over the transportation of recidivists allows us to examine the social dimensions of Albert de Mun's liberal Catholicism, and to relate these generally ignored ideals to the dilemma and strategies of a besieged conservatism searching for new ground to defend against anticlericalism. The debate over the recidivism law provoked all these major figures to relate their views on crime and deviance to their thinking as a whole. Their responses enlighten us not only on the politics of the 1880s, but on much of French parliamentary life in the period before 1914.

By the time the Opportunists gained control of the government in the late 1870s, the economic revival of the 1870s had begun to fade. The brief respite provided by the Freycinet Plan, which from 1878 to 1882 expedited public sector investment and the improvement of transport, gave way to a major financial debacle—the crash of the Union générale banking house—and a general economic crisis.[10] Industrial activity and investment fell off dramatically in 1882 and did not recover until near the end of the century. Allan Mitchell, who has calculated some of the balance of trade figures in this period, argues that they became negative for the first time in 1875, the gap gradually widening from that time forward.[11] The fact that French goods and services became increasingly less competitive abroad further contributed to stagnation and required citizens to pay more for foreign goods which were gradually taxed at higher and higher import rates. Though French statesmen could not have known it at the time, the economic events of the period 1875-1885 put a more or less permanent stamp on the commercial relationship of France with all her trading partners. A vicious circle in which low domestic growth rates exacerbated the adverse flow of foreign trade and vice versa was broken only by the upheavals of war and the recovery after World War II.

The most important factor contributing to the long-term economic doldrums was the poor situation of French agriculture. World agriculture prices were generally in decline during the last quarter of the century, but, owing to a variety of factors such as the failure of specialized crops and low investment in new technology, the drop in income hurt French cultivators more severely than most. Grain prices fell steadily throughout the last half of the century from a high of over 38 francs per quintal in 1855 to lows near 20 in the early 1890s.[12] The terrible phylloxera epidemic, which began in the late sixties, reached disaster proportions by 1880, altogether eliminating commercial viticulture in some regions of the Midi.[13] The value of agricultural properties dropped precipitously between 1882 and 1892, declining by about

[10] On the role the plan played in the struggle against depression see Yves Gonjo, "Le Plan Freycinet, 1878-1882: Un aspect de la 'grande dépression économique' en France," *Revue historique* (July-September 1972), pp. 49-79. For the politics of the plan see Elwitt, *The Making of the Third Republic*, pp. 145-162.

[11] Allan Mitchell, *The German Influence in France after 1870* (Chapel Hill: University of North Carolina Press, 1981), pp. 186-189.

[12] Figures are taken from Pierre Sorlin, *La société française, 1840-1914* (Paris: Arthaud, 1969), p. 53.

[13] For an account of the economic and social effects of the phylloxera in the Midi see Leo A. Loubère, *Radicalism in Mediterranean France: Its Rise and Decline, 1848-1914* (Albany, N.Y.: SUNY Press, 1977), pp. 96-107.

one-fifth during those years and by about one-third between 1881 and 1913.[14]

The social effects of this decline were devastating. During the Second Empire, when prices and population were still booming, two out of three Frenchmen lived on the land, and over half the population lived solely from farming activity. But this dense rural horde was able to maintain itself only through intensive polyculture cultivation and through the exploitation of marginal soils. When prices began to fall after 1855, so did the ability of the land to support its great numbers. Victimized first were the tiny cultivators, whose lands could no longer support large families. Also heavily affected were the rural artisans and *petits commerçants* who were thoroughly integrated into the web of rural commerce throughout France. Waves of rural emigration, with crests at 1860 and 1880, spread out in all directions from the most deeply affected zones.[15]

Before 1880 the most typical emigrant was an individual, a young artisan or day laborer looking for better days; after 1880 whole families, uprooted from their small plots by falling prices or harvest failure, were increasingly common. There were many variations in human motivation and in geographical impact in all this migration. Many migrants attempted to enter the flow of seasonal agricultural labor that had been a feature of rural life for time out of mind; but this was a temporary expedient at best during the long depression years. Eventually, the bulk of the post-1880 emigrants set its course toward regional urban agglomerations or toward Paris, but not with the high hopes of the emigrants of the 1850s and 1860s. There was no "light-heartedness," Pierre Sorlin has noted, where stagnation made urban jobs scarce too.[16] In the 1880s there was, in other words, no pull, only push. The agricultural migrant of that era had no labor organization to defend his interests, and the growing Radical and Opportunist network in the countryside listened to the prosperous farmers and the townsmen rather than the *gens sans aveu*. Between 1876 and 1911 three million of the agricultural classes quit the land for good.

The nature of the economic situation meant that emigrants did not often depart with a comfortable nest egg to tide them over until they

[14] Mayeur, *Les débuts de la IIIe République*, p. 82; Sorlin, *La société française*, p. 51.

[15] See Georges Duveau's comments on migration patterns and those of Daniel Faucher on the agricultural and technological reorientation that initiated them in Georges Friedmann, ed., *Villes et campagnes* (Paris: Colin, n.d.), pp. 163-166, 363-375. Loubère writes of a wave of emigration in the viticultural regions of the *Midi* after the period 1876-1881. *Radicalism in Mediterranean France*, p. 103.

[16] Sorlin, *La société française*, p. 56.

could find steady employment. They converged on areas of greater relative prosperity and followed the time-honored custom of begging for food and lodging. The dodges and devices used by vagrants to obtain provender are well known to historians of the early modern period. Some of these were something less than legal, often involving hoax, threat, or some combination of these.[17] It seems likely that these same techniques were employed by nineteenth- and early twentieth-century vagrants, but, despite the huge numbers involved (one study estimates 400,000 beggars were on French roads as late as 1904),[18] this is an area that social historians have only begun to investigate.[19]

Traditional Christian views of mendicancy assured medieval beggars of generous private and ecclesiastical charity, but the agricultural and demographic crises of the eighteenth century spelled the doom of the old system. Indeed, the old regime officials encouraged the growth of a network of *dépôts de mendicité* that were little better than jails where "dangerous" vagabonds could be detained without hearing. The Napoleonic Code reflected a continued concern about beggary by making both vagrancy and mendicity legal offenses. Articles 269 to 282 cover these offenses in the penal code. Vagabonds (*gens sans aveu*) were considered to be those who had "no certain domicile" or "means of subsistence," and who did not "habitually" exercise any "trade" or "profession." Mendicity was an offense when one was engaged in it in the neighborhood of a *dépôt* or some other source of charitable assistance. There were aggravated forms of begging that earned punishments longer than the three to six months of the simple offense (*délit*). These included the act of begging while carrying a weapon, while in disguise, or when furnished with tools to facilitate burglary. Violence or threats of violence were also aggravations carrying long prison terms.[20]

I have discussed the limitations of using the official statistics for those brought to trial, but the figures of vagabondage and mendicity (considered as a single offense in the *Compte générale*) are remarkably free

[17] See, in particular, Olwen Hufton, *The Poor of Eighteenth-Century France, 1750-1789* (London: Oxford University Press, 1974).

[18] Alex Vexliard, "La disparition du vagabondage comme fleau social universel," *Revue de l'Institut de sociologie*, 36 (1963), pp. 53-80.

[19] Michelle Perrot identifies the part-time occupations in cities that allowed vagabonds to live and lay claim to having work. The final decay of the apprentice system led to a "turn-over" employment of young workers that encouraged part-time labor and mobility, thereby contributing further to vagabondage. See "La fin des vagabonds," *L'histoire* 3 (July-August 1978), pp. 23-33.

[20] See articles 269 to 282 in Emile Garçon, ed., *Code pénal annoté*, 2d ed. by Marcel *Revue de l'Institut de sociologie*, 36 (1963), pp. 53-80.

56

from the kinds of wild swings that might reflect abrupt changes of attitude toward enforcement. The trends, more than in any other major category of crime, seem more or less directly related to economic trends and major migration patterns. Thus, the number of cases brought to correctional courts in the period 1846-1850 leaped to an average of 14,978 per year as against 7,993 in the five-year period of relative prosperity that immediately preceded.[21] Rates continued high during the period 1851-1855, but dropped to 10,893 in the 1856-1860 period, climbing back to a prewar high of 18,904 in 1868. The annual figure did not exceed 17,783 until 1879 when it reached 18,600. However, the beginning of the great depression was announced in 1880 when the number of trials was 20,456. The number climbed steadily throughout the 1880s, reaching the highest figure for the entire century in 1890, 35,301. The average for the decade was 29,363.

The average for the following decade, 1891-1900, dropped to 29,088, and in 1901-1910 fell even further to 22,500.[22] But the chief reason for the decline in trials of vagabondage and mendicity after 1890 seems to have been the suspended sentence law of that year, which had a tendency to lower judicial activity for these crimes. All we can say with any assurance, therefore, is that rates climbed dramatically through the 1880s before the sudden change in penal procedure in 1890. We know from many other sources that local officials were preoccupied during the whole period 1880-1900 with the growth in vagabondage and reported this concern to the administration.[23] The number of actual arrests is not known, but it was likely to have been much higher in any given year than figures for those brought to trial. Vexliard gives the number of arrests in 1905 as 50,000 a year when only 19,149 cases were brought to trial.[24]

Eugen Weber, discussing the extreme isolation and self-sufficiency of many villages in rural France, mentions their willingness to accommodate beggars from their immediate region but their fear and rejection of vagabonds from other areas.[25] No doubt, with so many migrants on the road, the importunities of *"chemineaux,"* whether

[21] "Résumé rétrospectif," *Annuaire statistique: Compte générale de l'administration de la justice criminelle* 52 (1936) (Paris: Imprimerie nationale, 1937), p. 47.

[22] Ibid., p. 48.

[23] Sorlin, *La société française*, p. 56; Eugen Weber, *Peasants into Frenchmen: The Modernization of Rural France, 1870-1914* (Stanford, Calif.: Stanford University Press, 1977), pp. 63-65.

[24] Vexliard, "La disparition du vagabondage comme fleau social universel," p. 53.

[25] Weber, *Peasants into Frenchmen*, p. 44.

57

accompanied by threats or not, were profoundly dreaded by settled folk. As far as the cities were concerned, we know that police and assistance services were terribly overstrained by the waves of jobless immigrants. It came to light in the debates over the recidivism bill that the Paris Prefecture of Police followed the practice of arresting suspected vagrants and then releasing them outside the city confines with a warning not to return. If they did return, there was no easy way of determining if they had been previously removed.[26] Not surprisingly, the recidivism bill was enthusiastically supported by conservative Parisian deputies, who believed that the new law would provide police with an exceptional weapon for dealing with these unwanted persons.

Unfortunately for these victims of agricultural stagnation, their plight coincided with a highly publicized increase in the rates of criminal recidivism. While the enlightened practitioners of the politics of moral order in the 1870s had found their great issue in moral rehabilitation and penitentiary reform, the Opportunists of the 1880s made the elimination of "recidivism" their main concern. Vagrancy and begging were merely the most numerous of the many crimes, it was alleged, that were committed by an "army" of recidivists that had become a menace to the Republic.

Those chiefly concerned about the rise in the number of crimes committed by repeat offenders could not use the assizes court records of serious crimes to prove their case. Indeed the numbers of recidivists convicted in assizes courts had actually begun to decline after 1875. In 1880 the lowest figure (1,459) since 1866 was recorded; through the rest of the century, the numbers of convicted repeaters never again attained the highs of the 1873-1875 period.[27] But the correctional courts, where the less serious crimes were tried, were yielding a higher number of recidivists each year after 1871. Though the numbers of cases brought to trial seems to have leveled off during the 1870s, the number of recidivists convicted had begun to grow, thereby reestablishing a trend, momentarily disrupted by the war, that had begun in the 1860s. Thus, in 1872, 57,118 recidivists were convicted, but in 1880 the number was 74,009. These numbers continued to grow rapidly in the 1880s and 1890s, reaching highs of over 100,000 between 1892

[26] Alphonse Bertillon, the inventor of an elaborate system of photographic identification for offenders, and an ardent supporter of the recidivism law, was moved to implement his ingenious identification system partly out of his desire to solve this problem. See his "L'identité des récidivistes et la loi de rélégation," *Annales de démographie internationale* (1883), pp. 1-18.

[27] "Résumé rétrospectif," in *Compte générale de l'administration de la justice criminelle* 52 (1936), p. 46.

and 1894, then declining slowly as the suspended sentence law began to take effect.[28]

Recidivism could be made to seem even more of a danger when the percentages of recidivists accused (*accusés*) of all offenses over the century were reviewed. Thus, 28 of every 100 individuals charged with a crime in the 1820s had previously been convicted. By 1881 this figure had climbed to 51 out of each 100 previously convicted.[29] On the basis of these figures, the critics of recidivism could argue that though the absolute number of crimes had not risen, these crimes were being committed by individuals who were being repeatedly recycled through the criminal justice system. Other aspects of the problem were duly noted by observers. Ferdinand Dreyfus pointed out in the debates of 1883 that although the rural areas were plagued with the crimes of recidivists, most of their crimes were committed in the cities. Paris was the most popular of these, with a rate of 53 for every 100 crimes, followed by 46 per 100 and 44 per 100 for cities of 100,000 and 30,000 respectively. Rural crimes were committed by recidivists at the relatively lower rate of 22 per 100.[30] Writing in the *Bulletin de la Société de statistique de Paris* in December 1882, Maurice Yvernès, the official government statistician, zeroed in on the vagrancy problem. Seventy-one of each 100 vagrancy offenses were committed by repeaters. Moreover, of all criminal accusations in 1880, 47 percent were "typical" vagabond crimes: vagrancy, begging, violating the ban against reappearing in the *arrondissement* of previous arrest, or other crimes committed while in a "state of vagabondage."[31]

The penal legislation that was eventually designed to cope with this "scourge" was the application of colonial transportation. Transportation, which had been used for political criminals under the Empire (law of 1852), had been first applied to common-law criminals by a law of 1854. Those who qualified for this sentence, however, had committed serious crimes requiring imprisonment at hard labor, at that time the most serious punishment after the death penalty in the penal code. The numbers sent to New Caledonia or Guyana under this law were small, and the convicts passed their terms in relative confinement

[28] Ibid., pp. 47-48.

[29] These are the figures used by René Waldeck-Rousseau in the Chamber debates. *Journal officiel*, "Chambre des députés," April 27, 1883, p. 779.

[30] Ferdinand Dreyfus, *Journal officiel*, "Chambre des députés," April 22, 1883, p. 700.

[31] Maurice Yvernès, "De la récidive," reprinted in *Bulletin de la Société générale des prisons* 7 (March 1883), pp. 316-328.

and under close guard. The legislators in 1881 were proposing a similar punishment for multiple convictions of crimes as common as begging.

There were several reasons for the choice of this particular punishment. But the excuse most regularly offered, and concurred in by the penal administration itself, was the utter insufficiency of the central prison system. The law of June 5, 1875, which was intended to crown the great prison reform movement of the July Monarchy, required that all French prisons be converted to cellular structures so that prisoners could undergo their punishment in twenty-four-hour isolation. This measure was motivated, of course, by the dominant reformist freewill philosophy that held imprisonment to be a form of correctional treatment for the moral rehabilitation of the fallen criminal. The state promptly began the gradual conversion of the *maisons centrales* to cellular design, and built new institutions according to the directives of the law. The departmental and municipal prisons, which were also directed to be converted, were to be financed out of local revenues, an initiative that failed completely, owing to the financial resistance of local authorities.

On the whole, jurists and the professionals of the penal administration maintained a clear loyalty to the full implementation of the law of 1875. A few legal treatises appeared in the late 1870s on the dangers of recidivism or on the growing menace of vagabondage and begging. But these either urged responses such as private patronage or more use of cellular imprisonment, or simply bemoaned the growth of this "social evil" for which there seemed to be no remedy in the penal code.[32] The liberal royalist Othenin d'Haussonville, a leading light in the penal reform commission of 1872-1875, wrote a series of articles on juvenile vagabonds and delinquents in 1878 and 1879 in the *Revue des deux mondes* in which he argued in favor of individual imprisonment, agricultural colonies, and private patronage societies.[33] A debate in the Société générale des prisons on the eve of the parliamentary debates on transportation revealed a clear majority of the discussants to have been supporters of patronage and imprisonment and wary of solutions that, in the words of one lawyer, were conceived in "salons" amid a

[32] See especially Emile Darnand, *Vagabonds et mendiants: Etude de droit pénal* (Paris: Leroux, 1876); T. Dumans, *De la récidive* (Caen, 1877).

[33] Othenin d'Haussonville, "L'enfance à Paris: Les vagabonds," *Revue des deux mondes* (June 1, 1878), pp. 598-627; "L'enfance à Paris: La mendicité," ibid. (June 15, 1878), pp. 891-927; "L'enfance à Paris: Les rendez-vous du crime—Les jeunes adultes et l'éducation correctionnelle," ibid. (January 15, 1879), pp. 346-377. See also Louis Sévin-Desplaces, *Récidivistes et patronage des libérés* (Paris, 1882).

state of public "exaltation."[34] Transportation, most argued, was an "expedient" that did not strike at the root of the problem or encourage the rehabilitation of its victims. In the same number of the society's *Bulletin*, the great reformer senator René Bérenger claimed that most recidivists were victims of society: "weak, cowardly, or discouraged, rather than truly incorrigible wrongdoers."[35] In his view recidivism was essentially a social problem which could not be effectively eliminated by simply punishing one generation unless the causes that would produce the next were removed.[36]

In spite of a strong current of continued support for prison reform, some voices within the legal community had been raised by 1883 in support of transportation. Their efforts received some important support from the budding "criminological" section of the medical profession, but despite the interest and attention of the medical community, the medicalization of deviance had made only limited progress. The notion of the deviant as a sick being, whose illness and cure were the special province of the doctor still had a decidedly ambiguous status, even within the confines of French medicine itself. Gradually, however, the traditional moral categories that had dominated discourse about unconventional social behavior were being eroded and replaced in a piecemeal fashion by more technical ones based on medicine and biology.

Crime in the old regime and during the Napoleonic era was, like crime in any age, a reflection of the society itself. Wealth and objects of value were not concentrated in particular places, so crime was largely a rural phenomenon. Bandits and highwaymen congregated at crossroads and inns to lie in wait for the traveler, who, rich or poor, was obliged to carry a large portion of his personal assets with him on his voyages. The wealthy man in this era protected his goods, his game and livestock, and his person by force of arms. Crime, therefore, like the justice that punished it, was summary, and often marked by great violence. However as wealth began to concentrate in cities during the early stages of industrial growth, the locus as well as the nature of crime began to change. This was nowhere as apparent as in Paris, which experienced a dramatic increase in its population in the first half of the century from less than 500,000 to over a million inhabitants.

[34] Raoul Lajoye, *Bulletin de la Société générale des prisons 7, séance* of January 13, 1883, pp. 4-5. See also the remarks of Georges Picot, abbé de Humbourg, and Eugène Greffier, pp. 11-15, 21-30.

[35] René Bérenger, "Moyens préventifs de combattre la récidive," *Bulletin de la Société générale des prisons* 7 (January 1883), p. 35.

[36] Ibid., pp. 35, 55-63.

Crime became less violent, but, concentrated within a smaller, more easily observed space, it seemed more frequent and more intense. Contemporaries identified crime with the growth of the huge floating population in the capital, christened the "dangerous" class to distinguish it from the "laboring" class which gained its bread by honest means.

As an object of study for philanthropists, social statisticians, and doctors, and a subject in the realist novels of Balzac and Sue, the "dangerous" classes were a source of anxiety and fascination for the urban bourgeoisie throughout this period. The dominant "philanthropic" discourse provided the pre-1848 political elite with an optimistic scheme for rehabilitating this criminal populace in a network of model prisons, but alongside this hopeful perspective, another darker vision flourished, both in social science and in fiction. This grimmer outlook portrayed the criminal as a savage living outside the limits of decent society, prey to vicious habits, prone to violence, and often physically deformed by the environment in which he lived.[37] Fear painted these stereotypes of the criminal with vivid strokes. Even the most optimistic of the philanthropists could not avoid language that, according to Catherine Duprat, emphasized negatives ("*not* moral, *not* sane, *not* normal"), extended these traits to the entire group ("they are all guilty, all vicious, all ignorant"), or denied them their common humanity ("a purely physical order of animality and savagery").[38]

As the place of internment of the most dangerous class of criminals, the forced labor camp (*bagne*) was an object of particular interest. The criminal who was condemned to a life of hard labor, chained by the leg or the neck to his comrades, had committed armed felony or some violent form of personal assault. The *forçat* was the archetypal villain for the French imagination until the final closing of the *bagnes* under the Second Empire. He was believed, by novelists, doctors, and journalists alike, to possess physical characteristics that could be classified according to the phrenological system of Franz Joseph Gall, and that placed him in a taxonomic slot somewhere between man and beast.[39] Hubert Lauvergne, a doctor at the *bagne* of Toulon during the July Monarchy, wrote the first "scientific" account of the criminal in 1841, *Les forçats considérés sous le rapport physiologique, moral et intellectuel*. Lau-

---

[37] See, in particular, Chevalier, *Laboring Classes and Dangerous Classes*.

[38] Duprat, "Punir et guérir," pp. 90-91.

[39] Victor Hugo uses phrenological language in *Claude Gueux* in connection with Gueux's fellow *forçats*. Foucault argues that the transport of *forçats* to the *bagnes* in closed conveyances after 1837 prefigured the replacement of the *bagnes* by modern prisons. *Discipline and Punish*, pp. 257-264.

vergne employed Gall's phrenology in an effort to correlate skull morphology with different kinds of criminals (assassins, felons, sex criminals, etc.) and with the precise moral and intellectual qualities peculiar to each category.[40]

Deterministic as this biological system appears to be, it is not proper to conclude that a phrenological system for classifying criminals was simply a bourgeois tactic to absolve society of any responsibility for motivating crime.[41] Indeed, most phrenologists appear to have believed that the so-called innate qualities, whose external manifestations appeared on the skull, could be shaped and improved by effort and through exposure to a better environment. Roger Cooter, who has studied the important influence of phrenology on British psychiatry between 1825 and 1845, has concluded that the adoption of Gall's ideas allowed a psychiatrist to become "a proto-social scientist studying an aspect of deviance, the knowledge from which was intimately connected with answers to other pressing social issues such as education and criminal reform."[42] Though a certain degree of medicalization of crime did take place before 1850, one can conclude that a medical discourse remained subordinate to the philanthropic discourse that dominated the era and, indeed, served to further the overall purposes of social reform.

At least until the Second Empire, French psychiatry remained more or less within the limits set by the procedural compromises of the early nineteenth century that marked the boundaries in criminal matters between the legal and medical realms. In practice, this meant that psychiatrists and medical experts were called to testify only on the

[40] Lauvergne and some of the other phrenological literature of this period are discussed by Zysberg in "Politiques du bagne, 1820-1850," in Perrot, ed., *L'impossible prison*, pp. 165-170. See also Ysabel Rennie, *The Search for Criminal Man, A Conceptual History of the Dangerous Offender* (Lexington, Mass.: D.C. Heath, 1978), p. 61.

[41] Zysberg, "Politiques du bagne, 1820-1850," in Perrot, ed., *L'impossible prison*, p. 170.

[42] Roger Cooter, "Phrenology and British Alienists, ca. 1825-1845," in Scull, ed., *Madhouses, Mad-Doctors, and Madmen*, p. 67. Catherine Duprat has shown that, no matter how deterministic the biological language used to characterize criminals might appear to be, it was not regarded as inconsistent with rehabilitation and moral expiation by the philanthropic luminaries of the Restoration. She quotes the medical imagery of one of the founders of the prison movement, A. de Laborde: "Prison discipline is a new science which fully takes into account man's physical and moral nature. Crime is an infirmity that one would badly mistreat if one limited oneself to amputation: one must know how to cure it." Duprat, "Punir et guérir," p. 89. Angus McLaren makes the same point in "A Prehistory of the Social Sciences: Phrenology in France," *Comparative Studies in Society and History* 23 (January 1981), pp. 13-16.

sanity of the "great monsters" of the annals of crime, not on the day-to-day criminal cases that were handled in the courts. To be sure, over the years psychiatrists developed diagnostic systems that enabled them to deal with the "hard" cases in which insanity did not manifest itself in permanent delusions, easily apparent to the eye of the layman, but expressed itself intermittently or in the guise of rational and consistent behavior. But diagnoses of "monomania" (Pinel and Esquirol), "lucid madness" (Trélat), or "intermittent insanity" (Bigot) were delivered as they were required in the courts. As Prosper Déspine wrote of these classes of insanity, though they operated to inhibit altogether the normal function of the moral sense, individuals affected by them could accomplish "very complex and intelligent acts reaching a goal that is perfectly specific and adjusted to circumstances; acts exactly similar to those that the ego commands on other occasions through the same apparatus."[43] The case to which Michel Foucault and his colleagues devoted a book-length study, *I Pierre Rivière*, offers a good example of the kinds of ambiguous circumstances that led to the intervention of experts. Addressing the apparent lucidness of Rivière's memoir documenting the events of the murders (which had convinced the provincial doctor of his sanity), the report argued that "the soundness of memory and the sequence in the ideas displayed in this narration do not rule out mental deficiency since it frequently occurs in the narratives of maniacs or monomaniacs writing out the history of their malady."[44] No doubt most psychiatrists believed that the insane were more likely than others to commit a crime, but this is not unusual in view of their belief that the very condition of madness presupposed an anesthesia of the moral sense.[45] It is more important to recognize that until the 1860s, with the exception of the work of B. A. Morel to which I shall return, psychiatric medicine made few special claims for jurisdictional rights over crime or criminals.

One of the first major demands for a change in the traditional relationship between medicine and criminality was voiced in 1863 at a

[43] Prosper Déspine, *Psychologie naturelle*, vol. I (Paris: Savy, 1868), pp. 490-491; see also Ulysse Trélat, *La folie lucide* (Paris, Delahaye, 1861); V. Bigot, *Des périodes raisonnantes de l'aliénation mentale* (Paris: Baillière, 1877). On monomania and legal medicine in general during the period 1840-1880, see Castel, *L'ordre psychiatrique*, pp. 174-182.

[44] Foucault, ed., *I Pierre Rivière*, p. 164.

[45] Marandon de Montyel quotes the mid-century psychiatrist Lunier as typical of that period: "I consider, in principle, all *aliénés* as dangerous, but must add that in fact there are numerous exceptions." "Les aliénés dits criminels," *Annales médico-psychologiques* (May 1891), p. 438; see also J. Christian, "Chronique," ibid. (November 1885), p. 377.

session of the Société médico-psychologique. Dr. Eugène Dally asked for nothing less than a total revision of the way that society treats criminals. Dally argued that most criminals, certainly all recidivists, were insane; they committed crimes out of "irresistible impulses," though their "love of evil for evil's sake" was often concealed beneath an apparently sane veneer.[46] He launched a full-scale attack on the "right to punish" based on the "metaphysical absurdity" of free will and individual responsibility. But he did not wish to eliminate the principle of responsibility entirely; he wanted to reconstruct it on a foundation of social danger whose rule of thumb would be that "each is responsible for his acts in proportion to the dangers these acts pose to society."[47] Thus, the aim of social policy with respect to criminals ought to be "preventive" and "repressive": "One must treat criminals as sick, having with regard to them neither hate nor anger nor the spirit of vengeance, and limit oneself to preserving society from the dangers their presence brings."[48]

Dally's paper appeared at a time when doctors at the fledgling Société d'anthropologie de Paris were attempting to apply the principles of phrenology and the localization of brain function to the identification of criminals. Paul Broca thought he could isolate the skull deformation that guaranteed the existence of certain kinds of abnormal brain—and therefore behavioral—disorders, and Georges Delesiauve was not contradicted after stating that "most convicts carry on their skulls the imprint of their vicious moral tendencies."[49] There was clearly some sympathy within the medical community for extending the frontiers of a criminal anthropology. Throughout the 1870s, and especially between 1879 and 1882, there were numerous efforts to build a systematic classificational system of criminal anatomy, largely a revamping of phrenological systems.[50] Still, the references to "satanic" or "neander-

---

[46] Eugène Dally, *Remarques sur les aliénés et les criminels au point de vue de la responsabilité morale et légale* (Paris, 1864), pp. 5, 14-15. This was a paper read at the Société médico-psychologique and first published in the *Annales médico-psychologiques* (September 1863). pp. 7-46.

[47] Dally, *Remarques sur les aliénés et les criminels*, pp. 5, 28-39.

[48] Ibid., pp. 4-5.

[49] Paul Broca, "Sur l'assassin Le Maire et sur la criminalité," *Bulletin de la Société d'anthropologie de Paris* (May 16, 1867), pp. 347-349; G. Delesiauve, "Discussion," ibid., p. 350.

[50] The most significant of these are Arthur Bordier, "Les crânes d'assassins," *Revue d'anthropologie 1879*, pp. 264-300; Paul Broca, "Le cerveau de l'assassin Prevost," *Bulletin de la Société d'anthropologie de Paris* (March 4, 1880), pp. 233-243; Armand Corre, "Sur quelques crânes de criminels conservés au Musée d'anatomie de l'Ecole de médecine de Brest," ibid. (August 4, 1881), pp. 638-654; Léonce Manouvrier,

thal" or "monstrously" shaped skulls cannot conceal the fact that there was an extraordinary reluctance to support Dally's radical departure from the traditional juridical basis of punishment.[51] His arguments, with some exceptions, were greeted by silence.[52]

In the following chapter I discuss the reasons for the unwillingness of the medical community to impose a new medical standard for the repression of crime during the 1880s. In the meanwhile, however, it is worthwhile to summarize a few general points about the extent of the medicalization of crime around 1880. First, it was by no means universally recognized that all criminals were insane. The only method for determining this fact that was regarded by doctors as reliable was a postmortem dissection that revealed massive brain lesions and thus the likelihood of serious impairment of mental function. Classificational schemes based on skull anatomy alone, or on the crania of living persons, always produced lively disagreement, even on the most fundamental principles.[53] Second, even where a consensus might exist on the insanity of a particular criminal, few doctors or psychiatrists were willing to conclude that the insanity had within it the germs of a particular criminal act. Finally, though some psychiatrists might be found in 1880 who were willing to advance the argument that some criminals were more constitutionally perverse than others, there was little agreement on how this might be determined, and there was virtually no support for Dally's view that repeated criminal acts were *in themselves* an adequate proof of some permanent criminal disposition.

There is little support, in brief, for the interpretation that the medical

---

"Discussions sur les criminels: Sur l'étude anthropologique des crânes d'assassins," ibid. (February 1, 1883), pp. 93-125.

[51] Ironically, Dally was himself hostile to the craniotomical efforts to classify criminals, as his interventions in various discussions indicate. He appears to have preferred a rather tautological definition whereby the best proof for criminal insanity is the very fact that a crime was committed. See *Bulletin de la Société d'anthropologie de Paris* (May 16, 1867) pp. 351-353, 378; ibid. (December 7, 1882), pp. 778-779; *Remarques sur les aliénés*, p. 19.

[52] Notable support for radical revision of the right to punish did appear in Gustave LeBon, "La question des criminels," *Revue philosophique* 22 (1886), pp. 515-539.

[53] See the inconclusive debates at the Société d'anthropologie de Paris. *Bulletin de la Société d'anthropologie de Paris* (May 16, 1867), pp. 347-378; ibid. (April 17, 1879), pp. 292-300; ibid. (March 4, 1880), p.243; ibid. (November 5, 1880), pp. 764-789. In her discussion of the contemporary "Grenier" episode, Jan Goldstein reveals the reluctance of the psychiatric establishment to engage directly the "free will" issue, though she also shows how the psychiatrists' scientific materialism began to take the more comfortable form of a militant anticlericalism. "The Hysteria Diagnosis and the Politics of Anti-clericalism in Late Nineteenth-Century France," *Journal of Modern History* 54 (June 1982), pp. 225-227.

community was aggressively engaged in promoting medicalization of crime at this time. Rather, an argument can be more convincingly made that the origins of the relegation bill of 1885 were political, and that its true authors were Opportunist Republicans. Their principal allies were the Opportunist press, elements of the magistracy, and a vast administrative apparatus that disposed of tremendous police and regulatory powers, now firmly in loyal Republican hands. The reasons for the support by centrist Republicans of this piece of legislation are more profound than a mere shortage of prison cells. Some of these reasons sprang from the short-term needs of an uneasy parliamentary coalition, but others were solidly rooted in the ideological tradition in which all Republicans had been nourished.

Opportunist Republicans, whose actions appear so self-serving to us now (and to their critics on the left and right in the 1880s), were passionately devoted to the history and idea of republicanism in their nation. During their years of opposition, militants searched the revolutionary past for "Republican" ideas that could be effectively used against dictatorship, the union of throne and altar, and the denial of essential liberties, and became, out of their need for a political program and a coherent ideology, diligent historians.[54] In the course of time Republicans of different political hues chose selectively from the past to suit their own dispositions. Thus, the young Jules Ferry blasted Jacobinism and the Committee of Public Safety for their attacks on individual liberty,[55] and the Opportunists generally upheld Danton over Robespierre in the martyrology of the Revolution. This selective approach to the Revolution later earned the reproaches of the Radical Clemenceau, who insisted that the French Revolution must be taken as a bloc or not at all.[56]

The disputes between Republicans over the actions and intentions of Republican ancestors gradually replaced the dialogue with Royalists and Bonapartists that had wholly absorbed Republicans until the 1870s. These ideological divergences ought not to be viewed simply as a screen for justifying pragmatic changes of political course. Most of the leading lights of republicanism—Ferry, Gambetta, Clemenceau—retained personal visions of the Revolution throughout their careers. Their views

[54] Paul Farmer, *France Reviews Its Revolutionary Origins: Social Politics and Historical Opinion in the Third Republic* (New York: Octagon, 1963), pp. 38-42.

[55] See the excerpts from a speech of 1866 reprinted in Barral, *Les fondateurs*, pp. 110-113.

[56] Clemenceau's speech in which he said "La Révolution française est un bloc" was made in the Chamber of Deputies on January 29, 1891; reprinted in ibid., pp. 113-116.

on the Convention or on the theories undergirding universal suffrage are important indications of their positions along a spectrum of republicanism where all the participants were conversant with a central body of discourse and facts.

It has been frequently pointed out that many of the Republican militants of the late nineteenth century mixed a good portion of Comtism in with Republican politics. Jules Simon, Jules Ferry, and Gambetta's lieutenant, Paul Bert, were among the best known of these, but Gambetta himself and many others in his entourage, not to mention Radicals like Clemenceau, had been exposed at some point or another to the ideas and methods of positivism.[57] It was quite common for Republicans of this generation to combine ideas of democracy and universal suffrage with Comte's notion of the inevitable victory of a "positive" stage of social and intellectual evolution which would doom religion and all its dependent institutions. Thus, a lay Republic that sought to replace religion with a "scientific" morality, while preserving the "natural" structures of the social order, could be regarded as a progressive force in history.[58] Republicans were convinced that political leadership belonged to those schooled in the methods of scientific politics. In practice these politicians combined a radical conception of democratic sovereignty with a biological notion of society that employed organic metaphors and stressed social solidarity.

The emergence of a "Republican" theory of punishment that included the political radicalism and social conservatism of the foregoing doctrines has not been the subject of systematic scholarly investigation. Some things are nonetheless quite clear. However crudely it was stated by Republican politicians in the heat of debate in the 1880s, there was a more or less coherent version of this theory in place by the late seventies. The chief intellectual figure in this development was the

[57] On this aspect of the thinking of the early Republicans see ibid., pp. 20-24; the chief work on Ferry's positivism is L. Legrand, *L'influence du positivisme dans l'oeuvre scolaire de Jules Ferry* (Paris: Rivière, 1961). Phillip Bertocci has discussed the connections between positivism and politics in this period, with special reference to Jules Simon in *Jules Simon: Republican Anti-Clericalism and Cultural Politics in France, 1848-1886* (Columbia: University of Missouri Press, 1978).

[58] Emile Littré, Comte's chief disciple (d. 1883) was the figure chiefly responsible for popularizing the conservative "Republican sociology" that influenced Gambetta and Ferry. His thought is still best elaborated in John A. Scott, *Republican Ideas and the Liberal Tradition in France* (New York: Octagon, 1966), pp. 92-105. Jan Goldstein has argued that French psychiatrists in this era supported the anticlericalism of the new regime with scientific explanations of the "hysteric" and "neurotic" foundations of religious belief. In return psychiatry received certain institutional benefits suitable to its expanding professional ambitions. "The Hysteria Diagnosis," pp. 209-240.

neo-Kantian philosopher Charles Renouvier. The later task of blending Renouvier's version of Enlightenment social contract theory with the more scientifically grounded organicism of the positivists fell to the liberal Republican philosopher Alfred Fouillée.

Renouvier's conception of the foundation of the state's right to punish was rooted in a neo-Kantian contract in which the associated parties agreed to move collectively toward the realization of certain ideals. The right to judge and to repress those who broke this contract flowed from the terms of the contract and was enforced by the representatives of the state power. Renouvier called this right the "right of personal defense," arguing it took both individual and collective forms.[59] The state had the responsibility of defending the "collective" form of private property, which Renouvier regarded as an extension of an individual's person. "Society's right over its members was," in Scott's words, "the collective exercise of the individual's right to self-defense."[60] By the time he published *Science de la morale* in 1869, Renouvier had pared away his earlier concern with the moralizing or expiatory function of punishment and rested his analysis entirely on the right of society to defend itself in the "state of war" that is the normal condition of modern life.[61]

Renouvier was suspicious of the biological determinism that was making its appearance in the 1860s and 1870s, and refused it any role in his voluntaristic system. Alfred Fouillée, however, younger and more sympathetic to modern biological and social science, attempted to harmonize classical contract theory with social determinism. The results of his early work, while they were philosophically wanting, made Fouillée the most popular "Republican" philosopher of the 1880s and 1890s. His efforts to preserve voluntarism within a system of "reparative" social justice that encouraged state intervention in behalf of the weak, laid the foundations of "solidarism" and were a chief influence in the development of a social welfare dimension to old-fashioned political Radicalism.[62]

In the course of a series of articles published in the late seventies,

[59] See "Du droit personnel de défense," *Critique philosophique* 2 (1872), p. 293.

[60] Scott, *Republican Ideas and the Liberal Tradition in France*, pp. 68-69.

[61] See the analysis of the evolution of Renouvier's views on punishment in Roger Picard, *La philosophie sociale de Renouvier* (Paris: Marcel Rivière, 1908), pp. 156-165. Renouvier specifically ruled out any "preventive" function for punishment because it entailed an "anticipated judgment" that abridged both the free responsibility of individuals and society's right to judge the acts of others only after they had broken the terms of the social contract.

[62] One of the best summaries of Fouillée's work is still in Scott, *Republican Ideas and the Liberal Tradition in France*, pp. 159-169.

later collected in *La science sociale contemporaine* (1880), Fouillée addressed himself to the problem of a theory of punishment that included both classical contractualism and modern naturalism. We must learn to admit, he wrote, the natural and determined basis of much crime, but without becoming either fatalistic or cynical. Instead, we should use the knowledge we gain in our study of the sources of crime to further society's collective ideal, in this instance by the elaboration of a theory of punishment that would justify the repression of crimes repugnant to those ideals. Since society was "at once an organism and a contract," responsibility could be either individual or social. It was individual when "the accused was aware of violating the social contract and the rights of others."[63] When the individual willfully violated the social contract, society's right to punish him flowed from that voluntary violation. But the right of *social* defense applied when the person accused, though personally without voluntary responsibility for his acts, constituted "a perpetual threat, [requiring] a perpetual responsibility toward society."[64]

Social defense, as Fouillée's theory had it, was society's natural right as an organism to protect itself against internal dangers. By replacing "the mystical right to punish by the scientific right of social defense," Fouillée was both striking a blow against expiatory, Christian theories of punishment, which he was anxious to discredit, and providing a foundation for a Republican system of penal repression that was more powerful and more "modern" than the old social contract theory alone. This new version of Republican contract theory provided, as we shall see, the chief justification for harsh measures of penal legislation throughout the 1880s and beyond. For many of its principal supporters the only issue it left unresolved was the absence of guidelines that could be used in determining when the "individual" and when the "social" criterion applied. A satisfactory solution to that problem, it is safe to say, was never reached.

Another intellectual element that figured prominently in the ideological heritage of Opportunism was a deeply felt contempt for *oisiveté* (idleness). A term with roots in physiocratic and Saint-Simonian social philosophy, it originally expressed the dislike of these economic reformers for the class of nonproducing *rentiers* whose self-indulgent and unwise use of income deprived the progressive industrial sector of

[63] Alfred Fouillée, "La pénalité et les collisions de droits d'après la science sociale contemporaine," *Revue des deux mondes* (November 15, 1879), p. 416. See also Fouillée's, *La science sociale contemporaine*, 6th ed. (Paris: Hachette, 1922), pp. 74-191; and *L'idée moderne de droit*, 2d ed. (Paris: Hachette, 1923), pp. 215-292.

[64] Fouillée, "La pénalité et les collisions de droits," p. 417.

necessary investment capital. This concept possessed an obvious political attraction to Republicans during their years of opposition to successive regimes dominated by a minuscule class of great financial notables. Gambetta's so-called Belleville program damned economic policy that provided "bounties to idleness"; the entire thrust of Republican economic policy throughout the seventies, culminating in the Freycinet Plan, was to win the favor of the mass of independent producers and farmers who were potential political supporters.

The practice of mixing metaphors of work with those ensuring the victory of the Republic were common. In a speech in Chambéry on September 22, 1872, Gambetta counseled, "Before producing anything, one must have the proper tool—all of you know this, since you are all workers—and, for us Republicans, the indispensable, the superior tool is the Republic."[65] Gambetta explicitly identified labor in a democracy as "the great agent of wealth, of peace, and of happiness. ... In a social situation in which most workers are already property owners, they will choose a Republican form of government, because democracy and Republic are associated like cause and effect."[66] The mass of producers, to be sure, included the capitalists and industrial allies of the Republican movement; the Opportunists in particular were not interested in setting class against class, but in outlining a policy of solidarity that would ensure social peace. But however outmoded the term *oisiveté* later became as a reproach to an aristocracy of finance, it was still a vital part of the Republican lexicon in the 1880s, capable of doing service against new enemies. Michelle Perrot has interpreted the late nineteenth-century war against vagabonds as a consequence of the need of modern capitalism for a disciplined work force.[67] The political elite's suspicion of *gens sans aveu* and its exaltation of the virtues of thrift, stability, and reliability are the expressions of "a society in the process of rationalization, which can no longer tolerate the marginal types who are proverbial time wasters."[68] While persuasive as far as it goes, this interpretation of vagabonds as the "last rebels" against the industrial order overlooks both the political origins of the Republican horror of idleness discussed above, and the powerful influence that Royalist "moral order" had on all debates on social issues in the 1870s.

In his study of French legitimism during the 1870s, Robert Locke attempts to deduce the "sociology of moral order" from the Royalist vision of rural society purged of its flaws and restored to a utopian

---

[65] Cited in Barral, *Les fondateurs*, p. 118.

[66] Speech in Auxerre, June 1, 1874, cited in ibid., p. 233.

[67] Perrot, "La fin des vagabonds," pp. 23-25.

[68] Perrot, "Délinquance et système pénitentiaire," p. 80.

condition. The Legitimist ideal postulated an association of family, religion, and a natural hierarchy of notables in which each participant filled a natural and organic role guaranteeing the stability of the whole. The most astute Royalist commentators were excellent observers of the social, economic, and administrative forces that were disrupting this natural utopia. They were particularly sensitive to those factors that increased rural migration or caused the breakup or uprooting of peasant families.[69] The great fear of the landed notables of the 1870s was, in the words of the comte de Melun, that the social situation that "stops the nomadic life which renders men heedless of the future, forgetful of the traditions of their home town, disrespectful of the opinions of those who have always known them" might be destroyed. "Property makes he who possesses it more tidy, more industrious; it removes him from fatal distractions, keeps him near his hearth, in the bosom of his family, and usefully occupies his leisure time."[70]

Locke emphasizes the tendency for Legitimists to refer to rural discontent in "purely pathological" terms such as "contagion" and "disease," and to lard their vocabulary with verbs "used in approval (*fixer* or *limiter*) or in opprobrium (*déraciner* or *déclasser*)—words that reveal minds longing for security."[71] Royalists had no monopoly on this language, however; it was resorted to regularly by Opportunist spokesmen for transportation and appears to have had a powerful appeal to all Frenchmen in this era of social change. Anxiety about the unpredictability and chaos provoked by widespread human migrations was symbolized in the terror of vagabondage expressed by contemporaries of both rural and urban provenance.

Thus, transportation had several factors in its favor as a means of dealing with a social problem that showed every sign of worsening. First, as we have seen, transportation already existed for certain categories of criminals, and several colonial dumping grounds were immediately at hand. Second, it was a "Republican" measure that had been first adopted (though never applied) by the revolutionary assemblies of 1790-1793 and the Constituent of 1848. Transportation provided, moreover, a striking doctrinal contrast with the penal preferences of

[69] Among these were economic policies encouraging the flow of capital out of rural areas, the growth of rural administrative jobs luring young peasants away from farming, and a host of changes, including military basing and recruitment and the growth of cabarets, that brought the disruptive effects of urban life to the countryside. Robert Locke, *French Legitimists and the Politics of Moral Order in the Early Third Republic* (Princeton, N.J.: Princeton University Press, 1974), pp. 147-172.

[70] Quoted in ibid., p. 156.

[71] Ibid., pp. 176-177.

royalism. The prison system sponsored by the Royalist-influenced reform commission of 1872-1875 relied on institutions that resembled monasteries and featured a mode of moral rehabilitation that was remarkably like Christian penitence. Republican punishment was made of sterner stuff, exiling from the fatherland those who violated the social and political contracts of free citizens, or who refused the work of honest laborers. Finally, transportation was expedient. It was allegedly cheaper than the huge penitentiary network required in the 1875 law, and it could be implemented immediately.

The proposed law aroused vigorous commentary by politicians, lawyers, and penal professionals, but only a few complaints that transportation might lie outside the Republican mainstream. The most anticlerical among them, such as Joseph Reinach, openly attacked the expiatory ideal that lay at the heart of imprisonment,[72] but others asserted that, by promoting work in the open air, transportation would encourage rehabilitation and allow "virtue" to flourish.[73] All used the most violent language, however, to condemn the communal prisons that were the lot of most French convicts. Employing a timely biological metaphor, Charles Bertheau, a public prosecutor, spoke of the "phylloxera of prisons" where new convicts find themselves locked in with "habitués and prison scum, mangy black sheep that threaten the whole herd with contagion; beggars, vagrants, and professional thieves."[74]

Vagabonds and beggars were singled out for special attention. Alfred Lagrésille, a public prosecutor in Nancy, wrote of the "law of work," and Charles Bertheau of "work, that holy law of the world," a principle being systematically violated, in Lagrésille's words, by an "invading horde of lazy no-goods, professional delinquents, true enemies of society."[75] Théodore Homberg, in his legal treatise on vagabondage, argued that "labor" was a "natural law imposed on all of humanity." Vagabondage, therefore, was not a crime *in se*, but a crime *in ommittendo*, that is, the formal crime was the *failure* to work;[76] for Lagrésille, the vagrant "is attached to nothing: that itself is his offense."[77]

The primary justification advanced for this extreme penalty was the

---

[72] Joseph Reinach, *Les récidivistes* (Paris: Charpentier, 1882), p. 59.

[73] Berteau, *De la transportation*, p. 86.

[74] Ibid., pp. 9-10, 35.

[75] Ibid., p. 11; Alfred Lagrésille, *Vagabondage et de la transportation* (Nancy, 1881), pp. 7, 78-79; see also the remarks of Georges Picot in the debates at the Penitentiary Society in 1883 concerning "the perverse natures of men born and corrupted in the great cities who reject all work," in the *Bulletin de la Société générale des prisons* 7 (January 1883), p. 15.

[76] Théodore Homberg, *Etudes sur le vagabondage* (Paris: Forestier, 1880), pp. 6-7.

[77] Lagrésille, *Vagabondage*, p. 79.

violation of the social contract.[78] Occasionally, biological language in the manner of Fouillée ("organism-germ," "organism-ulcer") was employed to characterize the relation of the recidivist to society.[79] Another metaphor with distinctly political overtones—a great favorite of Republican legislators during the debates—was that of society as nourishing breast (Marianne) who banished her wicked offspring when they gave offense.[80] Reinach posed the dilemma of the administration of justice in a democratic society in richly ironic terms, affirming that laxness is "for a democracy such as ours what religious indifference is for religion."[81] Few commentators failed to allude to the politico-military threat posed by the "legions" or the "armies" of recidivists recruiting their members from the "regimental depot" of the prison.[82] Memories of the upheavals of 1870-1871 were still vivid; Reinach made the connection with recidivism explicit. Citing the parliamentary inquiry that investigated the Paris Commune, he quoted the former prefect of police Gaston Macé to the effect that of every 100 participants in the March 18 insurrection, 25 were recidivists (25 of 100 women were prostitutes!). Fully 25,000 of the Communards who engaged in the civil war, he held, were also recidivists. And such, he warned, was the solidarity today of the army of recidivists that at a word from their nefarious leaders, they were prepared to descend on the capital to do battle with the Republic.[83]

Finally, each of these pre-1885 commentators employed some term with which he could make a distinction between "incorrigible" criminals (earmarked for transportation) and those salvageable beings destined for some more tender fate.[84] "Habitual delinquents versus occasional delinquents" was one favorite, "professional criminal versus accidental criminal" was another. The most idealistic of the early experts on transportation, Fernand Desportes, deplored the failure of the penal code to distinguish between "the criminal who commits his first crime in a moment of distraction, of despair, or of passion, and the inveterate repeater for whom crime is a profession; between the man whose crime,

[78] Ibid., p. 7; Berteau, *De la transportation*, p. 2; Homberg, *Etudes*, p. 3; Reinach, *Les récidivistes*, p. iii.

[79] Homberg, *Etudes*, pp. 3-4; Reinach, *Les récidivistes*, p. 14.

[80] Homberg, *Etudes*, p. 187.

[81] Reinach, *Les récidivistes*, p. iii.

[82] Bertheau, *De la transportation*, pp. 2-5, 16; Alexandre Bérard, *La transportation des récidivistes et les colonies françaises* (Lyon, 1885), pp. 5, 8.

[83] Reinach, *Les récidivistes*, pp. 30-35; see the remarks on the Commune by Charles Petit, *Bulletin de la Société générale des prisons* 7 (January 1883), p. 21

[84] See, for this distinction, Edmond Plauchut, "La loi des récidivistes et nos colonies," *Revue des deux mondes* (November 1, 1884), pp. 166-167.

blameworthy as it may be, is not dishonoring, and he for whose offense we must suppose the complete perversion of moral sense."[85]

By indicating the difference between "hardened" and salvageable offenders, these writers were not making an original distinction, but were following a long established tradition in the *politique criminelle* of recidivism. Arnould Bonneville de Marsangy, whose *De la récidive* (1844) was one of the foremost landmarks in a generation of great volumes on penal reform, was one of the first writers to insist that penal policy must distinguish between repeat and first offenders. Bonneville believed that a crime committed by a recidivist and the same one committed by a first offender ought to be punished differently, each earning a sentence based on the offender's judicial antecedents, that is, on "his own merits." Often recognized as the pioneer in focusing the attention of penologists on the criminal rather than the crime, Bonneville held that recidivism was proof of a grave degree of perversion, warranting much severer punishment than that appropriate for the relatively less perverted first offender.[86]

Though Bonneville de Marsangy was the pioneer in this field, the commentators of the 1880s were more influenced by a more recent classic by the Republican penologist, Hubert Michaux. Michaux's *Etude sur la question des peines* (1872) made popular the binary opposition of crime as accident and crime as profession and recommended transportation as a perfectly suitable punishment for the latter category.[87] Michaux was one of the few penologists of his generation who had little faith in cellular imprisonment, believing it led to madness. He coined a phrase much employed through the remainder of the century by opponents of the cell: "Many whose conscience we wished to save lost their reason instead."[88] Michaux warned against considering criminals as a "separate race," but in continuing the sort of distinction begun by Bonneville de Marsangy between first offenders and recidivists, Michaux employed language that strained the limits of the traditional concept of moral perversity. He used old-fashioned terms such as "l'ésprit du mal," but he also mentioned "mal du race ou de naissance," holding that some are "evil by instinct, by taste, by appetite, convicts by nature; others become so through poverty, the example of vice, or

---

[85] Fernand Desportes, *La récidive: Examen du projet de loi sur le rélégation des récidivistes* (Paris, 1885), p. 22.

[86] Bonneville de Marsangy, *De la récidive* (Paris, 1844), pp. ii-v. See André Normandeau, "Arnould Bonneville de Marsangy," in Mannheim, ed., *Pioneers in Criminology*, pp. 128-137.

[87] Hubert Michaux, *Etude sur la question des peines* (Paris, 1872), pp. 177-194.

[88] Ibid., p. 7.

through ignorance of the good." However they might become criminals, Michaux warned, "professional criminals" were no longer open to amendment. And "if society does not eliminate them, they will eliminate society."[89]

By the 1880s, the most inveterate Republican supporters of transportation were willing to reach into the clinic for the language they used to describe recidivists and to make the abyss that separated the "accidental" from the "professional" criminal practically unbridgeable. Recidivists were "moral lepers," who, "like the wild beast, have nothing but appetites." They were "monomaniacs" with "degenerate natures" who have descended so low on the social scale that they live among us "like savage beasts."[90] Joseph Reinach, one of Gambetta's chief lieutenants and editor of the Gambettist paper *La République française*, relied more heavily on clinical terminology than any of his nonmedical contemporaries. He discussed the "epileptic-alcoholics" among recidivists, and the "cerebral lesions" and "monomania" affecting many sex criminals.[91] He wrote that the distinction between the "accidental" and the "professional" criminal was "what a fever, which is curable, is to melancholia [*lypémanie*], which is not." Reinach did more than any other writer to make the old-fashioned term "incorrigible" interchangeable with the clinical one, "incurable." Transportation was the perfect solution for these recidivist "incurables" for the same reason the asylum was best for the madman: "They are, like all the insane, a grave danger to society, and must in equal measure be made powerless to do evil."[92]

The political origin of Reinach's language can be clearly demonstrated by a review of contemporary psychiatry, which by no means unanimously supported his views on the incurability of the mentally ill. Coincidentally, the psychiatric community was intensely engaged in debating this issue throughout the period 1881-1884 since the divorce bill being prepared by the first Ferry government included the insanity of one of the spouses in its original provisions. When the measure became law in 1884 the original insanity clause had been eliminated, owing largely to the depositions in 1882 of four of the

[89] Ibid., pp. 211-212, 198.

[90] Bertheau, *De la transportation*, pp. 9-11, and Homberg, *Etudes*, pp. 31, 243-244.

[91] Reinach, *Les récidivistes*, pp. 11, 138, 139.

[92] Ibid., pp. 10-11. In his effort to make a persuasive case for incurability, Reinach does violence to the syndrome of "lypémanie," a term that Etienne Esquirol used interchangeably with melancholy. Esquirol did regard the disease as partially inherited, but, far from being incurable, it was responsive to a number of therapeutic strategies which he discusses in great detail. See Etienne Esquirol, *De la lypémanie ou melancolie*, presented by P. Fédida and J. Postel (Toulouse: Privat, 1977), pp. 86, 149-165.

giants of French psychiatry: Blanche, Charcot, Legrand du Saulle, and Valentin Magnan. Their conclusions, as summarized in the chief organ of French psychiatry, the *Annales médico-psychologiques*, were that "the incurability of insanity could not be indicated with any assurance; ... facts have often thwarted such judgments and demonstrated their falsehood."[93]

These conclusions did not stand without opposition from within the community. The irrepressible Eugène Dally, president of the Société médico-psychologique in 1882, argued passionately in favor of the divorce measure to help "build a dike against the progressive degenerescence of our race."[94] Dally claimed to be shocked at the "solicitude" of his colleagues for the procreation of "individuals marked by hereditary symptoms" and the "diffusion of cases of madness."[95] In a lengthy report issued in September 1882, Jean Luys cited his own studies at the Hôpital de la charité to show that after men had suffered from chronic "dementia" for four years and women for five, according to "pathological laws concerning the lunatic's brain," a definitive incurability could be pronounced. Mocking claims that longstanding cases were often suddenly cured, Luys averred he had never seen one during his clinical experience, and knew of only three "questionable" cases in the literature.[96]

Dr. Esprit-Sylvestre Blanche, speaking for the majority, admitted it was occasionally possible to affirm with certainty that a case was incurable. But such cases usually involved illnesses of lifelong order, and could, on account of their obviousness, be eliminated as a factor in divorce by merely applying more rigorous medical standards for marital fitness.[97] Certainly, predisposition to madness was often hereditary, but Blanche did not regard that as a reason, even if the predisposition could be readily identified, to abandon hope of a cure. Taking the worst case possible, general paralysis with cephalic lesions, Blanche claimed to have seen occasional cures and remissions of a considerable

[93] "Chronique," *Annales médico-psychologiques*, 6th ser. 7 (May 1882), p. 354. The relative independence of French psychiatry, as expressed in this conclusion, is all the more remarkable in view of the alliance forged in this period between the Republican regime and psychiatry. See Goldstein, "The Hysteria Diagnosis," pp. 222-224.

[94] Eugène Dally, *Annales médico-psychologiques*, 6th ser. 7 (May 1882), p. 355.

[95] Ibid. 8 (July 1882), pp. 112-113.

[96] Jean Luys, *Annales médico-psychologiques*, 6th ser. 8 (September 1882), pp. 303-316, 331.

[97] E. S. Blanche, "La folie, doit-elle être considérée comme une cause de divorce?" *Annales médico-psychologiques*, 6th ser. 8 (July 1882), pp. 72-73.

length of time.[98] A. Giraud also responded to Luy's assertions about incurables with a lengthy study of "belated cures."[99] Other papers and debates during this same period on the likelihood of mental illness in the children of the insane seem to reveal a genuine reluctance on the part of psychiatrists to admit of incurability in all but the most extreme cases.[100]

In later years, as we shall see, French psychiatrists were more willing to pronounce confidently on the incurability of a large number of cases of mental illness and to ascribe an overwhelming portion of mental disturbances to heredity. But these developments had to await the victory of organicism, and in particular the great influence of its chief, Valentin Magnan, who, a proponent of psychiatry's ability to cure in 1882, became the prophet of an extreme neurological determinism for a later generation. In 1882 only a few voices within French psychiatry were willing to proclaim that some forms of insanity were incurable or to associate perversity and vice with "bad blood" or "predispositions." Nonetheless, their testimony, and the willful misuse of psychiatric terminology by advocates of transportation provided a substantial part of the justification for this measure of permanent exile. To those Republican politicians for whom the firm treatment of recidivists had become a political necessity, the worst possible account of their depravity was most useful.

The original project for transporting multiple offenders for simple misdemeanors (*délits*) originated within the Gambettist camp some time in 1880. It was a favorite project of the great man himself, who apparently regarded it as a pure expression of Republican penal principles. Transportation was on the agenda of the "*grand ministère*" but

[98] Ibid., p. 75.

[99] A. Giraud, "Contribution à l'étude des guérisons tardives," *Annales médico-psychologiques*, 6th ser. 9 (January 1883), pp. 68-91.

[100] See A. Giraud, "Médicine légale," in which he counsels medical experts to be cautious about relying on hereditary antecedents to pronounce nonresponsibility. *Annales médico-psychologiques*, 6th ser. 6 (July 1881), pp. 87-105. See also the interesting paper of Eugène Billod, "De la conduite à tenir quand on est consulté par un sujet qui se croit menacé de folie parce qu'il est issue de parents aliénés," ibid., 6th ser. 9 (May 1883), pp. 419-432. Billod's paper claimed, and in the debate that followed nearly all the participants agreed, that there was no certain "fatality," that serious morbid influences might express themselves in the offspring as "a simple nervous condition" (Dr. Jules Fournet, p. 465) or never appear at all, remaining merely a "predisposition" (Billod, p. 420). Dr. V. Bigot even made the optimistic assertion that if only one parent was tainted with hereditary "vice," the heredity of the healthy parent might "annihilate" the unhealthy heredity of the other, p. 461. Two of the luminaries of the preceding generation, Falret and Lunier, were cited by the majority as favoring its views, p. 468.

never reached the stage of formal proposal. Instead, Gambetta personally prepared the earliest legislative version of the bill and sent it off with some of the other unfinished business from his brief ministry in the fall of 1882, only months before his premature death.[101]

René Waldeck-Rousseau, who had been recruited by the Gambettists in 1880 as their expert on judicial affairs, became the rapporteur of the project in collaboration with another Breton Gambettist, Martin-Feuillée.[102] Waldeck-Rousseau had made a reputation for himself as a rigid authoritarian and centralizer while interior minister in the "great ministry." His report on the bill in December 1882 preserved the accents of the militant Republican social defense favored by the deceased "tribune." Waldeck-Rousseau fulsomely praised the work of the Republican legislators of the Revolution who did not hesitate to deprive of their rights those who had shown themselves undeserving, and to exile criminals and vagabonds far from the fatherland.[103] Waldeck-Rousseau struck a theme that sounded frequently throughout the debates to follow. We need, he affirmed, "a new punishment for the effective and energetic repression of these *incurables of vice*, of these *incorrigibles* of misdemeanor and crime, who, willfully, live outside the boundaries of society, struggle openly against it, and, through their repeated infractions, pose a serious and continuous threat to public tranquillity."[104] The logic of this argument, insofar as it has logic at all, is purely political. How, one wonders can an "incurable" and "incorrigible" criminal have "willfully" chosen to engage in open struggle with society? Yet, the statement effectively met two needs of Waldeck-Rousseau's program: it portrayed recidivists as deserving of punishment for having voluntarily broken the sacred social compact, and it described them as a species apart from the norm, and so unlikely of "cure" that one need feel no scruple against their lifelong exclusion from society.

Waldeck-Rousseau emphasized the vast wave of public opinion sup-

[101] For an account of Gambetta's activities in this period, see Joseph Reinach, *La vie politique de Léon Gambetta* (Paris: Alcan, 1917), pp. 112-116.

[102] Pierre Sorlin discusses Waldeck-Rousseau's "conversion" to Gambettism in *Waldeck-Rousseau* (Paris: Colin, 1966), pp. 198-199.

[103] René Waldeck-Rousseau, "Rapport sur la proposition de loi relative à la transportation des récidivistes," *Bulletin de la Société générale des prisons* 7 (January 1883), p. 74. He also asks the question posed by Fouillée, Renouvier, and other Republican thinkers: each individual has the right of legitimate self-defense against attack, why not society itself?, p. 78.

[104] Ibid., p. 73. My emphasis. Later, doubting the strength of the attachment of recidivists to the mother country, he reemphasized the "perversité absolue" of certain "incorrigibles," who were impossible to rehabilitate, pp. 78-79.

porting his bill, indicating with particular pride the 60,000 signatures gathered by the Masonic lodge, Travail et persévérante amitié. By the spring of 1883, as the Opportunist organ *Le siècle* pointed out, several provincial courts of appeal, and twenty-two departmental general councils had endorsed the transportation of recidivists.[105] It was also endorsed, not surprisingly, by many of the regional electoral committees which had supported Gambettist and Ferryist candidates. In Republican France prior to the full introduction of mass journalism, this was a typical cross-section of those sources of opinion on whose support a moderate regime could nearly always rely.

Parisian press opinion in the spring of 1883 split on the issue in predictable ways. The bill was opposed by the journals whose political hue was somewhere to the left of Opportunism. *La presse* mocked the proposal as the only way the government could find to populate the colonies.[106] *La lanterne* and Henri Rochefort's *L'intransigéant* called it the "political hobbyhorse of the Gambettists" and a "monument of Opportunist cruelty."[107] They left no doubt that this bill was a maneuver designed to strengthen the alliance of the moderates of the Republican center against their enemies on either extreme. The *Gazette des tribuneaux*, the voice of the legal profession, had strong doubts about the bill, and, on the right, *La croix*, while mocking the too-gentle sensibilities of the opponents of transportation, preferred to dwell on the "flood" of recidivism as God's punishment of the Republic.[108]

Moderate Republican papers and those a few shades to the right of the center supported the project with varying degrees of enthusiasm. *Le temps*, chiding the Opportunists for having yet made no reforms, advised them to pass this "reform" as a way of proving their ability to act firmly in a situation of "urgency."[109] The *Journal de débats* agreed, terming the transportation of incorrigibles one of the most "important judicial reforms of our times."[110] *Le petit journal* and *Le Figaro* also emphasized the crisis proportions of the problem in their remarks of support.[111] Far and away the firmest supporters were Reinach's *La République française*, which, *La presse* wrote, "has made of this law the

[105] "La loi sur les récidivistes," *Le siècle*, April 21, 1883.
[106] *La presse*, February 24, 1883. See also ibid., April 28, 1883.
[107] *La lanterne*, April 23, 1883; *L'intransigéant*, April 24, 1883.
[108] *Gazette des tribuneaux*, February 20, 1883; *La croix*, June 27, 1883.
[109] *Le temps*, April 17, 1883.
[110] *Journal de débats*, April 13, 1883.
[111] Thomas Grimm, "Les récidivistes," *Le petit journal*, April 28, 1883; "Les récidivistes," *Le Figaro*, April 27, 1883.

crowning of the Republican edifice of its dreams,"[112] and Waldeck-Rousseau's organ, *La réforme de Paris*. This short-lived sheet, whose sole reason for existence was the puffing of Waldeck-Rousseau and his allies, was by far the most extreme of the Paris newspapers on the issue of recidivism.[113]

Despite the support of much of Republican opinion, not all observers believed the law would pass.[114] It may have been the labor disturbances in the late winter that helped put the parliamentarians in a less compromising frame of mind toward vagrants. A wave of strikes in the fall of 1881 had signaled the rebirth of labor militancy after years of relative quiescence. The effects of the depression had been particularly damaging to building construction in Paris; by the spring of 1883, 26,000 workers in the housing trades were out of work. A demonstration on March 9, led by the notorious anarchist Louise Michel and her associates, degenerated into looting and window smashing around the place des Invalides. The leaders of the march were jailed and put on trial; they were eventually condemned in June to lengthy prison sentences, even though their complicity in the actual violence was far from proven to everyone's satisfaction.

For Michel's trial, and that in Lyon two months earlier of Peter Kropotkin and a group of anarchists accused of fomenting unrest in Lyon and Montceau-les-Mines, the 1872 law on international associations was invoked to ensure swift and certain convictions. The bourgeois press was in arms throughout the winter on this unhealthy conjunction of labor unrest and anarchism. Waldeck-Rousseau, who had become interior minister on February 21 in Ferry's second ministry, took the opportunity to elaborate the connections between recidivism and anarchy in *La réforme de Paris*. In a column headed "Anarchists and Recidivists," the paper warned that society would not yield to this "errant army of social revolt" composed of "miserable creatures driven to evil by a moral or physical deformity," but would attempt "not only to suppress these monsters, but also to cure them."[115] A conflation of "anarchists" with "bandits" and "recidivists," and later with "idlers," was made in connection with the rounding up of vagabonds in central

[112] *La presse*, April 27, 1883; see *La République française*, April 23, 1883; April 28, 1883; May 1, 1883.
[113] On the life of this typical *journal politique* see Sorlin, *Waldeck-Rousseau*, pp. 314-320.
[114] See *La presse*, April 24, 1883; "Les récidivistes," *Le Figaro*, April 27, 1883; *La lanterne* was predicting defeat as late as June 27, 1883.
[115] "Anarchistes et récidivistes," *Réforme de Paris*, March 1, 1883.

Paris.[116] The paper continued the assault in April on the army of 60,000 Parisian "robbers, bandits, killers, scoundrels ready for all crime; pimps, sneak thieves, armed to the teeth; a population that does not work."[117] The equation of crime, radical politics, and madness was underscored in March in the Chamber of Deputies by the new minister of the interior. In response to a request by the extreme left to amnesty the condemned anarchists of January, Waldeck-Rousseau denied that they were a "political party" or the "lost children" of republicanism deserving of pardon as political criminals. They were instead "a knot of agitators, a few evildoers, a few insane" whose recent provocations constituted a clear and present danger to the state.[118]

When the debate on transportation opened on April 22, Ferry's Republican cabinet of Opportunist "concentration" was two months old. By-elections earlier in the month had produced a few Radical victories, creating an atmosphere that caused the ever-cautious André Daniel to worry about the dissolution of the Gambettist party. Anticipating the terms of Ferry's October speech at Le Havre, Daniel believed that Opportunist discipline alone could prevent the nation from falling to "the double peril" of radicalism and monarchism.[119] Ferry's majority was a solid one by the standards of the time, but Prost and Rosenzweig, who have studied this assembly in detail, have shown that while the main issues of 1882 were still the Republic and clericalism, the rise of the new issues of working-class militancy, colonialism, and municipal government in 1883 threatened to divide the Republican coalition. Gambettists, and some of the members of Ferry's Gauche républicaine, found themselves obliged to choose between two emerging "republican" alternatives, one brilliantly articulated by Clemenceau and his Radical colleagues, and the other by Ferry's cabinet. In the words of Prost and Rosenzweig, this was a good example of the "logic" of a situation in which centrist deputies slid left or right "neither because of their own instability nor because of the pressure of their constituents' opinion. They had to move because their initial positions became too uncomfortable."[120]

[116] *Réforme de Paris*, March 5, 1883; "Récidivistes et anarchists," ibid., March 15, 1883; "Badauds et anarchistes," ibid., March 18, 1883. For an account of a Republic's right to defend itself see "La paix républicaine," ibid., March 12, 1883.

[117] "Botany-Bay," *Réforme de Paris*, April 23, 1883. Also see the biological imagery in Georges Grison, "Maximes de voleurs et d'assassins," *Le Figaro* April 18, 1883.

[118] Waldeck-Rousseau, *Journal officiel*, "Chambre des députés," March 20, 1883, pp. 664-665. François Cantagrel was moved to add, in response to Waldeck-Rousseau's reading of anarchist political tracts, "These are madmen, not criminals," p. 665.

[119] André Daniel, *L'année politique 1883* (Paris: Charpentier, 1884), pp. 151-152.

[120] Antoine Prost and Christian Rosenzweig, "Measurement of Attitude Changes

Though they would have preferred not to choose at all, there was a mild tendency, among the Gambettists especially, to slide to the left.[121] To keep his coalition intact for his reform of municipal government and his colonial program, Ferry sought issues that would unite his Opportunist colleagues by reminding them of their common heritage and interests. What better way than to adopt a piece of Gambettist legislation that would allow him the triple advantage of protecting public security, displaying "Republican" penal theory, and contributing to the colonial effort in unlikely portions of the world?

The version of the bill introduced on April 22 required the automatic sentencing, without discretion, of life transportation for "recidivists and habitual criminals" convicted of certain specified offenses. The relevant offenses were (1) convictions, in any order and within a period of ten years, for two *crimes* (felonies) carrying sentences of at least eight years and two *délits* (misdemeanors) carrying at least three months' imprisonment each; (2) convictions, within a period of ten years, for four offenses punished by at least three months' imprisonment each, falling into the following categories: theft, embezzlement, the destruction of trees and harvests, outrages of public decency, and the "habitual" corruption of minors; (3) five convictions, within a period of ten years, for vagrancy, of which one was for three months' imprisonment, or four convictions for vagrancy plus one for any of the offenses in category two above; (4) convictions for any six offenses, at least one of which carried a sentence of three months in prison.

One provision of the bill (article 6) changed the penal code's definition of vagrancy to disqualify both prostitution and "illicit games" as "trades" or "professions," thereby making both prostitutes and all varieties of street hustlers, however large their incomes, subject to the law. Transportation was to take place after the recidivist served out the term of his last conviction in a metropolitan penal establishment. It was an "accessory" punishment for life and would be served in New Caledonia, the Marquises, Phu-Quoc (off Vietnam), or Guyana. The bill punished escape attempts or crimes in the penal colony with close imprisonment, and made any pardon or other measure permitting return to France a virtual impossibility. Finally, the bill was mute on the nature or precise location of the *régime* to which the *"transportés"* would be subject, specifying provisionally that only "non-Europeans" would be sent to Guyana. The final arrangements on the type, if any, of penal institutions in the colonies, and the basis on which "rehabil-

---

among the Members of the French Chamber of Deputies, 1882-1884," in William O. Aydelotte, ed., *The History of Parliamentary Behavior* (Princeton, N.J.: Princeton University Press, 1977), pp. 127-128.

[121] Ibid., pp. 118-119.

itated" criminals might be granted land and send for their families was left entirely up to administrative decrees to be issued by the Naval and Interior ministries.

The first reading of the bill took place in late April and early May, and the second during the last half of June. During these first debates the principal spokesmen attempted to defend the bill on four primary grounds. First, recidivists were truly "incorrigible," and society had every right to protect itself against the danger they posed. Second, the bill's defenders indicated the Republican antecedents for the bill and praised it as a true "reform." It was also characterized as progressive in its aim to "regenerate" the recidivists, and, finally, was presented as a cog in the French colonial scheme, much as Australia had been for Britain. Opponents of the bill during these first readings were largely from the extreme left, the right confining itself to an occasional interjection. They countered all the arguments of the government and added other objections, in particular the bill's violation of equality and proportionality of punishment.

No debater challenged the facts of the growth of recidivism, though several leftists suggested that the overall figures for crime were hardly of crisis proportions. Nor did anyone question the right of society to a legitimate self-defense. This debate over criminal legislation is unique in the extraordinarily broad base of agreement on the philosophical foundations of punishment, and on the nearly total absence of disputes over statistics. More important was the willingness of all but the bill's most violent opponents to accept the great distinction between "accidental" criminals and the "professional," "incorrigible," or "habitual" ones. Both the principal government spokesman for the bill, Waldeck-Rousseau, and its new reporter, Gaston Gerville-Réache, built their cases firmly on this distinction. The "accidental" criminal, according to the bill's reporter, committed his crime under the influence of strong, but temporary emotions, while the "hardened" individual contemplated his crime coldly.[122] Waldeck-Rousseau elaborated this distinction, emphasizing both the willfulness of the "habitual offender" who "patiently" works to undermine society and his "incurability" and "natural perversity." By contrast, he pictured the poor devil who had "fallen" or committed an "infraction" in a "moment of anger" or "weakness" who appeared before the judge with his head lowered, filled with shame for his transgressions.[123]

[122] Gerville-Réache, *Journal officiel,* "Chambre des députés," April 27, 1883, p. 772.
[123] Waldeck-Rousseau, *Journal officiel,* "Chambre des députés," April 27, 1883, pp. 778-780.

84

Strikingly, some variation of accidental versus incorrigible was accepted by nearly all the bill's opponents, even those who allegedly believed that all crime would disappear with the elimination of poverty. Martin Nadaud, Philippe Jullien, Pierre Gomot, Georges Perin, Gustave Rivet, and many others employed this distinction in their remarks before the Chamber.[124] Even Georges Clemenceau, whose opposition to transportation was the most thorough and the most eloquent, did not deny that there were "habitual" criminals. However, he did argue that the vast majority of recidivists were merely men "on whom one had not acted effectively" by giving them some moral or economic support after they committed their first crimes.[125]

It is clear that the biological language favored by a minority of the penal and medical professionals of the era was popular with the Opportunist politicians.[126] Biological metaphors had the clear effect of helping to widen the gap between "accidental" and "habitual" criminals, and provided rhetorical and conceptual support for the discourse of social defense. Thus, Ferdinand Dreyfus spoke warmly of this law of "salubrity" and "purification" as a law of "social hygiene" that would destroy the "germs" of the "epidemic" of recidivism. These metaphors in turn fed anxieties that the "army" of recidivists might take up arms against the Republic. Opportunists complained about the "floating population" of recidivists "ready to join any public disorder or insurrection," or complained of the helplessness of society "faced with revolt" by the "reserve army" of criminals, especially when they "are moved by certain states of mind."[127]

Predictably, Republican supporters and opponents of the bill both claimed direct lineage with the revolutionaries of 1789 for their respective points of view. Opportunists cited the Republican doctrine of social defense and the Convention's transportation law of 1791, and

[124] Martin Nadaud, *Journal officiel*, "Chambre des députés," April 22, 1883, p. 697; Philippe Jullien, ibid., p. 703; Pierre Gomot, ibid., p. 707; Georges Perin, ibid., April 27, 1883, p. 777; Gustave Rivet, ibid., June 26, 1883, p. 1443.

[125] Georges Clemenceau, *Journal officiel*, "Chambre des députés," April 29, 1883, pp. 799-800.

[126] See the remarks of Claude-Marie Versigny, on the "monomania," "incurable perversity," and "moral perversity" of some recidivists. *Journal officiel*, "Chambre des députés," April 27, 1883, pp. 784-785; also Jullien's discussion of "physical and moral" symptoms of criminality, ibid., June 26, 1883, p. 1442; and Félix Granet, ibid., June 28, 1883, pp. 1479-1480. Ferdinand Dreyfus, ibid., April 22, 1883, p. 700; see also the remarks of Jean-Louis Camecasse, ibid., June 26, 1883, p. 1446.

[127] See the remarks of Ferdinand Dreyfus, Waldeck-Rousseau, Alphonse Labussière, and Louis Andrieux in *Journal officiel*, "Chambre des députés," April 22, June 26, and June 28, 1883, pp. 700, 779, 1450, 1493.

counted as their own Alexis de Toqueville and Alphonse de Lamartine, men of 1848 who had supported the exile of multiple recidivists.[128] Opponents of the bill, however, seem to have had much the better of this fraternal dispute over the past, both on the specific issue of transportation and on the general heritage of the Revolution. Charles Floquet reminded his colleagues that the code of 1791 decreed transportation only for multiple felonies, not for misdemeanors as in the present bill. It was, moreover, pronounced on a citizen by a jury of his peers, not, as was possible here, a lowly correctional judge. In 1791, he added, vagabonds were transported only for terms, and only then for a clear "refusal to work."[129]

Progress and humanity were repeatedly invoked by opponents; Clemenceau ended his long and eloquent address on April 29 by listing the penal reforms of "monarchist peoples who are undertaking the amelioration of laws that we, Republicans, do not dare touch." Where, he asked, are the liberal passions of the early Revolution? "They are here," he replied, "they are sleeping; and they must be reawakened." It is shameful, he said, that "we who lay claim to all the great and generous ideas that ennoble man, we who are trying to make him understand that he is perfectible, that he can improve himself, it is we who are returning to this medieval idea, we who are marching backward, who are renouncing the reforms of progress."[130]

In rebuttal, the defenders of the bill were hard pressed to pass off their measure of expediency as a reform. Waldeck-Rousseau tried to link transportation with "our great efforts" to reform education, and described the bill as a "first chapter" in a "great book" of penitentiary reform, an unusual argument in view of the fact that transportation was being presented as an alternative to cellular imprisonment.[131] A more popular argument seems to have been the claim that life in the penal colony provided just the proper situation to rehabilitate (*régénérer*) the hardened criminal. But this argument also had its obvious problems. No one could explain convincingly why work and life in the

[128] Fréderic Thomas, *Journal officiel*, "Chambre des députés," April 22, 1883, p. 704; Waldeck-Rousseau, ibid., April 27, 1883, pp. 777-778; Louis Laroze, ibid., April 29, 1883, p. 791.

[129] Charles Floquet, *Journal officiel*, "Chambre des députés," June 26, 1883, p. 1445.

[130] Georges Clemenceau, *Journal officiel*, "Chambre des députés," April 29, 1883, pp. 804-805.

[131] Waldeck-Rousseau, *Journal officiel*, "Chambre des députés," April 27, 1883, pp. 779-780. Clemenceau later predicted that transportation was an excuse *not* to build a penitentiary system. Ibid., p. 802.

outdoors were so apt a punishment for recidivists;[132] it was also a simple matter to point out how senseless it was to speak of "regeneration" for someone with a life sentence. Gustave Rivet, reminding his colleagues of Waldeck-Rousseau's laconic description of recidivists as "worthy of little interest," complained that the government was trying to have it both ways. What meaning, he asked sententiously, does rehabilitation have for a man "for whom the gates of the fatherland are eternally closed?"[133]

Though serious doubts about the financial and colonial advantages of the bill were raised, the major parliamentary challenges to the bill's integrity came in the form of proposed amendments to make transportation a discretionary punishment pronounced by presiding magistrates, or pronounced only after a jury verdict, even in correctional courts. The government met these proposals with the simple argument that magistrates and juries were notoriously lax in enforcing the law and that judicial discretion resulted, in any event, in unequal applications of the law, thus violating Republican principles.[134] Despite widespread fears that automatic sentencing would make a "machine" of the judge and a mockery of the aim of justice to amend wrongdoers as well as punish them, the government handily beat back these amendments. In so doing, the Chamber decided to ignore some important arguments. Louis Gatineau had argued that the choice of four consecutive offenses as the criterion for establishing life transportation could only be justified if it could be shown that no criminal had ever gone straight after four offenses. Otherwise, one had created only a "legal presumption," not a proof of incorrigibility.[135] Other commen-

---

[132] Former premier Richard Waddington attempted an explanation based on the notion that, their natures being extreme, recidivists required an extreme change of environment to rehabilitate them. *Journal officiel*, "Chambre des députés," May 2, 1883, p. 828. See also the defense of transportation by Louis Herbette, the commissioner of the penal administration, to the Chamber, ibid., May 1, 1883, pp. 815-818. Gerville-Réache was reduced to arguing that the number of crimes committed by liberated criminals in the prison colonies was much lower per capita than the crime rate in France. Ibid., April 2, 1883, p. 775.

[133] Gustave Rivet, *Journal officiel*, "Chambre des députés," June 24, 1883, p. 1425. Clemenceau no doubt enjoyed reproaching his fellow anticlerics in the government, pointing out that this punishment was a rigorous version of Christian damnation to eternal hell. Ibid., April 29, 1883, p. 802.

[134] See the arguments by Louis Laroze, *Journal officiel*, "Chambre des députés," April 29, 1883, p. 791; Gerville-Réache argued that when given the chance magistrates seldom opted for maximum penalties. Ibid., May 2, 1883, p. 836.

[135] Louis Gatineau, *Journal officiel*, "Chambre des députés," April 29, 1883, p. 793. Speaking for the Commission on Judicial Reform, Armand Rodat replied that

tators complained that the law would weaken repression as judges and juries would acquit rather than sentence petty criminals to life imprisonment. The proposed amendments were handily defeated, however, and the final vote of 431 to 45 with 45 abstentions indicates the strength of the government's majority, and the unwillingness of several Monarchists to join Clemenceau's Radical faction in a *politique de pire* against the Opportunists.

During the second deliberation, however, the Monarchists and many of the remaining Bonapartists joined the extreme left in either voting against or abstaining. Speaking for his colleagues on the right, Théobold de Soland repeated many of the arguments that had come earlier out of the mouths of Republican intransigents. It was, he said, a law of expediency with no proportionality, which lumped together criminals in arbitrary categories, replacing "individual responsibility by collective responsibility, and repression by virtue of common law by administrative repression."[136] This was, after all, not so different from the sentiments expressed in Clemenceau's great speech of April 29, 1883, in which he held Opportunists up to scorn for punishing a man for finding himself in poverty and ignorance.

While the Senate deliberated the bill in its turn, the general economic situation continued to worsen. Strike activity continued at a relatively high level and was met by the Ferry cabinet's determined resistance. After an alliance of extreme left, extreme right, and anti-Ferryists brought down Ferry's long ministry on March 30, 1885, a government of "Republican concentration" was formed under Henri Brisson's leadership to fight the October elections. In order to shore up the moderate alliance where it had been softest—the left flank—Brisson took as his interior minister François Allain-Targé, who, with Charles Floquet and Maurice Rouvier was of the "ministerial" group on the Republican left.[137] The fall of Ferry confirmed the willingness of the political extremes to work together, pointing out dramatically a need for Republican discipline to keep Opportunist momentum alive. Even more than in 1883, Republican moderates needed to show their constituents that they could be both reformists in the tradition of "true" republicanism and firm in the struggle against internal disorder.

In the Senate the defenders of the recidivist bill had been exposed to some embarrassing moments. Not only did a new study confirm that

---

a fourth offense was "ample proof" of "perversity" and that no system could ensure "mathematical" certainty. Ibid., pp. 794-795.

[136] Théobold de Soland, *Journal officiel*, "Chambre des députés," June 30, 1883, p. 1503.

[137] On this group see Kayser, *Les grands batailles du radicalisme*, p. 120.

New Caledonia was incapable of absorbing many more internees, but the Naval High Council ruled that Guyana was too unhealthy a site for a substantial European penal population. Waldeck-Rousseau defended the bill with some of his toughest language,[138] but in the end accepted an amendment that made it even more difficult to claim that colonial transportation would achieve either rehabilitation or colonization. Acknowledging the scarcity of good land in the proposed internship sites, the Senate proposed to make the liberation of internees conditional on the existence of adequate land for their self-sustenance. This decision, which would be left to the discretion of the penal administration, in effect opened the door for the inauguration of forced labor. Instead of being free, or at worst working collectively under contract for wages, internees would be subject to a heavily guarded work regime, augmented, in cases of refusal to work, by close incarceration. Not only did this mean a radical departure from the "ameliorative" aims of the original project, but, by making the climate and arability of the soil factors of less importance, it cleared the way for a more serious consideration of Guyana. The Senate, feeling electoral pressures of its own, voted to pass the bill on to the Chamber on February 13, 1885, by 189 to 18.

By the time the Chamber began consideration of the amended bill in May 1885, the atmosphere had become thoroughly politicized, press commentary was unusually bitter, and the defects of the bill were so well known that only the most rabid enthusiasts could ignore them.[139] Despite this inconvenience, some Opportunist papers shamelessly advertised the bill's political utility. The *République française* made the

[138] Waldeck-Rousseau resorted to pseudo-Darwinian language in his justifications of the harsh conditions in which internship would be served. "If . . . you make of him what I might call a pioneer of civilization, if you place him in a situation that will force him each day to struggle for his life against barbarians, you will have made of this man, who is presently in the lowest rank in society, the representative of a small measure of civilization." (From Senate debate, February 10-13); quoted in Daniel, *L'année politique 1885*, p. 19.

[139] For press opinion see Camille Pelletan, "Retour à l'âge de pierre," *La justice*, May 12, 1885; Jules Leveillé, *Le temps*, May 7, May 13, May 14, 1885; "Tout à la mer," *Le matin*, May 14, 1885; *Le petit journal*, May 10, May 11, 1885; *Le siècle*, May 10, 1885; Henri Conseil, "La Chambre des députés," *Le Gaulois*, May 13, 1885; Abel Peyranton, "Sentimentalité," *Echo de Paris*, May 13, 1885; *La République française* called the bill a measure of "public health" that would eliminate the "virus" of recidivism, May 11, 1885. One could read in the moderate Republican *Le siècle* that "one seems to forget that bad instincts are the effect of an innate or acquired physiological predestination, and that the man who is born or who becomes vicious is no longer able to change his ways when a long acquaintance with evil has confirmed his brain in depravity." *Le siècle*, May 12, 1885.

point that a coalition of "intransigents" and "clericals" were attempting to make the "Republic appear too impotent to apply energetic measures against this flood of abominable scoundrels [*grédins*]," and claimed the right to expel them "in the name of democracy."[140] *Le siècle*, the paper that was the most unswerving in its support of the bill, was also most explicit about its political advantages. Arguing that the final 1885 vote in favor of the bill was stronger than the vote in 1883, the paper hailed "the reconstitution of a great Republican majority" that would not support a "Republic of fantasies" in the next election, but the "practical and orderly Republic demanded by public opinion."[141]

The 1885 version of the relegation bill was different in certain important respects from the 1883 bill the Chamber had sent to the Senate. The amendment of the upper house requiring forced labor in the absence of adequate free land for internees was accepted, of necessity, by the Brisson cabinet. It had been shown convincingly that New Caledonia's available land would be quickly distributed to the first few cohorts of prisoners, and there was no question of claiming that the tropical wasteland of Guyana could support large-scale agricultural settlement. The government freely admitted these difficulties and acknowledged that the internees would have to be kept under tight surveillance and work discipline if colonial transportation were to be practicable. Though it could no longer pretend that the law was aimed at the rehabilitation of all recidivists, the administration claimed it was preserving the "principle" of the law by adding a new article that allowed an internee to be liberated from the work regime after six years of good behavior. The "most salvageable" convicts would thus be freed by special colonial tribunals and given enough land to support an independent existence.[142] In addition, the government loosened up slightly the provisions defining recidivism at the lower end of the catalogue of offenses. Thus, instead of convictions for six offenses, one of which carried a sentence of three months, the new version specified seven offenses of which two had to carry sentences of at least three months. Apart from this small concession, it would be difficult to say that the new version of the hierarchy of offenses punished by relegation was truly more generous.[143]

---

[140] *La République française*, May 11, 1885.

[141] "Un pas vers la concentration," *Le siècle*, May 14, 1885.

[142] See the remarks by the interior minister, François Allain-Targé; Paul Rousseau, the undersecretary of state for colonies; and Louis Herbette, the government's representative from the penal administration. *Journal officiel*, "Chambre des députés," May 10, 11, 1885, pp. 773, 776, 783-784.

[143] See the new version in *Journal officiel*, "Chambre des députés," May 13, 1885, p. 804.

Instead of softening the bill, admitting judicial discretion, or allowing juries to pronounce this life sentence, the government pursued another strategy. Allain-Targé, in his opening remarks, assured the Chamber that Bérenger's bill on parole would be the next item on the Chamber's agenda once the relegation law was passed. This long-delayed reform had passed the Senate in 1884 and was to be the carrot for those leftists for whom the upcoming elections were the stick. This measure, the interior minister assured his fellow Republicans, was the beginning of the "great social program" that would culminate in the building of a complete penitentiary system.[144] It was the clear implication of this concession that parole was a measure designed precisely for those first timers and "amendable" criminals whose offenses did not fall under the provisions of the relegation law. The logic of the situation encouraged supporters of the bill to make the contrast between potential parolees and the "hardened" offenders who deserved relegation as great as possible. Commissioner Louis Herbette explained that in committing itself to parole and penitentiary reform the government was following the dictum that "the forms and the character of criminality vary with the man; the crime is to the criminal . . . as the disease is to the sick individual."[145]

This pathological metaphor encouraged government spokesmen to make their case for the utter depravity of recidivists in biological terms. The criminal who has stolen four times, Herbette therefore asserted, "is not just a thief four times, he is a thief to the fourth power." His "degree of personal criminality" is therefore considerably elevated above that of the first offender, and he will certainly display the "complete deviation of the moral faculties" that makes of this individual an "incurable" whose state of "morbid physiology" leaves no room for rehabilitation.[146] The bill's reporter Gerville-Réache sustained this line of argument in his concluding remarks to the Chamber. We must not be, he said, like the surgeon, who, called upon to amputate a gangrenous limb, limits himself to prescribing a "tonic." Rather, we must "consider that we are in the presence of a true leprosy, a gangrene, and that we must extirpate it before it invades the social organism."[147]

Herbette and Gerville-Réache also made a virtue out of the labor regime required by the bill's latest version by praising it as the most appropriate punishment possible for vagrants and beggars whose "na-

[144] François Allain-Targé, *Journal officiel*, "Chambre des députés," May 10, 1885, p. 773.
[145] Louis Herbette, *Journal officiel*, "Chambre des députés," May 12, 1885, p. 781.
[146] Ibid., May 13, 1885, p. 796.
[147] Gerville-Réache, *Journal officiel*, "Chambre des députés," May 13, 1885, p. 808.

ture" it was to avoid work at any cost. Imagine, suggested Herbette, the prospect of freeing such individuals in the colonies where their propensity for laziness would make them a burden on the penal administration and their more energetic companions.[148] Gerville-Réache emphasized in his remarks the same distinction between the "single offense" of the first offender and the "series of acts" that confirmed the multiple offender in his "habit of vagrancy and begging linked to corruption and perversity."[149]

Two principal factors made it difficult for the bill's opponents to resist this strategy. First, while one might have expected the government's allies to biologize the corrigible-incorrigible distinction, it would seem counterproductive for their opponents to have done so too. Nonetheless, in trying to win concessions for amendments that would exclude certain crimes from the list of offenses punishable by relegation, several critics of the bill resorted to this distinction. Jean-Marie de Lanessan, arguing against the hard labor provisions for minor criminals, contrasted them with those criminals who the "conditions of heredity or milieu have rooted in vice and crime."[150] The old Republican doctor Emile Vernhès, who pleaded the case of the "vagrants" and the "lazy," refused to assimilate them to the "wild beasts" and "pathological cases" whose natures were so damaged that we should not worry about their fate.[151] Even the Monarchist reformer Albert de Mun fell into this linguistic trap, claiming that his intervention on behalf of "déclassés" and "the unfortunate" by no means made him sympathetic with "the cruelest and most inexorable of all, the professional criminals."[152]

By pleading in this manner for the exclusion of individuals they believed could be reformed, opponents of the bill merely reinforced the dubious legal premise on which it rested, namely the conflation of criminal and crime. The dilemma of all legal reformers of the classical nineteenth-century codes was that they could only reveal the blindness of the traditional system of judging each criminal act as identical, and therefore equally blamable, by drawing attention to how it was that

---

[148] *Journal officiel*, "Chambre des députés," May 12, 1885, pp. 782-783. Herbette has adopted here, of course, the argument that Granet had used in 1883 to demonstrate the unworkability of the original bill. This is just another instance of the government's ability to coopt the arguments of its enemies.

[149] Gerville-Réache, *Journal officiel*, "Chambre des députés," May 13, 1885, p. 808.

[150] Jean-Marie de Lanessan, *Journal officiel*, "Chambre des députés," May 10, 1885, p. 776.

[151] Emile Vernhès, *Journal officiel*, "Chambre des députés," May 12, 1885, pp. 791-792. Vernhès claimed "special authority" in this matter as a medical doctor.

[152] Albert de Mun, *Journal officiel*, "Chambre des députés," May 12, 1885, p. 788.

the criminals who committed these identical acts were in fact different from one another in motivation, social situation, or degree of mental alienation. But this strategy of judging the criminal rather than the crime could lead, as it did in this case, to a situation in which those who managed to have their criminal stereotypes integrated into the discourse of crime and punishment could then practically ignore the purely legal issues at the heart of the matter.

The Napoleonic legislator had constructed a hierarchy of crimes with vagrancy and beggary at the very bottom, subject to the judgment of correctional tribunals and warranting prison terms only under exacerbating circumstances. Serious crimes, according to the rule of proportionality, deserved harsher punishment. But by breaking with the classic doctrine whereby the punishment must be proportional to the crime, and by making it fit the criminal instead, the legislator of 1885 had confounded the intentions of the framers of the code. The debaters spent the vast majority of their time discussing criminals; the punishments they finally approved were devised for a certain kind of criminal called a recidivist rather than for the crime he committed. This fundamental shift in emphasis allowed a seven-time loser for misdemeanors to be sentenced to the same punishment as a murderer or someone convicted two times for armed robbery. Even René Bérenger, the greatest late-century penal reformer and a violent opponent of the recidivism law argued for his parole bill before the Senate in the same corrigible-incorrigible language that justified Waldeck-Rousseau's project. Parole, he said, preserved the first offender from contact with essentially perverse men, irremediably corrupted."[153] The nature of the criminal was a new determinant in the elaboration of penal legislation in the last half of the century, and the construction of that nature was by no means a monopoly of lawyers and magistrates. By 1885, as we have seen, medical doctors, journalists, and the politicians themselves could influence what that criminal's nature was to be.

A final reason for the Opportunists' smashing success on this bill was their cunning political strategy of divide and conquer. At every turn government speakers gratuitously baited their Monarchist opponents with anticlerical jibes. Herbette taunted Monsignor Freppel, the bishop of Angers, with the alleged indiscretions of prison chaplains, posing as the defender of freedom of conscience against the "forced hypocrisy" of mandatory religious service. This tactic even managed to engage Clemenceau, who told of having attended mass at Mazas prison for "the only time in my entire life," in a brief encounter with

[153] René Bérenger, *Journal officiel*, "Sénat," March 22, 1884, p. 750.

the Royalists.[154] This incident and countless other diversions, including allegations of real-estate manipulations by New Caledonian monasteries, served to stoke the anticlerical fires on the Republican left at a time of political danger to the Opportunists. The Conservatives for their part displayed a truly ludicrous inability to distinguish between serious and gratuitous attacks, responding with alacrity to the clumsy and often repeated Opportunist witticism that it seemed strange to see believers in eternal damnation object to a mere sentence of transportation for life.[155]

The Monarchists took a much greater share in the opposition to the bill than they had done in 1883. The irrepressible Freppel made forceful points about the need for judicial discretion in the bill and resisted anticlerical baiting with great aplomb. Albert de Mun, who was at this time anxious to have his own brand of social Catholicism incorporated fully into the Monarchist cause, spoke eloquently on the origins of crime in poverty and ignorance, duplicating many of the points Clemenceau had made in his great speech in 1883.[156] De Mun managed some of the best bons mots during the debate, calling the bill a "deporting machine which obeys an arithmetic calculation."[157] It was also de Mun who recalled Hugo's description of Guyana as "the dry guillotine."

Though the extreme left and the Conservatives agreed on many points, neither was particularly at ease in this temporary alliance, made all the more uncomfortable by the anticlerical climate created by the Opportunists. The divide-and-conquer strategy no doubt won over to the government's cause some waverers from the left-center. Allain-Targé's promise to support the parole bill must have won over even more. But most, one suspects, were persuaded by the nearness of the elections, by the wave of opinion created by the dominant Opportunist political machine, and press, and by a certain conception of the recidivist that and penetrated the discourse of *politique criminelle* during the early 1880s.

[154] To this comment, Rochefoucauld, duc de Bisaccia responded, "You have scarcely profited from it," allowing Clemenceau the final rejoinder: "That proves the institution is worthless (fresh laughter on the left)." *Journal officiel*, "Chambre des députés," May 12, 1885, p. 782.

[155] See the discussion following Adolphe Lelièvre's remarks, *Journal officiel*, "Chambre des députés," May 10, 1885, pp. 768-769; other incidents of this sort were provoked by Jules Horteur, ibid., May 10, 1885, p. 765; Gerville-Réache, ibid., May 13, 1885, pp. 800, 807.

[156] See Ben F. Martin, *Count Albert de Mun, Paladin of the Third Republic* (Chapel Hill: University of North Carolina Press, 1978), pp. 31-55.

[157] Albert de Mun, *Journal officiel*, "Chambre des députés," May 12, 1885, p. 787.

In the end, the only concession made by the government was the requirement that a *rélégué* must have committed at least two crimes more serious than simple vagrancy, though this might be as minor an offense as carrying a weapon. The final margin of the vote was greater than in 1883, 383 to 52, with that many more abstaining. Only Radicals and Royalists actually voted against the bill.

Having passed one of the most Draconian pieces of legislation in French history, the Chamber immediately passed, with minimum debate and by voice vote, Europe's most liberal parole law. The British law, passed two years before, did not allow parole for punishments shorter than five years. The French law allowed half of the punishments for any length of time to be excused, and it allowed the liberation to be definitive on expiration of parole and the crime to be erased from the criminal's dossier. The administration also agreed to implement thorough procedures for evaluating good behavior in the prisons and increased the government stipend to patronage societies on a per capita basis of treatment.[158]

These two apparently contradictory pieces of legislation were in fact intimately dependent on one another. The one was the price for the other in strictly political terms, but their practically simultaneous passage cannot be reduced to a simple political bargain. They also reflected two faces of Republican ideology in the nineteenth century—the Opportunist and the Radical—which would continue to stare, Janus-like, in opposite directions for many years to come. They also spoke to two different types of criminal, indeed, practically two different species of humanity who would be, from that time on, irrevocably separate.

Colonial transportation was maintained throughout nearly the whole of the life of the Third Republic, ending only in 1938 after the revelation of scandals in the *bagnes*, as they continued to be popularly called. "Relegation," the supplementary punishment for recidivists invented in May 1885, continued in law until 1970, though it was served in "metropolitan" prisons after 1942.[159] In the first years of its life the law was vigorously applied. One thousand six hundred and ten recidivists were transported in 1886, 1,737 in 1887, and 1,734 in 1888. But these annual contingents were nowhere near the figure of 5,000 that had been predicted by the originators of the measure, and the figures dropped off rapidly after 1888. In 1889 only 1,109 were sent, and in

[158] The law was adopted July 17, 1885. For the whole text, see *Journal officiel*, "Chambre des députés," July 18, 1885, pp. 1517-1518.

[159] The history of this legislation is discussed in Léauté, *Criminologie et science pénitentiaire*, pp. 93-94, 211. See also O'Brien, *The Promise of Punishment*, pp. 258-296, and Wright, *Between the Guillotine and Liberty*, pp. 134-139.

the next two years 994 and 940, respectively. The figures fell to 629 in 1900, 520 in 1903, 515 in 1908, and 477 in 1911.[160] It is clear from the statistics that neither assizes juries nor correctional magistrates were enthusiastic about enforcing the law, and so they availed themselves of the various strategies at their disposal for evading the automatic application of the sentence, just as the opponents of the bill had predicted. Relegation to New Caledonia was halted in 1896, making insalubrious Guyana the sole depository of those deemed unsalvageable by society. Women were no longer sent after 1907; the climate was regarded as too hard on them, and there was no longer any life left in the myth of a colonial renaissance created by the labor of "rehabilitated convicts." As much a monument to Opportunism as schools and anticlericalism, relegation limped on through the life of the Republic, a useful solution for the overflow from metropolitan prisons.[161]

As Patricia O'Brien has recently argued, the relegation law signified that by 1885 a clear break had been made with the older association of crime with poverty. Without abandoning altogether the notion that poverty was a contributing cause to lawbreaking, observers were more likely to explain criminal behavior as an effect of criminal "associations" and "occupations" or as a consequence of the nature of the criminal. The rise of criminology in the 1880s helped to consolidate these ideas because "it encouraged and supported the shift in the analysis of criminogenic factors."[162] The following chapter explains how and why this shift took place.

[160] See the figures in the following volumes of the *Comte générale de l'administration de la justice criminelle*: 16 (1895), p. 29; 22 (1902), p. 86; 25 (1905), p. 106; 30 (1910), p. 85; 33 (1913), p. 79. Léauté, unaccountably, gives slightly different figures, though he also cites the *Comte générale. Criminologie et science pénitentiaire*, p. 211.

[161] Foucault's only mention of the 1885 law, to my knowledge, is in the *Power/ Knowledge* volume, p. 225, where he says that the French invented the notion of irredeemable citizens as potential colonial settlers in the relegation laws. Apart from its failure to mention the clear precedence of the British in this matter, this statement underestimates the earlier influence of French transportation laws and overestimates the influence of medical ideas (the statement is made in the context of a discussion of degeneracy).

[162] O'Brien, *The Promise of Punishment*, p. 295.

CHAPTER IV

Heredity or Milieu: The Born-Criminal Debate and the Foundations of Criminology

The 1880s and early 1890s were a time of extraordinary intellectual effervescence and doctrinal combat within the international legal community. During this period a major effort was mounted in Europe to reform the classical freewill penal codes which were regarded by progressives as having outlived their time, and to include within them measures allowing the state to adapt punishment (treatment) to the criminal rather than the crime he committed. Legal progressives were joined by doctors, social scientists, and other interested experts in assembling reliable knowledge about the nature of criminals and criminal behavior that would aid them in making the best presentation of their case. The reformers founded an International Union of Penal Law in 1889 that held annual congresses and acted as a clearinghouse for useful information and as a forum for debate. Vigorously opposed by the conservative legal and penal establishment, the reformers were able to make only partial and piecemeal changes in the codes and procedures before 1914. They did, however, manage to lay the intellectual foundations for the more successful efforts of the next generation. And, by inviting contributions from outside disciplines, the reform movement acted as a catalyst in the formation of a body of criminological knowledge with scientific pretensions.

French thinkers played no small role in these developments. Edouard Gauckler and Emile Garçon, were, with the German Franz von Liszt, the Belgian Adolphe Prins, and the Dutchman G. A. Van Hamel, the leading lights in the International Union. The French were equally influential within the burgeoning discipline of criminology. To a great degree French doctors, philosophers, social scientists, and jurists set the stamp on criminological thinking that it possesses to this day: the view that the social environment plays the most important role, in the long run, in shaping the actions and nature of the criminal. They

97

helped to rally European opposition to Cesare Lombroso's conception of a biologically determined "born criminal" by providing some of the most influential refutations of the research of the Italian school and by demonstrating a canny political sense of the feasible limits of penal reform.

Within France, as we shall see, the intellectual ferment provoked by these movements had the effect of making crime and criminality topics of universal public interest for over a decade. Though the debates over penal reform and the existence of "criminal man" ended in a temporary victory for the moderates and those who favored environmental theories of crime causation, the ironic effect of this speculative upheaval was to advance the application of medical ideas to crime and criminality, and, by extension, to other forms of deviance, considerably beyond the stage represented by the decade or so prior to 1885. A simultaneous progression of medicalization and environmental (sociological) explanations of crime was possible because of the pervasive influence of native scientific traditions that harmonized rather than opposed these developments. A neo-Lamarckian conception of heredity and descent and the theory of degeneration were the principal intellectual elements that allowed this accommodation to take place.

The criminology that emerged from this unique blend of French intellectual traditions was thoroughly eclectic, composed of contributions from experts in penal law, doctors of legal medicine, psychiatrists, and social scientists. Though the intellectual foundations of the new discipline were laid, as these matters go, in a remarkably brief space of time, the scientific claims that were made for criminological knowledge were bold and far-reaching. The assurance that criminological knowledge had scientific status guaranteed, in turn, a sympathetic hearing from French jurists and penal reformers; historically, the tradition of French *politique criminelle* had always encouraged legal experts to square new legislation with the "facts" about criminality.[1] The extraordinary mixture of sociological and biological determinism in the intellectual contours of this new discipline, and the striking collaboration of doctors, lawyers, and social theorists in its construction provided French criminology with a curiously ambiguous ideological identity. Experts on crime and criminality could find in criminological knowledge, as the occasion demanded, reasons for optimism or for pessimism, for rehabilitative intervention or for helplessness. Thus, a tide that ran firmly toward rehabilitation and the reshaping of criminogenic

[1] On French *politique criminelle*, see Leon Radzinowicz, *In Search of Criminology* (Cambridge, Mass.: Harvard University Press, 1962), pp. 65-67.

milieux in the late 1880s, flowed in the opposite direction in the more pessimistic era after 1895.

I intend in this chapter to relate the history of the debates from which criminology was born in the late 1880s and early 1890s. I discuss the various scientific ideas that gave the so-called French school its unique identity and show that, despite overwhelming public agreement at the time in favor of a social theory of crime, a comprehensive medicalization of criminal deviance took shape that could subsequently undergird a rigid biological determinism, though one different in tone and in content from the Lombrosian "heresy" it replaced. Crime was the second of the major varieties of deviance, after insanity, to be medicalized and converted into a social pathology; once it could be shown how criminals were in part biological anomalies, it proved a relatively simple matter to medicalize other kinds of deviance as well.

The first shot fired in the great criminal debates of the 1880s and 1890s was the publication in 1876 of Cesare Lombroso's *L'uomo delinquente*. From his anatomical studies of Italian soldiers, the young army doctor asserted that he could distinguish between the criminal and "normal" recruit on the basis of certain gross morphological characteristics. He followed up his slender first edition with an enlarged volume of 1878 in which he extended his anatomical probe into several Italian prisons, classifying convicts according to groups of anomalies of his own invention. Though he had yet to work out all the implications of his new system, Lombroso did not conceal the fact that his findings presented a serious challenge to classical penal theory. Lombroso explained the physical deformities of his born criminals not just in terms of "atavism," a hereditary regression to the behavior and appearance of a primitive human ancestral type, but as the morbid consequence of epilepsy, a syndrome about which very little was known at that time.

The best way to sample the fantastic hopes and limitless enthusiasm that moved the young Lombroso is to quote him on his first "empirical" proof of atavism, the discovery of an especially primitive median occipital fossa in the skull of a famous Italian brigand:

> This was not merely an idea, but a revelation. At the sight of that skull, I seemed to see all of a sudden, lighted up as a vast plain under a flaming sky, the problem of the nature of the criminal—an atavistic being who reproduces in his person the ferocious instincts of primitive humanity and the inferior animals. Thus were explained anatomically the enormous jaws, high cheekbones, size of the orbits, handle-shaped or sessile ears found in criminals, savages and apes, insensibility to pain, extremely acute sight, tattooing, excessive idle-

ness, love of orgies, and the irresistible craving for evil for its own sake, the desire not only to extinguish life in the victim, but to mutilate the corpse, tear its flesh, and drink its blood.[2]

Appointed professor of legal medicine at the University of Turin in 1876, Lombroso quickly gathered together a group of ardent young doctors and lawyers, among whom numbered Enrico Ferri, Raffaelle Garofalo, and many other young Italians who soon became the stalwarts of the new *scuola positiva*. They founded a journal in 1880, the *Archivio di psichiatria ed antropologia criminale*, giving them an Italian forum for their work. By 1885 two monographs had appeared that completed the major philosophical foundations of the school, Garofalo's *Criminology* and Ferri's *Criminal Sociology*. Though there were divergences over minor issues, the Italian school enjoyed a surprising degree of unity on the main principles of Lombroso's original findings: the preponderant role of hereditary factors in criminal behavior, the existence of identifiable and morphological characteristics in criminals, and the conviction that various pathological influences—atavism, epilepsy, moral imbecility—controlled the appearance of "criminal" physiological manifestations.[3] Until Lombroso's death in 1909 even those members of the school who, like Ferri, gave significant emphasis to social and economic influences in crime, rallied to the master's side when public controversy was most heated. Solidarity was even more complete on issues regarding criminal responsibility, sentencing and incarceration, and methods of treatment.

In the reformist atmosphere that prevailed among legal and penal authorities in the 1880s, the Italian criminal anthropologists possessed a "scientific," coherent, and revolutionary program for defending society against the rising tide of recidivism. The Lombrosians, who were the earliest and most outspoken spearhead of criminal anthropology, made no effort to spare the freewill philosophy that underlay the

[2] This is an account written retrospectively by Lombroso in his introduction to Gina Lombroso-Ferrero, *Criminal Man According to the Classification of Cesare Lombroso* (New York: G. P. Putnam's Sons, 1911), pp. xiv-xvi.

[3] On divergences within the school see Hermann Mannheim's "Introduction" in Mannheim, ed., *Pioneers in Criminology*, pp. 1-35. On Lombroso and the Italian school in general see Hermann Mannheim, "Lombroso and His Place in Modern Criminology," in *Group Problems in Crime and Punishment* (London: Routledge and Kegan Paul, 1955), pp. 69-85; Marvin E. Wolfgang, "Cesare Lombroso," in Mannheim's *Pioneers in Criminology*, pp. 232-291; Francis Allen, "Raffaelle Garofalo," in ibid., pp. 318-340; and Thorsten Sellin, "Enrico Ferri," in ibid., pp. 361-384. Taylor, Walton, and Young have a useful section on Lombroso's doctrine as ideology in *The New Criminology*, pp. 31-44; Stephen Jay Gould has devoted a section of *The Mismeasure of Man* (New York: Norton, 1981) to Lombroso, pp. 122-142.

European legal and penal establishments. From the outset of their debates with penologists in their own country, the Lombrosians adopted a combative tone characterized by its extreme determinism and materialism. To a degree those Italian intellectuals who embraced militant positivism after 1870 were attempting to inject intellectual animation into the comparatively dreary atmosphere of the Italian *postrisorgimento*. The romanticism and political idealism that had dominated Italian cultural life until unification had postponed the introduction of the cult of the scientific method that had made extraordinary headway elsewhere in Europe during the previous two decades. But when it finally arrived, as Benedetto Croce lamented, "hardly anyone dared to admit that he was engaged in philosophical investigations and thought; everyone boasted instead of studying science and working as a scientist."[4]

Although elsewhere in Europe the lines between free will and determinism in criminality were by no means drawn as sharply as in Italy, by 1885 there had emerged two distinct doctrinal alternatives. On one side were the defenders of the old classical codes, who were largely jurists and penal authorities, and on the other were those for whom criminal anthropology provided the unifying focus—doctors of psychiatry, neurologists, and doctors of legal medicine. In 1885 there was no readily available model that might breach the gulf between the prevailing scientific and moral evaluations of crime. Yet, within five years or so the foundation had been laid for a body of criminological theory that could securely occupy that middle ground. It generated enough reliable knowledge to meet the needs of psychiatrists and doctors of legal medicine; it supported the claims of the reformers of the classical codes that more attention must be paid to the criminal than to the crime he committed; but it also proved minimally acceptable to the freewill philosophers and jurists in its treatment of criminal de-

---

[4] Benedetto Croce, *A History of Italy: 1871-1915*, trans. Cecilia M. Ady (New York: Russell & Russell, 1963), p. 130. No doubt positivism achieved rapid progress after 1870 in Italy, but it would be a mistake to infer from the idealist Croce that all levels of Italian intellectual culture were equally affected. Rather, it appears that the relatively slow development of science in Italy after 1870, while it did not protect Italian scientists from an extreme variety of positivism, more or less guaranteed that the "cult" would not have great prestige or influence in other areas. If anything, the relative intellectual isolation of the scientific and medical communities reinforced their commitment to a militant positivism. This explanation may help indicate why the split between the jurists and doctors was more notable in Italy than anywhere else in Europe in this period. For a discussion of the background to these developments see Giorgio Candeloro, *Storia dell'Italia moderna: Lo sviluppo del capitalismo e del movimento operaio*, vol. 6 (Milan: Feltrinelli Editore, 1970), pp. 283-289.

terminism. Of greatest importance was the ability of the new school both to sell itself to the jurists and to combat convincingly the excesses of the Lombrosians. Against the coherent program of the Italians, the new theoretical focus had to provide more than a mere alternative; it needed an aggressive and self-justifying popular and scientific posture that would not only convince the specialist, but be attractive and comprehensible to the enlightened public. The theoretical cluster of ideas that emerged to fill this need went by many names, but it can be generally characterized as a sociological or environmental interpretation of the origins of criminality. The notion that crime was nurtured in the social milieu could be traced back at least as far as Thomas More, and charity and welfare authorities had understood the relationship between poverty and crime for centuries. But the contributors to this new theory of crime brought a systematic and rigorous approach to the environmental interpretation that moved considerably beyond the old formulas and into the domain of the modern social sciences.

The leaders of this new movement were mostly French. Although contributions came later from theorists elsewhere, it was the French who first picked up the gauntlet thrown down by Lombrosian biological determinism. Once the challenge was joined by French jurists and doctors, the way was cleared for jurists throughout Europe to express support and interest. For reasons I examine later, the international legal community and much of the public favored the French interpretation over the Italian; the victory of the social interpretation was rapid and remarkably thorough. No doubt the positive school of Italian criminology continued to uphold its position in Italy, and even enjoyed limited successes elsewhere, especially in South America. But its role in influencing the shape of criminal law and penal reform in general had nowhere near the grand effect originally envisioned by Lombroso. Writers on the history of criminological theory generally have held that the Lombrosian interpretation was not empirically demolished until the appearance in 1913 of Charles Goring's important statistical refutation, *The English Convict*.[5] This is largely a hindsight view, however, which perhaps naively assumes that empirical, especially statistical, arguments are nearly always superior in doctrinal struggles to positions argued from nonstatistical evidence. In fact, the most damaging blows had been dealt to the Lombrosian dogma well before the

[5] For this view see George B. Vold, *Theoretical Criminology* (New York: Oxford University Press, 1958), p. 52; H. E. Barnes and Negley H. Teeters, *New Horizons in Criminology*, 2d ed. (New York: Prentice-Hall, 1951), pp. 143-144; and Edwin D. Driver, "Charles Buckman Goring," in Mannheim, ed., *Pioneers in Criminology*, pp. 429-442.

turn of the century, and the subsequent ability of the Italian school to influence judicial or legislative authorities, or public opinion, was sorely diminished.

In 1885 the fortunes of the Italian school were at their very highest point. In the fall of that year, the interior circle of the Lombrosian group convened the First International Congress of Criminal Anthropology in Rome. They hoped to attract a broadly European representation to the congress and outshine the meetings of the Third International Penitentiary Congress, the rival organization of freewill jurists also meeting in Rome. At stake for the Italians attending each congress was the possibility of influencing the direction of the new Italian penal code, then in a state of preparation, by a show of general European unanimity. The congress was dominated numerically by Italians; otherwise the French were best represented, but no English and only a few German and Eastern European delegates made the journey. Though disappointed at the poor attendance, Italian delegates spoke confidently about the existence of Lombroso's born criminal. Some opposition surfaced at the outset, however, when the French doctor of legal medicine, Alexandre Lacassagne, ventured a direct criticism of the Italian system, in which he was joined by his French colleague, the psychiatrist Emile Magitot, warning against the gratuitous use of such "unproved" words as "atavism" and "Darwinism."[6]

Later, in the meeting of November 20, Lacassagne threw the first real bombshell of the congress. Rejecting an arch-Lombrosian defense of atavism by Giuseppe Sergi, Lacassagne pointed out the absurdity of associating apparently primitive anatomical characteristics with a pathological predisposition to crime. Such reasoning, he said, was merely a kind of projected guilt by association which branded any individual unlucky enough to possess one or more of these features with "an indelible scar, an original sin." He reminded the congress how such a notion must appear to legislators and jurists who are told that their only future resort is to "do nothing but cross their arms, or construct prisons or asylums in which to gather these misshapen creatures."[7] Lacassagne's sensitivity to the reaction of politicians and jurists was

---

[6] *Actes du premier congrès international d'anthropologie criminelle* (Rome, 1885), p. 113.

[7] Ibid., pp. 165-166. In a later session Lacassagne reproached Lombroso for his notion of "larval epilepsy" on similar grounds: "I believe that it would be a great danger for the future of criminal anthropology to use before a jury or magistrate a comparison or words whose exact worth or meaning might not be understood." Ibid., p. 275.

unique in the congress; it exemplified a crucial difference between French and Italian criminologists in the years to follow.

Lacassagne then constructed a brief argument in which he told the congress that the emphasis of criminal anthropology to that time was entirely incorrect. "The important thing," he said, "is the social milieu. Permit me a comparison drawn from a modern theory. The social milieu is the mother culture of criminality; the microbe is the criminal, an element that gains significance only at the moment it finds the broth that made it ferment."[8] This simple metaphor, drawn from Pasteurian bacteriology, was the first rallying cry to the sociological interpretation of crime and was repeatedly quoted in later years by enemies of extreme biological positions. Denying that special physical characteristics were exclusive to criminals, Lacassagne posed an optimistic social initiative for eliminating crime against the "immobilizing fatalism that inevitably falls from the anthropometric theory." And, to emphasize his contention that each society had a moral obligation in the reformation of "vicious" criminal environments, Lacassagne articulated his celebrated aphorism: "Les sociétés ont les criminels qu'elles méritent."[9]

The Frenchman's frank comments drew a vituperative response from the Lombrosians that was altogether characteristic of positivism in its most militant humor. The Neapolitan Giulio Fioretti described himself as "profoundly surprised" by Lacassagne's sentiments, adding, "The criminal type is a fact definitely ascertained by science. On this point discussion is not at all admissible."[10] Nor were other commentators willing to concede any flaws in the theory of the born criminal; all cited the extraordinary sense of agreement on the issue that prevailed at the congress. Significantly, none of Lacassagne's antagonists was satisfied with merely repeating the facts that had been used earlier to support their position. Stung by the implication that their views encouraged a fatalistic attitude toward crime, the Italians defended their "progressive" stance by appealing to the naturalistic and scientific foundations of their school. But as compelling as their arguments may have been to convinced partisans, they could hardly have mollified the fears of the jurists at the penitentiary congress. Ferri, for instance, spoke proudly of his "scientific materialism" as the "way of progress," and defended the humanitarian aspects of his system, which by removing born criminals from society would operate as a melioristic device of "artificial selection."[11] Raffaelle Garofalo made the extraordinary claim

8 Ibid., p. 166.
9 Ibid., p. 167.
10 Ibid., p. 168.
11 Ibid., pp. 171-173.

that because of criminal anthropology, "moral responsibility and the proportionality of the punishment to the crime, these two pivots of penal law, are disappearing from our system, and one can truly say that penal science has been renewed from top to bottom." We are powerless against the "moral monstrousness," he continued, "that one can recognize in infancy and against which all efforts of education and the milieu are hopeless."[12]

Later presentations made equally salient points. Enrico Morselli, appropriating arguments from social Darwinism, summarized his arguments on violent death by saying, "Suicide and homicide are the same: elimination of the weak (applause)."[13] Later, arguing for capital punishment, not in the outmoded interest of social vengeance, but with the positivist formula of "social defense," another Lombrosian alleged that "the most absolute guarantee, and the most effective for social security . . . is represented by his [the capital criminal's] death."[14] Lombrosian criminal science invariably defended the eugenical service its doctrine would perform through the systematic "elimination" of the criminally unfit by overseas transportation, perpetual imprisonment, or death. Jurists, who had traditionally argued for capital punishment on retributive and moral grounds, were understandably uncomfortable with a mode of reasoning that denied the validity of normative or ethical judgments.

Other members of the Italian school openly suggested that the inexorable advances of empirical science would destroy the freewill position altogether if the "metaphysicians" did not consent to absorb the principal Lombrosian reforms. Lombroso himself concurred warmly with the demand to make "metaphysical" notions of criminal responsibility more "scientific," and remarked austerely that "it is not with sentiments that one rules a society."[15] A belligerent speech by Raffaelle Garofalo insisting on the "immensity" of distance between the "idealists" and the "positive school" was met with a measured riposte by a lone observer from the penitentiary congress who argued that though the classical school was ready to admit exceptions for insane persons under criminal

[12] Ibid., pp. 174-175.
[13] Ibid., p. 204.
[14] Ibid., p. 340. In supporting Sylvius Venturi's demand for "social selection," Garofalo called it "a logical consequence of the naturalist theory applied to penal science" and the result of a "purely scientific point of view." "Be logical," he concluded, "and don't let yourselves be influenced by [humanitarian-sentimental] considerations of an inferior order," p. 343. Not all Lombrosians supported the death penalty. Ferri, for instance, thought isolation of the criminal was adequate to ensure social defense.
[15] Ibid., pp. 184-185.

indictment, it deplored the general philosophical incursions into free-will theory so characteristic of the spirit of the congress.[16] Lombroso's Austrian disciple Moritz Benedikt brushed off that warning by speaking of the inevitable triumph of science over law and derisively mocking the classicists whose "cult is ready to fall."[17] In subsequent years, the Lombrosians paid dearly for these intemperate attacks on the legal cornerstone of free will. By the time the next congress met in Paris four years later, the likelihood of a favorable public reception for their work had begun to fade.

The Paris congress of 1889 was the occasion of a stunning public reversal in the fortunes of the Lombrosian theories. A gathering that was more truly international than the Rome congress witnessed an avalanche of hostile criticism push Lombroso and his colleagues into a defensive posture. While some of the commentators disputed the Lombrosians on their own anatomical grounds, by far the most effective criticisms were of a logical and methodological type, not infrequently accompanied by mocking or ironic overtones. Lombroso was his own worst enemy in the whole fiasco—blustering and vague in self-defense.

The French were foremost in the assault: Léonce Manouvrier and Paul Topinard, anthropologists in the independent Ecole d'anthropologie of Paris; Paul Brouardel, professor of legal medicine at the Paris Medical School, the criminal judge and sociologist Gabriel Tarde, and the ubiquitous Lacassagne. The papers and comments of Manouvrier were particularly damaging. He compared Lombroso's theories to the disgraced phrenology of Franz Joseph Gall, accused Lombroso's criminal type of being a sort of "ideal harlequin," and subjected the Italian efforts at statistical analysis to a rigorous examination.[18] Tellingly, he pointed out Lombroso's failure to collect measurements within discrete series according to race, sex, and class, and dismissed the value of statistics on criminal anomalies that were never compared with equally broad samples of "honest" men. Manouvrier was particularly incisive on the difficulty of arriving at any valid definition of "honest," ob-

[16] For Garofalo's speech, see ibid., pp. 305-317, and for the Italian lawyer Righi's reply, pp. 317-320.

[17] Ibid., pp. 321-322.

[18] Almost all of the *Actes* and *Procès-verbaux* of the Paris congress were reprinted in Lacassagne's journal, the *Archives d'anthropologie criminelle et des sciences pénales* (later the *Archives d'anthropologie criminelle et de médecine légale*). The discussion section in the *Archives* is often more complete than that in the *Actes* of the congress. For Manouvrier's remarks, see *Archives d'anthropologie criminelle* 4 (1889), pp. 540-541. A complete version of Manouvrier's paper may be found in the *Actes du deuxième congrès d'anthropologie criminelle* (Paris, 1889), pp. 5-13.

serving that the category generally included great numbers of "knaves, intriguers, and brutes" whom the law does not qualify as criminal.[19] He concluded ironically by accusing Lombroso of having done anthropology the disservice of "criminalizing" anatomical characteristics: "One will only be able to console himself at being a born criminal by remembering that he is an honest man even so."[20]

Paul Topinard, director of the Ecole d'anthropologie, disputed Lombroso's contention that his favorite—indeed his first—anatomical "criminal" trait, an enlarged *fossette occipitale*, was indicative of any inherent abnormality.[21] Topinard denied that Lombroso's work deserved the title of anthropology, and he proposed that the congress substitute a new name of his own coining, criminology, for criminal science.[22] At another juncture, Gabriel Tarde asked Lombroso why it was, since female skulls often showed the same "criminal" anomalies as those of men, there was so little female criminality, and Dr. Valentin Magnan, head of the Saint Anne Asylum in Paris, challenged Lombroso on the crucial matter of whether criminal anatomical characteristics could be observed in young delinquents.[23] This last issue was a crucial one for the Lombrosian orthodoxy, since the Lombrosians held that early identification and isolation of juvenile criminals would be a major factor in crime prevention.

Together with the critical dismemberment of Lombrosian dogma, the French and their allies depended on two major strands of argument: the unacceptability of Lombrosian theories to the legal community, and the thesis that crime was not provoked by hereditary factors alone but rather by factors in which the social milieu played an immediate or indirect role. Nearly every anti-Lombrosian commentator, whether jurist or doctor, referred to the conditioning effect of the social environment in encouraging criminal careers. Misery, poverty, lack of opportunity, and vice and alcoholism in parents were among the favored causes. If criminals seemed to display a few more anatomical peculiarities than others, Lacassagne observed, it was be-

[19] *Archives d'anthropologie criminelle* 4 (1889), p. 534.

[20] Ibid., p. 542.

[21] Ibid., p. 554. Moritz Benedikt, who had moved away from a dogmatic Lombrosian position after 1885, added to Topinard's remarks on the *fossette* by saying, amid general hilarity, "It is easy to make hypotheses: why not say the *fossette* indicates a predisposition to hemorrhoids for example?," ibid.

[22] See Topinard's proposal in the *Actes du deuxième congrès d'anthropologie criminelle*, p. 34.

[23] Tarde, *Archives d'anthropologie criminelle* 4 (1889), p. 543. See Magnan's paper and the orthodox Lombrosian rejoinder of Dr. Romeo Taverni, in *Actes du deuxième congrès d'anthropologie criminelle*, pp. 20-32.

cause the "evil of misery and deprivation" acted to deform and mottle its victims in tragic fashion.[24] Even Enrico Ferri's system, which claimed to balance "biological" and "social" causation equally, was dismissed as "arbitrary" by the unrelenting Manouvrier, who had been trained as a doctor and educated as an anthropologist under the renowned Paul Broca, and was emerging as the most pugnaciously articulate spokesman for the French.[25]

In contradistinction to the Italian majority at the 1885 congress, the French and their allies were careful to tread lightly where the implications of their work touched on matters within the domain of current criminal procedure. They resisted suggestions that classifications of "criminals" by juridical anthropologists could be substituted for the normal sentencing procedures, though they agreed that exposing jurists to legal medicine was necessary.[26] In general, the environmentalists made every effort to harmonize freewill doctrine and other projects dear to the classical school, such as individual cellular imprisonment, with their own suggestions for reform.[27]

In his closing address to the congress Paul Brouardel made direct reference to the many rebuttals suffered by the "apostles" of Lombroso and trusted that they would benefit by resubmitting their theories to the crucible. He wondered openly whether an extreme determinism was serving the interests of humanity, when "the child who believed himself lost would never make any effort toward the good." He concluded by saying, "This remark puts us face to face with practicality, and we feel that though, philosophically, we are free to sort through these principles, . . . we risk alienating society by attempting to apply them."[28]

Before the last session closed, however, the angry Italian contingent demanded that a commission be formed to make a comparative anatomical study of one hundred criminals and one hundred honest men and present its findings to the next congress. Much later, when it became clear that the French-dominated commission had decided against completing the study, the Italians voted not to attend the third con-

[24] *Archives d'anthropologie criminelle* 4 (1889), p. 535.

[25] Ibid., p. 561. Dimitri Drill, a Moscow lawyer, seconded Manouvrier in his attack on Ferri.

[26] See Paul Brouardel's and Moritz Benedikt's comments in ibid., pp. 566-567.

[27] Gabriel Tarde, "Les anciens et les nouveaux fondements de la responsabilité morale," *Actes du deuxième congrès d'anthropologie criminelle*, pp. 54-58; and G. A. Van Hamel, "Du système cellulaire considéré au point de vue de la biologie et de la sociologie criminelle," ibid., pp. 70-75.

[28] *Archives d'anthropologie criminelle* 4 (1889), pp. 587-589.

gress, held in 1892 in French-speaking Brussels. Thwarted in their efforts, the Lombrosians angrily protested in an open letter that the new congress was "barren of any foundation of facts" and lacked any basis for a "truly scientific and conclusive discussion."[29] In his report on the 1889 congress to Lombroso's *Archivio di psichiatria*, Ferri attempted to discount the opposition to the biological theory of crime as merely a "strategic reaction" to the presence of the strong Italian delegation and implied strongly that the preference for speaking "only in general terms about social conditions easily visible to everyone" revealed an empirical weakness in the arguments of a sociological interpretation.[30]

Ferri and his colleagues were convinced that theoretical revolutions in science could only follow new discoveries in empirical research, a view that illustrates that for the most simplistic late nineteenth-century positivists induction had a mythic rhetorical appeal even when—one is tempted to say especially when—it did not figure as a working methodology. Statistical approaches and quantification also enjoyed great prestige as scientific novelties.[31] But conceptual changes in the social sciences grow out of the confluence of numerous factors, many of them extrascientific, that participate in shaping the contours and value structure of new research areas. Even if the Lombrosian contributions had not been flawed by logical and empirical shortcomings, the possibility of a rapid and thorough victory of their ideas would have been unlikely in the face of the unified hostility and distrust of European jurists. Though the opponents of the Italians in the development of criminal science were no less insistent about the scientific nature of their work, and often as deterministic in their assumptions, their more practical approach to the problems of reform proved ultimately decisive for their interpretation. In France, where the successes of the sociological school were most complete, there were domestic intellectual and social influences that smoothed their way. While the sociological theory of the period 1885-1900 may appear relatively primitive to modern observers, the refutation of the notion of the born criminal in favor of a broader environmental interpretation was an impressively convincing accomplishment.

The role of French theorists in turning back the Lombrosian tide was much greater than is generally acknowledged. Not only were the

[29] *Actes du troisième congrès d'anthropologie criminelle*, pp. xiv-xvii.

[30] Enrico Ferri, "Il II congresso internazionale di antropologia criminale," *Archivio di psichiatria, scienze penali ed antropologia criminale* 10 (1889), pp. 546-547.

[31] Stephen Jay Gould has discussed the "allure of numbers" for early anthropology in *The Mismeasurement of Man*, pp. 73-82.

French the first to oppose Lombroso in a systematic way, but their efforts were distinguished by a rare blending of professions and points of view, including those of jurists, moralists, doctors of legal medicine, anthropologists, and psychiatrists. Elsewhere, especially in Italy, the medical-scientific and legal communities were more divided by their allegiances to the conflicting interpretations. The unity of these elements in France ensured the French school its international prestige and remarkable effectiveness. Especially for France in the late nineteenth century, even an informal integration of these generally disparate elements suggests that special forces were at work beneath the surface to ensure the defeat of the common enemy.

Thus, with few exceptions, French doctors, anthropologists, and alienists reacted with apparent horror to the extreme anatomical determinism displayed at the Rome congress of 1885. Two of the French doctors at the congress reported in distressed terms on the Italian's savage attack on free will. Emile Magitot wrote from Rome that he was unconvinced in the matter of a criminal type and preferred to follow the classicist Beccaria and the notion of social causation rather than yield to the "excessive pretensions" of the Lombrosian position.[32] In a report on the Rome congress to the lawyers and penal authorities of the Société générale des prisons, Dr. August Motet stressed social factors in crime as opposed to the "false route" of criminal anthropology and reminded the members of the need for moral responsibility, "because there is no society possible without responsibility."[33] Théophile Roussel, an important penal reformer and politician, welcomed the doctors into the freewill camp and had words of praise for "the sense of moderation, of scientific reserve, and of respect for the legislative domain that the action of the French members of the congress manifested."[34]

The unacceptability of extreme biological determinism to jurists and legislators was immediately apparent to students of criminal phenom-

[32] See the reprinted version of Magitot's 1885 letters to *Le national*, in E. Magitot, *Lettres de Rome* (Havre, 1894).

[33] August Motet, "Rapport sur le Congrès d'anthropologie criminelle de Rome," *Bulletin de la Société générale des prisons* 10 (January-February 1886), p. 132.

[34] Théophile Roussel, "Rapport," *Bulletin de la Société générale des prisons* 10 (January-February 1886), p. 134. The failure of the Lombrosians to compromise with Italian jurists led to the utter rejection of Lombrosian positions in the new criminal code promulgated in 1889. See Luigi Lucchini, *I simplicisti (antropologi, psicologi, et sociologi) del diritto penale—saggio critico* (Turin, 1886). Also Albert Desjardins, "La méthode expérimentale appliquée au droit criminel en Italie," *Bulletin de la Société générale des prisons* 10 (December 1886), pp. 1043-1064; 11 (January 1887), pp. 50-62; 12 (January 1888), pp. 15-38.

ena in France. To prevent a hiatus in their relations with the legal community, French criminologists hoped to minimize any apparent threat to free will and criminal responsibility in their studies on the origins of criminal behavior. They found that sociological explanations of crime, while preserving the overtones of a mild determinism, nonetheless maintained in the eyes of jurists a commitment to individual responsibility that did not challenge the historic principles of penal repression. It is also likely that a sociological interpretation of crime was regarded as complementary to the classical assumption of an intimate relationship between misery, vice, and crime.

The stakes were substantial for the French anthropologists, psychiatrists, and doctors of legal medicine who were the primary enemies of the Italian school. Anthropology in France was gradually moving away from the physical-morphological concerns of Broca's day and toward a more cultural and ethnological orientation.[35] The French anthropologists most in favor of this new direction were reluctant to be associated with an extremely dogmatic new "science" in which the word anthropology figured so prominently. This concern explains Paul Topinard's repeated insistence that the name of the new science be changed to criminology. For the brief time that they were engaged in the fray against Lombroso and in favor of a social explanation of crime, the anthropologists were among the most effective combatants, inasmuch as they could meet the positivists on their own grounds. Manouvrier and Topinard ceased their polemics soon after it was clear that the danger had passed, but not before they had set in motion a new interest in crime in primitive societies that was later exploited by Emile Durkheim and his followers.

French doctors of legal medicine were in an even more precarious situation. Legal medicine in France had been born officially during the medical reforms of the French Revolution. One of the original twelve chairs at the Paris Medical School was devoted to legal medicine and the history of medicine; the subject was part of the regular course of study for third-year (later fourth-year) students for the medical degree.[36] As we have seen, after 1832 forensic experts or psychiatrists were asked to testify in court on the mental condition of accused criminals. Gradually, legal medicine became a specialty of its own, notably at Paris and Lyon, where institutes attached to the medical schools

---

[35] Donald Bender, "The Development of French Anthropology," *Journal of the History of the Behavioral Sciences*, 1 (April 1965), pp. 139-151, and Fred W. Voget, "Progress, Science, History and Evolution in Anthropology," ibid. 3 (April 1967), pp. 132-155.

[36] Coury, *L'enseignement de la médecine en France*, pp. 114-115.

trained medical doctors in forensic techniques and "criminal" psychiatry.[37] After years of agitation a special *diplôme* was instituted in 1903, to be granted after a course of study in Paris in "legal medicine and psychiatry."

To an increasing extent in the nineteenth century, the income and professional status of these experts in mental responsibility depended upon their friendly relations with magistrates and their credibility with the public that sat on criminal juries. They were painfully aware that their role in judicial proceedings had no specific statutory support and existed only at the pleasure of the presiding judge. Yet, their status as experts relied to a large degree on the scientific and technical knowledge that they were able to command. In the daily exercise of their functions, they were caught in the well-known bind of making the content and the form of their expertise palatable to laymen without sacrificing the scientific basis on which their judgments presumably rested. Their problem involved obtaining recognition for the reduced responsiblity of insane criminals without alienating jurists or juries with excessive claims for massive institutional reforms as the Lombrosians had done in Italy. In supporting a sociological interpretation of crime, the forensic and psychiatric expert found an intermediate position that allowed him to argue within a moderately deterministic scientific context acceptable to the legal community, but from which he could build arguments in favor of individual cases of more serious irresponsibility.

A coordinated movement to establish a scientifically acceptable social explanation for crime against the claims of the Italian school began in earnest the year after the Rome Congress of Criminal Anthropology. In the *avant-propos* of his new criminological journal, Alexandre Lacassagne counseled that the *Archives's* work would not be fruitful if done "in the spirit of denigration or destruction for those existing laws that constitute one of the most precious parts of mankind's intellectual heritage."[38] His contemporaries saw Lacassagne as an aphoristic synthesizer of anti-Lombrosian proverbs and founder of the "Lyon school" of criminology.[39] As professor of legal medicine at the University of Lyon, Lacassagne built a faculty of sociologically oriented doctors whose

[37] Henry Coutagne, "L'exercice de la médecine judiciaire en France," *Archives d'anthropologie criminelle* 1 (1886), pp. 25-58. Also Alexandre Lacassagne's retrospective, *Des transformations du droit pénale et le progrès de la médecine légale de 1810 à 1912* (Lyon: Storck, 1913).

[38] Alexandre Lacassagne, "Avant-propos," *Archives d'anthropologie criminelle* 1 (1886), p. 6.

[39] Jules Dallemagne, *Les théories de la criminalité* (Paris: Masson, 1896), pp. 156-157.

writing and teaching gained for Lyon a major voice in the social interpretation of the French school. His own opposition to Lombroso began
long before 1886. *Les tatouages* (1881) was an exhaustive examination
of tattooing in which he concluded that Lombroso's association of tat-
toos with atavistic criminality was unwarranted.[40] He elsewhere opposed the linking of a criminal type with primitive man, preferring to
account for crime by reference to the social milieu.[41]

Over the next few years Lacassagne set his colleagues and pupils at
Lyon to work on problems relevant to the sociology of crime and
opened the pages of the *Archives* to anti-Lombrosian perspectives. Many
of the results were of a high quality and have proven to be extraordinarily durable contributions. Charles-Marie Debierre in his *Le crâne
des criminels* took direct issue with many of Lombroso's anatomical dog-
mas.[42] Henry Coutagne's study of the influence of occupational categories on types and frequencies of crime was a kind of classic which
later influenced Tarde and others in their writings on the criminal as
a professional type.[43] Emile Raux prepared an impressive statistical
study of juvenile crime in the Lyon region in which he drew direct
correlations between crime rates and the socioeconomic conditions prevailing in the poorer sections of the city. He made particular reference
to the disastrous effect on juveniles of paternal unemployment or de-
sertion and other influences disturbing stable family organization.[44]
Armand Corre explored Lombroso's assertion that criminals and prim-
itives were synonymous. His detailed study of criminality in the French
colonial holdings led him to the conclusion that far from having a
beneficial effect on native crime rates, the arrival of French rule precipitated a rapid rise in crime, the result of native imitation of French
colonials and the drastic interference with normal cultural patterns.[45]
In this connection Paul Topinard's comparison of Lombroso's views
on criminals with the cultural egoism European voyagers manifested

[40] "Imitation," he concluded, was the most likely cause. Alexandre Lacassagne,
Les tatouages—étude anthropologique et médico-légale (Paris: J. B. Baillière, 1881), p.
115.

[41] Alexandre Lacassagne, "L'homme criminel comparé à l'homme primitif," reprint of an address to the Société d'anthropologie de Lyon (Lyon: Storck, 1882).

[42] Charles-Marie Debierre, *Le crâne des criminels* (Lyon: Storck, 1895).

[43] Henry Coutagne, "De l'influence des professions sur la criminalité," *Archives
d'anthropologie criminelle* 5 (1889), pp. 616-640.

[44] See Emile Raux, "L'enfance coupable," *Archives d'anthropologie criminelle* 5 (1890),
pp. 221-258, and *Nos jeunes détenus: Etude sur l'enfance coupable* (Lyon and Paris:
Storck, 1890).

[45] Armand Corre, *L'ethnographie criminelle* (Paris, 1894).

toward primitive tribes is apt.[46] On the whole, by dispensing favorable and unfavorable reviews to friends and enemies, but above all by maintaining good relations with jurists and penal authorities, the coterie associated with the *Archives* managed to advance its cause considerably.[47]

The closest and most valuable ally of the Lyon school was the jurist-sociologist Gabriel Tarde. Perhaps more than any other single figure Tarde provided the theoretical structure for a social interpretation of crime. Though his system was a very personal one, at times convoluted and infused with his peculiarly intense moral outlook, Tarde's eventual academic success as professor at the Collège de France and as a prolific author of sociological theory is well known;[48] but he spent the bulk of his early career in criminal concerns, first as a provincial judge and later as head of the statistical section at the Ministry of Justice.[49] He was a skillful debater and inveighed articulately against the Italians at the international congresses. The aphorism he delivered at the 1892 congress remains one of the most oft-quoted characterizations of Lombroso: "I compare Lombroso to coffee, which does not nourish, but at least stimulates and prevents one from dying of inanity."[50]

In his *Criminalité comparée* (1886) Tarde took an important first step toward combatting anatomical studies of the born criminal. He did not provide new information of his own, but merely compared all the statistical measurements made on criminal morphology by the Italians and others, most of them sympathetic to Lombroso's goals. He found not only considerable variations in figures for the most popular physical anomalies but substantial disagreement about which stigmata were crucial to hereditary criminality. Everyone, it seems, had his favorite atavism. Though these arguments were probably the most damaging,

[46] "They find all the faults imaginable and no quality whatsoever." Paul Topinard, "L'anthropologie criminelle," *Revue d'anthropologie* 2 (1887), p. 685. Other products of the Lyon school are Emile Laurent's *L'année criminelle (1889-1890)* (Paris, 1891) and *L'anthropologie criminelle et les nouvelles théories du crime*, 2d ed. (Paris: Société des Editions Scientifiques, 1893).

[47] For a far-seeing discussion of the tasks for students of crime in the years to follow, including surveys of the relation of local studies to the evolution of penal law and social and political institutions, see A. Lacassagne, "Programme d'études nouvelles en anthropologie criminelle," *Archives d'anthropologie criminelle* 6 (1891), pp. 565-567.

[48] See Terry N. Clark's preface to *Gabriel Tarde: On Communications and Social Influence* (Chicago: University of Chicago Press, 1969).

[49] The best study of Tarde's criminal theories is that of Henry Geisert, *Le système criminaliste de Tarde* (Paris: Domat-Montchrestien, 1935). Also see Margaret S. Wilson Vine, "Gabriel Tarde," in Mannheim, ed., *Pioneers in Criminology*, pp. 282-304.

[50] *Actes du troisième congrès d'anthropologie criminelle*, p. 335.

Tarde also directly disputed Lombroso's theory of atavism and the contention that epileptoid tendencies were common in born criminals, ridiculing Lombroso's belief that the values common in criminal subcultures were better explained by hereditary than by sociological reasons. Tarde also offered a psychosociological explanation of crime that depended on social imitation and showed that crimes followed patterns of fashion, which crystallized into customs and habits and became characteristic behavioral traits of criminal-social milieux. In *Criminalité comparée* and his later *La philosophie pénale* (1890) Tarde suggested a theory of moral responsibility based on individual identity and social similarity. He hoped to avoid a fruitless debate over free will and determinism by making responsibility and subsequent punishment an automatic reflection of the extent to which an individual's actions were consistent with his personal and social images.

Tarde quickly became friendly with Lacassagne and the major figures in the Lyon coterie, and they in turn welcomed his philosophical turn of mind and superb debating skills. In 1893 he became coeditor of the *Archives* with Lacassagne.[51] On the whole Tarde was remarkably successful in maintaining a stable balance between the appearance of a careful empirical method in his own work and a frontal assault on the philosophical pretensions of positivism. His unique synthesis, in denying science the possibility of moral reductionism, had the effect of allowing empiricism to coexist with traditional moral values.[52] This rare marriage enabled the French school to avoid a direct confrontation with the legal and religious establishment while gaining the respect in France and abroad of those who hoped to bring greater scientific rigor to the study of criminal phenomena.

Certainly of equal value in the growth of a French opposition to the Italian positivists were the efforts of French anthropologists to disassociate themselves from Lombroso's dogmatic craniometry. Paul Topinard took issue with Lombroso's concept of type, arguing that anthropology had learned to distinguish between the "mesological" (physical) type that issued from certain geographical and physical surroundings over millennia, and the "social type, resulting from social distinctions, differences of occupation, the ways and type of life engendered by civilization."[53] The latter type, though it might create small

[51] See Alexandre Lacassagne, "Gabriel Tarde," *Archives d'anthropologie criminelle* 24 (1909), pp. 895-906.

[52] In this connection see Tarde's "Positivisme et pénalité," *Archives d'anthropologie criminelle* 2 (1887), pp. 32-51, and also "Les actes du congrès de Rome," ibid. 3 (1888), pp. 66-80.

[53] Topinard, "L'anthropologie criminelle," pp. 660-661.

morbid effects and influence behavior, could not create a uniformity of influence that would transmit an ensemble of physical traits from one generation to the next. The "artificial assemblage of characters," which Lombroso called a type, Topinard wrote, is the product of a scientific imagination that would call a race brachycephalic when 60 percent of its members were dolicocephalic. As far as the notion of atavism was concerned, "between the human species and its phylogenetic ancestors, between the present races and the primitive races, all continuity has disappeared. The wire, having lengthened and become thinner has broken . . . a multitude of races have interposed and have disappeared."[54]

Léonce Manouvrier, Topinard's brilliant colleague at the Ecole d'anthropologie of Paris, offered some especially effective rebuffs to the Lombrosians in several skillfully prepared presentations. As did Topinard, he challenged the nature and manner of collection of cranial indices. Lombrosian statistics, he pointed out, were gathered without reference to a randomly selected control group of noncriminals.[55] And how, he asked, can one identify measurable pathological anomalies, even granting they appeared with any frequency, with social roles, socially defined? Moreover, Lombroso's examples are merely the criminals who have been caught: "Would one, if he wanted to study the commercial spirit, the military spirit, the ecclesiastical spirit, measure the heads and count the stigmata of bankrupt businessmen, the occupants of police jails, or interdicted priests?"[56] For Manouvrier the central problem remained one of confusing social definitions with anthropological ones in arriving at some appreciation of the concept of normality.[57]

[54] Ibid., p. 683. Stephen Jay Gould has also briefly discussed the anthropological rebuttals in *The Mismeasurement of Man*, pp. 132-139.

[55] Léonce Manouvrier, "Les crânes des suppliciés," *Archives d'anthropologie criminelle* 1 (1886), pp. 128-132.

[56] *Actes du troisième congrès d'anthropologie criminelle*, p. 175.

[57] Manouvrier drew these common-sense conclusions from the following dilemma: "When one reflects on the innumerable multitude of acts of violence and of willful violations of common law that are committed each day from the top to the bottom of the social scale, without speaking of the acts of injustice and brigandage committed by societies themselves under the cover of religious, political, or social necessities . . . one is obliged to ask himself if the imprisoned criminals do not simply constitute a category of lawbreakers more easily apprehendable by law or police, more particularly dangerous, perhaps, for public tranquillity, and too exclusively sacrificed, in any case, as a sort of scapegoat to assure to the law an indispensable sanction. Thanks to this tribute paid to morality at the expense of men considered criminals by the law, the others are able to call themselves honest men by legal definition, as well as all their acts that are most contrary to morality. . . . In the

A more predictable reaction in support of a sociological explanation of crime came from the social scientists within the Durkheimian orbit. Though the work of Durkheim and his followers came a bit late to aid their countrymen in the early stages of the struggle against Lombroso, some trenchant critiques of the Italian school from the Durkheimian point of view did appear before the turn of the century.[58] Most of Durkheim's own work in this area was also completed by 1900.[59] No doubt Durkheim had his disagreements with rival proponents of sociological causation, especially Tarde, but there can be no doubting their sense of unity against biological determinism in criminality.[60]

A final bridge, if one were indeed necessary, between the sociological students of crime and classical penal theorists in France was provided by a group of popular writers on criminal matters whose main object was to use the new sociological theories to bolster traditional concepts of free will and responsibility against the threat of Lombrosian determinism. These jurists, lawyers, and penal authorities were trusted members of the legal establishment. In an earlier era this sort of author would have confined his remarks on the causes of crime to "vice" or "misery," but by 1890 he had a growing body of sociological literature to support him. Writers of this ilk were by no means thoroughgoing

---

matter of theft, there are diverse shrill and hazardous forms which lead many of those who practice them to prison, but there is a whole crowd of others no less obnoxious, that the law ignores or protects; this doesn't startle good society too much, provided especially that these others have succeeded so well that morality and success are all tangled together." Ibid., pp. 174-175.

[58] See Durkheim's review of L. Gunther's *Die Idee der Wiedervelgeltung in der Geschichte und Philosophie des Strafrechtes* in *L'année sociologique 1896-1897* (Paris, 1898), p. 350; Gaston Richard, "Sociologie criminelle," ibid., pp. 393-394; Richard's review of Corre's *L'ethnographie criminelle*, ibid., pp. 409-416, and other reviews in which he touches on the Lombrosian theory, e.g., pp. 419-450. See Paul Fauconnet, review of Raymond Saleilles's *L'individualisation de la peine* in *L'année sociologique 1897-1898* (Paris, 1899), pp. 360-362. And see Gaston Richard, "Les crises sociales et les conditions de la criminalité," in *L'année sociologique 1898-1899* (Paris, 1900), pp. 15-42.

[59] Most important are *De la division du travail social* (Paris: Alcan, 1893), *Les règles de la méthode* (Paris: Alcan, 1895) and "L'évolution des deux lois pénales," *L'année sociologique 1899-1900* (Paris, 1901), pp. 65-95.

[60] See especially Tarde, "Criminalité et santé sociale," *Revue philosophique* 39 (1895), pp. 148-162; and Emile Durkheim, "Crime et santé sociale," ibid., pp. 518-523. Later, Durkheim remembered Tarde's criminology in this way: "But in order to understand its full significance, it is necessary to place it in the epoch in which it was conceived. This was the time when the Italian school of criminology exaggerated positivism to the point of making it into a kind of materialistic metaphysics which had nothing scientific about it. Tarde demonstrated the inanity of these doctrines and reemphasized the essentially spriritual character of social phenomena." "Sociology," in *La science française* (Paris: Imprimerie Nationale, 1915), p. 382.

social scientists, but they were the heirs of a respected tradition of *politique criminelle* begun by writers such as Charles Lucas, Bonneville de Marsangy, and Hubert Michaux.[61] Shortly after the Rome congress of 1885 the French Academy of Moral and Political Sciences offered a prize for the best manuscript on the most recent principles of penal philosophy. In reporting the prize in 1888, Emile Beaussire praised the two winners' careful elaboration of the new sociological doctrines on the "natural history" of criminality and their forthright opposition to the theories of the born criminal.[62] Georges Vidal and Louis Proal were legally trained defenders of freewill theory who felt that the search for "social laws," in Vidal's words, must be as scientific as possible without falling prey to the absurd pretension that had plagued the Italians of reducing philosophy to science.[63] About this time Vidal began teaching a course at the Toulouse law faculty on criminology and criminal law that eventually blossomed into the Institut de criminologie et des sciences pénales.[64]

By 1889 the Paris law faculty had empowered Henri Joly to teach a similar *cours libre*, the immediate progenitor of the Paris Institut de science pénale (1906). As a Catholic writer on crime and social issues, Joly was a passionate opponent of Lombrosian determinism. Both his *Le crime—étude sociale* (1888) and *La France criminelle* (1889) integrated freewill theory with the findings of Tarde, Manouvrier, Lacassagne, and other members of the French school.[65] Another Paris law professor, René Garraud, who was later to write a ground-breaking treatise on French penal law, also stood by the sociological school in 1886 and used language that extended sociological determinism as far as any lawyer in the period dared.[66]

By far the most convinced believer in free will in the French legal

[61] The great classic of this tradition in the era of our concern was Raymond Saleilles' *L'individualisation de la peine* (Paris, 1898). He laboriously integrated the findings of the "French school" into his treatise.

[62] Reported by Georges Vidal, *Principes fondamentaux de la pénalité dans les systèmes les plus modernes* (Paris, 1890), pp. 1-6.

[63] Ibid., pp. 20-23. See his later *Cours de droit criminel et de science pénitentiaire*, 2d ed. (Paris, 1902). Also Louis Proal, *Crime et la peine* (Paris, 1892).

[64] On the institutionalization of the sociological perspective in French criminology, see Denis Carroll, Jean Pinatel, et al., *Les sciences sociales dans l'enseignement*, vol. 7: *Criminologie* (Paris: Presses Universitaires de France, 1956), pp. 111-121.

[65] See especially pp. 1-22, 102-161, 277-308, and 328-384 in *Le crime—étude sociale* (Paris: Cerf, 1888); and pp. 56-96, 170-179 and 199-200 in *La France criminelle* (Paris, 1889).

[66] René Garraud, "Rapports du droit pénal et de la sociologie criminelle," *Archives d'anthropologie criminelle* 1 (1886), pp. 9-21.

system was the *juge d'instruction*. His task of extracting the motives for a crime in direct confrontations with the accused operated as a working presumption of the existence of reason and conscious responsibility. Thus, when Adolphe Guillot, chief *juge d'instruction* in the Department of the Seine, and one of the most celebrated jurists of his era, embraced the French school, sociology might be said to have truly arrived. He continued to use the conventional rhetoric of the classicists—"it is easier to do evil than good"— but for his opposition to Lombroso and in his need for a convincing alternative explanation, he relied on Manouvrier, Tarde, and others.[67]

The relative ease with which a working compromise was obtained between scientists, philosophers, and jurists cannot be explained simply in strategic or purely professional terms. The common effort to defeat the Lombrosian heterodoxy was securely rooted in native scientific traditions that by the 1880s had become widely influential in France beyond the boundaries of specialized science. Neo-Lamarckian heredity and degeneration theory provided a matrix of scientific concepts and language that was comprehensible enough to appeal to nonscientists and sufficiently fruitful empirically to meet the scientific criteria of specialists in a variety of biological, medical, and social science disciplines. Indeed, as I later argue, these concepts became so profoundly imbued with a common cultural meaning for most literate Frenchmen and women in the *belle époque* that they seem to have gained a practically ideological stature in the era. Degeneration theory in particular served to provide a continuum between biological and social thought that makes nonsense of the usual efforts to distinguish between them, and was so culturally useful that it could explain persuasively all the pathologies from which the nation suffered. Leaving aside for later chapters an account of these general developments, I would like to discuss the scientific origins of these concepts and the manner in which they were used in the debates on crime.

By the mid-nineteenth century a thoroughly French tradition of evolutionary *transformisme* existed which accounted for the nature of species change across a broad spectrum of biological disciplines. This tradition, based on the hereditary theories of the eighteenth-century naturalist Jean-Baptiste Lamarck, was so well rooted in the life sciences that Darwinian evolution, first introduced in the 1860s, failed to gain a firm foothold in French scientific thought. Though Lamarckian con-

[67] Adolphe Guillot, *Les prisons de Paris et les prisonniers* (Paris: Dentu, 1889), esp. pp. 9-15, 103-131, 136-144, and 491.

cepts were employed throughout the century in anthropology, histology, physiology, embryology, paleontology, botany, and general zoology, they experienced a marked revival in 1870-1873 as part of the nationalist reaction to the military defeat of 1870. Intrusions of Darwinian schemes of "evolution by natural selection" were combatted vigorously from a neo-Lamarckian point of view and treated in such a way that Darwin could be congratulated for providing the final proof of Lamarck's theory.[68]

The ruling ideas in this neo-Lamarckian *transformisme* were borrowed from early nineteenth-century embryology where many of the most convincing early proofs for the notion of species evolution had been initially formulated. Central to this tradition was the conception of the embryo's "organic economy," a kind of solidarity of the internal components of the organism which served it in the constant task of adaptation to changing environments. In the Lamarckian explanation, the organism possessed an interior force that helped it to determine "the conditions in which it accepted combat."[69] The organism's "accommodation" to an environment was, in a sense, negotiated between these *"solidaires"* components and the milieu in a way that made an internal equilibrium with an efficient division of labor an *a priori condition of successful adaptation.* In her survey of the nineteenth-century life sciences, Yvette Conry treats species change as embryological evolution writ large, writing that in the work of the physiologist Charles Robin "Lamarckian transformism is the zoological projection of embryological evolution."[70] The persistence of this concept in biology helps explain the importance of equilibrium models both for late nineteenth-century biology and for French social theorists seeking analogues in life forms.

Darwin's doctrine of natural selection, when it was not simply misunderstood, was generally rejected on the grounds that it was a mere a posteriori narration of biological events *explaining* nothing. Darwinism, which viewed heredity as the problem of the perpetuation of variants, was in conflict with the French notion which treated heredity as a *"force* of reproduction."* The irreducible element of teleology in the mechanism of French heredity encouraged a "conservation of initial directions," to borrow a phrase of the neo-Lamarckian *transformiste* Félix Le Dantec. According to this teleological process, adaptation was not blind; rather, environmental changes posed a problem for the

[68] Yvette Conry, *L'introduction du Darwinisme en France au XIXe siècle* (Paris: Vrin, 1974), pp. 39-40, 311.

[69] Ibid., pp. 43-44.

[70] Ibid., p. 418.

organism which it was obliged to solve by limiting the production of inadaptive variations, and by learning new functional behavior which reestablished "equilibrium" between itself and the environment. The notion of organic economy was crucial to this process for it allowed the problem of biological survival to be reduced to a problem of internal organization.[71] Once habituated to a new functional relationship ("vivre, c'est s'habituer" in Le Dantec's words),[72] the organism acquired the ability to pass on this new organization to its offspring. In what may have been as much a cultural as a scientific statement, Amedée Coutance contrasted a Darwinian conflict model with one based on a Lamarckian equilibrium: "Struggle is disorder, uncertainty, and ruin; equilibrium is harmony, design, and conservation."[73]

But what if the environment alters in such a way as to produce responses from the organism that are successful in the short-run task of adaptation, but potentially dysfunctional to the organism in the long run—in other words, an adaptation that the organism experiences as a pathology? It was this "problem"—a modern one with an intellectual history of its own—that produced degeneration theory.

The earliest French theorists of degeneracy were doctors with special interests in mental pathology. The two earliest texts were Prosper Lucas's *De l'hérédité naturelle* (1847) and B. A. Morel's *Traité des dégénérescences* (1857), the latter of which became the *font et origo* of the theory. In Morel's schema, an organism adapting to a pathological environment concealed this pathology as an "aptitude" or "tendency," but later generations experienced it as a worsening physical and nervous disorder of a morbid type. Left unchecked, degeneration would result in sterility and finally death, Morel's concession to the continuing relative health of the rest of the population. Mental pathologists who wrote after the publication of Morel's classic gradually elaborated and refined the process by which mental aberrations were inherited in degenerational syndromes. Henri Le Grande du Saulle's *La folie héréditaire* (1873), Théodule Ribot's *L'hérédité psychologique* (1873), J. Déjérine's *L'hérédité dans les maladies du système nerveux* (1886), and Charles Féré's *La famille*

---

[71] Ibid., pp. 317-323.

[72] Félix Le Dantec, *Science et conscience* (Paris: Flammarion, 1908), p. 76.

[73] Amedée Coutance, *La lutte pour l'existence* (Paris, 1882), p. 508. As Conry has described the extrascientific outlook on Darwinism, "Darwinism appears to isolate organisms while undermining all their essential affective and social guarantees." Conry, *L'introduction du Darwinisme*, p. 423. According to Georges Canguilheim this conception of internal equilibrium became the touchstone of organic health and viability in the nineteenth-century French life and medical sciences, informing, most significantly, Claude Bernard's notion of the "internal milieu" of vital forces characteristic of the living organism. *Le normal et le pathologique*, pp. 11-68.

névropathique were in a direct line of descent from Lucas and Morel. They extended the implications of degeneracy more widely to include inherited "sentiments" and emotional states of a pathological type and built up an impressive array of clinical anecdotes.

The introduction and growing popularity of the concept of degeneracy in mental medicine, with its emphasis on organic symptoms and heredity, were hardly random events. The concept's introduction coincided with a growing crisis in the diagnostic and therapeutic model favored by Pinel and Esquirol, who were the dominant influences in French psychiatry until the 1860s. Robert Castel has explained this crisis as an ironic effect of psychiatry's efforts to construct a new technical basis for its specialization. The nosologies of early psychiatry stressed the careful observation of signs and symptoms of madness and eschewed speculations that attempted to locate the roots of mental disorders in the organism itself.[74] The weaknesses of this essentially nonmaterialistic outlook were not lost on many of Pinel's and Esquirol's medical contemporaries. First, and most obviously, to the extent the new specialty diverged from general medicine, it abandoned the particular claim to scientific expertise that had been the original justification for its monopoly in the care of the mentally ill. Second, even before the rise of the new "scientific" medicine in the 1860s, many psychiatric practitioners were convinced that many forms of mental illness could be traced to organic sources. As a consequence, for some time—Castel says until the early 1870s—many French psychiatrists employed two "codes" in their clinical work: one, analytical, sought to locate mental disorders in organic causes; the other, therapeutic, continued the moral treatment along the original lines laid down by Pinel.[75]

The mid-century scientific revolution in the life sciences, led by Claude Bernard, spelled the doom of this awkward bifurcation and reunited the analytic and therapeutic "codes" under one rubric. Between 1855 and 1870 there were a number of breakthroughs in pathological anatomy, cell histology, and neurological physiology. Claude Bernard, Jean Luys, and Charles Robin were the main figures in this effort to push the frontiers of the physical sciences deeper into the sciences of life. These developments coincided with the efforts of neurologists at the Paris mental hospitals (Bicêtre, Salpétrière) to explain nervous diseases as effects of brain and nerve lesions. Also at this time, Paul Broca at the Bicêtre launched his researches on the cerebral localization of mo-

[74] Castel, *L'ordre psychiatrique*, pp. 108-111.
[75] Ibid., pp. 113-118.

tion and sense skills.[76] The staffs of these two distinguished psychiatric hospitals were largely responsible for the training of the generation of psychiatrists who placed the study of mental disease on a new, "scientific" basis. It may be that the psychiatry of the previous generation had strayed too far from the technical aspects of medicine, and that the specialty needed a strong infusion of scientific materialism to justify its continued monopoly of the treatment of mental illness. Whatever the immediate cause, there is no denying the tenacity and militancy of the new views.

Even before many of the above developments had taken place, B. A. Morel had laid down the general theoretical lines that the new orientation would follow. It was not Morel, however, but a young clinician trained at the Salpétrière, Valentin Magnan, who was primarily responsible for the adaptation of organic theories of degenerative mental illness to the neurological science of the day. Appointed head of the Bureau of Admissions at the new Saint Anne Asylum in Paris in 1867 at the age of thirty-two, Magnan was the key figure in a generation of mental pathologists who regarded the laboratory as a valuable resource for psychiatry. The doctrine of organicism that was the product of this generation's work was the controlling paradigm in French and European mental medicine from the early 1880s until the eve of World War I.

Magnan's leadership of this new theoretical paradigm was not the consequence of any unusual personal qualities he possessed, nor of his control of a network of university patronage, for he never held a university chair in his specialty. Rather, Magnan was a prolific worker and publisher whose activities covered the entire spectrum of mental medicine. He did careful laboratory work on the effects on animals of various drugs and intoxicants, including cocaine, alcohol, and absinthe. Indeed it was primarily owing to his findings on the extremely toxic effects of absinthe that it was finally banned in most European countries by 1918. He also worked intensively on epilepsy and idiocy and did a massive study in 1874, *De l'alcoolisme*, on the contribution of alcohol to insanity. He was best known, however, for his attempt to separate the study of nerve lesions from localization theory and orient it toward a doctrine that stressed the general degradation of all nervous tissue in degenerative illnesses. This allowed him to square neurological pathology with Morel's notion that successive generations of degenerates

---

[76] An excellent source for these developments written by an observer sympathetic with "scientific" psychiatry is Paul Sérieux, *Valentin Magnan: Sa vie et son oeuvre* (Paris: Masson, 1921), pp. 9-18. See also Henri Baruk, *La psychiatrie française de Pinel à nos jours* (Paris: Presses Universitaires de France, 1967), pp. 43-47.

experienced a progressive weakening of vital energy across a range of mental and physical functions.[77]

Magnan also created an elaborate, widely used nosological system in which the emphasis was not on classifying the signs and symptoms of autonomous psychological syndromes as in the theories of Pinel, but rather on *explaining* symptoms by certain causes in the hereditary makeup or environment of the afflicted individual and making them intelligible by their appearance within an aprioristically devised syndrome that progressed to ever-worsening effects. As one of the main figures in organicist psychiatry explained this difference, the old school "uses classifications that are too exclusively symptomatic. . . . Others, and by this we mean more modern authors (Morel, Magnan), have on the contrary made an effort to take into consideration, in their construction of types and nosological groups, the etiology and the advance of mental disease."[78]

In his most concise definition of degeneration, Magnan wrote that it was "a pathological state of the organism which, in relation to its most immediate progenitors, is constitutionally weakened in its psychophysical resistance and only realizes in part the biological conditions of the hereditary struggle for life. That weakening, which is revealed in permanent stigmata, is essentially progressive, with only intervening regeneration; when this is lacking, it leads more or less rapidly to the extinction of the species."[79]

From the outset of the debates on the born criminal, degeneration theory possessed a clear potential for occupying a middle ground between the atavistic criminal of Lombroso and the abstractly free man of the voluntarist metaphysicians and jurists. Degenerate syndromes were set in motion, after all, by pathological environments; though biological causes (and accompanying morphological symptoms) might be advanced as the *proximate* sources of criminal behavior, these could be explained as the products of some temporally *distant* social environment that shaped criminal behavior in a more general way. Second, since degeneracy was an illness that advanced in stages, it was possible

[77] On these aspects of Magnan's work, see Sérieux, *Valentin Magnan*, pp. 28-75.

[78] Gilbert Ballet et al., *Traité de pathologie mentale* (Paris, 1903), p. 2.

[79] Valentin Magnan and Paul-Maurice LeGrain, *Les Dégénérés* (Paris: Rueff, 1895), p. 79. The phrase "struggle for life," as used here and elsewhere by French scientists has been systematically misunderstood as a sympathetic gesture to the Darwin-Spencer model of evolution wherein organisms of the same species compete with one another to determine which among them are the fittest to survive. Instead, the phrase refers to the struggle of the individual organism to adjust its organic economy to achieve a successful adaptation: in this process the competition for scarce resources with members of the same species was only one of several requirements.

to argue that it did not extinguish the autonomous will, and therefore the penal responsibility of its victims, until the final phase of degeneration was reached. Indeed, there are clear signs that Léonce Manouvrier and others were hoping to capitalize on this quality of degeneration theory well before the Rome congress.[80]

The utter hopelessness of Lombrosian atavism was opposed by Manouvrier, Topinard, and others whose neo-Lamarckian outlook prevented them from accepting the notion that progressive evolution had altogether ceased for a whole class of humanity. None of us, Manouvrier insisted, escapes the constant influence of the milieu over his daily acts, or its simultaneous effects on the adaptive process of inheritance.[81] The unhealthy social and physical environment that produced degeneracy could be purged of its pathological features and have a positive and formative influence on the individuals living within it. The psychiatrist Charles Féré argued this point in his influential text of 1888, *Dégénérescence et criminalité*, attacking Lombroso's unwarranted identification of degeneracy with particular "criminal" anomalies. A criminal degenerate, he insisted, was produced in an unhealthy milieu that overstimulated him, led him to a state of exhaustion (*épuisement*), and lowered the resistance of his will to the "impulses" of criminal temptations.[82] Paul Brouardel closed the Paris congress of 1889 with words that underscore his endorsement of these views on the origins of crime and his optimistic belief that a solution was at hand: "that for the good of humanity we must have but one enemy to combat: crime; that we must find the solution to but one problem, the amelioration of the social milieux in which degenerates are born, in which they are cultivated, and out of which criminals develop."[83]

Even before the explosion of writing on criminal degeneracy in the 1880s, philosophical exponents of free will found that the ability of degeneration theory to account for the "moral monstrousness" of modern France made it compatible with traditional moral views on crime. Ludovic

[80] See especially the remarks of Orchansky, *Bulletin de la Société d'anthropologie de Paris* (December 7, 1882), pp. 778-789, and Léonce Manouvrier, "Discussion sur les criminels: Sur l'étude anthropologique des crânes d'assassins," ibid. (February 1, 1883), pp. 97-99.

[81] See Manouvrier, *Actes du troisième congrès d'anthropologie criminelle*, p. 182.

[82] Charles Féré, *Dégénérescence et criminalité* (Paris: Flammarion, 1888). See especially the chapter on "épuisement et criminalité," pp. 85-96. On the environmental origins of degeneracy, see pp. 120-129.

[83] Paul Brouardel, *Archives d'anthropologie criminelle* 4 (1889), pp. 589-590. Brouardel's complete argument in favor of replacing Lombroso's atavism with degeneration is in "Le criminel," *Gazette des hôpitaux* 63 (March 20, 26, April 3, May 1, 8, 20, June 3, 26, July 3, 1890), pp. 242-243, 530, 577-579, 669-671.

Carrau argued that the enfeebled inhibitions of the degenerates in Morel's theory were an effect of "the identity of milieux, influences of all sorts, which are able to act on the successive generations of the same family . . . misery, hate of society, laziness, bad examples, the impossibility of rehabilitating a dishonored name . . . the patrimony of shame and reprobation handed down by the father or the ancestors."[84] Catholic commentators were also well disposed to degeneracy as an explanation for crime in a "rotting civilization." One writer directly identified degeneration with the "moral egoism" of our "decomposing" society, but drew the comforting conclusion that since the cause of this degeneracy was moral, so was its cure.[85] In general, even the most violent Catholic opponents of Lombroso's biological determinism routinely explained the occasional physical abnormalities displayed by criminals as the consequences of morbid milieux.[86]

The ease with which degeneracy theory was accepted by nonmedical observers as a convincing explanation for the physical and mental qualities of criminals was surely a decisive factor in its successful replacement of Lombroso's conception of atavism. It left open the hope that "degenerate" environments might be ameliorated, and it was clearly regarded by jurists as a less direct threat to individual penal responsibility than Lombroso's criminal man. Degeneration also enjoyed the advantage, as George Vold has pointed out, of "bolstering the common sense, man-on-the-street conclusion that criminals are what they are because they don't know enough to understand the hazardous nature of criminality, or the satisfying rewards of a law-abiding life."[87]

Medical and scientific specialists certainly interpreted this friendly public response as a sanction to expand the explanatory dimensions of degeneracy as far as possible. By degrees, particular "atavistic" or "primitive" anatomical features were successfully decriminalized, and

---

[84] Ludovic Carrau, "La folie au point de vue psychologique," *Revue des deux mondes* (October 15, 1877), pp. 856-857.

[85] Hippolyte Martin, "Le bilan criminel de la France (1825-1888)," *Etudes religieuses, philosophiques et littéraires* 57 (September 15, 1982), pp. 92-93. See in addition Hippolyte Martin, "Le type criminel: Sa genèse et sa mort," ibid. 58 (February 15, 1893), pp. 264-290, and "Le bilan criminel de la France (1825-1888)," in ibid. 56 (June 15, 1892), 210-232. For a supporting Catholic position which explicitly states the consistency of sociological determinism, degeneracy, and free will, see Dr. G. de Lassus, "Les théories de la criminalité aux congrès d'anthropologie criminelle," extract from *Revue de Lille*, November 1897 (Paris, 1898).

[86] See Joly, *Le crime*, pp. 289-292, 373; le comte d'Haussonville, "Le combat contre le vice," *Revue des deux mondes* (April 1, 1887), p. 580; Guillot, *Les prisons de Paris*, pp. 103-113, 137-144.

[87] Vold, *Theoretical Criminology*, p. 78.

a successful attack mounted on the epilepsy-crime connection so dear to the Italian school.[88] Degeneracy became the most respectable scientific theory for explaining crime, scoring great successes at the Congresses of Criminal Anthropology of 1889, 1892, and 1896;[89] it was even adopted in modified form by the Lombrosians themselves.[90] The great generality of the theory allowed it to satisfy the doctors on the *symptoms* of criminality, particularly the mental aberrations of criminals, and to convince the social scientists that degeneracy could be regarded as a special case of *social causation*.

Degeneration was, however, a theory of medical, indeed of psychiatric provenance; its technical terminology was used primarily by doctors and was applied by nonmedical students of crime only in the most general way. During the heat of the battle against the Lombrosian heresy, French doctors were openly encouraged by their nonmedical allies to enlarge the scope of their activities. They responded with such alacrity to this carte blanche that degeneration became an indispensable concept in all thinking about criminology before World War I. Militant positivists within the medical community like Eugène Dally had demanded a fuller participation by doctors in criminal justice since the 1860s, but the developments of the 1880s and 1890s could not have occurred on the scale or with the thoroughness they did without

[88] The principal texts documenting these developments are Laurent, *L'anthropologie criminelle*; Dallemagne, *Les théories de la criminalité*; Xavier Francotte, *L'anthropologie criminelle* (Paris: Baillière, 1891). Charles Féré, *Les épileptiques et les épilepsies* (Paris, 1890), pp. 420-425.

[89] For the 1889 congress see the remarks on pp. 535, 561-562, 567, 582, 588-589 in "Compte-rendu du Congrès de Paris," *Archives d'anthropologie criminelle* 4 (1889), pp. 522-589. In 1892 the principal statements were M. G. Jelgersma, "Les caractères physiques, intellectuels et moraux reconnus chez le criminel—ne sont d'origine pathologique," *Actes du troisième congrès d'anthropologie criminelle*, pp. 32-36; Léonce Manouvrier, "Etude comparative," ibid., pp. 171-182; P. Cuylits, "L'origine morbide des caractères reconnus chez les criminels-nés," ibid., pp. 240-244; Drs. Emile Houzé and Leo Warnots, "Existe-t-il un type de criminel anatomiquement determiné?" ibid., 121-127. See also the comments by Dr. Dekterew, Paul Garnier, and Adolphe Prins, ibid., pp. 247, 281, 268. For the 1896 congress, see P. Naecke, "Considerations sur la psychiatrie criminelle," *Congrès international d'anthropologie criminelle—Compte rendu* (Geneva, 1897), pp. 1-10; M. B. Alimena, "Relation entre la prédisposition héréditaire et le milieu domestique pour la provocation du penchant criminel," ibid., pp. 48-49; Maurice de Taets and G. de Baets, "L'éducation des fils des criminels," ibid., pp. 90-93; R. Garofalo, "Quelle classification des criminels pourrait-on adopter?," ibid. pp. 145-151; C. Lombroso, "Le traitement du criminel-né et du criminalöide," ibid., pp. 320-325.

[90] Steven Jay Gould traces the retreat in *The Mismeasure of Man*, pp. 132-135; see Rennie, *The Search for Criminal Man*, pp. 68-78; and Marvin E. Wolfgang, "Cesare Lombroso," pp. 258-271.

widespread initiatives from outsiders. Skirmishing between doctors and jurists on the issue of responsibility continued in later years, but it was less intense and less permeated with either-or issues than in the period 1885-1895.

There were, however, some serious consequences, many unattractive to jurists and penologists, that were the result of having invited doctors to participate more fully in criminal justice. First, criminal behavior was thoroughly psychiatrized, or psychiatry was thoroughly criminalized—it is difficult to say which. Charles Féré was virtually alone in holding that degenerate criminals had certain physical "stigmata" lacking in the "simple madman"; in general psychiatrists played down morphology and strove for more nuanced criteria.[91] The most popular characterizations focused on will pathologies. According to the reasoning of Théodule Ribot, the French exponent of this concept, consciously directed willpower was the last of the mental qualities appropriated phylogenetically in mankind's slow evolution from savagery. It was, accordingly, the most fragile of his mental powers and the first to disappear in individuals afflicted by mental disorders of organic (that is, degenerate) type.[92] The absence of willpower made it less likely that the degenerate criminal could resist the allure of easy money or the sordid temptations of debauchery. A huge technical literature was generated that attempted to identify clinically the criminal variations of will pathology.[93]

Second, it became common to locate the "criminal-madman" somewhere on a scale of insensible gradations that ranged from "the most bestial idiocy to the most subtle instability."[94] This spectrum of degenerate criminality was regarded as both a behavioral and a legal continuum, the degree of seriousness of mental incapacity corresponding

[91] Féré, *Dégénérescence et criminalité*, p. 53.

[92] Théodule Ribot, *Les maladies de la volonté* (Paris, 1884). Ribot explained the connection of human will with its organic foundations in the following way: "Volition is not an event coming from no one knows where; it drives its roots into the depths of the unconscious and beyond the individual into the species and the race. It comes not from above, but from below: it is a sublimation of the lower instincts," p. 150.

[93] The most significant items of this literature, which virtually dominates medical criminology, are Féré, *Dégénérescence et criminalité*, pp. 85-96; Emile Laurent, "Les maladies de la volonté chez les criminels," *Annales médico-psychologiques* (November 1892), pp. 404-428; Marandon de Montyel, "Les aliénés dits criminels," ibid. (May 1891), pp. 434-450; Laurent, *L'anthropologie criminelle*, pp. 158-175; Henri Thulié, *La lutte contre la dégénérescence et la criminalité*, 2d ed. (Paris, 1912); G. L. Duprat, *La criminalité de l'adolescence* (Paris, 1909); Marandon de Montyel, "De la criminalité et de la dégénérescence," *Archives d'anthropologie criminelle* 7 (1892), pp. 221-244.

[94] Henri Thulié, "Assistance des dégénérés supérieurs," *Revue philanthropique* 1 (May 1897), p. 45.

to the seriousness of the crime. Thus, the Dutch criminologist Van Hamel proposed a classification scheme in 1892 that ranked criminals from "occasional" to "incorrigible," his assumption being that "the more horrid the crime, the more likely the presence of degeneracy."[95] Though French psychiatrists could not be said to have reduced criminality to madness, they extended the boundaries of mental medicine far enough that the commission of a criminal act became grounds for suspecting the presence of insanity.

Finally, despite the optimistic posture that doctors had adopted during the 1880s, which had minimized criminal nonresponsibility and presented a hopeful perspective on the reshaping of criminogenic environments, the prevailing emphasis of their work was to link crime more closely to heredity, and thus to pessimism. Varieties of criminality were gradually annexed to insanity, and thus controlled by the concept of biological determinism that gripped all of French psychiatry during the heyday of organicism between 1885 and 1910. "Perverts," "degenerates," and other "regressive" types were regarded as in the grip of "iron laws" of hereditary transmission, which, as Conry has written, "were a substitute by default for an unknown causality and an impossible therapeutics, expressing at once the dream and the illusion of a mastery of the phenomena, at least to the extent that the invention of rules normalized them and made possible some measure of predictability."[96] The psychiatrist Georges Heuyer, who was a young man when criminal degeneracy was still au courant, later recalled the way in which the degenerate child was viewed:

> The child born of parents in a good state of health is not predisposed to crime; if he becomes a criminal, it is under the influence of a pathological situation in the parents. He is born with a congenital problem in his brain operations which takes the form of an emotive instability with obsessive preoccupations, and which is able, in certain circumstances, to lead to crime. A bad education has on him a more pronounced influence than on the normal individual. More than others, degenerates were predisposed to offense or crime, and these predispositions manifested themselves from infancy. Mental degenerescence is a kind of selection, but a selection against the grain.[97]

[95] *Bulletin de l'Union internationale de droit pénal* 4 (1892), pp. 295-297.

[96] Conry, *L'introduction du Darwinism*, p. 328.

[97] Georges Heuyer, "Le point de vue de la médecine psychiatrique," *Revue des sciences criminelles* (1964), p. 738. See, in addition, Jean Pinatel's discussion of the role of degeneracy theory in criminology, "Aperçu de l'histoire des doctrines criminologiques," ibid. (1953), pp. 336-346.

The growing preponderance of irresistible biological impulses, particularly in the diagnoses of perversity in young criminals around the turn of the century,[98] helped bring on the "tutelary complex" about which Jacques Donzelot has written so eloquently in *The Policing of Families*. The so-called reform of juvenile justice in 1912, which resulted in a separate system of juvenile courts for minors, forged, in effect, a new alliance between judge and psychiatrist, making final "the completion of a migration that had brought the psychiatrist from the minor and infrequent role of last resort for difficult cases to that of declared instigator of the lowliest judicial decisions."[99] By the first decade of the twentieth century, the medicalization of crime had made the doctor an indispensable figure in the treatment of juveniles, displacing both "paternal correction" and traditional legal processes in the "punishment" of young delinquents.[100]

But this is to anticipate a degree of medical influence in criminal justice that, during the debates over the born criminal, did not yet exist. To read the medical and criminological literature of the 1880s and early 1890s is to be persuaded both of a widespread sense of agreement on the social origins of crime and of a deeply felt optimism that a remodeling of the environment would dramatically curtail criminal and antisocial behavior. When the International Union of Penal Law was formed in 1889, its founding statutes insisted that "the mission of penal law is the struggle against criminality understood as a social phenomenon," warning that the union "reserves especially vis-à-vis the positivist Italian school a complete liberty of criticism."[101] As we have seen, sociological explanations of crime were the only realistic foundation on which a unity of doctors, social scientists, and jurists could be achieved, and which might combat successfully the threat of a total uprooting of the traditional system of criminal justice. The danger

[98] The growth of concern about "perversity" may be found even before 1900: H. Thulié, "Premières mésures à prendre contre le développement de la criminalité infantile," *Revue philanthropique*, 3 (July 1898), pp. 289-311; Louis Albanel and P. V. LeGras, "L'enfance criminelle à Paris," ibid. 4 (February 1899), pp. 385-400; Marandon de Montyel, "Les pervers et leur assistance," ibid. 20 (January 1907), pp. 273-309.

[99] Donzelot, *The Policing of Families*, p. 150. On the "tutelary complex" see esp. pp. 117-151.

[100] On the slow evolution of "paternal correction" toward this "modern" form see Bernard Schnapper, "La correction paternelle et le mouvement des idées au dix-neuvième siècle (1789-1935)," *Revue historique* 263 (April-June 1980), esp. pp. 345-349.

[101] *Bulletin de l'Union internationale de droit pénal* 1 (1889), pp. 4, 20.

passed, at least in its Lombrosian guise, sociological theories of crime have continued as the source of intellectual consensus for criminological experts within these different fields, even though doctors, social scientists, and jurists have pursued their own independent lines of research. Criminology is unique among modern social science disciplines in having foundations that were more intellectual than practical. The "social" interpretation of crime in its twentieth-century form, however, is a pale reflection of the far-reaching claims of this theory in the 1880s when, as the Marxist criminologist Willem Bonger later recalled, criminology called the entire social system into question.[102]

The French school, which was so essential to the victory of the environmental theory of crime, provided the indispensable "scientific" ideas for the defeat of Lombroso's atavistic and epileptoid criminal. These ideas, as we have seen, had a medical and biological provenance; they also had unique explanatory qualities that could account for the social origins of biological features. In view of the uses to which degeneration theory was put after the 1880s, one must revise the remarks of the French criminologist Jean Pinatel, who wrote of the early history of criminology "that while organizing itself methodologically after the example of medicine, criminology is not medicine. The delinquent is not, as a general rule, a sick being but a social case."[103] It might be more accurate to say, "The delinquent is . . . a sick being *and* a social case." Brought in to play an ad hoc role in social theory in the 1880s, the medical idea of degeneration gained dominant status as a cultural theory of national decline in the following decades.

[102] Willem A. Bonger, *Criminality and Economic Conditions*, trans. Henry P. Horton from 1905 French ed. (New York: Agathon Press, 1967), p. 176. This classic Marxist text on criminal problems has special praise for the French school, pp. 148-176.

[103] Jean Pinatel, "De Lacassagne à la nouvelle école de Lyon," *Revue de science criminelle et de droit pénal comparé* (1961), p. 156.

CHAPTER V

Metaphors of Pathology in the *Belle Epoque*: The Rise of a Medical Model of Cultural Crisis

Is it contradictory to link together the terms *"belle époque"* and "cultural crisis"? Can a period whose literature, music, and art reached pinnacles arguably as high as those in any other era in French (or European) culture have coincided with a profound and widespread concern with illness and decline? Leaving aside the questions of the origins of the term *"belle époque"* as a convention of literary and art historians, or of the period 1885-1914 as a roseate memory of a reign of survivors from the *ancien régime*, it is clear that the thirty years preceding the war were years of social and political conflict. No doubt one can find reasons for viewing the era as one of progress, and there are indeed many hopeful material indices. Industrial production, in the doldrums from the late 1870s, showed marked improvement after the mid-1890s. Gross national product, respectable enough as a raw percentage, was near the very top of industrialized nations when considered per capita.[1] Beginning in 1905 the French economy entered its most productive expansionary cycle since the late 1850s. Monetary stability was notable throughout the period, and real wages, after rising from 1873 to 1896, remained more or less steady until 1914.[2] Meat and wine had become substantial parts of working-class family budgets, and illiteracy among men had fallen to 6 percent by 1900. After a century of fits and starts France had finally achieved something like a "normal" economic growth rate, accompanied by most of the attendant social benefits. Nonetheless, most students of the period have begun their work with some sort of disclaimer indicating that they have not been taken in by the "image" of the era. Thus Jacques Chastenet with his disingenuous portrait of

---

[1] Madeleine Rébérioux, *La République radicale? 1898-1914* (Paris: Editions du Seuil, 1975), pp. 196-200.

[2] Georges Dupeux, *French Society 1789-1970*, trans. Peter Wait (London: Methuen, 1976), p. 176.

the solid, patriarchal chief of state Fallières, issued the subsequent warning: "In reality it was a tense and anxious epoch."[3]

But why did it seem so to contemporaries? In the normal course of things, even "positive" and "progressive" statistics, when mediated by the consciousness and sensibility of the era, seldom produced an optimistic effect. The temper of the times tended toward malaise and even pessimism. Decadence was a favorite literary theme which had its echoes in ethical philosophy and political speculation, thus fortifying the interpretation that the ebullience and *joie de vivre* of the *belle époque* was a last feverish eruption of a dying culture, or the bittersweet pleasure of being the "last of a series."[4] This was not an insight confined to aesthetes. In his book on suicide (1897), Emile Durkheim warned his fellow citizens that "we must not be dazzled by the brilliant development of sciences, the arts and industry of which we are the witnesses; this development is altogether certainly taking place in the midst of a morbid effervescence, the grievous repercussions of which each one of us feels. It is then very possible and even probable that the rising tide of suicide originates in a pathological state just now accompanying the march of civilization without being its necessary condition."[5]

There are two essential reasons why favorable material indices were minimized. First, for each series of statistics displaying French advances, there were, as we shall see, many more that revealed stagnation or, worse, regression; moreover, even the most progressive figures were not impressive when measured against the achievements of other industrial nations.[6] Second, as Durkheim also pointed out, there was

[3] Jacques Chastenet, *La France de M. Fallières* (Paris: Fayard, 1949), p. 8.

[4] For the literary, philosophical, and social themes of decadence, the studies of A. E. Carter and Koenraad Swart are still quite useful. A. E. Carter, *The Idea of Decadence in French Literature, 1830-1900* (Toronto: University of Toronto Press, 1958); Koenraad Swart, *The Sense of Decadence in Nineteenth Century France* (The Hague: Nijhoff, 1964). Renato Poggioli has brilliantly described the atmosphere of apocalyptic activism in the *fin-de-siècle* artistic avant-garde in *The Theory of the Avant-garde*, trans. Gerald Fitzgerald (Cambridge, Mass.: Harvard University Press, 1968).

[5] Emile Durkheim, *Suicide: A Study in Sociology*, trans. John H. Spaulding and George Simpson (Glencoe, Ill.: Free Press, 1951), p. 368.

[6] The statistics on raw economic productivity are well known. From a position rivaling England in industrial production in 1800, France had fallen to fourth in the world in 1914. For the comparative figures on coal, steel, and energy output see David Landes, *The Unbound Prometheus: Technological Change, 1750 to the Present* (Cambridge: Cambridge University Press, 1969), pp. 432-433. On the putative decline in French science and technology in this period see Harry Paul, *The Sorcerer's Apprentice* (Gainesville: University of Florida Press, 1972). See also the excellent discussion of the "decline" debate in the French scientific and technical community

another and more important measure of national well-being that could not be easily quantified: "For a society to feel itself in good health, it is neither sufficient nor always necessary that it use a lot of coal or consume a lot of meat, but it is imperative that the development of all its functions be regular, harmonious, and proportioned."[7] The possibilities for subjective judgments in this equilibrium model of national health are obvious. Functions are regular compared to what, harmonious when viewed against what disharmony, and proportioned in what scale of things?

The primary reason for the appeal of an essentially medical model of health was its appropriateness for a nation whose vital statistics revealed several alarming trends. Chief among these were the disquieting figures on population. Though the first signs of a leveling off of the high population growth characteristic of eighteenth-century Europe were noticed as early as the Restoration, it was not until the Second Empire that the growth began to slow dramatically in comparison to other European states. From 1872 to 1911 the French population grew from 36,101,000 to only 39,605,000, an average increase of 89,700 per year, less than one-third the annual growth rate of the period 1821-1846. During the same period (1872 to 1911) the German population grew by 600,000 a year, and increased in size by 58 percent to France's 10 percent. Spain grew by 20 percent, Italy by 30 percent, Austria-Hungary by 38 percent, Great Britain by 43 percent, and European Russia by 78 percent.[8] When mortality finally began to fall below 800,000 per year the number of births was not long in following, plunging to a prewar low of 746,000 between 1911 and 1913. During one five-year period (1891-1895) deaths exceeded births by 300, and there were several years after 1890 when the growth was negative: 1890, 1892, 1895, 1900, 1907, and 1911.[9] Writing just after the war of 1914-1918 Michel Huber said of France: "The pathological weakness of its birthrate distinguishes the French population from all other European peoples."[10] The great responsibility for the slow growth lay with a lagging

---

in Mary Jo Nye, "The Issue of Scientific Decline: Is Quantitative Analysis Enough?" *Isis* (forthcoming).

[7] Emile Durkheim, "Suicide et natalité: Etude de statistique morale," *Revue philosophique* 26 (1888), p. 447.

[8] André Armengaud, *La population française au XIX⁰ siècle* (Paris: Presses Universitaires de France, 1971), pp. 47, 108.

[9] Ibid., pp. 47-51.

[10] Michel Huber, *La population de la France pendant la guerre* (Paris: Presses Universitaires de France, n.d.), p. 81. On the long-term nature of the crisis see Francis Ronsin, *La grève des ventres: Propagande néo-Malthusienne et baisse de la natalité française (XIX-XX siècles)* (Paris: Aubier, 1980), pp. 11-27.

birthrate, though it is also true that the mortality rate was absurdly elevated for the general standard of living in France in the period.

The birth problem did not lay in too few marriages—France boasted a marriage rate near the top in Europe—but in an excessively low marital fertility. The "Malthusian family" produced only 2.2 children in 1900 and 2.0 in 1914. Birthrates fell more quickly in the cities, falling just below the composite rural birthrate for the first time on the eve of the war. These rates, coupled with the higher mortality rates of urban milieux, gave many towns negative growth rates through the last thirty years of the century.

And what of "moral" statistics? It is more difficult to judge the relative weight of these figures because of the varying definitions and modes of data collection that were employed throughout Europe. But there were several trends that, in absolute terms, seemed alarming enough to contemporaries to warrant their serious concern. Some of these worrisome trends were strictly medical in nature. In the 1890s, for instance, just as victories over cholera and smallpox were being claimed, tuberculosis and syphilis became grave concerns. Doctors, members of the hygiene professions, and many other leaders of public opinion began to speak and write about the dangers to the social organism posed by these diseases as if they were discovering them for the first time.[11]

The most serious problem, if we can judge by the flood of documents attesting to contemporary concern, was alcoholism. It was a widely documented fact that the French were the European leaders in per capita alcohol consumption: in the period 1901-1910 they consumed 17 liters per capita of pure alcohol per year to 15 in Italy, 12.5 in Belgium, and 11.5 in Switzerland.[12] Simplified licensing procedures for *débits de boissons* in the 1880s had led to a growth of drinking establishments, giving France more of these outlets than any other country in the world. Paris led the way for the world's great cities with 11.25 *débits* for every one thousand residents. French politicians had always enjoyed a cozy relationship with the distilling lobby, ensuring low taxes and minimal obstacles for the expanding production of *eaux de vie* and absinthe during the last quarter of the century. In spite of growing public concern about alcohol consumption, prosecutions for

[11] See Alain Corbin, "Le péril vénérien au début du siècle: Prophylaxie sanitaire et prophylaxie morale," and Gérard Jacquemet, "Médecine et 'maladies populaires' dans le Paris à la fin du XIXᵉ siècle," in *L'haleine des faubourgs, Recherches*, no. 29 (December 1977), pp. 245-283 and 349-364.

[12] Michael R. Marrus, "Social Drinking in the Belle Epoque," *Journal of Social History* 7 (1974), pp. 120-128.

public drunkenness declined from 75 per million in the period 1876-1880 to 50 per million in 1901-1905, a "logical consequence," in the words of one commentator, "of the scandalous tolerance in our country for the powerful corporation of cabaret owners."[13]

Because of the complexities of compiling and analyzing figures on mental illness, crime, and suicide, it is not possible to state with accuracy where France stood in relation to other countries in these social pathologies. Contemporaries were usually not timid in using alarming comparative statistics, however, and regularly interpreted absolute increases as certain proof of worsening conditions. Thus, for whatever cause, it is certain that the population of insane asylums increased dramatically faster than the general population in the last third of the century, moving from 49,589 in 1871 to 100,201 in 1911.[14] And, as Durkheim pointed out in 1897, though suicide rates were on the increase everywhere in Europe, those in France showed practically the highest rate of growth, increasing between 1826 and 1888 by 385 percent, or from about 2,000 per year to about 8,000 in the decade of the 1880s. This growth continued in the first fifteen years of the twentieth century, reaching yearly figures between 9,300 and 10,300.[15] Even after allowing for the range of "normal" expressions of social pathology that he permitted in his social theory, Durkheim regarded this increase as dangerously high.

The data on voluntary homicide were much less clear-cut. Howard Zehr gives a percentage of 9 for the decline in persons tried for homicide between 1830 and 1900, a figure that is even higher when figured in per capita terms.[16] There was, however, an abrupt rise in first-degree homicide figures just after the turn of the century that particularly alarmed contemporaries. From figures averaging around 450 per year in the 1893-1903 period, homicides climbed to an average of 611 in the decade before the war.[17] Contemporaries could also read the general figures on crime as supporting the growth theory of social pathology. When all crimes against property from the 1820s on are av-

[13] Dr. Lowenthal, "La criminalité en France," *Revue du mois* 6 (October 10, 1908), pp. 410-413. On the comparative laxness of French prosecution, see Maurice Yvernès, "L'alcoolisme et la criminalité," *Journal de la Société de statistique de Paris* 49 (November 1908), pp. 400-419.

[14] "Assistance," *Asile d'aliénés: Annuaire statistique, 1913* (Paris, 1914), p. 33.

[15] Durkheim, *Suicide*, p. 367. The data for the period 1900-1914 may be found in the "Résumé rétrospectif," *Compte générale de l'administration de la justice criminelle* 52 (1936), p. 48.

[16] Zehr, *Crime and the Development of Modern Society*, pp. 114-115.

[17] These averages are computed from the "Résumé rétrospectif" in the *Compte générale de l'administration de la justice criminelle* 52 (1936), pp. 46-47.

eraged together, including those tried in the correctional courts, there was an increase in offenses reported to the police of 230 percent, and at least a 60 percent gain in property crimes going to trial.[18] Personal assaults also rose in the last quarter of the century. In the decade 1875-1884 an average of 25,611 cases were tried yearly on this charge. This figure had increased, however, to 34,655 yearly by the decade of 1895-1904.[19] Other studies have noted an increase in the number of recidivists apprehended for crimes in urban areas and a general rise in juvenile delinquency near the century's end.[20]

On the whole, sexual crimes seem to have declined slowly during the century. Public anxiety about assaults on minors remained at a high level, however, and concern about prostitution and its role in spreading syphilis made the period from 1890 to 1914 the "golden age of venereal peril." Thirteen to 15 percent of Parisian males were alleged to be infected, and one million individuals nationwide.[21] As we shall see later, syphilophobia was accompanied as a general rule by a fear of perverse (or merely active) sexuality and abhorrence of pornography and sexually explicit entertainment. French printers had supplied most of European pornography for generations, with the consequence that the mother tongue of Bossuet and Racine was the language par excellence of European erotica. The fascination with the perverse, which was a major theme in the "decadent" and symbolist literature of the eighties and nineties, often spilled over into lucrative pornographic hack work: Apollinaire, poet and pornographer, produced a sizable quantity of erotica for profit (and by inclination). But if there was some precedent for ignoring French leadership in the dirty book trade, there was less tolerance for the *belle époque* brand of nude display and erotic dialogue that appeared in the cabarets and little theaters of the capital, and in the grand revues of the Moulin Rouge, Olympia, and Folies Bergères.[22] These new forms provoked the appearance of lawsuits, press campaigns, and congresses designed to counteract their influence, and put the *service des moeurs* on a footing of constant mobilization.

France had her problems, no doubt, and citizens of any society might

[18] Zehr, *Crime and the Development of Modern Society*, p. 36.

[19] These are my averages from the "Résumé rétrospectif" in the *Compte générale de l'administration de la justice criminelle* 52 (1936), pp. 47-48. These are the crimes that contemporaries most often linked to the rise in alcoholism.

[20] Denis Szabo, *Crimes et villes* (Paris: Cujas, 1960), p. 38; Yak-Yon Chen, *Etudes statistiques sur la criminalité en France de 1855 à 1930* (Paris: n.p., 1937), pp. 15-16.

[21] Corbin, *Les filles de noce*, pp. 387-388.

[22] See Patrick Waldberg on the nude theater, *Eros in la Belle Epoque*, trans. Helen R. Lane (New York: Grove Press, 1969), pp. 90-100. On the pornography tradition see Zeldin, *France, 1848-1945*, vol. 1, pp. 309-312.

have been expected to feel alarm at this formidable range of "illnesses" attacking the nation's vitality. But many other European nations were plagued with high rates of alcoholism, disease, mental illness, suicide, and "modern" forms of immorality without undergoing an anxiety crisis about national health like the one that occurred in France. What distinguished the French reaction to these typically modern problems of urbanizing and industrializing societies was the existence in France of two images of the fatherland that had practically ideological status in the nineteenth century.[23] These models, against which all progress, or decadence, was measured by contemporaries, were the image of France as it used to be and the image of the relative status of France and Germany. In the course of the geopolitical developments of the period after 1850 the two images became so inextricably linked that no judgment about the stature of France could be made without some reference to the relative stature of its neighbor *outre-Rhin*. By the end of the century, "the German menace was regarded as the sign of French decadence."[24]

It is a commonplace of French history that the "idea" of France has provided the necessary ideological apparatus for warring political factions throughout the modern period. The Monarchist idea consisted of a king, a union of throne and altar, and the dispersion of political power into the hands of landed notables. The Bonapartist idea recalled an authoritarian political regime, a subordinate but "official" church, and a certain military-imperial veneer. And there was of course the idea of the French Republic: Jacobin state centralism, anticlericalism, and popular sovereignty. If Theodore Zeldin's recent argument about the richer vein of analysis being the study of forces uniting the French is correct, what is common to all three of these "ideas" of France? Assuredly, it is France as La Grande Nation, the premier military power on the continent and the richest, most populous and economically advanced state in West and Central Europe. Contained in the skein of historical memories within each of these "ideas" lay an enormous pride in the expansion of French arms, culture, and institutions.

Following the humiliating defeat in 1870 at the hands of Prussia, French images of France as it used to be and of newly united Germany underwent some necessary revision. The new nation, already possessed of a much larger population than France in 1870, also had a more

[23] Victor Nguyen, "Situation des études maurrasiennes: Contribution à l'histoire de la presse et des mentalités," *Revue d'histoire moderne et contemporaine* 18 (1971), p. 516.

[24] Claude Digeon, *La crise allemande de la pensée française 1870-1914* (Paris: Presses Universitaires de France, 1959), p. 431.

The flirt, to her admirer, Count G. of Stockholm: "My dear, I consent
to marry you, but you must promise me that we will have no children.
My motto is: Reproduction is forbidden, even for Sweden and Norway."
by Villemot, *Gil Blas*, March 1, 1901, p. 1

substantial birthrate and demonstrated an astonishing capacity for economic growth that allowed it to surpass France in most significant areas by the 1890s. In Claude Digeon's account of French intellectual reaction to Germany, it was the literary generation of 1890 that felt the first clear signs of "a profound anxiety, a consciousness of weakness, a concern about decadence, an obsession with diminution."[25] By the 1890s the image of the lost provinces had begun to take a characteristically corporeal, biological form. Thus, explains Digeon, for Maurice Barrès, "it is certain that the detachment of these two provinces contributed precisely to the orientation of the Lorrainer's reflections toward the idea that the fatherland was first a soil, a frontier, and men, and that it was conditioned by both human and material realities."[26] Such organic metaphors and typologies increased in popularity throughout the remaining years of the century; by 1914 they exercised a kind of linguistic imperialism over all efforts to compare the situations of the two nations. One could dispute degrees of illness or health within this clinical frame of reference, but there was no easy way to avoid the medical model of analysis that it invariably entailed.[27]

The "master pathology" in the spectrum of pathologies afflicting France was the sluggishly growing population. It was in this domain that the relative disadvantages of the French were most readily apparent and the geopolitical effects most redoubtable. Lucien Prévost-Paradol, writing at the time of Bismarck's consolidation of the North German Confederation, worried about France preserving

[25] Ibid.

[26] Ibid. The "scientific" study of national character was a veritable industry in France in the thirty years before World War I. Writers specializing in various national "organisms" explored the virtues and vices of other European nations and America in a kind of prefiguring of twentieth-century racism. See Gustave LeBon, *Lois psychologiques de l'évolution des peuples* (Paris, 1894); Alfred Fouillée, *Esquisse psychologique des peuples européenes* (Paris, 1903). Jacques Bardoux was the most noted anglophile. See his *Essai d'une psychologie de l'Angleterre contemporaine*, 2 vols. (Paris, 1906, 1907). Firmin Roz and especially Paul de Rousiers found much of interest in the American character. Georges Sorel, much moved by the latter's idealization of the American captain of industry, contrasted the vigorous American entrepreneur with his conservative French counterpart in *The Illusions of Progress*, trans. John and Charlotte Stanley (Berkeley: University of California Press, 1969), pp. 200-206. See Firmin Roz, *L'énergie americaine* (Paris, 1910) and Paul de Rousiers, *La vie americaine* (Paris, 1892).

[27] In his *Les disciplines de la France* (Paris, 1908), Paul Adam treated the national types of other nations as cuttings that could replenish the French root: "We must not neglect to create in our elite the spirit of risk, the power of the Americans, the spirit of enterprise, the power of Germany, the spirit of solidarity, the power of England," p. 75.

a material place and a physical force worthy of our rightful pride, deserving still some consideration from the other peoples of the earth, and retaining the respect, the glorious name, our old France deserves . . . it is to the most numerous nation that the highest military and political rank belongs along with all the material and moral advantages that flow from it. Any projects or hopes to keep France in its relative rank in the world must be considered to be absolutely chimerical if they do not take as their point of departure this maxim: the number of French must rise rapidly enough to maintain a certain equilibrium between our power and that of the other great nations of the world.[28]

At about the same time, the French medical and scientific community was engaged in spirited discussions on the relative *quality* of the population; it was in this context that the notion of degenerescence as a social question was first raised. It was conceded that the French were less fertile than their neighbors and as a population significantly older, but few were willing to conclude that this signified any inevitable degeneration.[29] Nonetheless, it was generally conceded that, in the face of a relative diminution in absolute numbers, the "productive and intrinsic worth" of the population assumed an increased importance. Thus, "the fatherland is not in danger at present; it offers a population powerful in numbers and in the productive and personal worth of its individuals, but it is in danger for the future, and, in place of sleeping tranquilly, we must remain alert and act with energy and in a spirit of patriotic foresight."[30]

As the figures on French natality worsened in the 1890s, there gradually appeared a huge contemporary literature on the problem. In his classic review of this literature, Joseph Spengler broke down the causal explanations that were most commonly used into two great categories: involuntary and voluntary.[31] In the first category he considered the explanations that seemed to him entirely biological. These included causes that weakened the "genetic instinct" of the race to reproduce itself, manifested by a depression of "natural fecundity," or the prac-

---

[28] Lucien Prévost-Paradol, *La France nouvelle* (Paris: Michel Lévy Frères, 1868), pp. 409-410.

[29] See the debate reported at the Academy of Medicine, "Sur la prétendue dégénérescence de la population française," *Revue des cours scientifiques* 4 (April 13-20, 1867), pp. 305-311, 320-331.

[30] These are the remarks of Félix-Henri Boudet at the Academy of Medicine reported in *Revue des cours scientifiques* 4 (June 29, 1867), pp. 494-496.

[31] Joseph J. Spengler, *France Faces Depopulation* (Durham, N.C.: Duke University Press, 1938), pp. 135-174.

tices of deferring birth, active contraception, abortion, and infanticide. Spengler found that the favored causes in this category were racial ones, whereby formerly fecund and "pure" races intermixed under the social conditions of modern democracy and thereby lost, in their new genetic identity, the capacity to procreate.[32] Of secondary importance were causes based on equilibrium models, wherein some form of genetic energy essential for reproduction was gradually lost in the movement of the social organism from a homogeneous condition to a heterogeneous form characterized by specialization and division of labor.[33]

In the voluntary category Spengler listed the causes that he felt French writers believed to admit of conscious or rational control. Among these was social capillarity, a process in which individuals exchanged the social limitations of high birthrates for the lucrative advantages of upward mobility. Another voluntary argument was popular with the LePlayans and with those who preferred the generalized notion of "civilization" as the most powerful explanation. In this account of the argument, Paul Leroy-Beaulieu makes the inevitable reference to Germany: "The children of our families, one or two in number, surrounded with indulgent tenderness, with debilitating care, are inclined to a passive and sedentary life, and do not but exceptionally manifest the spirit of enterprise and adventure, of endurance and perseverance that characterized their ancient ancestors and which the sons of prolific German families possess today."[34]

Revealing a certain circularity of argument, all these positions tend to burst the bonds of Spengler's voluntary-involuntary dichotomy, expressing instead a belief in a very generalized sociological determinism that initiated all these mechanisms, hereditary and social alike. In the causal accounts offered for low birthrates, there was a characteristic compression of biological and social-environment arguments that, as we have seen, was typical of neo-Lamarckian explanations of organic pathologies. No matter how writers on depopulation explained the "will" to reproduce as having weakened, they invariably regarded it as an "instinct" that was transmittable and closely knitted into the fabric of social life.

[32] The best instance of this argument is Georges Vacher de la Pouge, *Les séléctions sociales* (Paris, 1896).

[33] Spengler, *France Faces Depopulation*, pp. 138-140. See especially E. Maurel, *De la dépopulation en France: Etude sur la natalité* (Paris, 1896) and Alfred Fouillée, *Psychologie du peuple français* (Paris, 1898).

[34] Paul Leroy-Beaulieu, *La question de la population* (Paris: Alcan, 1911), pp. 350-351.

When we recall that the primary symptoms of degeneration were held to be a weakening of the vital forces of its victim and an inability to exercise willpower, we are encouraged in the suspicion that depopulationist writers at the turn of the century had adopted the theoretical apparatus of degeneracy to account for the grievous decline in the birthrate. In his review of the literature, Spengler found that depopulationist writers seldom applied their theories to individuals, but "reasoned in terms of the French people as a collectivity."[35] This fact strongly suggests that by the 1890s degeneracy was no longer simply a clinical theory of abnormal individual pathologies, but a *social* theory of persuasive force and power. We have already seen how degeneration provided an explanation of both crime and mental illness in terms that experts believed to be consistent with sociological explanations. By the 1890s, the theory was being widely employed as an explanation for the whole range of pathologies from which the nation suffered: alcoholism, prostitution and pornography, suicide, and the incapacity (or unwillingness) to procreate.

All these pathologies were taken seriously by contemporaries, but the population problem was clearly the master pathology among them. The profound feelings of anxiety about the decline of French power after the disastrous defeat by Prussia were articulated by degeneration theory as concern about the quantity and the quality of the French population. On account of the neo-Lamarckian idea of inherited characteristics, each case of individual pathology could be regarded as both a symptom and a cause: a symptom that a syndrome of degeneracy was unfolding, and a cause of future—worse—cases. Thus, the degenerate was endowed with a double power. He (or she) was a painful reminder of the weakness of the "race," and a living assurance of its continued decline.

As we have seen, the generality of degeneration theory, and its tendency to telescope biological and social causes, made it possible for observers to pass easily from a case of individual "degeneracy" to degeneration as a collective problem. It enabled them to see in the alcoholic, the prostitute, or the criminal a symbol of France's tenuous hold on great power status. But the reverse reasoning was also possible. Any consideration of the state of the nation, its absolute or its relative status, inevitably brought to mind the separate social manifestations of degeneracy. This mode of thinking, as we shall see, encouraged the appraisal of social problems from the point of view of *national interest*,

[35] Spengler, *France Faces Depopulation*, p. 9.

thrusting, as it were, issues of domestic health and external security into an identical frame of analysis.

One can demonstrate how the relation between national problems and individual cases functioned by following in some detail the gradual application of degeneration theory—much as I have already done with crime—to these different pathologies. There is a certain amount of artificiality involved in analyzing separately the development of medicalization in each of these domains. Though each "pathology" had a set of medical and lay specialists who concerned themselves largely with their chosen field, connections were regularly made between them. Every pathology was, after all, an expression of the same syndrome, and, as we have seen, both a cause and a symptom of others. They became so hopelessly confounded with one another and with degeneration itself, in both the technical and the popular literature, that they were in practice virtually interchangeable.

Suicide in the nineteenth century was an object of study for moralists, social statisticians like A. M. Guerry and Adolphe Quetelet, and psychiatrists. Medical specialists attempted very early in the century to annex suicide to mental illness. J. P. Falret's *De l'hypochondrie et du suicide* appeared in 1822, and in his *Des maladies mentales* (1838), Etienne Esquirol treated suicide as a definite symptom of mental disorder.[36] By the last half of the 1800s, there was a huge medical literature on this topic, discussed in great detail by Emile Durkheim in his classic treatment of self-destruction in 1897. Durkheim identified two principal kinds of psychiatric explanations of suicide. The oldest, suicidal monomania, he regarded as outdated by modern medical standards, since it was no longer permissible to argue that a single faculty could be alienated without the others also being affected.[37] But he also rejected the theory that held suicide to be an episodic expression of some general condition of insanity. Why, he asked, must we consider the insane to be different from others who kill themselves for "external" reasons? We need not accept psychiatric explanations for "insane" suicides if we can show that their acts have other more likely causes. Thus, "dejection and depression" are no proof of madness, because "the normal

[36] Etienne Esquirol, *Des maladies mentales*, vol. I (Paris, 1838), p. 639. See also Alexandre Brierre de Boismont, *Du suicide et de la folie-suicide* (Paris, 1856). Anthony Giddens discusses this early literature in "The Suicide Problem in French Sociology," *Studies in Social and Political Theory* (London: Hutchinson, 1977), pp. 322-332.

[37] Durkheim, *Suicide*, pp. 59-62.

person who kills himself is also in a state of dejection and depression like the mentally alienated."[38]

Of course, Durkheim was at pains to demonstrate the great role that social causes played in suicide, and, by extension, in all other individual behavior. He was, however, only partially successful in wrenching suicide away from the domain of medicine; psychiatry has continued to exercise its claims on the field of suicidal behavior to the present day. However, Durkheim's reputation as a founding father of modern sociology has to a great extent been based on the apparent accomplishment of bearding the psychiatric lion in his own den: demonstrating convincingly that the vast majority of suicides could be explained sociologically.[39] Durkheim's reputation was well deserved, but nonetheless he was not immune to the allure of biological theory. Indeed, as I hope to show, some important premises of Durkheim's social theory of suicide are derived from neo-Lamarckian assumptions about heredity, and from degeneration theory. As I have argued elsewhere at greater length, Durkheim's obsession with suicide and other forms of social pathology made his thinking amenable to the well-established definitions of the normal and the pathological that underlay nineteenth-century French biology and medicine.[40] If we can demonstrate the extent to which this luminary of sociological realism was dependent on a medical model of social analysis, we will have moved closer to confirming the extraordinary intellectual attraction it exerted on Durkheim's contemporaries.

In a little-known paper of 1888, Durkheim treated the question of the relationship of suicide and birthrates. Affirming at the outset the pathological nature of large increases in the suicide rate, Durkheim asked with mock innocence whether or not one could reach a similar conclusion about birthrates if it could be shown that high suicide rates varied regularly with natality. Though Durkheim was interested in validating the well-known association of high suicide rates with societies whose birthrates and population density were high, he was particularly concerned with the opposite case, that is, a high suicide rate that was associated with an abnormally *low* birthrate. By demonstrating the

[38] Ibid., pp. 65-66.

[39] See on this point, Philippe Besnard, "Durkheim et les femmes, ou le suicide inachevé," *Revue française de sociologie* 14 (September 1973), pp. 37-40; Jack D. Douglas, *The Social Meaning of Suicide* (Princeton, N.J.: Princeton University Press, 1967), pp. 47-48; Steven Lukes, *Emile Durkheim: His Life and Work* (London: Penguin, 1973), pp. 213-222.

[40] See my "Heredity, Pathology, and Psychoneurosis in Durkheim's Early Work," *Knowledge and Society*, vol. 4 (1983), pp. 103-142.

pathological nature of *both* high and low birthrates, Durkheim could substantiate his definition of social health as a "temperate zone" lying between extremes; but he could also conclude that current French natality was morbid. He constructed an index of "physiological growth" by subtracting the number of deaths in a year from the number of births, excluding immigration as inapplicable to the "active" population. Comparing this "biological" rate within a large number of categories with the corresponding suicide rate, Durkheim was able to show that towns and the liberal professions, where the lowest "growth" existed, were struck with the highest figures of self-destruction. Owing to the "parallelism of their development, the abnormal nature of the one reveals the abnormal nature of the other."[41] No doubt, he concluded, a low birthrate is a tragedy for a society, but "it is in addition a pity and an evil for individuals. Not only is a society that grows regularly stronger and more capable of maintaining itself against rival societies, but its members themselves have a greater chance of surviving. Their organism has more vigor, more force of resistance."[42]

Durkheim identified the common cause underlying both these pathological conditions as a disruption of the equilibrium of "vital force" in a society that served as the stable milieu in which individuals lived. However, in an argument that would later reappear in *Suicide*, he held that "this lack of equilibrium may have either organic or social causes. At one time it is the individual himself who is affected, and his functions are degraded and altered, while the milieu is healthy; at another time it is the milieu itself that is not normal. To speak truly it is very probable that there is no suicide where the two causes are not working simultaneously. A perfectly intact organism will resist the milieu, and if the milieu has nothing pathological about it, the morbid germs that may be concealed in the organism are not able to develop."[43]

Then, in an effort to establish the primacy of sociological causation, for which he campaigned in all his work, Durkheim had resort to a typical neo-Lamarckian explanation, merging the biological and social realms in a thorough fashion:

> It is true that the departments in which there are most suicides and the least births are also those that have the most insane. But that proves only that madness, like suicide and the birthrate, does not result uniquely from individual and accidental variations, but, for a good part, from social causes. Tainted nervous systems do not mul-

[41] Durkheim, "Suicide et natalité," p. 450.
[42] Ibid., p. 460.
[43] Ibid., p. 461.

tiply themselves in a group only by means of unfortunate cross-breedings and hereditary predispositions, but also from the bad sociological conditions in which they find themselves placed. *Organic causes are often social causes transformed and fixed in the organism. There are thus social causes common to suicide and natality which are able to explain their relation.*[44]

This passage offers proof that Durkheim subscribed to the heredity theories of French biologists, and that he acknowledged the possibility that organic defects in individuals were frequently the result of social pathologies acting, as it were, at a distance. His willingness to include insanity as an effect of "bad sociological conditions" only seems to underline further Durkheim's resemblance to the mental pathologists of the end of the century.

In 1888 the part of the social environment about which Durkheim was most concerned was the family, the primary social *and* biological component in the human heritage. The taste for "material ease" was invading the "pleasures of common life" natural to families. Though these changing "preferences" could be observed in "la morale populaire," they "express themselves most often in an *instinctive* and *unreflective* manner; but what matter? Deliberated or not, they do not change their nature."[45] Durkheim clearly implies in this passage that a weakening of the birthrate stems from a weakening of the "esprit domestique," which in turn makes individuals more vulnerable to self-destruction. The sentiment of domesticity, Durkheim continues, is part of the nature of the human organism, fixed there by "evolution." It is part of the moral structure of society; it is no less part of the biological constitution of individuals. Durkheim demonstrated his debt to contemporary biological theory in his concluding section, in which he mixes physiological metaphors and his personal brand of moral fervor. "In the family the individual is a part of a compact mass with which he is unified [*solidaire*] and which multiplies his strength [*forces*]: his power of resistance is thus augmented. He is stronger for the struggle to the extent he is less isolated. Where on the contrary families are rare, poor, or meager, individuals are less closely joined to one another, allowing spaces between them where there blows the cold wind of egoism which freezes the heart and weakens the courage."[46]

In his classic *Suicide*, Durkheim continued his battle against wholly psychiatric explanations of suicide. Together with the logical and in-

[44] Ibid., pp. 461-462. My emphasis.
[45] Ibid., p. 462. My emphasis.
[46] Ibid., p. 463.

ternal criticisms already mentioned, Durkheim made the point that he had already raised in 1888, namely that insanity "is partly a social phenomenon."[47] This claim cannot simply be explained away as a polemical device, nor is it entirely enlightening, as Gurvitch and others have done, to accuse Durkheim of having constructed in this matter a "false dichotomy" between the "individual" and the "social," and to claim that he failed to recognize the "reciprocity" of their mutual influence.[48] It would be far more accurate to say that, far from locating society and the individual in separate ontological realms, he merged those realms to a point at which the boundaries between them, in his conception of social causation, practically disappeared.

In a similar fashion, Durkheim refused to make hard and fast distinctions between normal and pathological phenomena, holding that one could only, in the fashion of the physiologists, measure quantitative differences along a scale of infinite variations. As a consequence, "suicides do not form, as might be thought, a wholly distinct group, an isolated class of monstrous phenomena, unrelated by a continuous series of intermediate cases. They are merely the exaggerated form of common practices."[49] By the same token, in the motivations of suicides there is a "gradual shading from normal and deliberate acts to illusions and automatic impulses."[50] To make this biological conception of the normal and the pathological work smoothly in his theory of suicide, Durkheim borrowed a popular clinical idea from psychiatry, neurasthenia.

Neurasthenia, a term invented by the American physician George M. Beard to account for "American" nervous problems, was readily integrated into the nosologies of French psychiatry in the 1880s. In practice, the series of "nervous" and physical symptoms associated with neurasthenia were regarded as signs of the onset of degeneracy. The standard medical text on neurasthenia, Proust and Ballet's *L'hygiène du neurasthénique*, appeared in 1897, the same year as Durkheim's *Suicide*. The authors describe the symptoms as "weakness," "suggestibility," lowered "resistance," inability to sustain concentrated, willful activity.[51]

[47] Durkheim, *Suicide*, p. 58, n. 2.

[48] Anthony Giddens summarizes this argument in "The Suicide Problem in French Sociology," *Studies in Social and Political Theory*, pp. 328-329.

[49] Durkheim, *Suicide*, p. 45.

[50] Ibid., p. 66.

[51] Adrien Proust and Gilbert Ballet, *L'hygiène du neurasthénique* (Paris: Masson, 1897), pp. 1-2, 75-78. Jan Goldstein discusses the incorporation of the "intermediary zone" of neuroses into mental medicine by French psychiatrists in the 1870s in "The Hysteria Diagnosis," pp. 216-218.

Proust and Ballet trace the origins of neurasthenia to a "struggle for existence" in the modern world, which provokes "an incessant and exaggerated exaltation of the nervous system."[52] They also suggest that, though the malady might be successfully treated if caught at an early stage, it might also be the first step toward a progressive and hereditary degeneration that has "irresistible consequences." To a greater extent than Durkheim, Proust and Ballet and many of the other standard medical commentators on the syndrome emphasized the great range of physical infirmities to which these "weakened" neurasthenics were susceptible; they were anxious to identify the "intoxicants" in the environment—alcohol, venereal disease—that could help initiate neurasthenia.[53] Durkheim, by contrast, focused his attention on the *social* effects of the illness and did not attempt to locate specific viruses in an environment that he regarded as *generally* pathological. Despite these differences of emphasis, there is a remarkable amount of agreement between Durkheim and the mental pathologists of his day on the social origins of this illness. They all believed its incidence to be on the rise in modern civilization.

Neurasthenia, according to Durkheim, lies in the "intermediate stages" between mental alienation and a "perfect equilibrium" of intelligence. The neurasthenic is not insane, and is capable of deliberation, but is nonetheless a type commonly found among suicides. He is extremely sensitive and impressionable, his nervous system is in a "weakened state," and his feelings are always in "unstable equilibrium."[54] A product of cities and our intense modern civilization, the neurasthenic is ironically the person most easily victimized by the "mêlée" of modern life because his refined nervous system feels stimulations beyond the range of sensitivity of the "normal" organism.

The repeated "hammer" of these shocks keeps the neurasthenic's "mental organization" in constant disarray so that it cannot become stable, but is constantly being "destroyed and swept away."

Life in a fixed and constant medium is only possible if the functions of the person in question are of equal constancy and fixity. For living means responding appropriately to outer stimuli and this harmonious correspondence can be established only by time and custom. It is a product of experiments, sometimes repeated for generations,

[52] Proust and Ballet, *L'hygiène du neurasthénique* pp. 10-12.

[53] Ibid., pp. vi, 15-24, 35, 37. See also, Léon Bouveret, *La neurasthénie*, 2d ed. (Paris: Baillière, 1891); Fernand Levillain, *La neurasthénie* (Paris: Maloine, 1891). In Chapter Nine I examine the therapeutic strategies used to treat neurasthenia.

[54] Durkheim, *Suicide*, p. 69.

the results of which have in part become hereditary and which cannot be gone through all over again every time there is necessity for action. If, however, at the moment of action everything has to be constructed, so to speak, it is impossible for this action to be what it should be. We require this stability not only in our relations with the physical environment, but also with the social environment. The individual can maintain himself in a society definitely organized only through possessing an equally definite mental and moral constitution. This is what the neurasthenic lacks.[55]

As it is a lesser form of insanity, Durkheim asks, may we not study neurasthenia to see whether it varies with the social suicide rate? Since statistics on neurasthenia were not known, Durkheim proposed an "indirect" solution that is in perfect accord with degeneration theory: "Since insanity is only the enlarged form of nervous degeneration, it may be granted without risk of serious error that the number of nervous degenerates varies in proportion to that of the insane, and consideration of the latter may be used as a substitute in the case of the former. This procedure would also make it possible to establish a general relation of the suicide rate to the total of mental abnormalities of every kind."[56]

Durkheim then attempts to demonstrate that there is an *inverse* relation between suicide rates and insanity, using sexual, religious, and national differentials. But, astonishingly, his conclusion is not to dismiss neurasthenia as a causal influence on suicide, but to detach it from insanity and claim it as a secondary social cause for self-destruction. Neurasthenics, in short, have no *intrinsic* predisposition to suicide; indeed they are not "essentially asocial" in nature: "Other causes must supervene upon their special organic condition to give it this twist and develop it in this direction. Neurasthenia by itself is a very general predisposition, not necessarily productive of any special action, but capable of assuming the most varied forms according to circumstances. It is a field in which most varied tendencies may take root depending on the fertilization it receives from social causes."[57]

[55] Ibid.

[56] Ibid., p. 70.

[57] Ibid., p. 77. As proof of the "ambiguous power" of neurasthenia, Durkheim offers the extraordinary example of the affinities between French and Russian writers, notably their delicate nervous systems and "lack of mental and moral equilibrium." But, he argues, different social consequences flow from this similar organic condition: Russian literature is idealistic, "excites faith and provokes action," while "ours prides itself on expressing nothing but deep despair and reflects a disquieting state of depression," p. 77, n. 30.

Those most protected from suicide are those whose moral sentiments are anchored most firmly in institutions that provide for them the necessary degree of "solidarity" to resist suicidogenic currents. Thus, the average man, whose moral sentiments are more or less identical to the collective type, though very general and much more weakly felt, benefits from the stabilizing hereditary makeup that is itself a product of the social milieu of that type. Durkheim argues circularly by saying that the more stable and slowly evolving this collective type is, the more equilibrium it enjoys, and the more likely it is to pass on moral sentiments to its members that have become "fixed" in the type through habituation and repetition. Thus, the identity between individual and society is in part biological and hereditary, and nowhere more so than in stable societies.[58]

Durkheim concluded this argument by directly appealing to the analogous ideas held by "contemporary zoologists" on the individual's relations to the species. They have abandoned the notion that the species "is only an individual perpetuated chronologically and generalized spatially." Variations become specific only in rare and doubtful cases. In reality, the fixing of new characters originates in the race: "The distinctive characteristics of the race change in the individual only as they change in the race in general. The latter has therefore some reality whence come the various shapes it assumes among individual beings, far from its consisting simply of a generalization of these beings."[59] This passage conforms nicely to the concept of social evolution propounded in *The Division of Labor*, to Durkheim's continued adherence to the neo-Lamarckian concept of organic economy as the determining factor of adaptation, and to his concept of equilibrium as the touchstone of normality in the individual and in society.

Durkheim clinches his argument by showing how this model explains who it is that commits suicide:

The hypercivilization breeds the anomic tendency and the egoistic tendency also refines nervous systems, making them excessively delicate; through this very fact they are less capable of firm attachment to a definite object, more impatient of any sort of discipline, more accessible both to violent imitation and to exaggerated depression. Inversely, the crude, rough culture implicit in the excessive altruism of primitive man develops a lack of sensitivity which favors renunciation. In short, just as society largely forms the individual, it forms him to the same extent in its own image. Society, therefore, cannot

[58] Ibid., pp. 318-319.
[59] Ibid., p. 320.

lack the material for its needs, for it has, so to speak, kneaded it with its own hands.[60]

But these neurasthenic individuals, whose mental constitutions are shaped by the social conditions of "hypercivilization," do not kill themselves simply because they are neuropathic; instead, as Durkheim demonstrates throughout his book, they kill themselves because they are driven to do so by suicidogenic currents that are social in nature and that "call" their victims from among these neurasthenics because these individuals offer "less resistance" to them. One can explain this or that suicide by appeal to a clinical diagnosis of neurosis or alcoholism, but one can explain suicide rates only by reference to social conditions. In Jack Douglas's formulation of Durkheim's notion of cause, the individual is the "material" cause of his suicide, but society is the " 'efficient cause' that is the 'active' and only 'real' cause of suicide."[61]

Though some of these psychiatric connections in Durkheim's theory of suicide must be demonstrated to the modern reader, they were very much part of the working assumptions of most psychologists and sociologists of Durkheim's day. If Tarde, René Worms, and a host of psychologists objected to the book, it was on account of the appearance of an extreme sociological determinism in Durkheim's theory. His theory struck at two contemporary shibboleths. By apparently allowing little role for individual motivation, he offended the proponents of free will among the psychologists, and, by boldly encroaching on the

[60] Ibid., p. 323.

[61] Douglas, *The Social Meaning of Suicide*, p. 348. The line of argument I have followed above is nearly altogether overlooked in the secondary literature on *Suicide*. The most astute commentators, Giddens and Lukes, recognize that Durkheim allowed a certain degree of social influence on the psychological nature of the suicide-prone individual, but both reproach him for failing to develop this insight. Lukes says that "Durkheim did not see the wider implications of this insight of his own thought as a whole, pushing back the boundary between the 'organico-psychic' and the 'social.' " Lukes, *Emile Durkheim*, p. 219. Lukes also misunderstands the use Durkheim makes of the concept of disequilibrium in the psychology of the individual suicide; see pp. 219-220. Giddens also argues that this insight remains "undeveloped" and in his "A Theory of Suicide" presents his own psychology of the suicidal personality because Durkheim's "limited" one reveals so little of the "dynamics of motivation that might be involved." Giddens, "The 'Individual' in the Writings of Emile Durkheim" in *Studies in Social and Political Theory*, p. 287; "A Theory of Suicide" in ibid., pp. 304-305. Pope, whose treatment of *Suicide* is most extensive of all, made no effort whatsoever to define Durkheim's understanding of the term "neurasthenia," so his accusations that Durkheim wrongly used the concept in establishing the social nature of suicide are altogether beside the point. Whitney Pope, *Durkheim's Suicide: A Classic Analyzed* (Chicago: University of Chicago Press, 1979), pp. 160-162.

DISCUSSION WITH THE DOCTOR

"So my dear man, you who represent one of our average adults, you wish to know the effect of absinthe on our poor species? Well . . ."

"The 'green fairy' is a mixture of alcohol, colored with spinach, some parsley, essence of hyssop, tincture of tumeric, some indigo, essence of anise and aniseed tree . . ."

"Listen; the basis of the green liqueur is made from nine essences: essence of absinthe, fennel, hyssop, anise, aniseed tree, melissa, angelica, wild marjoram, and mint. A cubic millimeter of three of those chief elements injected into a rabbit provokes convulsions followed by death!"

"The six other essences are not convulsives, it is true, but they are intoxicants! They produce sleepiness, torpor, loss of memory, intellectual laziness, a dazed condition, the complete destruction of willpower, and brutishness . . . This is the aperitif of three-quarters of the French!"

"A hundredth of a millimeter injected into a rooster makes a perfect milksop, if I may so express myself!"

"Man's most noble conquest, with an injection of a half-centimeter of that mixture, is not long in demonstrating all the symptoms of epileptic idiocy followed by a terrible death."

"As for the pig, sir, one might say he is man himself!"

"A bull injected with the mixture loses his most precious qualities and his . . . prestige. What a matter to think on in this era of depopulation!"

"It's frightening!" says the man who represents the average adult. And he goes to his usual cafe to take his twice-daily dose.

by Emmanuel Poiré, *Gros et détail* (Paris: Plon-Nourrit, 1907), p. 20

territory of the psychiatric theories of "insane suicide," he aroused the ire of the alienists.[62]

There is no doubt, in any case, that Durkheim's treatment of neurasthenia appears to be located directly at the juncture of social and biological theory in France at the end of the nineteenth century. As we have seen, the use of categories of human heredity and of mental pathology to explain *social* phenomena was an element in his social theory from the outset, and played an important role in his *Suicide*. Since he was passionately interested in founding a science of sociology that was free from the need to rely on explanations derived from other disciplines, Durkheim's inclusion of neurasthenia in his social theory of *Suicide* can be best explained on the grounds that he regarded it as ultimately a *social* phenomenon. Nor, in treating this "lesser form of insanity" as social in origin, was Durkheim wrenching neurasthenia out of its clinical and psychiatric context; the medical account of neurasthenia was identical in all important respects to Durkheim's.[63]

Considered as a social issue, suicide never attained the level of public concern of other pathologies. Suicide was a private act which no amount of public intervention was likely to influence. Moreover a successful suicide, though it might be a symptom of degeneracy, in interrupting the hereditary link, could not be a cause as well. The same could not be said about alcoholism. In the second half of the nineteenth century more harm was attributed to alcohol than to any other environmental "intoxicant." Alcohol earned the hearty disapprobation of moralists and of doctors; even those who were willing to defend the "digestive"

[62] On the opposition to Durkheim's theory see Giddens, "The Suicide Problem in French Sociology" in *Studies in Social and Political Theory*, pp. 322-332, and Lukes, *Emile Durkheim*, pp. 316-318. One of his best critics was Durkheim's own collaborator Maurice Halbwachs, whose *The Causes of Suicide* proposed certain modifications in Durkheim's theory. Halbwachs argued that insanity and suicide were independent rather than inversely related as Durkheim had insisted. However, as had Durkheim before him, Halbwachs denied that there were many true "insane suicides" and essentially relegated most minor mental troubles (including neurasthenia) to the category of "social" causes. He also denied that neurasthenia was an exclusively upper-class illness; its equivalent could be found among the lower classes "in the form of habitual drunkenness," p. 285. In general, Halbwachs seems to have adopted Durkheim's standard of the normal-pathological continuum, and the equilibrium conception of an individual's successful adaptation to his milieu, pp. 266-267. Maurice Halbwachs, *The Causes of Suicide*, trans. Harold Goldblatt (New York: Free Press, 1979), esp. pp. 247-290.

[63] I have shown how these themes are expressed in most of Durkheim's other early work, including *The Division of Labor* and *Rules of Sociological Method* in "Heredity, Pathology, and Psychoneurosis in Durkheim's Early Work," pp. 118-124.

or "hygienic" virtues of wine, were critical of the distilled spirits consumed in huge quantities by the French after 1870.

Before the defeat of 1870 and the Commune, there was little medical interest in the effects of alcohol consumption. Until the term alcoholism was coined by the Swedish physician Magnus Huss in 1852, drunkenness (*ivresse, ivrognerie*) was the only way to characterize extreme states of inebriation. Indeed, medical concern about the problem was at such a low ebb in 1852 that although the Academy of Sciences awarded Huss a major prize for his identification of alcoholism as a chronic disorder, the prize reporter, while admitting there were plenty of drunks in France, denied there were any alcoholics.[64] The war with Prussia and the Paris Commune ended this benign indifference with a vengeance. The immediate postwar period was marked by an extraordinarily high degree of anxiety about alcohol. An inquiry led by Dr. Jules Bergeron attributed the Commune to "a monstrous outburst of acute alcoholism."[65] Concern about the military effectiveness of French troops showed up in Dr. Jules Lunier's first report to the new Société française de tempérance (1872) in which he warned that "the future of France is at stake."[66] A law repressing public drunkenness, enacted in 1873 though not enthusiastically enforced, was testimony to the widespread belief that excessive drink had weakened the fabric of French life. Susanna Barrows has written that this outburst of postwar activity "owed less to scientific research than to psychological factors—anger, fear, humiliation, and guilt."[67] These psychological factors must, however, have worked on doctors with a special force.

Doctors appeared on the rolls of antialcoholic organizations in disproportionately large numbers from the very start of the movement's growth. Of the 382 members of the Société française de tempérance in 1873, 120 either practiced or taught medicine; a steering committee composed of the principal officers of the French antialcohol groups numbered 9 doctors among its 26 members.[68] The largest and most influential of the *ligues* was Dr. Paul-Maurice LeGrain's Union française

[64] Cited in Marrus, "Social Drinking in the Belle Epoque," p. 117.

[65] Jules Bergeron, "Rapport sur la répression de l'alcoolisme," *Annales d'hygiène publique et de médecine légale* 38 (1872), p. 6.

[66] Cited in M. J. Gaufrès, "Les origines de l'antialcoolisme en France," *L'alcool* 7 (February 1902), pp. 28-32.

[67] Barrows, "After the Commune," p. 205.

[68] These figures are provided by Jacqueline Lalouette, "Discours bourgeois sur les débits de boisson aux alentours de 1900," *L'haleine des faubourgs, Recherches*, no. 29 (December 1977), pp. 316-317.

antialcoolique, which published a periodical, *L'alcool*, whose columns were open to concerned medical specialists.

Apart from providing the indispensable "scientific" cachet needed by these groups, the widespread presence of medical specialists helped minimize sectarian disputes between Protestant and Catholic organizations. LeGrain, for his part, made every effort to smooth over differences and coordinate activities between rival groups.[69]

Though a medical point of view was present from the outset of the antialcohol crusade, the medicalization of alcoholism developed gradually through the last decades of the century. Valentin Magnan's study of 1874, *De l'alcoolisme*, established a firm link between alcohol and madness by demonstrating the physical effect of intoxication on nervous tissue. E. Gendron's medical thesis studied the effects of alcohol use on a family over several generations, concluding that a tendency of a degenerate type to take alcohol in excess was inherited by the children of alcoholic parents. In his *Alcoolisme héréditaire* (1880) Gendron argued that descendants inherited a threshold of alcoholic degeneracy which they then voluntarily lowered by drink in their lifetimes, thereby passing on a decreased threshold to their own offspring.[70] LeGrain popularized these concepts in *Hérédité et alcoolisme* (1889) and *Dégénérescence sociale et alcoolisme* (1895). He argued in the latter volume for the classical degenerational cycle of B. A. Morel in which the breeding line becomes sterile in the fourth generation of alcoholics.[71]

If these consequences were not grim enough, other dangers awaited the alcoholic. LeGrain articulated the logic of the medical outlook, saying, "And if alcoholism is increasing at the same time as criminality, has not one the right to establish a causal relationship between these two facts as one has already done between alcohol and madness?"[72] The master pathology of depopulation was also very much in the fore-

[69] LeGrain's group welcomed Catholic support in 1898 and 1900. See "Un mouvement catholique," *L'alcool* 3 (April 1898), pp. 57-60 and "Un mouvement catholique," ibid., 5 (February 1900), pp. 26-30.

[70] E. Gendron, *Alcoolisme héréditaire* (Paris, 1880).

[71] Paul-Maurice LeGrain, *Dégénérescence sociale et alcoolisme* (Paris, 1895), pp. 1-46. Degeneration theory's role in alcoholism lasted longer than its influence on other social pathologies. See Jacques Borel, *Du concept de dégénérescence à la notion d'alcoolisme dans la médecine contemporaine: Les campagnes antialcooliques de 1865 à 1965* (Montpellier, 1968).

[72] Paul-Marie LeGrain, "L'année du crime et l'alcool," *L'alcool* 2 (May 1897), p. 61. On the alcohol-crime relation see Paul Masoin, *Alcoolisme et criminalité* (Paris, 1891); G. L. Duprat, *Les causes sociales de la folie* (Paris, 1900); and Paul Jacoby, *Etude sur les sélections chez l'homme*, 2d ed. (Paris: Alcan, 1905).

ground of antialcoholic writings in the 1890s as figures for both problems worsened.[73] In this connection, LeGrain and his colleagues warned about the inability of alcoholic mothers to breast-feed their children, and a huge body of medical literature, based on degenerational assumptions, was devoted to the dangers of both bottle feeding and wet-nursing.[74]

Alcohol abuse was pictured ultimately as a national and patriotic issue. Antialcohol activists, relying on figures that indicated a higher medical rejection rate for French military inductees than German ones, and a decline in the average height of French draftees since 1800, focused much of their propaganda on the evils of drink in the frontier garrisons.[75] A popular poster released by LeGrain's Union française antialcoolique connected alcohol to all the nation's pathologies in an unsurpassingly morbid escatology: "The fatherland is in danger: alcohol is a poison. France offers us the disheartening spectacle of a nation rushing pell-mell toward decadence through alcohol." It causes "suicides, crimes, mental illness . . . ruins morality, and weakens the army."[76] As Jacqueline Lalouette has shown, the tireless campaigns to present such propaganda in the schools and in military barracks, even if it did not always discourage drinking, implanted firmly the beliefs about the terrible biological effects of alcohol in the minds of students and soldiers.[77] By degrees, a matter that had been traditionally re-

[73] Maurel's *De la dépopulation de la France* made alcoholic degeneracy a special concern, as did L. Salomon's *L'alcool et la dépopulation de la France* (Paris, n.d.). See also A. Coutaud, "La dépopulation et l'alcoolisme," *L'alcool* 1 (June 1896), pp. 90-92.

[74] Paul-Marie LeGrain, "De l'impuissance croissante des femmes à allaiter leurs enfants," *L'alcool* 5 (November 1900), pp. 164-166. LeGrain insisted that "thousands" of infants died yearly from artificial feeding. F. Martin-Ginouvier, "Stigmates physiques et moraux de la nourrice mercenaire sur son poupon éxpliqués d'après le Guedisme," *Revue philanthropique* 6 (March 1900), pp. 549-555. Violent emotions could also be transmitted from the wet-nurse, with dangerous consequences as one thesis of 1904 argued. Pierre Loyer, *Les émotions morales chez les nourrices et leur retentissement sur le nourrisson* (Paris, 1904). On advice to mothers written by medical specialists, see Lalouette "Discours bourgeois sur les débits de boisson," pp. 325-327.

[75] Victor Margueritte, "La première des cultures," *Le Journal*, October 24, 1908. A. des Cilleuls, "La population française en 1800 et en 1900," *La réforme sociale* 40 (1900), p. 833. Charles Humbert, "Le cabaret à la caserne," *La Grande revue* 48 (April 10, 1908), pp. 417-435. Lalouette, "Discours bourgeois sur les débits de boisson," pp. 322-324.

[76] *L'alcool* 1 (August 1896), pp. 126-127.

[77] Lalouette, "Discours bourgeois sur les débits de boisson," pp. 240-241.

garded as a vice of the lower classes, or as a political issue owing to the incendiary combination of alcohol and left-wing ideology in the cabaret, became a *medical* and *national* problem of grave dimensions.[78]

The most complicated conjunction that degenerational theorists succeeded in popularizing in the *fin de siècle* was the link between venereal disease, prostitution, and "liberated" (read perverse) sexuality. An analysis of the medicalization of this set of relationships has the particular virtue of illustrating the extraordinary identity that was achieved between conservative moral judgments and science. Of course, I have drawn attention in the other pathologies I have discussed to the typically strong connection between conventional moral views and the outlook of the medical theorists who addressed themselves to deviant behavior. But the medicalization of prostitution and sexuality dramatizes to a far greater degree than with other forms of deviance the remorseless transformation of private activity into behavior that could be legitimately judged by standards of "public" hygiene.

No doubt the prevailing model of Victorian respectability lent itself very well to the public regulation of private sexual comportment. The point has been very effectively made that the middle-class elite could expect considerable benefits to accrue from a conversion of the lower orders to the standards of thrift, sobriety, and continence that presumably characterized bourgeois behavior.[79] As Gramsci and other theorists have argued, moral hegemony is a good deal more efficient in producing conformity and obedience than a regime relying on political power or naked dictatorship. But in France at the turn of the century we are far removed from a calm atmosphere in which moral exemplars or traditional exhortation could be expected to produce useful effects. Unregulated sexual behavior was not simply perceived as a threat to moral order but as a biological menace to the social organization itself. The very seriousness of the problem called for a discourse of medical pathology that could not only encompass the fearsome proportions of the threat but locate its origins and propose its cure.

As Alain Corbin has shown in his brilliant study of French prostitution, early nineteenth-century commentators on the oldest profession,

[78] On this earlier bourgeois outlook and its transformation see Barrows, "After the Commune," pp. 205-206, and Lalouette, "Discours bourgeois sur les débits de boissons," pp. 342-343.

[79] Peter Cominos has explained the power and appeal of this model of respectability in "Late Victorian Sexual Respectability and the Social System," *International Review of Social History* 8 (1963), pp. 18-48, 216-250.

THE GOOD DAUGHTER

"Young and pretty as you are, you ought to be ashamed to leave your old mother without a drop to drink."

"Ah, parents don't know the sacrifices one makes for them."

"Saved! Thank God! My mother will have some wine!"
　　　　　by Jehan Testevuide, *Gil Blas*, February 28, 1902, p. 4

such as Parent-Duchâtelet, regarded it as an "excremental" phenomenon whose existence protected the social organism from infection, much as a boil on the surface of the skin harmlessly isolates bacteria from systemic circulation.[80] Such a view encouraged the elaborate regulatory system of prostitution that prevailed during the July Monarchy and after, and the treatment of prostitutes as helpless children requiring the *tutelle* of state supervision and care. From the outset of its creation, doctors played an important role in the administrative regulation of the *maisons de tolérance,* whose inhabitants were inscribed in the dossiers of the vice squad and subject to regular medical inspection. Any actual repression of prostitution was confined to the unregistered clandestine streetwalkers who, for the most part, confined their activities to the popular quarters of towns and cities.

Gradually, however, the old supervisory structure began to break down as the demography of prostitution changed and new patterns of sexual behavior emerged. "Clandestines" grew in number and began to spread into the central and bourgeois districts of urban areas. Prostitutes found it possible to attach themselves to cabarets and hotels, or rented apartments for more "modern-style" meetings with their clients.[81] Meanwhile, a vigorous liberal abolitionist campaign was begun in the mid-1870s; its leaders sought to end definitively the degrading "closed" regime and the official protection of vice, and were especially critical of the administrative-medical partnership that was the heart of the old system. The liberals organized a Ligue française pour le relèvement de la moralité publique in 1883 that was dominated by Protestant intellectuals and pastors, and mounted an effective campaign directed at both municipal and national officials.[82]

The abolitionists initially benefited from the clear rise after 1871 of public anxiety about the easy going attitude toward prostitution of public officials. As had happened in so many domains, the events of 1870-1871 encouraged a reevaluation of the overall relationship of prostitution and society. The changed geopolitics of population lent credence to the liberal argument that the liberation of thousands of women from the chains of servitude would free them for productive and patriotic motherhood; the high moral tone of the 1870s was in full accord with the abolitionist claims that official toleration legitimated and encouraged the further expansion of debauchery.[83] Unfortunately for the liberal cause, the medical community, theatened by the loss of

[80] Corbin, *Les filles de noce,* pp. 15-17.
[81] Ibid., pp. 176-180, 210.
[82] For liberal agitation see ibid., pp. 316-344.
[83] Ibid., pp. 37-44, 331-333.

a valued professional prerogative, was able to make the same sorts of promises with greater force and a more powerful imagery.

Medical research on syphilis in France and elsewhere had reached a high level of sophistication by the late 1870s. Clinical studies had investigated the disease's stages, fully documenting the horrible effects of untreated syphilis. Doctors Philippe Ricord, Toussaint Barthélémy, Charles Mauriac, and Alfred Fournier were the principal French medical "syphilographers." In addition to doing clinical studies, some of these writers attempted to ascertain whether the "venereal peril" was increasing and to collect information on the social factors that influenced its spread. Not surprisingly, they vigorously stressed the important role prostitutes played in circulating the virus, because, Corbin believes, they wished to reassert their control, challenged by liberal abolitionism, over this domain of public hygiene.[84] Stressing that no matter where it might end up, syphilis "always comes from the street," Barthélémy proposed a strategy that became the manifesto of the forces of "neoregulation": "Cleanse the low-down places (the streets, sidewalks, bars, dance halls, and cafes) and you will cleanse the rest . . . cleanse the great cities and you will cleanse the whole country. Cleanse all the capitals and you will cleanse the world."[85]

Throughout the 1880s Alfred Fournier filled his writings, popular and scientific, with clinical anecdotes about personal tragedies brought about by venereal infection: virgins whose bodies were covered with syphilitic lesions, fiancés who killed themselves rather than risk infecting their beloved, and murderous fathers-in-law who avenged themselves on the husbands of their victimized daughters.[86] As early as 1882, in a meeting of the Statistical Society of Paris, prostitution was mentioned as having an inverse relationship to population growth;[87] Fournier made a similar point in an important speech in 1885 to the Academy of Medicine.

Though doctors had long made much of the "syphilis of the innocents"—infants infected by their mothers—it was not until toward the end of the 1880s that it became common to allege that syphilis, even in "cured" or latent cases, was hereditary. In this virulent form it was immune to the standard iodide and mercury cures, and was christened "parasyphilis," owing to its tendency to take the form of a number of disfiguring and debilitating diseases. In the course of the 1890s, héré-

[84] Ibid., pp. 362-364.
[85] Quoted in ibid., p. 364.
[86] Cited in ibid., pp. 366-367.
[87] *Séance* of May 24, 1882, *Bulletin de la Société de la statistique de Paris* 23 (July 1882), p. 181.

"Ah, doctor, she was from such a good family."
by Jan Duch, *Gil Blas*, November 8, 1900, p. 4

dosyphilis became simply another of the powerful "intoxicants" that could initiate degenerative syndromes leading to the standard moral disorders and eventual sterility.[88] Described in this way syphilis could escape its traditional lower-class identity and become a terrifying social peril. The novels of Huysmans and the plays of Ibsen had already treated middle-class syphilitics for avant-garde readers, but the mass of the literate public had to await the appearance on the Paris stage of Eugène Brieux's *Les avariés* (The Spoiled Ones) in 1902. In this *succès de scandale*, Brieux addressed the infection of a young wife, daughter of a deputy, by her husband, and the subsequent birth of their syphilitic child. The play had an optimistic conclusion, but the dangers of venereal infection were handled by Brieux with merciless realism.[89]

Fournier and a number of his fellow doctors took advantage of this

[88] See in particular, Alfred Fournier, *Danger social de la syphilis* (Paris, 1905) and Edmond Fournier, *Les stigmates dystrophiques de l'hérédosyphilis* (Paris, 1898). On the construction of this new discourse see Corbin, *Les filles de noce*, pp. 285-290, and Corbin, "Le péril vénérien au début du siècle," pp. 247-258. The former prefect of police, Gaston Macé, urged closer regulation of prostitutes as a protection of "the very life of the race, the first resource of all countries." *Le gibier de Saint-Lazare* (Paris, 1888), pp. 298-299.

[89] Corbin, *Les filles de noce*, pp. 395-397. Corbin reviews other popular syphilophobic literature in detail; see pp. 297-402.

high tide of syphilophobia to found a Société française de prophylaxie sanitaire et morale in 1901 as a lobbying organ for their hygienic crusade.[90] Trumpeting the dangers of depopulation, the Société de prophylaxie identified prostitution and extramarital sex as the chief causes of venereal maladies. They recommended two courses of action: the institution of a new hyperregulatory regime for prostitution, replacing the discredited and ineffective system then in place; and second, a rigid code of sexual comportment that confined all sexual activity to marriage, so that motherhood might become a "duty rather than a destiny." In the words of Alfred Fournier, "If humanity manages this return to innocence and the golden age, the days of syphilis will be numbered."[91]

Corbin has noted a temporary reversal in the liberalization of sexuality during this period, which may well have been a consequence of the reigning syphilophobia of the turn of the century. It had several important effects. First, it encouraged the utter medicalization and therefore marginalization of the prostitute. Prostitution was assimilated directly into degeneration or was mixed up with Lombrosian ideas to create the ludicrous notion of the "born prostitute." Prostitutes were characterized as displaying "moral insanity"; the "lack of shame" they exhibited in their liaisons became in itself an incriminating symptom of this hereditary disorder. Second, the sexuality of "degenerate prostitutes" became *in se* pathological and regressive.[92] Thus, in the words of Dr. Thulié, "their destiny is to be delivered over to deplorable excesses, to undergo the most abominable miseries, and to fall into the most shameful and abasing degradations whose torments are marked by the perpetual pursuit of new pleasures and the incessant satisfaction of their erotic frenzy."[93]

[90] Fully 751 of the founders were doctors, dentists, or pharmacists. See ibid., p. 391.

[91] Alfred Fournier, *La Ligue contre la syphilis* (Paris, 1904), p. 25.

[92] On the "born prostitute" and the "degenerate prostitute," see Corbin, *Les filles de noce*, pp. 436-452. See also Emile Laurent, "Prostitution et dégénérescence," *Annales médico-psychologiques* (May 1899), pp. 353-370.

[93] Henri Thulié, "Premières mésures à prendre contre le développement de la criminalité infantile," *Revue philanthropique* 3 (July 1898), p. 303. Like Thulié, most observers saw worsening degeneracy affecting women by miring them ever more deeply in "female" crimes like prostitution. Some, however, believed that degeneracy recognized the emerging equality of the sexes by bringing women, in the last stages of the disease, to the same condition as men. See Pauline Tarnowsky, *Les femmes homicides* (Paris: Alcan, 1908). In the imagery of the times, these iconoclastic women represented a sinister danger to male "force," that mysterious creative energy that in some symbolic way constituted the basis of male dominance in *fin-de-siècle* society. The repressed subliminal foundations of bourgeois life were presumably challenged

Third, sexuality itself underwent a thoroughgoing medicalization in this period. As usual, degeneration theorists led the way in these developments. In a seminal study of this process, Georges Lanteri-Laura shows how the definition of sexually normal behavior was made to adhere rigidly to popular evolutionary notions about species survival and adaptation. In typically reductionist fashion, procreation itself became the norm and sole aim of sexual behavior; pleasurable activity beyond the basic act was therefore "without biological justification" and qualified in the new nosologies as "obsessive" or "perverse."[94] Not surprisingly, Magnan's classification of sexual perversion made rapid progress in France, where anxiety about low birthrates was unusually high, despite the so-called French tolerance for sexual diversity. Magnan's schema broke with the tendency of the previous generation to be content with a description of the act itself, by way of showing how it was typical of the genre. Magnan showed how a particular sexual act was typical, not of other acts of the same sort, but of a stage in the development of a degenerate individual. His system had a natural advantage in medical testimony before a magistrate. Comparing Lasègue's old manner of analyzing exhibitionism with Magnan's, Lanteri-Laura writes:

> The way Lasègue went about the examination of exhibitionists remained centered on the act itself and became, therefore, somewhat tautological: its medical identity was by no means evident, and the magistrate risked not being convinced of the sickness. With Magnan, the tautology ceased: the interest of the case was no longer limited to the acts themselves; the clinician identified the elements that would establish that the acts in question belonged in a morbid category, guaranteed, not by the acts themselves, but by other signs of mental instability. The illness was thus neither a manner of speaking nor a simple analogy, but a functional alteration of the central nervous system.[95]

---

by women not restricted to "normal" roles. Thus did Emile Pourésy warn in his *La gangrène pornographique* (1907) that "the sweet poison of lips, the delicious and divine sap that spills out of the mouth of a woman in a kiss is the poison that destroys our force, our will, enervates us, maddens us, renders us slaves, like Samson in the arms of Delila." Quoted from Pourésy's book by J. Ernest-Charles in "La vie littéraire," *Le grand journal*, September 25, 1908, p. 400.

[94] Georges Lanteri-Laura, *Lecture des perversions: Histoire de leur appropriation médicale* (Paris: Masson, 1979), pp. 40-41.

[95] Ibid., pp. 51-52. On Magnan's attempt to identify particular perversions with particular stages of brain and neurological disorder, see pp. 47-50.

In describing how sexuality came to be medicalized, Michel Foucault has identified in diagnoses of abnormal sexual practice at the end of the nineteenth century the same relation of cause and symptom that I have shown to have operated in other pathologies at that time: "There was scarcely a malady or physical disturbance to which the nineteenth century did not impute at least some degree of sexual etiology. From the bad habits of children to the phthises of adults, the apoplexies of old people, nervous maladies, and the degenerations of the race, the medicine of that era wove an entire network of sexual causality to explain them."[96]

More important still was the social meaning of a "science" of sexuality to contemporaries: "Claiming to speak the truth, it stirred up people's fears; to the least oscillations of sexuality, it ascribed an imaginary dynasty of evils destined to be passed on for generations; it declared the furtive customs of the timid, and the most solitary of petty manias, dangerous for the whole society; strange pleasures, it warned, would eventually result in nothing short of death: that of individuals, generations, the species itself."[97]

Finally, the generalized anxiety about unconventional sexuality spilled over into organized purity crusades against particular abuses. The so-called white slave trade,[98] pornography, and theatrical nudity were vigorously attacked by coalitions of medical specialists and laymen with altogether complementary aims. The inveterate reformer Senator René Bérenger organized a Fédération des sociétés contre la pornographie in 1905. He orchestrated press conferences and public meetings, and urged fellow citizens to press lawsuits against abuses of public decency. Jules Delahaye, a deputy from Maine-et-Loire, personally filed suit against a show featuring two women exchanging caresses at the Petit-Palais, a scene he alleged to find particularly revolting to his sensibilities. Bérenger himself filed several successful suits against dance hall nudity in the summer of 1908 in an excellent example of personal sacrifice for the larger cause.[99]

The purity crusaders were successful in shutting down a few shows, but their successes were transitory; nudity on the stage continued and the healthy trade in pornography flourished. But with this "pathology" as with alcoholism, the significance of the movement, as I have suggested, lay in its ability to associate the object of its dissatisfaction with a syndrome of more admissible biological or social pathologies, and to

---

[96] Foucault, *The History of Sexuality*, vol. 1, p. 64.

[97] Ibid., pp. 53-54.

[98] On this little-known phenomenon see Corbin, *Les filles de noce*, pp. 405-436.

[99] Waldberg, *Eros in La Belle Époque*, p. 99. *Dépêche de Toulouse*, July 21, 1908.

present its arguments in such a way that the vilified behavior was both a symptom of malady and a cause. Dr. Lucien Nass, a medical doctor and publicist who had made a career from his "scientific" characterizations of French leftists as psychotic monsters, wrote a treatise in 1909 on the problem of nudity in the theater in which he emphasized the morbid nature of the phenomenon and the extreme danger it posed to the mental health of its customers.[100] The campaign to retain regulation of prostitution was a good deal more successful, however. By 1906 the abolition movement, though it had expected success only a few years earlier, was all but dead. The new alliance of doctors and of moralists à la mode managed to bring about an intensification of surveillance, a rise in arrests of "clandestines," and longer prison sentences that kept prostitutes effectively out of circulation.[101]

Purity and hygiene crusaders also took aim at the vigorous French neo-Malthusian movement, whose leaders preached the moral and economic virtues of small families. The Ligue de la régénération humaine, founded in 1896 by Paul Robin and his associates, disseminated information about contraception and female reproduction in conferences, public speeches, and its paper, *Génération consciente*. It may seem to us that in a country with the lowest birthrate in the world, such a movement was only preaching to the converted. But neo-Malthusian propaganda was motivated by largely political aims, connected closely to the economic self-interest of the working classes and the education and political liberation of women.[102] Hygiene crusaders objected violently to the flood of neo-Malthusian literature on birth control, labeling it pornographic and demoralizing. The antipornographic organizations seem to have spent a disproportionate amount of their energy combatting birth control measures and abortion, harassing distributors and publicists with lawsuits, and lobbying for laws prohibiting neo-Malthusian writings outright.[103] This kind of activity clearly reveals

[100] See Lucien Nass and A. J. Witkowsky, *Le nu au théâtre* (Paris, 1909). His studies on political pathologies (with Dr. Cabanès) are *Névroses de l'histoire* (Paris, 1908) and *La névrose révolutionnaire* (Paris, 1906). Rémy de Gourmont, reformed aesthete, performed this sort of operation with the dubious passion for gambling he observed in his contemporaries. Gambling, "analogue au alcool," manifested itself in "automatism," loss of consciousness, and in some cases extreme "collective hysteria." This state of mind was in turn conducive to other questionable obsessions, resistance to which was dangerously lowered by the gambling mania. "La passion du jeu," *Dépêche de Toulouse*, July 18, 1908.

[101] Corbin, *Les filles de noce*, pp. 476-477.

[102] On the origins and aims of neo-Malthusianism see Ronsin, *La grève des ventres*, pp. 42-73.

[103] On the legal efforts of these groups see ibid., pp. 137-148.

the depopulation anxieties that lay beneath the obsessive puritanism of these groups.

It is very likely that the most effective of the hygiene groups were those that spoke most clearly in the language of the master pathology itself. Repopulationist agitation was largely initiated by the respected demographer Jacques Bertillon, who had been appealing for larger families in his scholarly books on the French population since the 1880s.[104] Bertillon founded the Alliance nationale pour l'accroissement de la population française in 1896; he formed it in the mold of the great political leagues of the period, making it a clearinghouse of information, an exchange for public speakers and conferences, and an aggressive lobbying and fund-gathering organization. By virtue of its avowed purpose, the Alliance nationale concerned itself with all the pathologies, moral and medical, that its leaders believed were sapping the will and the capacity of the French to reproduce. They did so in a mood of moral outrage and tragic pessimism. In language worthy of an Old Testament prophet, Bertillon mourned that "the worst of it is that France will be dishonored. History will be fully justified in saying that she died of two ignoble vices: the crime of Onan and drunkenness."[105]

Yet, the medical perspective was always very much in evidence. By the end of the first decade of the twentieth century, the list of depopulationist writings identifying alcoholism, prostitution, pornography, crime, and the hereditary forms of tuberculosis, arthritis, and syphilis as "cause-symptoms" of low birthrates was long and growing longer.[106] Industrialists gave huge donations to support anti-Malthusian propaganda; in 1909 when the Académie des sciences morales offered a prize for the best work on depopulation, twenty-two book-length man-

---

[104] Among Bertillon's books are *Calcul de la mortalité des enfants du premier âge* (Paris, 1887); *De la dépopulation de la France et des remèdes à y apporter* (Paris, 1896); *Le problème de la dépopulation* (Paris, 1897); *La dépopulation de la France, ses conséquences, ses causes, mésures à prendre pour la combattre* (Paris, 1911).

[105] Quoted without reference in Ronsin, *La grève des ventres*, p. 126.

[106] The main periodicals were *Le relèvement social*, the paper of the Ligue française de la moralité publique; *Pour la vie*, the organ of the Ligue française pour le relèvement de la moralité publique; and the *Bulletin* of Bertillon's Alliance nationale. The most influential books were Paul Bureau, *La restriction volontaire de la natalité et la défense nationale* (Paris, 1913); Henri Clément, *La dépopulation en France* (Paris, 1910); Georges Deherme *Croître ou disparaître* (Paris, 1910); Charles Gide, *Rapport sur la moralité publique* (Melun, 1903); René Lavollée, *Les fleaux nationaux: Dépopulation, pornographie, alcoolisme, affaiblissement moral* (Paris, 1909); Edmonde Piot, *La dépopulation* (Paris, 1902); L. Vuillermet, *Le suicide d'un race* (Paris, 1911).

167

uscripts were received.[107] Medical themes and depopulation were incorporated into the solidarist programs of the Ecole des hautes études sociales, and in 1912 the Musée sociale sponsored a congress on "pornography, neo-Malthusian propaganda, and their repression."[108] Meanwhile journalists followed the statistics on population with close attention—much as we do now for economic indicators—for evidence of trends in national health.[109] As tensions with Germany mounted and birthrate figures worsened, anxieties about military disaster helped encourage a turn in repopulationist rhetoric toward overtly racist themes.[110]

The politicians were late to fall into line, perhaps because of the embarrassment of urging others to reproduce while their own families remained small.[111] However, a parliamentary commission was formed in 1902 to study the problem, and though it disbanded in the positive growth years 1904-1906, it quickly reconstituted itself when the data from the negative year 1907 became known. Various pieces of legislation were proposed: reducing the age of marriage without parental consent, legitimizing the children of adulterous liaisons, and encouraging larger families.[112] But a law of 1907 reducing the formalities of civil marriages, which led to a temporary spurt in marriages, did not produce any corresponding change in the marriage fertility rate, the root of the problem after all.[113] Only after the demographic disaster of the war did the government move, in 1920, to punish the dissem-

[107] See the summary of these works by Henri Joly in *Séances et travaux de l'Académie des sciences morales et politiques* 172 (1909), pp. 106-130.

[108] Ronsin *La grève des ventres*, pp. 126-127.

[109] A typical newspaper editorial of this sort appeared in *Le temps* on January 9, 1902. The writer was willing to celebrate the 400,000 or so growth in population in the five-year period 1896-1901, as it compared so favorably to the negative growth rate of the previous five years. This suggests, he tentatively offered, that those who speak of the "loss of vigor of our race" or of "degeneration" may be mistaken.

[110] Ronsin, *La grève des ventres*, pp. 125-126; see also the documents collected by André Armengaud, *Les Français et Malthus* (Paris: Presses Universitaires de France, 1975), pp. 105-106. A French Eugenics Society was founded in 1912 by a coalition of doctors, social scientists, and politicians. For an overview of the movement see William Schneider's "Toward The Improvement of the Human Race: The History of Eugenics in France," *Journal of Modern History* 54 (June 1982), pp. 268-291.

[111] A fact not lost upon the neo-Malthusians: André Armengaud reproduces a poster of the neo-Malthusian Ligue de la régénération humaine listing the presidents of the Third Republic from Thiers to Poincaré and the number of their children: "Four children for nine couples! What a beautiful lesson of social foresight and of parental prudence for an unfortunate proletariat plunged into misery, filth, and ignorance." *Les Français et Malthus*, pp. 52-53.

[112] The text of one of these laws is in ibid., pp. 62-63.

[113] Armengaud, *La population française au XIXᵉ siècle*, pp. 48-49.

ination of birth control "pornography" with jail terms. Public officials did move against prostitution, and certain varieties of outrages against public decency. The government also initiated new legislation on the hygiene of urban housing, and, as we shall later see, made official inquiries on the connections between alcoholism, mental illness, and suicide.[114]

The various hygiene groups I have discussed seem to have concerned themselves with so-called single issues. But such a notion would be as mistaken for *belle époque* France as it is for the antiabortion or school prayer groups in the United States today. In practice, there was an extraordinary overlapping of interests in these movements. The repopulationists found antipornography arguments useful in the struggle against the sex manuals of their neo-Malthusian enemies; antialcohol groups took comfort from the temperance platforms of other hygienists; and those seeking to regulate prostitution profited from the familialist rhetoric of all those who hoped for a rise in birthrates. More important, the medical model that was quickly gaining acceptance in France explicitly linked together the pathologies weakening the nation in a single degenerational syndrome. It must have been difficult for contemporaries to think about one of these issues without having the others immediately called to mind. Certainly, the Parisian journalist who witnessed a little girl call a correctional magistrate a "cow" could not resist brooding over the consequences of such behavior in the language of the clinic: "The plague rages on, and there must be a vaccine against its virus, because, in the end, though it is regrettable that the French are not making many children any more, it is certainly not at all desirable that they make them like the little cow girl."[115]

Such ruminations could also be heard from on high. In his book *The Rules of Sociological Method* (1895), Emile Durkheim offered a challenge to Republican statesmen in purely medical terms: "It is no longer a matter of pursuing desperately an objective that retreats as one advances, but of working with steady perseverance to maintain the normal state, of re-establishing it if it is threatened, and of rediscovering its conditions if they have changed. The duty of the statesman is no longer to push society toward an ideal that seems attractive to him, but his role is that of the physician: he prevents the outbreak of illnesses by good hygiene, and he seeks to cure them when they have appeared."[116]

[114] See for much of this activity, Georges Cahen, *L'autre guerre: Essais d'assistance et de prévoyance sociale (1905-1920)* (Paris: Berger-Levrault, 1920).

[115] A. Claveau, "La petite pègre," *Le Figaro*, January 11, 1902.

[116] Emile Durkheim, *The Rules of Sociological Method*, 8th ed., trans. Sarah A. Solovay and John H. Mueller (Glencoe, Ill.: Free Press, 1938), p. 75.

By the turn of the century, a medical outlook of *bio-pouvoir* had thoroughly penetrated popular consciousness. A medical theory of degeneration was so successful in integrating the palpable and familiar litany of social pathologies into a discourse of national decline that it escaped the terminological prison of the clinic to thrive in the arena of public debate. The events of the remaining years before the war would ensure that this thoroughly modern perspective would not fade away.

CHAPTER VI

The Politics of Social Defense:
Violent Crime, "Apaches," and the Press
at the Turn of the Century

In the early summer of 1908 *Le Figaro's* literary editor Maurice Leudet interviewed the celebrated Italian criminologist Scipio Sighele, who was visiting Paris to promote his new book, *Littérature et criminalité*. The interview passed quickly to topical matters of great concern to Leudet. What did Sighele make, he asked, of the infamous child murderer Jeanne Weber, whose case was currently being heard in an assizes court of the capital? "Certainly a degenerate," replied Cesare Lombroso's former disciple, a type against which society "must learn to defend itself." Sighele reflected further on the unusual difficulty of social defense in this advanced state of civilization. Modern society, of its own nature, he observed, creates a greater number of degenerates than ever before, while so softening our sensibilities and customs that we lack the will to deal properly with them. He pointed out the enormous statistical increase in "the insane, alcoholics, and criminals" since 1830, musing that such things make us all regret the simple life that reigned before our civilization became so complex.[1]

With these words, Sighele illustrates usefully the major themes that I wish to argue dominated thinking about deviance from the 1890s until the First World War. There is, of course, a continuation of the medical idea of degeneracy as the common link between these various pathologies, an idea that is tossed off casually in the middle-class press without any accompanying explanation. The subject of Leudet's concern, Jeanne Weber, was by no means a typical criminal for this period except in the sense that she was a violent criminal; this fact, taken together with Sighele's claim that "increases" in these pathologies had taken place, signals a rising anxiety about the potential *violence* inherent

[1] Maurice Leudet, "Crimes et littérature—Conversation avec M. Scipio Sighele," *Le Figaro*, May 16, 1908.

in all forms of deviance. Sighele's suggestion that there is an inverse relationship between the increase of degeneracy and a society's willingness to treat it with the firmness it deserves perfectly expresses the dilemma that most contemporaries believed they faced: new and more dangerous forms of deviance were taking shape, but the traditional institutions and processes of repression were unable to cope with them. By compensation, however, Sighele also proposed the principle on which he and many of his contemporaries believed a new philosophy of punishment must be based: social defense.

The historical convergence of these themes is the subject of this chapter. I wish to argue that although one can ascertain that each of these themes existed even before the turn of the century, the full effects of their union could only be appreciated fully during the period 1905-1908. The extraordinary series of external and internal crises that occurred in this brief era combined to produce an unusually high level of public concern about security and to raise questions about the nation's ability to respond effectively to a growing German military and diplomatic assertiveness. In this atmosphere of anxiety, one might reasonably expect the threshold of public tolerance for deviance to be particularly low. Indeed, there are clear signs that popular attitudes, and in some instances the treatment of deviants, became much tougher during this period. Perhaps more surprising is the fact that the leaders of this reorientation were medical or scientific experts on deviance, in some cases the same individuals who had fought the good fight against Lombroso over a decade earlier in favor of a rehabilitative and humane outlook on crime and mental illness. This intervention of the experts helped crystallize a pervasive though vague sense of public disquiet into a full-fledged movement of ideas.

I do not wish to argue that medical and criminological experts precipitated this change of course alone, or simply acted in order to extend their professional hegemony more broadly or deeply into the realm of public policy. By the period 1905-1908, a language of national pathology which regarded crime, mental illness, or alcoholism as signs of national debility was no longer a monopoly of medical specialists. By this time, as I hope to show, the influences running between the lay public and the professional community were thoroughly reciprocal. In their capacity as the guardians of public hygiene, doctors and other specialists responded with great sensitivity to the needs and the concerns of popular opinion and public officials, integrating new sources of anxiety into a medical model of cultural crisis. In turn, those who shaped opinion and public policy in France for the most part heeded the promptings of experts and responded enthusiastically to the technical formulas they devised. There were limits, as we shall see, to a full reciprocity of the language of medical pathology, which prevented its attaining a perfect exchange value, but mutual adjustments were readily managed.

By the end of the first decade of the twentieth century there were clear signs in France that the usual dialectical relationship between domestic order and external security had become infused with a medical perspective. The outlook on deviance, on the other hand, had become profoundly politicized. Suffice it to say that these developments did not contribute to flexibility or moderation in either politics or medicine.

The continued and intensified application of medical ideas to new areas of deviance in the decade or so prior to 1905 helped to strengthen the credibility of the politics of internal security and promote suspicion of marginal elements in French society. Vagrancy, which, as we have seen, was a source of grave concern in the early 1880s, continued an apparently ineluctable increase through the last decade of the century. Beginning around 1895-1896 there was a clear rise in public concern, marked by a flood of legal writings, legislative proposals, and editorials, cresting around 1900 but extending well into the next decade. During this period vagrancy was thoroughly medicalized. In the years just preceding passage of the relegation law, the reader will recall, medical professionals made only modest efforts to comprehend vagrancy and mendicancy in technical terms. At that time the construction of an image of the vagrant as an incurable was largely the work of the politicians. By the 1890s, however, the growing popularity of a medical model of deviance had encouraged medical specialists to apply the model to a wider array of subjects.

For the phenomenon of vagrancy, as for the other varieties of deviance I have discussed, doctors provided medical explanations in response to direct requests for their expertise. Since the Parole Law of 1885, an increasing burden, in part mitigated by state subsidies, had fallen on the private patronage societies which had undertaken to find jobs and support for former criminals. Most of these groups were founded in the 1870s when the hopes for prison reform were still running high, and their leaders were often liberal Catholics or Protestants, philanthropists, or magistrates anxious to moralize society. But the growth in numbers of parolees provoked regular reminders from some patronage leaders that they were by no means obliged to invest

173

time and resources in individuals who were not socially redeemable.[2]
The rule of thumb that was generally used to make distinctions between
salvageable and nonsalvageable individuals was of a familiar variety:
first offenders were "the most interesting," while repeaters were deemed
"unworthy of interest."[3]

At the Third National Patronage Congress (1896) Senator René
Bérenger called for recognition of a clearer distinction between "incorrigible" and "repentant" ex-convicts. He chose to contrast an "incorrigible vagabond" who was a "habitual thief living from plunder"
and the confused fellow whose "good intentions" of holding a job were
thwarted by society's suspicions.[4] Other speakers and presentations at
the 1896 congress drew attention to the rapid growth and "social danger" of vagrancy and begging; a general discussion of the issue yielded
agreement that there were clear differences between the "accidental"
vagrant and the "habitual" one who was "irremediably gangrenated."[5]
A local Bordeaux physician, Philippe Tissié, whom we will later encounter in the sports movement, stepped forward with a medical distinction. Tissié posited the existence of a "social vagabondage," which
was "conscious" and motivated by "imitation" or "cerebral fatigue,"
and a "pathological" variety, which was "unconscious" and engaged in
by "alcoholics, epileptics, idiots, and general paralytics."[6]

While it is not clear how useful such characterizations might have
been to the practical work of the patronage societies, they were employed with increasing frequency at the end of the century in the
philanthropic literature, particularly after the suspended sentence law
of 1897 released a new flood of clients for "rehabilitation."[7] There can
be little doubt that patronage leaders, already overburdened with work,
believed that vagrants constituted unusually formidable cases for social
reassimilation, and they expressed their doubts in the available lan-

[2] Francis Turcas, *Premier congrès national du patronage des libérés* (Paris, 1894), p.
75.

[3] J. A. Raux and Henry-Louis Berthélémy, *Deuxième congrès national du patronage
des libérés* (Lyon, 1895), pp. 13-15, 121.

[4] René Bérenger, *Troisième congrès national du patronage des libérés* (Bordeaux, 1896),
pp. 65-68.

[5] This last is the remark of Georges Tellier in "L'engagement dans l'armée des
mendiants et des vagabonds," *Troisième congrès national du patronage des libérés*, p. 79.
For a general discussion see pp. 220-234.

[6] Philippe Tissié, *Troisième congrès national du patronage des libérés*, pp. 225-226.

[7] Speakers at the Fourth National Congress of 1897 addressed this problem in
particular. See the presentations of George Vidal, Félix Voisin, and Louis Rivière,
Quatrième congrès national du patronage des libérés (Lille, 1898), pp. 50-63, 149-155,
300-308.

guage of medical pathology. Many of these discussions appeared in the *Revue philanthropique*, which replaced the old-fashioned *Annales de charité* in 1897 with a more modern, medical perspective. Doctors and laymen alike employed the language of hereditary incurability and degeneration to an unprecedented degree. Most emphasized the need for social defense against this grave menace, laying special stress on the violent instincts of vagrants.[8] In two long studies of juvenile vagabonds in Paris, Louis Albanel, a magistrate, and Dr. P. V. LeGras argued that only medical specialists could distinguish "refractory monsters marked by their illness" from the ameliorable, warning, in a sinister new vein, that only such measures could preserve France from another Sedan or Commune.[9] The demoralizing condition of vagrancy, they averred, "nourishes in the brains of individuals who were children only yesterday the conception of hideous crimes, executed with a savage ferocity and a revolting indifference."[10]

In the large body of literature on vagrancy that appeared between 1897 and 1908, medical themes play a predominant role, even in the legal theses written on the problem during that period. The principal Lombrosian work on the subject, Florian and Cavaglieri's *I vagabondi* (1895) attracted a few French adherents to the thesis that vagrancy was an atavistic "nomadic tendency" that recapitulated the instinctive cravings of mankind's wandering prehistory.[11] On the whole this explanation found little favor; most commentators seem to have favored the sort of mixture of social, hereditary, and "moral" causes (pornography, debauchery, family influences) that could be easily accommodated to degeneration theory.[12] The standard French treatment, Marie

[8] See, in particular, Gustave Drouineau, "Les enquêtes sur le vagabondage," which held vagabonds responsible for the typhus epidemics of 1894-1895. *Revue philanthropique* 1 (June 1897), pp. 321-336; Loys Brueyre, "Du vagabondage, de la mendicité," ibid. 2 (December 1897), pp. 196-213; Louis Rivière, "Le patronage des vagabonds," ibid. 3 (July 1898), pp. 330-334 and "Le délit de mendicité" ibid. 4 (April 1899), pp. 641-668; Alfred Lambert, "Un étrange délit: Le vagabondage," ibid. 4 (February 1899), pp. 453-464.

[9] Louis Albanel and P. V. LeGras, "L'enfance criminelle à Paris," *Revue philanthropique* 5 (July 1899), pp. 296-297.

[10] Albanel and LeGras, "L'enfance criminelle à Paris," *Revue philanthropique* 4 (February 1899), p. 398.

[11] See Armand Marie and Maurice Hamel, "Vagabondage et folie," reprinted from the *Deuxième congrès national d'assistance* (Rouen, 1898), pp. 1-2; Armand Pagnier, *Du vagabondage et des vagabonds* (Paris: Maloine, 1906), pp. 144-146. Henri de Varigny gave these views a warm reception in *Le temps*, March 3, 1900.

[12] Hubert DuPuy, *Vagabondage et mendicité* (Paris: Larose, 1891); André Dalesme, *Du vagabondage* (Limoges, 1900); Fernand Chauteau, *Vagabondage et mendicité: Les plaies sociales* (Paris: Pedone, 1907); Charles LeRoux, *Le vagabondage et mendicité*

The "vagabond" painted.

The same in real life.
    by Emmanuel Poiré, *Gros et détail* (Paris: Plon-Nourrit, 1907), p. 20

and Meunier's *Les vagabonds* (1908), postulated three great classes of vagrancy: those of social and economic origin; "morbid" vagrants (including neurasthenics, hysterics, epileptics, special varieties of degen-

---

(Pithiviers, 1908). For especially graphic accounts of juvenile vagrancy, see Eugène Testut, *Les vagabonds mineurs* (Paris, 1908), pp. 6-8, 74-77, 129; in *Le vagabondage des mineurs* (Mayenne, 1899), Jean Hélie writes that the child vagabond, "far from being inoffensive, is often a redoubtable being; his overheated imagination is easily capable of the most abominable conceptions," p. 13.

"That's papa . . . If you could see how sturdy he is at home!"
by Abel Faivre, *Le Figaro*, September 25, 1907

erates, and alcoholics); and "ethnic" vagrants, comprising collective mystics and barbarian invaders, a category of only historical significance.[13] While it may be an exaggeration to claim, as Donzelot has done, that from 1890 to 1900 the vagabond was the "universal of mental pathology, the prism through which all the categories of madness and abnormality could be distributed,"[14] the vagrant most certainly assumed a prominent place in the medical sideshow of national pathologies.[15]

[13] See Armand Marie and Raymond Meunier, *Les vagabonds* (Paris, 1908), and the useful summary of their analysis, "Les vagabonds au point de vue psychologique," *Revue des idées* 4 (July 15, 1907), pp. 577-594.

[14] Donzelot, *The Policing of Families*, p. 130; see also the comments of Michelle Perrot in "La fin des vagabonds," *L'histoire* 3 (July-August 1978), pp. 23-33.

[15] Discussions beginning in 1907 in the Chamber about the "nomad" problem

The other medicalized forms of deviance of the 1890s cut closer to the bone of French political life. Anarchism in France entered the phase of "propaganda by deed" with a vengeance in 1892. Anarchist newspapers had long counseled would-be revolutionaries in the art of making bombs, but, apart from reports of occasional grand gestures against foreign despots, the French public was innocent of first-hand knowledge of anarchist violence. However, between 1892 and 1894 bombs were placed near the dwellings of public officials, thrown into the Chamber of Deputies, and exploded in numerous public places. Sadi Carnot, the president of the Republic, fell to an anarchist's knife on June 24, 1894. Emile Henry and Auguste Vaillant were names whose utterance not only struck fear into the hearts of countless politicians and magistrates, little used to regarding themselves as moving targets, but also, as contemporaries testified, terrified middle-class urbanites, who perceived these deeds as dangerously random.[16]

The problem with anarchism, from the point of view of those attempting to find the means to repress it, was that it attacked *all* forms of authority in society, while claiming the legal immunity traditionally associated only with acts against the political arm of the state. Throughout the nineteenth century French penal law had recognized a distinction between common-law crimes and political crimes. Political criminals were usually treated more leniently: capital punishment for political crimes was abolished in 1848, and, in practice, long jail terms were amnestied well before their legal termination. The brief though deadly serious Boulanger episode, and the fearsome generality of anarchist violence provoked Republican legislators to exempt anarchists from the usual protection of political ecumenism. To meet this threat, the politicians passed the *lois scélérates* between 1892 and 1894, which specifically defined anarchist activities as offenses in common law against society (*délits sociaux*) punishable by death.

As Machelon has shown, French legal experts abandoned the "subjective" theory of political crime which had traditionally considered the motivations of the violent act and replaced it with one that punished only its effects.[17] They justified this course of action in part with the

---

finally resulted in a law of 1912 which instituted a new regime of surveillance of vagabonds, requiring, among other things, the carrying of an "anthropometric" card with vital measurements and unique morphological features. See Machelon, *La République contre les libertés*, pp. 399-400n; also, François Vaux de Foletier, *Les Bohemiens en France au XIXᵉ siècle* (Paris: J. C. Lattès, 1981), pp. 182-189.

[16] Jean Maitron, *Ravachol et les anarchistes* (Paris: Julliard, 1964), pp. 10-14; Machelon, *La République contre les libertés*, p. 404.

[17] Machelon, *La République contre les libertés*, pp. 408-410. Barton L. Ingraham does

argument that anarchists were by nature a separate species of humanity whose crimes, far from being motivated by political principles, were an expression of both derangement *and* the wanton depravity of common criminals.[18] That a conflation of crime and madness could be made with such ease is testimony both to the general influence of the medicalized criminology of the era, and to the rise of a unique genre of medical theory devoted to the specific category of political criminality.

The most important text of this sort was published in 1891 in Italian by Lombroso and Laschi, and translated into French the following year as *Le crime politique et les révolutions*. Lombroso and Laschi attempted to separate true "revolutions," led by "honest" idealists, from "revolts," "sedition," and other antisocial acts, which they held to be motivated by a range of abnormal causes. Their typology of "political delinquents" ran the familiar Lombrosian gamut from "born criminals" and "insane criminals" to "occasional" and "passionate" political offenders.[19] An important French literature, stressing monomania or degeneracy, developed rapidly after the publication of Lombroso's book.[20]

Anarchy moved on to other pastures after its experiment with propaganda by the deed. But there are two aspects of this brief episode in the history of anarchism and the medicalization of deviance that are important for this study. First, there was a definite tendency in this instance for legal experts and politicians to characterize a group of political extremists in the biopsychological terminology that had previously been reserved for marginal social elements. Second, as Machelon has shown, many contemporary observers, in the name of the doctrine of "social defense," advocated dispensing with the usual judgments about the mental responsibility of offenders in view of the alleged threat they posed. In his words, "it was of primary importance that penal law be adapted to the ends of preserving organized society against the aggression of a virtual subhumanity. Thus, all legislative

---

not recognize the subjective-objective distinction, but does acknowledge that these laws marked a distinct change in emphasis from the nineteenth-century tradition. *Political Crime in Europe: A Comparative Study of France, Germany, and England* (Berkeley: University of California Press, 1979), p. 181.

[18] Machelon, *La République contre les libertés*, pp. 404-406.

[19] Cesare Lombroso and R. Laschi, *Le crime politique et les révolutions* (Paris, 1892), pp. 17-20, 60-68, 164-165. See also the extensive summary of their views in Léauté, *Criminologie et science pénitentiaire*, pp. 271-289.

[20] P. Boilley, *Les trois socialismes, anarchisme, collectivisme, réformisme* (Paris: Alcan, 1895); Jean Crocq, *L'état mental des anarchistes* (Paris, 1894); A. Hamon, *Psychologie de l'anarchiste-socialiste* (Paris: Storck, 1895); Louis Proal, *La criminalité politique* (Paris: Alcan, 1898); *Documents et études sociales sur l'anarchie* (Lyon: Storck, 1897).

measures destined to facilitate the combat against anarchism found themselves justified in advance."[21] It is unlikely, in any event, that Ravachol and his colleagues could have been saved from the guillotine, but one suspects that whether it functioned as ideology or as rationalization, clinical language made the killing of political criminals a more palatable affair.

Once the discourse of medical pathology had been applied to the most heinous political extremists, it was a relatively easy matter, as I have argued elsewhere, for zealots to expand that discourse to include a large number of less aggressive political movements. Indeed, the social and political upheavals of the 1890s and the following decade spawned a new science of collective psychology in which crowd behavior was described as a collective version of individual mental anomalies. Following the same classification procedures perfected earlier for individual criminals, Gabriel Tarde, Gustave LeBon, Scipio Sighele, and others speculated on the "criminal" propensities and penal responsibility of crowds.[22] The best known of these theorists, Gustave LeBon, later developed his ideas on the pathological nature of radical political movements at some length, relying heavily on crowd theory and degeneracy as the "scientific" underpinning of his work.[23] The events of the period 1900-1914 provided a fertile soil in which speculations about pathology could take deep root.

There are two lenses through which I would like to examine the attitudes of contemporaries toward deviance: capital punishment and criminal responsibility. These issues are addressed in detail in subsequent chapters, but I must first explain why they resonated so strongly in the minds of French men and women just after the turn of the century. Why, in other words, did subjects whose usual appeal was limited to philosophers and magistrates attract, for a brief moment, the attention of educated opinion in the whole nation? The answer lies in the bedrock of French middle-class mentality.

It is certainly the case that the years 1906-1909 represented simply another chapter in the *grande peur* of the French bourgeoisie. Louis

---

[21] Machelon, *La République contre les libertés*, p. 411. See also p. 411, n. 52.

[22] Scipio Sighele, *La foule criminelle*, 2d French ed. (Paris: Alcan, 1901); Gustave LeBon, *La psychologie des foules* (Paris: Alcan, 1895); Albert Abbo, *Les crimes des foules* (Marseille: V. Colombani, 1910).

[23] See my *The Origins of Crowd Psychology: Gustave LeBon and the Crisis of Mass Democracy in the Third Republic* (London and Beverly Hills: Sage, 1975), pp. 59-122. See also Susanna Barrows, *Distorting Mirrors: Visions of the Crowd in Late Nineteenth-Century France* (New Haven: Yale University Press, 1981).

Chevalier has shown how in the 1840s the vague malaise of the propertied classes took the form of a fascination with and revulsion against the *classes dangereuses* of Paris, and led to an apparently insatiable appetite for tales of their vices, origins, and numbers. Although it might be claimed that this well-known period of class tension had been preceded in French history by numerous episodes of collective anxiety or hysteria, most notably the *grande peur* of 1789, the decade of crisis 1840-1850 is distinguished by its modern penchant for setting in motion a species of fact gatherers and administrators whose device might have been, as Michel Foucault has suggested, "savoir et pouvoir." There appeared in the 1840s a middle-class fear that knew its objects, located and defined them, and took prudent measures of self-protection.

If fear remained an independent variable throughout the century, the objects of fear varied with the times. As Pierre Sorlin has written, after the 1840s people were no longer occupied with "dangerous classes" but with "dangerous individuals," actually "groups of dangerous individuals," as Sorlin's own examples show.[24] In the 1870s it was fear of "pimps," in the 1880s recidivists, and in the 1890s, as we have seen, anarchist assassins. Though Sorlin does not mention it, the first decade of the twentieth century had its own genuine objects of fear. These were the infamous "apaches," whose characteristic crime was the violent street crime: the knife blade between the ribs, and urban ambush.

The rise of a new form of violent criminality might in itself be sufficient cause to investigate capital punishment, since, as Paul Savey-Casard has written, "the history of the death penalty was inevitably linked to the history of fear."[25] Moreover, as capital crimes were violent crimes, the question of how to punish them raised to the fore the issues of violent behavior and the responsibility of a violent criminal for his crime. But the mass of law-abiding and property-owning Frenchmen and Frenchwomen had additional cause for experiencing fear in this "complex and often strangely confused era."[26]

As the reader may recall, Ted Gurr has argued that no historical justification can be found for assuming a direct relationship between public disorder and crime. On the other hand, they are often *perceived* as related "and are often treated as if they were similar. Both threaten some people's sense of well-being, and both lead to concerted demands for the re-establishment of 'order.' "[27] As Gurr points out, an earlier

[24] Sorlin, *La société française, 1840-1914*, vol. 1, p. 122.

[25] Paul Savey-Casard, *La peine de mort* (Geneva: Droz, 1968), p. 110.

[26] Jacques Chastenet, *Histoire de la troisième République: Jours inquiets et jours sanglants*, vol. 4 (Paris: Hachette, 1957), p. 20.

[27] Gurr, *Rogues, Rebels and Reformers*, p. 10.

research tradition on these problems merely assumed that the social conditions producing crime and collective disorder were identical. Recent work, as we have seen, has largely overturned that assumption. Those who lived through the heroic era of French revolutionary syndicalism, however, did not enjoy the benefits of hindsight.

French labor was especially active in these years, having completed a period of notable centralization and coordination just after the turn of the century. The high-water mark of strike activity was 1906, with record numbers of strikers and days struck, but "strike intensity" was also high in 1907. "Intensity" fell in 1908, but the number of strikers that year remained abnormally high.[28] Stearns has argued that the goals of the strikers in this period were the traditional ones of better wages and working conditions; no doubt settlements appear to reflect these strictly economic aims.[29] But Tilly and Shorter have argued for a kind of politically coordinated inspiration for these years of exceptional activity, actuated by a combination of confidence gained from recent organizational and political advances and bitterness at some unusually rigid opposition from a government workers had imagined might be more sympathetic to their interests.[30] Whatever motives moved strikers to this unprecedented activity, it is certain that militant ideologists were willing to see in the demonstration of collective vigor an endorsement of the revolutionary general strike. From the level of high theory in Georges Sorel's *Réflexions sur la violence* (1906), and in the grass-roots syndicalist press, arguments were advanced about the revolutionary potential inherent in strike action.[31] The "mode of presentation" of the bourgeois press, which related the "facts" of labor unrest to the public, laid a heavy stress on the violence and revolutionary aims of strikers.[32] The press reached new heights of hysteria just before the May Day marches of 1906, spreading unease far and wide.

In any event the conservative press did not have to invent the danger presented by militant labor out of whole cloth in 1907. Paris was plunged into darkness in small installments in March as a consequence of the

[28] Michelle Perrot, *Les ouvriers en grève: France, 1871-1890*, vol. 1 (Paris: Mouton, 1974), p. 51. "Intensity" is an index that takes into account the number of strikers and the number of days they are on strike.

[29] See Peter Stearns, *Lives of Labor: Work in a Maturing Industrial Society* (New York: Holmes and Meier, 1975), pp. 305-317.

[30] Charles Tilly and Edward Shorter, *Strikes in France, 1830-1968* (Cambridge: Cambridge University Press, 1974), pp. 118-120.

[31] See F. F. Ridley, *Revolutionary Syndicalism in France* (Cambridge: Cambridge University Press, 1973), pp. 182-187, 213-219.

[32] Perrot, *Les ouvriers en grève*, vol. 1, p. 35.

first electrical workers' strikes. In the spring and early summer of 1907 the first great union of agricultural workers, the Confédération générale viticole, demanded relief from the disastrous effects of overproduction and the questionable manufacture of wines of high degree from inferior grapes.[33] Though the *révolte des vignerons* was by no means exclusively a movement of the agricultural proletariat of the Midi, it had the overtones of an emotional religious revival and was marked by unusual mass meetings and manifestations. There was also a distressing mutiny of an infantry regiment, the first such episode in recent memory, and a damaging blow to the image of the new "Republicanized" army of the post-Dreyfus period.

The Clemenceau ministry dealt with these developments smoothly and firmly, indeed more firmly than the political left had assumed in view of Clemenceau's program and the nature of his parliamentary coalition. In April the prime minister announced that public employees did not enjoy the right to unionize or strike. This issue had been hanging in the air for several years, and tentative efforts at organization by the *instituteurs* had been tolerated if not officially sanctioned by earlier ministries. Clemenceau's pronouncement confined public employee organizations to the benevolent and mutual-aid activities of the pre-1884 period. It helped earn him the title "Le premier flic de France" and provoked one of the great debates with Jaurès that marked his long ministry. Clemenceau was able to recoup some of his prestige with the left through his reintroduction of the controversial income tax, but it was abundantly clear to all that Clemenceau in power was a "new" Clemenceau who would act resolutely against all threats, real and imagined, to public security.

Clemenceau harshly repressed the inevitable challenges to the antistrike rule in the spring of 1906. He did, it is true, turn a deaf ear to demands by the right and an increasingly large number of fellow Radicals for a complete disbanding of the CGT, (Confédération générale du travail). But the Draveil-Vigneux strike, broken by force in May 1908, brought forth the charge by the prime minister that the strikers were "revolutionaries" cultivating "antipatriotism" and "anarchy."[34] The still more brutal repression by troops of the construction workers' strike in the Paris suburb of Villeneuve-Saint-Georges in July left dead and wounded workers on the field of "battle" and their leaders in jail. The vigor of the government's response to labor manifestations,

[33] On this episode see Felix Napo, *La révolte des vignerons* (Paris: Privat, 1971).

[34] Gaston Monnerville, *Clemenceau* (Paris: Fayard, 1968), p. 332. For a detailed treatment of Clemenceau's attitudes toward labor in this ministry see Jacques Julliard, *Clemenceau, briseur des grèves* (Paris: Julliard, 1965).

on the grounds of illegality or a threat to public order, increased from 1906 to 1908. From having been a mediator between capital and labor throughout much of the nineteenth century, and by all appearances a fairly equitable one, the French state found itself after 1900 an employer, cleaving ineluctably to the side of capital. As the head of a vast network of public services that showed growing signs of restiveness, the state acted as would any employer suspicious of worker combinations; yet, as Clemenceau's rhetoric testifies, the state did so not in the name of a particular interest intent on preserving its rights, but in the name of national interest, speaking for the people as a body. It is not difficult to understand how, in this highly charged atmosphere, striking government workers became traitors, and striking private ones their fifth column.

The intrusion of language appropriate to national-security matters into the domestic context is highly significant. It inaugurated a period of mutual overlap in rhetoric and imagery between foreign and internal categories and a definite growth in the exchange value of concepts stressing national solidarity. This is the origin of the period of nationalist revival about which so much has been written, but about which there still seems to be so much confusion. One thing seems certain enough: the truth of Eugen Weber's argument that the recrudescence of nationalism was not simply the product of internal crisis but needed the connection with foreign affairs.[35]

J.-P. Peter has written that from the first conflicts of the Dreyfus affair the nation experienced a long period of internal division which finally resulted in "the growth of an instinct of self-preservation in a divided society whose conflicts condemned the national organism to an extreme fragility."[36] This sense of division was prolonged into the era following Dreyfus's pardon, taking on a violent and confrontational nature the period 1898-1905 had never known. But this later period of conflict was different from the previous one in two principal ways. First, the new divisions were not between two strata of the property-owning classes of the nation, as they had been during the Dreyfus affair, but between propertied and propertyless, capital and labor. This was a division not only unequal in numbers, but also in resources, political power, and access to the most influential channels of communication. The second difference was in the relative calm of the Dreyfus period in foreign affairs. From Fashoda to Tangiers (1898 to

---

[35] Eugen Weber, *The Nationalist Revival in France, 1905-1914* (Berkeley and Los Angeles: University of California Press, 1959).

[36] J.-P. Peter, "Dimensions de l'affaire Dreyfus," *Annales: Economies, sociétés, civilisations* 26 (1971), p. 121.

1905), the Foreign Ministry was in the hands of Théophile Delcassé, who guided France to a closer union with Great Britain and made great strides in the colonial domain. The first resulted in the initial military and political discussions between France and Great Britain that eventually bound them closer than either had believed possible; the second led to a tentative though certain policy of assertiveness in Morocco, the last uncompleted link in France's vast West and North African empire.

It was the spark of Tangiers that helped ignite the sense of "fragility" in the national organism of which Peter has written. The kaiser's personal diplomacy in Morocco was apparently aimed at placing a series of obstacles in the way of French progress to a protectorate and was based on the assumption, however misguided, that his personal actions in the Moroccan arena from 1905 to 1911 were strengthening his own hand at home and Germany's abroad. The resignation of Delcassé on June 6, 1906, provoked a higher level of anti-German sentiment in France than had appeared in many years. But it also led to a period of uncertainty in foreign affairs that was to mark the entire period before 1914; the grave internal difficulties of the Russian monarchy were by no means entirely offset by French promotion of a colonial accord in August 1907 between her two ertswhile allies.

The Clemenceau ministry kept the military and diplomatic pressure on in Morocco, but harbored an increasingly suspicious and hostile attitude toward Germany. Clemenceau himself was, of course, on principle anti-German and regarded a strong French Moroccan policy as a check to German expansion in general. The Casablanca affair of October 1908 helped considerably to spread this view in French political and journalistic circles.[37] At the end of October some German deserters of the Foreign Legion tried to leave the country with the connivance of the German consular official at Casablanca. Their apprehension by French officials led to a protest to Germany and a counterprotest by the Germans in defense of their nationals. The affair was eventually arbitrated successfully, but at the end of October and beginning of November, and for some weeks afterwards, tension ran high, bringing unprecedented jingoism and demands for firm resistance from press and politician alike. This combination of new political

[37] E. Malcolm Carrol's still valuable study on public opinion and foreign policy holds the Casablanca incident to have been a turning point after which none of the parties—even Jaurès's Socialists—could doubt the political significance of Morocco. *French Public Opinion and Foreign Affairs, 1870-1914* (New York: Century, 1931), pp. 227-230. See also Oron J. Hale, *Germany and the Diplomatic Revolution: A Study in Diplomacy and the Press* (Philadelphia: University of Pennsylvania Press, 1931).

divisions, internal social upheaval, and diplomatic insecurity was the background against which the penal establishment, the politicians, and the general public discussed the question of how the nation should punish crimes of blood.

If the period 1906-1908 ended on a note of tumult and uncertainty, it began in a spirit of Republican consolidation and the promise of a political new deal. The Republican coalitions that had governed France until the Dreyfus period had eschewed egalitarian social or economic projects and had confined their progressivism to the building of a politically enlightened secular state. Under moderate Republican leadership, the period 1880-1900 produced a fully comprehensive system of state education, and a general broadening of the political and civil rights of individual citizens. Opportunists and Progressives had defended the Republic against the old right and the new caesarism of Boulangism, and guided the regime through the humiliation of government scandal and advantage seeking. During the Dreyfus period the Republic was ruled by a series of governments of Republican defense wary of the threats, both real and imagined, from the center-right faction of anti-Dreyfusards. The old Opportunist Waldeck-Rousseau began this period with his coalition cabinet of 1899, which included all strains of Republican opinion including the first Socialist to hold cabinet rank in France, Alexandre Millerand. The era ended with the ministry of the Radical Emile Combes in 1905. The major pieces of legislation of the period were designed as disciplinary measures against the anti-Dreyfusards: the army was "Republicanized" and the period of service reduced to two years; the schools finally secularized; the church was separated from the state and its principal religious orders disbanded.

In the months just before the passage of the separation law (in December 1905), some timid social legislation did appear, notably old age assistance to those over seventy (life expectancy in France at this time was less than sixty), and the eight-hour day in the mines. Combes introduced the progressive income tax, but the large number of conservative Republicans, not to mention conservative "Radicals," on whom his majority relied did not allow it more than token parliamentary progress.

The governments of the 1902 parliament were governed by the so-called *bloc des gauches*, the offspring of Waldeck-Rousseau's cabinet of Republican defense of 1899. This parliamentary coalition was only nominally either a bloc or a leftist movement. Party identities and loyalties in this period were too loose for the bloc to be more than an electoral organization ensuring a centrist or leftist victory in close contests with right-wing candidates. On the political spectrum the bloc ran from the Socialists on the left, through radical socialism and radicalism, to the Alliance démocratique on the right. But most cabinets from 1902 to 1906 included a large component of Radicals and "Progressists" or members of the Alliance, so egalitarian legislation was effectively excluded. So long as the bloc's principal concern was to limit the power of its putative foes in the Affair—the Catholic church and the officer corps—the parliamentary coalition remained viable. Once "victory" over these ancient enemies of the Republic was achieved, however, the centrifugal forces within the bloc were gradually unleashed.

Madeleine Rébérioux marks the death of the bloc in parliament with the confirmation vote of the Rouvier ministry of January 1906.[38] Rouvier, an opponent of the income tax and a member of the Alliance démocratique, made his appeal for office in the familiar terms of Republican solidarity behind the separation law, just voted in December and not yet effectively implemented. One hundred fifty-four Socialists and Radical Socialists withheld their votes, and a full half of the votes of confidence came from the right and from the "dissident" Radicals who had parted company with the bloc much earlier. The business of elections was at hand, and the bloc was revived long enough to present closed ranks at the polls, though, as Goguel points out, without any positive legislative program, and for the Radicals, "less from conviction than out of a desire to be elected."[39] The cabinet that fought the elections was led by the Radical Sarrien and heralded Georges Clemenceau's first appearance in power at the Ministry of the Interior.

The elections were a huge success for the left-wing segment of the ailing bloc. Sixty seats were lost by the Monarchist, Ralliée, and Nationalist parties, and some visible dissident Radicals lost their seats. The Nationalist movement, which had won city council seats in Paris in 1900, and parliamentary seats in 1902, was nearly completely liquidated.[40] The big winners were the Radical-Socialists, now the largest group in the Chamber with 132 seats. The socialist SFIO (Section française de l'internationale ouvrière), running for the first time on a unified parliamentary platform, increased its number of seats to fifty-nine; its potential for legislative pressure in the leftist drift increased

[38] Rébérioux, *La République radicale*, pp. 106-108.
[39] François Goguel, *La politique des partis dans la IIIᵉ République*, 3d ed. (Paris: Editions du Seuil, 1958), p. 129.
[40] On the short-lived career of the Nationalist movement see D. R. Watson, "The Nationalist Movement in Paris, 1900-1906," in David Shapiro, ed., *The Right in France, 1890-1919* Saint Antony's Papers, no. 13 (Carbondale: Southern Illinois University Press, 1962), pp. 49-84.

dramatically. If a common legislative program could be found, Radicals, Radical-Socialists, and Socialists had the votes to rule alone for the first time in the history of the Third Republic.

The Sarrien cabinet reintroduced the income tax in the reopening of the new session in June, and in July presided over the passage of the obligatory day of rest, long a Radical and Radical-Socialist objective. In October the ill Sarrien presented his resignation and suggested Clemenceau as his successor. In *L'humanité* Jaurès lent the support of the extreme left, confident that a Radical-Socialist legislative program would be passed that would lead the nation into the "foyer" of socialism. Clemenceau promptly dropped the members of the Alliance démocratique who had been his colleagues in the Sarrien ministry, Raymond Poincaré, Eugène Etienne, Georges Leygues, Louis Barthou, and the old Radical Emile Bourgeois. They were replaced by loyal Radicals and Radical-Socialists, among them Guyot-Dessaigne at Justice, Joseph Caillaux, a proponent of the income tax, at Finances, the martyred Picquart at the War Ministry, and Clemenceau's intimate, Stephen Pichon, in the Foreign Ministry. A new Ministry of Labor, created as a reward for the burgeoning left, was filled by the former executive administrator of the SFIO, René Viviani. "Would an era of hegemonic radicalism," asks Rébérioux, "supported by the Alliance démocratique, succeed that of the bloc?"[41]

Clemenceau's legislative program was announced in November 1906.[42] It included nationalization of the failing Western Railway, workers' pensions, the income tax, an injury compensation scheme, the ten-hour day, the vow to continue the work of separation in the schools, and the abolition of the death penalty. The program was the most daring ever introduced by a ministry in modern French history, and, despite the partial and relatively timid nature of some of the proposals, was met by a storm of vituperation from the press of the center and right. As Malcolm Anderson has written, "although the practical effects of the old-age pensions, nationalization of the Western Railway and income tax were small, the principles on which they were based were important—the redistribution of wealth, the right of the state to take over sections of the economy, and progressive taxation."[43] These measures, sponsored by a Republican regime that had for nearly thirty years displayed anticlericalism, secular education, and a self-serving doctrine

[41] Rébérioux, *La République radicale*, p. 110.

[42] For the published program see the *Revue politique et parlementaire* (December 1906), pp. 604-608.

[43] Malcolm Anderson, *Conservative Politics in France* (London: Allen and Unwin, 1974), p. 44.

"What are you complaining about, bourgeois? . . . Caillaux will take much more! . . ."   by Jean-Louis Forain, *Le Figaro*, March 4, 1907

of parliamentary sovereignty as its most progressive features, symbolized an apparently decisive break with the past.

Placed among all these epochal issues, the abolition proposal did not attract much initial comment, though at the very least one would have imagined the humanitarian rhetoric of the proposal to have been a red flag to the journalistic watchdogs of the right. As quoted in the *Gazette des tribunaux*, the language of the official bill seems a curious survival of the liberalism of the July Monarchy. Capital punishment was alleged to be "an unjustifiable cruelty, a survival of the past, and the last bloody trace of the law of an eye for an eye." France must, it continued, put itself in step with "the progress of customs and the evolution of science."[44] The editors of the *Gazette*, who could in general be assumed to speak in the interests of the French magistracy and public prosecutors, echoed the sentiments of the government in their editorial. Thus, while they acknowledged that there would be some public criticism, the time for the nation to be an example to humanity had come. France could no longer tolerate the contradiction of "society

[44] *Gazette des tribunaux*, November 10, 1906.

189

itself assaulting human life, while nonetheless proclaiming its intangible and sacred character."[45]

In these first responses it was not unusual for commentators to appeal to both humanitarianism and science as twin justifications for abolition. Stéfane-Pol's confident article "The End of the Death Penalty" claimed that abolition not only had the support of all criminologists but was squarely in the French humanist tradition.[46] Within the criminological community, Dr. F. F. Falco cited the new "respect for the person of the criminal" as the germ of penitentiary science in the nineteenth century and the foundation of abolitionism.[47] The association of science with human progress was an important feature of the debate of 1906-1908 and was uttered without embarrassment by public figures of the greatest importance. But, as we shall see, this association did not inspire the confidence it had in earlier years; it had a defensive and timid posture that would have seemed unfamiliar to a crusader of the 1820s like Charles Lucas.[48] By the turn of the century, the confident alliance of science and humanity that had prospered through much of the century, which had been the midwife of the Republic and the inspiration for countless reforms, was deeply troubled. A parting of the ways was at hand.

In 1906, however, evidence for this dénouement was scarcely visible. Indeed, in 1906 the gross statistics of crime and violence were usually read in an optimistic light. As we have seen, there were some disturbing long-term trends in theft, and for cases of minor assault tried in the correctional Courts. In the decade 1875-1884 an average of 24,611 cases were tried yearly on this charge; in the decade 1895-1904 this increased to 35,655 per year.[49] However, if we recall the 9 percent drop in first-degree murder in the nineteenth century, and consider

[45] Ibid., November 11, 1906.

[46] Stéfane-Pol, "La fin de la peine de mort," *La grande revue* 39 (September 1, 1906), pp. 456-462.

[47] F. F. Falco, "Origine de l'organisation pénitentiaire internationale," *Bulletin de la Société générale des prisons* 31 (January 1907), pp. 144-146.

[48] Paul Savey-Casard identifies the high-water mark of abolitionism as the period 1810-1870. After 1870 "the partisans of the scaffold raised their heads, proposed new arguments, discovered new horizons; they spoke of elimination and selection. And public opinion, instead of evolving in a progressive direction, as one might have anticipated, ceased to respond to proposed reforms as it had done a century earlier." *La peine de mort*, p. 109. Another contemporary observer, Emile Durkheim, discerned a clear trend in the diminution of the "intensity" and "violence" of punishments in 1901. See "Deux lois de l'évolution pénale," *L'année sociologique* 4 (1901), pp. 65-95.

[49] My figures from "Résumé rétrospectif," *Compte générale de l'administration de la justice criminelle* 52 (1936), pp. 47-48.

that the decade 1885-1894 averaged 512.8 homicides a year and the one ending in 1905 just 460, we can see there was some basis for optimistic assessments.[50]

The Justice Ministry's official statistician, Maurice Yvernès, reporting on trends through 1906, wrote that in general crime was losing its violent and "archaic character" and was taking on more of the aspects of ruse and cunning typical of "civilized" societies. He chose to characterize the gross crime statistics just reviewed as displaying a growth of "petty criminality" and a decrease of "serious criminality."[51] In their extended survey of 1906, Etienne Martin and Alexandre Lacassagne also remarked on the relative decline of violent crimes in past decades. They based this assessment on the figures from crimes actually tried, figures that were much more favorable to an optimistic reading than those for unindicted cases, which were nearly five times as numerous.[52] They also saw reason for optimism in the figures on recidivism, the great issue of the 1880s, where some notable declines in rates were occurring.[53] However, they did remark at great length on what they took to be serious if slightly less visible problems of "voluptuous criminality," in particular pornography and other crimes offensive to public morality.

Lacassagne, who had led the fight against Lombrosian determinism in the 1880s, was still an optimist in 1906. Now the most influential figure in French criminology, Lacassagne was still convinced that the reshaping of "degenerate" environments was the best way to deal with crime.[54] He had adopted the concept of "social defense" to justify the isolation of "incorrigible" or "dangerous" criminals who were unameliorable, but social defense also included the ideals of education and ambitious social engineering, so his views had not dramatically altered since his days on the barricades against Lombroso.

[50] My figures from ibid., p. 46.

[51] Maurice Yvernès, "Statistique criminelle," *Journal de la Société de statistique de Paris* 48 (October, November, December 1907), pp. 330-343, 370-379, 403-409. Quotations from pp. 408-409.

[52] Alexandre Lacassagne and Etienne Martin, "Les données de la statistique criminelle," *L'année psychologique* 12 (1906), pp. 465-468.

[53] The figures for the appearance of recidivists in the court were indeed strikingly improved. In the assizes courts, recidivists convicted of new crimes fell from an average of 1,673 in the decade 1875-1884 to 1,292 in the decade ending in 1904. In the correctional tribunals the numbers had fallen to the 80,000 per year range in the five years 1900-1904 from highs above 100,000 per year in the early 1890s. My figures from the "Résumé rétrospectif" in the *Compte générale de l'administration de la justice criminelle* 52 (1936), pp. 46-48.

[54] Lacassagne and Martin, "Les données de la statistique criminelle," pp. 470-476.

More to the point, Lacassagne denied that penal repression was an effective mode of social defense. He quoted with approval the remarks of the minister of justice in his annual report of 1905 to the effect that the general diminution of criminality was all the more remarkable for coming at a time when there was "a general tendency toward the softening of punishment. One may rightfully attribute this tendency to the moralizing action of our more enlightened reforms in the penal code, as well as the various welfare institutions which have improved the material well-being of our population."[55] Even more germane to our topic, he and Martin concluded their essay by denying the deterrent virtue of capital punishment with a quotation attributed to Voltaire: "An executed man is no good to anyone."[56]

Yet, when the statistics on violent crime for the year 1905 were released they may have given pause to even the most optimistic observers. One year does not constitute a trend, so little was made of the fact that first-degree homicides had increased from 512 in 1904 to 597. There had been yearly variations nearly as large before: for instance the leap from 494 to 553 between 1888 and 1889, a year of political turmoil. But these figures had not excited comment at those times, nor did they in 1906. The close observer may have found other cause for alarm, however. The figure 597 was the highest since the "hungry forties" nearly three-quarters of a century earlier. It followed a decade, as we have seen, when only two of ten years exceeded 500, and one year, 1901, fell as low as 390, the smallest total since the war year of 1870.[57]

What is more, assaults resulting in serious injury or death (tried before the assizes courts) in 1905 jumped to 228, the highest figure since 1869, and only the second year above 200 in that category since 1885. Assaults with less serious consequences were also up slightly in 1905 to 35,796, the highest figure since 1900. Contemporaries could not know it yet, but the period beginning just after the turn of the century, excluding the war years, and continuing until 1922 was one of upward bulge in the number of homicides. From 1905 to 1914 homicides averaged 613 a year, contrasted to 460 a year in the previous decade. They then fell to more "normal" figures after the demobilization years. This upward movement in homicides cannot be accounted for by better policing, new statistical procedures, a change in the criminal code, or any of the other explanations that sometimes apply in

[55] Ibid., p. 468.

[56] Ibid., p. 476. The more likely origin is Rousseau's *Social Contract*, Book II, Chap. V.

[57] "Résumé rétrospectif," *Compte générale de l'administration de la justice criminelle* 52 (1936), p. 46.

connection with other crimes. Homicide, as all commentators agree, is the least affected by secondary influences of all crimes, the most often reported, investigated, prosecuted, and convicted. In this area alone the published judicial statistics are fairly good sources for real crime rates.

Howard Zehr has cited this slight upward trend without explaining it, and notes, in addition, that a similar trend occurred in the German homicide rate at about the same time. Since the rate in France fell after 1922 to pre-1905 rates, it might be more accurate to call this bulge, in Zehr's words, "an unusual cycle in homicide" rather than a trend.[58] Although it might be too much to say that a special effort to locate the causes of this cycle should be made, the simultaneous rise in the rates in Germany suggests the possibility that similar forces were at work and invites a comparative study. Certainly the decade 1905-1914 was a tumultuous one in France with a high rate of strike activity and several violent confrontations between strikers and the forces of order. But, the confrontations aside, the strike rates were not appreciably different from the previous decade. The years 1903-1908 were years of especially high strike "intensity," in Michelle Perrot's usage, but after 1908 when the intensity of strikes declined, the homicide rate stayed up.[59]

Emile Durkheim, ever a careful observer of social pathologies, had some interesting things to say about homicide in his Sorbonne lectures of this period.[60] Since homicide was "a crime of irreflection, of spontaneous fear, and of impulsiveness," murder rates tended to rise during wars and political crises when collective passions were running high.[61] Durkheim adhered to the biologists' linear scale of normal to pathological; thus "immorality is not the simple contrary of morality any more than sickness is the opposite of health; both the one and the other are merely different forms of the same state, the two forms of moral life, and the two forms of physical life."[62] By the same token, the intensity with which society reacts to murder also varies proportionally with the "level of passion" in the "collective consciousness." Durkheim stressed the dialectical nature of this response by the social

---

[58] Zehr, *Crime and the Development of Modern Society*, p. 115. Zehr also notes an increase in crimes against persons at the end of the century, pp. 84-137; McHale and Johnson see this trend peaking in the decade 1896-1905. McHale and Johnson, "Urbanization, Industrialization, and Crime in Imperial Germany," pp. 211-215.

[59] Perrot, *Les ouvriers en grève*, vol. 1, p. 51.

[60] Emile Durkheim, *Leçons de sociologie: Physique des moeurs et du droit* (Paris: Presses Universitaires de France, 1950); Lukes, *Emile Durkheim*, p. 263, n. 46. Published only in 1950, these lectures were composed and revised between 1903 and 1916.

[61] Durkheim, *Leçons de sociologie*, pp. 140-141.

[62] Ibid., p. 141.

organism, arguing that vengeance and pity were inversely related: each, in its most extreme expression, necessarily excluded the other.[63] It seems likely that Durkheim, when he formulated this idea, had the social turbulence and wild pendulum swings of opinion of this era very much in mind.

Such speculative accounts do not, however, take us very far, suggestive though they may be. It was Durkheim's conception that the social organism's "reaction" to the violent crime of murder is like a primitive reflex (indeed it *is* a primitive reflex), unmediated by the rich plenitude of social life. It is only when one reduces one's focus to the fine grain of contemporary events that one encounters the symbols, the stereotypes, and the information processes that channeled the sentiments of middle-class rage and fear in precise directions. No one thinks about violence in the abstract. Any historical society shapes conceptions of its objects of fear out of images presented by everyday culture; it uses these images as a kind of shorthand, until, by degrees, the images come to symbolize violence itself, collapsing metaphor into sign. One of the images to conjure with from 1907 to 1909 was the name Albert Soleilland. The story of his brutal crime is a useful way to introduce this period.

The Erbeldings were middle-aged Alsatian immigrants who had lived in the capital long enough to regard themselves as Parisians. Erbelding *père* was a skilled engraver; he and his wife and five children lived in the rue Saint Maur in the eleventh *arrondissement* of the city's east side. Nearby in the rue de Charonne lived a friend of the family, Albert Soleilland, his wife of two years, and their infant son. In January 1907 Soleilland was in his mid-twenties, about the same age as the eldest Erbelding son, and was working as a part-time day laborer. He had apprenticed himself for a while to Erbelding as an engraver but had given it up the previous year on account of unsatisfactory progress. He seemed content to live largely on his wife's earnings as a clerk in a corset shop. Soleilland did not adjust well to having so much free time, however. A minor theft was traced back to him, and he was scheduled to appear in correctional court in February.

He had taken to spending his time with the Erbeldings and seemed to have a special fondness for their youngest child, eleven-year-old Marthe. Mme. Erbelding allowed Albert to walk her daughter in the neighborhood or escort her to popular entertainments in the quarter. One day near the end of January Albert offered to walk Marthe to a *caf'-conc'* in the late afternoon. As he told it, he left her briefly to run an errand and could not find her when he returned. Since he seemed terribly distraught, there was no reason to assume that he had any role in the girl's disappearance; he cooperated in every way with the search. Finally, on February 9, after nearly two harrowing weeks, the family learned that Marthe's body had been found at the baggage *consigne* of the Gare de l'Est. The shock and horror of the Erbeldings were deepened when they learned that Albert Soleilland had led the police to the corpse and admitted to the killing.

As was the rule in violent crimes, the Paris press devoted bold headlines to the affair and faithfully reported the grisly details to its readers. Press coverage was led by the *Petit Parisien*, which alleged on the ninth that Soleilland was a "satyr" who had killed this "little girl" in "a sadistic fury."[64] Two days later the papers reported the results of the official autopsy. The staid *Gazette des tribunaux* contented itself with saying that the girl had been violated in the "most odious" fashion imaginable,[65] but the *Petit Parisien* and most of the rest of the popular press offered their readers all the details. The immediate cause of death was an incision from ear to ear in the girl's throat, though the body bore the marks of multiple knife wounds. But she had also been raped, her genitals had been mutilated, and she had been partly eviscerated.[66]

Albert, who had babbled incoherently from the moment of his first confession, appeared before a *juge d'instruction* on the twelfth; in the presence of an intent crowd of journalists, he gave his own version of the events. He admitted taking her to his apartment and caressing her in a way that exceeded previous familiarities. When she objected and screamed, "I lost my wits and mechanically cut her throat." He claimed that he then lost consciousness, and when he awoke, took her body in a large canvas sack to the Gare de l'Est. He denied having raped her or making other lascerations on her body, averring that someone else must have done it while he was unconscious.[67]

The day before Soleilland's court appearance the *Petit Parisien* printed an interview with a "famous psychiatrist" about the likelihood of an insanity plea by Soleilland's court-appointed lawyer. The unnamed doctor was reluctant to commit himself positively on the precise nature of Soleilland's mental condition, but opined that the very extremity of the act suggested the presence of "what one calls vulgarly an erotic insanity." He cautioned, however, that this was not madness "in the exact sense of the word." On the same day the alienist's interview

[64] *Petit Parisien*, February 9, 1907.
[65] *Gazette des tribunaux*, February 11, 1907.
[66] *Petit Parisien*, February 11, 1907.
[67] Ibid., February 13, 1907.

appeared, the paper hinted darkly that indignant crowds would apply the "lynch law" if the state did not do its duty. The paper's position on the matter of an insanity plea was unambiguous: "The theoreticians who speak of the physical degeneracy of murderers forget that when one kills a rabid dog, one does so to prevent him from biting."[68]

In the popular presentation of this gruesome crime, a scenario was enacted in which violent crime was treated not from on high, as an abstract question on the justice of the scaffold, but from below, out of the simpler justice of the life of the streets. First a violent crime was presented in lurid detail by the mass press with a mixture of fascination and disgust. Next, an expert medical witness's comments on the psychological state of the murderer were subjected to the journalist's disdain. Finally, there came a direct threat of popular intervention if the criminal was not dealt with in an appropriate way. In general, the crime of Soleilland was treated with an impatience and indignation that were unusual even for this period of yellow journalism. As we shall later see, public outrage reverberated for well over a year after Soleilland's own fate had been decided. The contemporary fame of the "satyr," as he came to be known, grew until this pathetic young man became the equal of such criminal luminaries as Cartouche, Lacenaire, and the infamous Troppmann, without achieving, significantly, the romantic allure that surrounded their names. Convicted, but pardoned by "father pardon" Fallières, Soleilland spent the rest of his short life at hard labor in Guyana, more remembered as a symbol of judicial leniency than as a paragon of ferocity.

Like the name Soleilland, the word "apache" became a word to conjure with. But even more than the rapist-killer of the rue de Charonne, the dreaded apaches achieved a mythic status that cut across class, political, and educational lines to become a universally recognized sign of random terror and violence. The Soleillands of the world, who preyed on little girls, threatened the peace and inner security of the family and haunted the dreams of anxious parents. But the apaches threatened everyone, young and old alike. And where the Soleillands were rare, the apaches were ubiquitous. First identified in Paris, they spread to the countryside; there was not a provincial town that did not have its apaches, nor the simplest peasant who had not heard of their terrible deeds. They became in France in our period the sign and symptom of wanton cruelty, disorder, and unpredictability. Who were these apaches? How did they win their reputation for cruelty?

To begin with the name, French knowledge of American Indians

[68] Ibid., February 12, 1907.

was limited to the novels and romances about the American wilderness, which were a staple part of the literary diet of the European reading publics. The French had no equivalent of the German Karl May, whose novels captivated the central European bourgeoisie in the last third of the nineteenth century; most French fiction about American Indians came from translations of American and English classics, from James Fenimore Cooper and the Scot Henry Mayne-Reid. The Indian subject matter of such novels followed, in the course of the century, the western expansion of the American frontier. The Mohicans and Iroquois, the Indians Europeans encountered in the first half of the century, were gradually replaced by Sioux, Blackfeet, Crow, Pawnee, and other Plains Indians of the West. These redoubtable horse warriors engaged in bloody internecine strife, took hostages, and claimed the scalps of opponents defeated in battle or individual combat. Of the last subdued tribes, the Apaches resisted the white man's presence most fiercely. The last battles of the Apache wars of the 1890s were the stuff of which adventure fiction is made, and a generation of European readers eagerly followed this last stand of indigenous Americans. Of all the American Indians, wrote the French journalist Paul Matter, "the bloodiest, the cruelest, and the most terrifying were the Apaches."[69]

As was true of so much of *belle époque* popular culture, the happy inspiration to borrow the name of this fierce tribe came from a journalist, Arthur Dupin, who covered crime for the mass circulation paper *Le journal*. In the first half of 1902 Dupin chronicled in his paper the story of a rivalry between two street gangs of the eastern Paris suburbs. His columns revealed that these gangs possessed a whole culture—language, dress, customs—redolent of gypsy bands or the warring clans of Corsica. To his good fortune Dupin found that at issue between the leaders of two rival gangs were the affections of a strikingly statuesque woman who wore her mass of blond hair piled in soft layers. Thus was born the legend of the *"casque d'or"* for whom men were killed and pitched battles fought in a kind of atavistic resemblance to the dark side of chivalric courtly love, or so Dupin's romanticized accounts pictured the events.[70] Dupin invented the term "apache" for the members

[69] Paul Matter, "Chez les apaches," *Revue politique et littéraire*, 5th ser. 8 (November 16, 1907), p. 626.

[70] Read Dupin's accounts in *Le journal* of the "apache wars" between January and December of 1907, when one of the principals in the wars was brought to trial for murder. See also Armand Laroux, "La vraie casque d'Or" in Gilbert Guilleminault, ed., *La belle époque* (Paris: Denoël, 1958), pp. 73-118. The "casque d'or" affair has had some survivals. A film, *Le casque d'or*, starring Simone Signoret, and based on the incident, was made in 1952. The apache dance, purportedly a wild love-venge-

APACHE HISTORY

"Love you, Gontran? . . . but you do not seem to me very . . . substantial."

"You understand your roles?"
"Yes, boss!"

"Your money or your life!!!"

"Ffutt!"

"Do I appear to be substantial now?"

"Oh, yes!"

by Sardena, *Gil Blas*, February 27, 1903, p. 4

of these groups as he learned more and more of their violent mores and extralegal means of self-support. What began as a popular romantic epic ended in an acutely heightened sense of the grave danger presented by these suburban marauders.

Who were the apaches? It seems certain enough that Dupin and the other journalists who wrote of their exploits were not inventing these exotic beings from whole cloth. Apaches were the product of a crisis in the demographic and social history of the capital similar to the one chronicled for the first half of the century by Louis Chevalier. The overcrowding, lack of sanitation, and inadequate water supplies in the old *arrondissements* of Paris during the period of rapid growth from 1800 to 1850 began in the 1870s to affect the working-class *arrondissements* on the northern and eastern part of the city and the ring of tiny villages that lay just beyond the walls. The period 1880-1914 was the great period of industrial expansion in this zone, and the population grew apace. As had been true of the center city in the 1840s, a grave housing crisis developed in the working-class districts. An inquiry of 1912 revealed that of 2,900,000 Parisians only half were well housed; 1,000,000 lived in "insufficient" space, and 300,000 lived in quarters in which at least one family was confined to a single room. At least 45 percent of those most poorly housed lived in the new suburbs.[71] Water, electricity, sanitation, schooling, and other amenities also arrived too little and too late to improve the living standard before 1914. The greatest growth in the density of these areas followed the economic boom that ran from 1896 to 1914.[72]

As they had in the 1830s and 1840s, the insalubrious living conditions of the new quarters attracted the attention of concerned social statisticians and philanthropists. Studies conducted by the Academy of Sciences, the Musée social, and other groups showed a mortality rate 30 percent higher than the central *arrondissements*. A cholera epidemic that carried off a thousand Parisians in 1892 took a full one-third of that number from three *arrondissements*, the eighteenth, nineteenth, and twentieth.[73] In a preface to O. Dumesnil's book of 1890 on work-

---

ance dance done in Belleville-Charonne cabarets in 1900, has been a standard of popular dance routines ever since. See also Michelle Perrot's useful account of the origins of the "apaches" in "Dans la France de la belle époque, les Apaches, premières bandes des jeunes," *Les marginaux et les exclus dans l'histoire* (Paris: Union générale d'éditions, 1979), pp. 387-407.

[71] Sorlin, *La société française*, p. 124.

[72] Jean Bastié, *La croissance de la banlieue parisienne* (Paris: Presses Universitaires de France, 1964), pp. 188-199. Rents in these new districts increased 15 to 20 percent faster than the cost of living, especially from 1905 to 1914.

[73] Sorlin, *La société française*, p. 124.

ing-class housing, Jules Simon wrote: "Society is in a state of war against the plague. I am speaking about a permanent plague that the various types, cholera, smallpox, influenza, aggravate from time to time."[74] The gross social effects of this situation also figured heavily in arguments for some kind of amelioration. A new law being debated in the Chamber in 1908 to provide state guarantees for private building loans in the afflicted areas provided the supporting argument that it would reduce "promiscuity, tuberculosis, and alcoholism."[75] The age and sex structure of the new suburbs also changed markedly. In the growing suburban town of Ivry, less than one-fourth of the inhabitants were over forty years old and males heavily outnumbered females. In addition, in 1882 26 percent of the population could not read or write.[76] Nor were these problems unique to Paris. Most of the great provincial towns, led by Marseille, also experienced overcrowding and bad sanitation. Epidemics struck the growing suburbs of these towns as hard as those of Paris.

Most of the inhabitants of the new suburbs were immigrants from the French countryside, but a sizable portion came from demographically more fertile neighbors to the south, Italy, Spain, and Corsica. Indeed, it was a favorite theory of the Parisian journalists that the gang warfare and ritual vendettas that were common to apache mores were manifestations of the violent customs in their countries of origin. But one does not need such theories to account for the violent patterns of criminal behavior in the new suburbs. The populations of these areas were relatively poor, lived in overcrowded conditions, were under-employed, and were predominantly young and male. The fact that many of these suburbanites were recent arrivals from relatively underdeveloped countries or regions of France simply underscored their differences from the more stable populations of the central city, encouraging stereotyping and casual generalization. When the number and intensity of strikes began to rise dramatically in the late 1890s, a large share of them took place in the recently industrialized suburbs. The classical nineteenth-century strike, centered in the industrial regions of the northeast or the Midi, had been a geographically remote affair for most French city-dwellers. But in 1906 strike activity in the Paris suburbs, which involved 29 percent of all strikers in that year, overshadowed that in the provinces.[77] The Paris suburbs of Villeneuve-

[74] Quoted in Bastié, *La croissance de la banlieue parisienne*, p. 192.
[75] Ibid., p. 193.
[76] Sorlin, *La société française*, p. 116.
[77] Tilly and Shorter, *Strikes in France*, p. 120.

Saint Georges and Draveil-Vigneux were the hot spots of strike activity and confrontation throughout 1907 and 1908. Thus, there were multiple reasons for city dwellers, particularly Parisians, to fear the outlying districts of their towns. They appeared to be governed by criminal violence or its labor equivalent, direct action, and had become, in Michelle Perrot's words, "the failure of urban history, and the terror of the middle class."[78]

The code word for all the threatening activity that pullulated in the suburbs of French cities in our period was "apache." Journalists wrote that the "apaches are kings" of the suburbs[79] or exclaimed with wonder that a broken-hearted young lover who had gone walking at night in the sinister districts of the capital to commit "apache suicide" had failed to find an obliging murderer.[80] Apaches were seen in the outskirts of Toulouse,[81] in Marseille,[82] in Lille,[83] and in Lyon,[84] and provincial papers carried detailed stories of the deeds of the Parisian apaches. In Paris it made good copy for journalists to cover the exploits and customs of apaches in these years.

In 1907 Paul Matter accompanied a squad of the "mobile brigade" into the suburbs on one of its nightly raids of *bal musettes* frequented by apaches. The young apaches were summarily rounded up, taken to the nearest police station, searched for weapons, and checked for violation of parole. Lacking cause for either of these offenses they were simply booked as vagrants.[85] Matter emphasized their vulgar behavior and drunkenness, their greasy hair, the outmoded gallantry of their dress. He noted that "in all of them, what is most striking is their glance, which is angry and false, cowardly and cruel, cynical and full of hate, a clear reflection of their souls."[86]

The very popular literary review *Lectures pour tous* went to the effort of hiring several rough-looking characters and a photographer to obtain some "typical" events in the lives of apaches for its article on youth and suburban crime: there are apaches standing around a campfire

[78] Perrot, *Les ouvriers en grève*, vol. 1, p. 220.

[79] Jean Frollo, "L'apache-roi," *Petit Parisien*, April 7, 1907.

[80] Albert Delvallé, "L'homme qui n'a pas vu d'apaches," *Le petit journal*, July 19, 1908.

[81] "Nos apaches" and "Histoires d'apaches" in *Dépêche de Toulouse*, August 6, 7, 1908.

[82] *Le petit Provençal*, July 4, 1908 and *Le petit Marseillais*, July 4, 1908.

[83] *L'echo du nord*, November 4, 1908.

[84] *Le progrès de Lyon*, July 2, 1908.

[85] Matter, "Chez les apaches," p. 628.

[86] Ibid.

drinking, with pistols and knives at their belts; there are two sinister youths waiting in ambush for a victim on a deserted street corner; there is a night debauche in a *bal musette*; there are two men fighting with knives; and there is a staged photograph of a band of armed men attacking a merchant in his wagon. The text of the story emphasized the "barbaric cruelty" of their lives, their prison records, and the elaborate initiation rites of the apache bands: to join one had to kill a member of an enemy "tribe" in combat, kill a *sergent de ville*, or perform some other heinous deed worthy of the group's respect. Leaders of the groups, according to *Lectures pour tous*, had to meet four conditions: they must have spent "three years in prison, know how to work the streets, speak argot in three languages, and kill for a friend."[87]

Provoked by the endless tales of apache exploits and the senseless crime of Albert Soleilland, even the staid *Gazette des tribuneaux*, so sanguine a year before about violent crime, began to note a change in the atmosphere. The criminal statistics for 1906 indicated that crime was "on the rise, or was at the very least of a much more audacious variety."[88] The editors of the *Gazette* also praised unstintingly the efforts of the purity crusader René Bérenger in his war to crush pornography and "cleanse the streets," proclaiming that "ministers, senators, deputies, magistrates, newspapers, citizens, virtually everyone is in agreement with his efforts."[89] Significantly, they also resorted to the imagery of national solidarity and social defense in their preachments about the electrical workers' strike of early March 1907: "In the national community and, to speak in a more limited manner, the city, all functions are in some sense unified, and the principle that must regulate them is that of respect for the carrying out of those agreements [that are] the axis of all social life."[90] This constellation of arguments was repeated with far greater force and effectiveness between 1907 and 1908 in the mass circulation press, which succeeded in making an issue of Soleilland and his banally violent crime, and turning the emphasis on *apachisme* from the romance of courtship habits to the real fear it posed to a settled and "normal" life.

It is difficult for us today to appreciate fully the great influence that newspaper culture played in *belle époque* life. Television allows us to be visually present at a news event and to be presented with the opinions of the participants in their expressive and gestural context, and it is

[87] "Les conscrits du crime," *Lectures pour tous* 10 (July 1908), pp. 831-832, 835-837.

[88] *Gazette des tribunaux*, March 3, 1907.

[89] Ibid., February 24, 1907.

[90] Ibid., March 15, 1907.

possible to underestimate the role the print media could play in the formation of opinions and attitudes. The press in our period was at a unique intersection of its history. By the turn of the century the last pockets of illiteracy were being eliminated, and direct access to print was possible where only an oral culture had once flourished. Still, before 1914 none of the modern image media—cinema, radio, television—had emerged to challenge the supremacy of the printed word, and the journalist had nearly absolute sway.[91]

In the first half of the century newspapers were a phenomenon of the large towns. Although they did sometimes penetrate to the countryside, where they were passed from hand to hand or read aloud in the village tavern, they usually contained only political news. The great events of the day reached the countryside tardily and usually by word of mouth. By the 1870s, however, the new mass circulation daily had joined political and popular sources of information into one format, revolutionizing the manner in which news was presented. The press revolution followed the contours of the literacy explosion, spreading from town to countryside with astonishing speed and relentless thoroughness.

The ultimate source of the flow of information was the capital. In 1905 Paris had two major dailies with weekly supplements, the *Petit Parisien* and the *Petit journal*, with more than a million daily readers. By 1911 80 percent of the daily printing of the *Petit journal* went to the provinces as did 65 percent of the *Petit Parisien*. The invasion of the rural domain was so complete that a priest complained that the "*Petit Parisien* is the holy scripture of the countryside."[92] The major provincial papers also underwent a notable increase in readership between 1890 and 1914, and some of the larger towns—Marseille, Lyon, Lille—had by 1900 a range of political opinion to rival Paris. Still, most news was generated in Paris or filtered through Paris sources. In this period news gathering was still primitive. News agencies like Havas were still embryonic by modern standards, and only a few of the big Paris dailies maintained foreign correspondents. Provincial dailies, with the exception of the *Dépêche de Toulouse*, relied on the Parisian press of similar political outlook for their news releases, as did many of the

---

[91] Pierre Albert, et al., eds., *Histoire générale de la presse française* (Paris: Presses Universitaires de France, 1967) vol. 3, p. 244. As Pierre Guirol has written, "what is more: in the countryside, where for many reading was neither a need nor a habit, the daily paper or the weekly is more than a form of privileged culture; it is the only form of culture." "Présentation, problèmes d'histoire de la presse," *Revue d'histoire moderne et contemporaine* 18 (1971), p. 485.

[92] Quoted in Weber, *Peasants into Frenchmen*, p. 470.

lesser Paris papers.[93] News in *belle époque* France consisted of a few central shouts and hundreds of echoes.

Eugen Weber has described how this remarkably centralized apparatus managed to rapidly supplant the traditional and popular sources of information in the countryside. The almanacs, little volumes of the *bibliothèque bleu*, and *canards*, which had nourished provincial curiosity since medieval times and made the book peddler a familiar sight on rural roads, were replaced by the illustrated supplements and serialized novels in the Paris dailies.[94] If format changed, however, content remained the same. The heavy emphasis on the lives of the saints and other subjects dear to Catholic popular culture had disappeared, but other subjects equally dear and no less miraculous were served up in generous portions. These subjects touched on themes that had deep roots in rural France and thus for recent emigrants to the cities. Weber has graphically described some of the themes he found in the *canards* that were continued, in slightly altered appearance, in the mass papers: "Greed for the money that middle-class victims of crime had carried or concealed; the suspicion of all strangers and of travelers, who have good cause to fear for their lives themselves; . . . the venting of collective fury on some victim; the murder of children by parents and of parents by children; gang rapes; innocence condemned and sometimes saved; . . . Most country crimes took place in the mountains and woods; but from these accounts the roads and inns were no safer. Above all, fear, fear, fear: of brigands, thieves, rape, fire, hail, floods, rabies, epidemics, violence of all sorts."[95]

Georg Simmel has written eloquently about the origins of modern journalism and the dialectical relationship between the journalist and his audience;[96] there is no reason to doubt that the phenomenal growth of newspaper circulation was a consequence of the journalist's knowledge of his public, in large part only a generation or two removed from illiteracy. Another factor made the dialectic one of mutual influence. Even with their pathetically small staffs, the big dailies realized small profits as they cut their prices and advertising fees to drive up subscriptions and drive out competitors. But rivalry was so fierce between the big Paris dailies that they began the first experiments in

[93] Janine Ponty, "La presse quotidienne et l'affaire Dreyfus en 1898-1899: Essai de typologie," *Revue d'histoire moderne et contemporaine* 21 (1974), p. 213.

[94] Weber, *Peasants into Frenchmen*, pp. 463-466.

[95] Ibid., p. 460.

[96] As Simmel wrote, the journalist directs opinions, "but he is nevertheless forced to listen, combine, and guess what the tendencies of the multitude are." *The Sociology of Georg Simmel* (Glencoe, Ill.: Free Press, 1950), pp. 185-186.

creating news that we have come to know so well as the media event. Sports events were approaching the top of the list, this period standing at the beginning of the time sport would become the "opium of the masses" rather than a pastime for the leisure classes. Each paper offered a prize for the automobile, bicycle, airplane, and balloon races it had promoted and promised its readers "exclusive" interviews and coverage. On the day of a big race front-page banner headlines screamed out the victor and the number of dead and injured (the races were dangerous affairs), and featured a retouched photograph of driver and vehicle. It is a generally unchronicled and unappreciated fact that between 1900 and 1914 mass national sports audiences were created by the efforts of a handful of enterprising organizers and writers.

Sports were a new topic for exploration, but the mass press also had other, more traditional subjects to feed to its voracious readers. Avoiding political controversy which might offend their heterogeneous public, the information dailies followed "the cult of the army, the colonial movement, the memory of Alsace-Lorraine, and the hate of Germany."[97] It is true enough that these subjects could be politicized, but what of their other favorite topics, the celebration of bourgeois virtues and crime?[98]

Bourgeois and crime are a true binary opposition; in linguistic and conceptual terms each notion is dependent on the other for the fullest meaning. We have already seen how widespread were other binary terms in the technical and medical literature: normal-pathological, sane-insane, moral-immoral. As journalistic tools the binaries served, in Frederic Jameson's words, as "a technique for stimulating perception."[99] That is, they enhanced the possibility of a reader's understanding in familiar terms a superficially unique or unusual situation. They were used generously in journalistic discourse to clarify and enhance narrated events.

The problem for the journalist was to find a way to present the various terms of these simple oppositions in a fashion that would maximize their appeal. As an information broker dealing with a minimally literate audience, he had above all to avoid abstractions or complicated descriptions. In the words of Bensman and Lilienfeld, "he is likely to look for the specific image, illustration, symbol, anecdote, or event that illustrates his point; and having found and presented that symbol, he

[97] Albert et al., eds., *Histoire générale de la presse*, vol. 3, p. 298.

[98] These are the two other favorite topics mentioned by the editors of ibid., p. 298.

[99] Frederic Jameson, *The Prison-House of Language: A Critical Account of Structuralism and Russian Formalism* (Princeton, N.J.: Princeton University Press, 1972), p. 113.

is likely to allow the symbol or succession of symbols to convey his point without presenting the abstract argument."[100] He attempts to find "the image of the personality that embodies the idea, and deals with the image or personality in place of the idea."[101]

In the highly competitive environment of *belle époque* journalism, these requirements for simple communication were carried to extremes: information was scarce; simplification was necessary for the readers' sakes; vilification and negative characterization had the greatest resonance; sensational personalities, particularly those who could be pictured in the most diabolic manner possible, were the central figures. There were obvious consequences for objectivity and accuracy of presentation in this atmosphere. One of these problems may have been the effect that the description or labeling of something could have on explanation and causal attribution. David Kanouse has written: "First, the language used to describe events and actions frequently contains implicit attributions in itself. Second, the level of generality used in describing a given phenomenon is likely to influence the level of generality at which the phenomenon is explained. Pertinent details and facets that are omitted in description are unlikely to be reinstated in explanation."[102] The simpler the characterization, therefore, the simpler the explanation of its causes.

Bensman and Lilienfeld also point out that what begins as an organizational and communicational necessity for journalists—the presentation of "the case study" or concrete example—ends as a "habit of mind" which militates against any analysis of the problems and circumstances that generated the case study.[103] Where anecdote plays an important role in the presentation of an idea, there is a strong likelihood that the "image" or "stereotype" suggested by the anecdote will become continuous with its cause. The stereotype will become self-explanatory.

Other factors encouraged the phenomenon of the self-explanatory stereotype. As attribution theorists tell us, observers display regular tendencies in their explanations of the behavior of others. Lacking information on the motives and environmental influences on the actor,

[100] Joseph Bensman and Robert Lilienfeld, "The Journalist," in *Craft and Consciousness: Occupational Technique and the Development of World Images* (New York: John Wiley, 1973), pp. 209-210.

[101] Ibid., p. 211.

[102] David E. Kanouse, "Language, Labeling and Attribution," in Edward E. Jones, et al., eds., *Attribution: Perceiving the Causes of Behavior* (Morristown, N.J.: General Learning Press, 1972), p. 133.

[103] Bensman and Lilienfeld, "The Journalist," pp. 221-222.

observers tend to attribute cause to "the stable dispositional properties of the actor."[104] That is, actions are explained by some "trait" the actor presumably possesses rather than by his choice among various alternatives presented by environmental circumstances. A *belle époque* journalist often wrote stories with little solid information at his disposal. As we have seen, he favored the exploitation of individual personalities in particularly violent acts. As Fritz Heider has written, violent "behavior . . . has such salient properties that it tends to engulf the entire [explanatory] field rather than be confined to its proper position as a local stimulus whose interpretation requires the additional data of a surrounding field."[105]

These circumstances certainly encouraged the sorts of stereotyping, dispositional explanations, and negative attributions that operated in the crime reporting of the *belle époque*. The demonic acts of individuals like Soleilland and the exploits of the notorious apaches were the inevitable fare of the journalism of the period. They could be negatively portrayed and anecdotalized. Their acts were sensational and out of the ordinary. And best, they were their own explanations, no mean advantage for front-page stories where compression was a virtue. An "apache" was, quite simply, an "apache." A story of an apache's killing or wounding someone needed no other explanation or description, since it was his nature to act thusly. Soleilland was a "satyr," and "satyrs" rape and disembowel their victims.

For some insight on how the press treated violence in this period, let us look at the major Paris daily, the *Petit Parisien*, over a period of some months in 1907. The paper's 1.5 million daily printings made it the world's largest newspaper. Crime had always been high on the *Petit Parisien*'s list of topics, but the editors must have thought that subscription opportunities were in the offing; in early 1907 they increased the space devoted to crime stories dramatically. The Soleilland murder

[104] Edward E. Jones and Richard E. Nisbett, "The Actor and the Observer: Divergent Perceptions of the Causes of Behavior," in Jones et al., eds., *Attribution*, pp. 80-81. By contrast, the authors find that the actors tend to explain their *own* behavior in a nuanced and environmentally disposed fashion, emphasizing the force of circumstance in deciding among alternatives set before them.

[105] Fritz Heider, *The Psychology of Interpersonal Relations* (New York: Wiley, 1958), p. 54. On the tendency of negative evaluations to dominate positive ones in post hoc assessments, see David E. Kanouse and L. Reid Hanson, "Negativity in Evaluations," in Jones, et al., eds., *Attribution*, pp. 47-62. Jones and Nisbett argue in "The Actor and the Observer" that "once we have labelled an action as hostile it is very easy to move to the inference that the perpetrator is a hostile person. Our language allows the same term to be applied to behavior and to the underlying disposition it reflects," p. 90.

kicked off the campaign successfully, the paper reporting every detail and rumor of the case. Sensing a grand cause in the forthcoming issue of abolition of the death penalty, they began in March an "inquiry" into various celebrities' opinions on the question. Every few days a special column, nestled amid headlines announcing the deeds of criminals, reported these findings. Thus on April 1, with a special column devoted to the opinions of theatrical personalities, there appeared the headline "Another Policeman Killed by the Apaches," naming a "twenty-year-old apache" as the killer.[106]

The following day, under the promising heading "Insecurity," an editorial demanded more police for the apache-infested suburbs, alleging them to be in an "insurrectional state against society," populated by individuals "who repudiate work of all kinds."[107] On the fifth, Louis Parisot, a Socialist in the department council declared his opposition to the death penalty in the regular column, reporting as his reason the need for a society "of love and good will." While insisting on his impartiality the interviewer commented, "it would be salutory to know whether certain natures are not altogether resistant to love and good will."[108] On the seventh Jean Frollo wrote under the heading "The Apache-King" that killers could be had in the suburbs for forty centimes, and that "one kills there for the simple pleasure of it, because murder has become a sport."[109]

On the sixteenth under "Struggle against the Apaches," the paper supported the prefect of police's demand for blank warrants to search and seize those in the "army of crime." And in a special article on the death penalty, E. Montclar quoted the former prefect of police, Goron, as having reversed his former stand against capital punishment, now supporting the supreme punishment for apaches.[110] Without mentioning that the inquiry the paper had been conducting had not produced a clear majority of celebrities in favor of punishment by death, Montclar declared his certainty that the majority of the paper's readers certainly favored it. Finally, Jean Frollo's editorial on the nineteenth, "The Last Brigands," contained the choice lines, "The apaches of our Parisian suburbs represent a type in the last phase of degenerescence."[111]

Albert Soleilland's trial began on April 20. The paper gleefully re-

---

[106] *Petit Parisien*, April 1, 1907.
[107] Ibid., April 2, 1907.
[108] Ibid., April 5, 1907.
[109] Ibid., April 7, 1907.
[110] Ibid., April 16, 1907.
[111] Ibid., April 19, 1907.

ported an expert witness's confirmation of his mental responsibility, claiming that the young man was a "monster" who had "cynically" denied that any doctor could call him responsible for the killing of Marthe Erbelding.[112] The verdict and death sentence on July 23, 1907, were met with joyous approbation.[113]

A new note crept into the reporting of crime in these months, with sinister overtones and grave portents for the future. An editorial in the *Petit Parisien* of April 5, "The Gap," described the enormous gulf between those who supported private property and the "collectivists" who favored the "criminal" theory of direct action. Singling out the Independent Socialists who had condemned violence, the paper praised their recollection "that they are Frenchmen" as an "overwhelming voice of patriotism."[114] Jean Frollo wrote an attack the following day on antimilitarism, arguing that it was a "law of nature" that "any organism that ceases to act in its own defense . . . must weaken and die."[115] And on the seventh he wrote that apaches followed "the philosophy of direct action, putting into practice counsels offered by the thinkers of avantgarde parties such as M. Georges Sorel in his *Réflexions sur la violence*."[116] These new themes amalgamated crime, apaches, direct action, and antimilitarism as a series of oppositions to patriotism, the army, and an organic conception of social solidarity.

Apparently in despair over the failure of its celebrity interviewees to register a victory for the correct position on capital punishment, the *Petit Parisien* decided on a new gambit to "test" opinion. The occasion for this new experiment was the inevitable pardon of Soleilland on September 14. As President Fallières had commuted all capital crimes to life at hard labor in the previous two years, there was no reason to expect anything different in this case. The paper tried to keep its readers in a state of suspense about the outcome of the decision, and when the pardon was announced, proclaimed that "the death penalty is effectively abolished in France."[117] The "savage attacks" and "repeated crimes" demanded action. The paper continued a sustained campaign against crime through September, alleging "civilization" to be in danger from the "monstrous acts" and the "orgy of blood" of recent months. One problem, the paper insisted, was the ability of

[112] Ibid., April 20, 1907.
[113] Ibid., July 23, 1907.
[114] Ibid., April 5, 1907.
[115] Ibid., April 6, 1907.
[116] Ibid., April 7, 1907.
[117] Ibid., September 14, 1907. Fallières commuted to hard labor all twenty-nine capital condemnations in 1906, and all forty-one in 1907.

clever defense lawyers to use the "insanity plea" for "so-called madmen." This was, said an editorial, "obsession, mass obsession," and it suggested that perhaps "even a partially insane individual may be punished."[118]

On September 29 the paper announced its scheme: "Great Referendum of the *Petit Parisien*. The Question of the Death Penalty." Since the results of this referendum are universally known, and taken quite seriously even nowadays, its methods deserve to be better understood.[119] The paper denied that this was a political issue, but accompanying the announcement of the referendum was an editorial appealing directly to fear, mentioning "brigands, apaches . . . sinister phalanxes," blaming the whole inspiration for abolition on men with "so-called humanitarian sentiments."[120] Throughout the entire period of the referendum, editorials denounced crime, and articles played to the grandstands.[121]

As it happens the entire referendum was a promotional scheme in the best *belle époque* tradition. There was to be a concurrent "artistic contest" with prizes given in several categories for the most attractive picture postcards sent from each department of France. One was to write yes (for abolition) or no (for maintenance) on the back of a postcard showing the beauties of one's home department and send it to the paper's offices in Paris. However, as mailing dates were to be rotated (to expedite handling), one had to read the paper daily to know when to send the card.[122] Warnings not to miss one day were repeated ad nauseam. There was one more catch. To be eligible for the "artistic contest" one had to have voted with the ultimate majority! There seemed little doubt what the paper's opinion was, or what its editors thought the majority of the French believed, so one knew in advance the right position. When the results were announced on November 5, there must have been little doubt about the outcome: 1,083,655 voted no and only

[118] Ibid., September 23, 1907.

[119] Bonnefous calls the referendum "legitimate indignation" for Soleilland's crime. *Histoire politique de la troisième République, 1906-1914*, vol. 3 (Paris: Presses Universitaires de France, 1956), p. 112. Rébérioux, *La République radicale*, p. 144. A short but useful study of the referendum has been made by A. Cannavo, "Le référendum du 'Petit Parisien' sur la peine de mort" (Paris: Centre de formation des journalistes, n.d.), multilith.

[120] *Petit Parisien*, September 29, 1907.

[121] On October 15 an editorial appeared denouncing the "monster" Soleilland and ridiculing the doctor who called him mentally irresponsible. Ibid., October 15, 1907.

[122] On all these details see Cannavo, "Le référendum du 'Petit Parisien.' "

328,692 yes in favor of abolition. The *Petit Parisien* had managed both to promote a favorite hobbyhorse and to sell a few extra papers.

In documenting any situation in which there seems to have been a profound shift of opinion, it is always difficult to know how much of the shift is the result of spontaneous perceptions of change in material conditions, and how much has been manipulated or even manufactured by so-called opinion leaders. Even in the case of a seriously flawed polling procedure like that of the *Petit Parisien*, there is no way to be sure that the poll might not have produced similar results even without the coaching and demagoguery in which the paper openly indulged. Blatant manipulation could not sustain a mood of deep concern about crime unless there was other testimony about the gravity of the situation readily available to those who followed public affairs in a rudimentary way. In 1907, and still more the following year, there was growing evidence that other segments of French opinion supported the views of the *Petit Parisien*.

The most vocally concerned members of the public at the end of 1906 and the beginning of 1907 were the members of the assizes court juries. Until a law of 1909 democratized the selection process for juries, these bodies were filled by good bourgeois who paid sufficient taxes to have their names appear on the departmental rolls. It is not surprising to see them, property holders and admirers of public order, protesting against any measure they believed might threaten the security of their property and their persons. But between 1906 and 1908 jury members protested with an unusual vehemence against the proposed abolition of capital punishment. By May 1907 the newspapers were reporting that twenty-five of the nation's assizes juries had submitted petitions to the Minister of Justice requesting the withdrawal of the abolition bill.[123] As additional juries joined the list of petitioners in the following months, their names were widely announced in the papers and in favorably disposed periodicals.[124] By late 1908, the overwhelming majority of departmental juries had joined the list.

Jury opinion is not an easy thing to measure. Many forces are at work in the courtroom of a criminal trial, and it is not always apparent which of the elements present—prosecution, defense, magistrate, jury, public opinion—played the most important role in influencing the outcome of a single trial or a group of them. One can, of course, read through the dossiers of individual trials, as Mary Hartman has done

---

[123] *Le journal*, May 19, 1907; *Gazette des tribunaux*, May 13-14, 1907.

[124] The *Archives d'anthropologie criminelle*, antiabolitionist by mid-1907, reported each new adhering jury. See "Pour la peine de mort," announcing the demand by the jury of the Vaucluse department, 22 (1907), p. 662.

for *Victorian Murderesses* (1977), but even if one read a representative sample—an awesome task—it is a subtle business trying to explain jury verdicts from the internal evidence of the trial. What, after all, is a "typical" trial? Each murder has its special combination of circumstances that makes it unique. Jury opinion is a particularly elusive subject in the history of crime.

The statistical rates of jury decisions—condemnations, acquittals, extenuating circumstances—are only marginally helpful. Condemnation rates in the assizes courts are remarkably uniform in the late nineteenth century, falling only slightly from 1881. From 1901 to 1906, they averaged about what they had the previous decade: 68 percent. There was, to be sure, a climb to 70 percent in 1907, a percentage not breached for over a decade, but the rate fell again in 1908 to 66.8 percent and to 63.2 percent and 62.5 percent the next two years.[25] Not much can be made of this.

The figures on acquittals of those accused of committing crimes where death was or might have been the result are also of little help. In 1905 33.87 percent of those accused of a range of mortal crimes and attempted crimes (attempted murder, attempted assassination) were acquitted. The number dropped to 30.18 percent in 1906, rose to 35.03 percent in 1907, and peaked at 39.68 percent in 1908. Thus juries condemned a higher percentage of blood criminals before capital punishment became an issue than afterward. It is true that the acquittal rate for assassinations (first-degree murder) for these four years is lowest (15.5 percent) in 1907, the first full year of jury protest, being 21.1 percent, 19 percent, and 23 percent in 1905, 1906, and 1908.[126] But, if juries were determined to bring their disapproval of the lax punishment of violent crime to bear on the criminal justice process, it is not apparent from acquittal and condemnation rates.

The figures on the granting of extenuating circumstances are more revealing of a certain trend in jury behavior in this period. Abolitionists tended to argue during the debates on capital punishment that jurors were increasing their verdicts of extenuating circumstances because they had less taste for harsh punishment than jurors once had. If this was so it cannot be discerned from the general assizes statistics on serious personal and property crimes. There is a slight drop in the percentage of cases in which extenuating circumstances were granted

[125] My averages from "Résumé rétrospectif," *Compte générale de l'administration de la justice criminelle* 52 (1936), p. 46.

[126] These are my averages. They are taken from the respective volumes of the *Compte générale de l'administration de la justice criminelle*: 25 (1905), p. 96; 26 (1906), p. 76; 27 (1907), p. 116; 28 (1908), p. 89.

between 1871 and 1913. The decline is very small before 1907: 68.4 percent for the decade 1871-1880, 66.3 percent for 1881-1890, 65.8 percent for 1891-1900, and 65.7 percent for the period 1900-1906. However, in 1907, the first full year of jury protest, and a year of crisis of faith in expert testimony, the percentage fell to 61.8 percent. It was 61.8 percent again in 1908, rose to 64 percent in 1909, and fell within the 60-62 percent range from 1910 to 1913.[127] This may be a significant figure, coinciding as it does with a high-water mark in public concern about a crisis in criminal repression. Jurors may have been less tolerant of appeals for extenuating circumstances in general, mental incapacity among them, during this period; the drop in the rate in 1907 may reflect a conscious determination to lengthen sentences and imprison those who might have otherwise received medical or psychiatric aid.

But if this is so, it is also true for magistrates' decisions in the correctional courts, where juries were not an element of the criminal justice process. Extenuating circumstances in the correctional tribunals were granted at an increasing rate from 1871 to 1900. The rate, 46.2 percent in the decade 1871-1880, rose to 52.5 percent in 1881-1890, and to 55.2 percent from 1890 to 1900. It dropped from that time, however, to an even 50 percent from 1901 to 1906, and to even lower rates in the years before the war. It was 49 percent in 1906, 50 percent in 1907, and around 47 percent thereafter.[128] These figures seem to indicate that the forces working on juries to grant extenuating circumstances less often apparently worked on correctional magistrates as well. We still cannot say with certainty that this statistical trend adds up to some consciously determined change of attitude by juries and magistrates. Still, these individuals were also literate and informed citizens who in matters of crime and punishment were likely to be especially sensitive to shifts in public opinion. If not, then they had the courage to act on their changing convictions, certainly a more profound indicator of the depth of that conviction than any poll.

Veteran court reporters, who sat year after year through the spectacle of assizes trials, and the testimony of assizes judges and trial lawyers are other sources for jury opinion. Marcel Harduin, the crime writer for *Le Figaro*, complained in 1902 about the "neurotic" Paris juries who were so full of indulgence for the authors of crimes of passion.[129] But Edgard Troimaux, one of the most popular crime journalists of the *belle époque*, wrote in 1908 that juries were no longer as

[127] My averages from "Résumé rétrospectif," *Compte générale de l'administration de la justice criminelle* 52 (1936), pp. 46-47.

[128] My averages from ibid., pp. 47-48.

[129] Marcel Harduin, *Le Figaro*, January 11, 1902.

sympathetic as they once had been to pleas on these grounds.[130] However, for what it is worth, Henri Robert, the greatest criminal lawyer—and manipulator of juries—of his generation, argued in the 1907 Penitentiary Society debates that juries were quite willing to find extenuating circumstances while the death penalty was being implemented, but now that it was proposed to abolish it, they demanded its maintenance. This was so, he argued, because there is a "jury mentality" which has "a craving to confound authority."[131] In the end, the flood of jury petitions in 1907-1908 protesting abolition—and, by extension, Fallière's pardons—may be our best gauge of jury opinion.

Doubtless, the strength of public opinion alone, whether or not one considers it to have been manipulated, could account for a substantial part of the impetus for tougher treatment of violent crime. In 1907-1908, however, lay opinion was largely supported, if not directly led, by both the legal and the medico-criminological specialists. The importance of this support, I wish to argue, does not lie in the simple endorsement of the death penalty or in demands for stiffer punishment for violent criminals; a fair majority of both groups could be heard arguing for such measures throughout the early Third Republic, even at the height of the debate with the Italian school. Rather, the significance of the specialists' participation in this change of attitude was the role they played in helping to introduce and legitimate a new discourse on violence and on the logic of capital punishment. There were two primary features of this discourse that, ineluctably, entered the flow of public and political debate on violence and punishment. One, put simply, is the short-circuited logic that wants to have it both ways; that is, to claim that murderers are utterly animalized, but that there is still some virtue in retaining the guillotine. Second, there is a noticeable slide in the matter of justifying punishment from a determination grounded in classical questions of individual responsibility, to a notion of social responsibility anchored in social defense. As we shall see in later chapters, the allure of this discourse was such that scarcely anyone, even those who endorsed most passionately the struggle for abolition and the humanization of punishment, could escape its widening coils.

In February and March of 1907, only a few weeks after Albert Soleilland's rape-murder of Marthe Erbelding, the Penitentiary Society devoted two of its regular sessions to a discussion of the government's

[130] Edgard Troimaux, *L'echo de Paris*, November 13, 1908.
[131] *Bulletin de la Société générale des prisons* 31, *séance* of February 27, 1907, p. 313.

proposal to abolish the death penalty.[132] Joseph Reinach, sometime reformer and Radical deputy, put the case for abolition. He offered an essentially eclectic position, mentioning judicial error and the non-deterrence of the guillotine, putting greatest emphasis, perhaps, on the erosion of public support for the "medieval atavism" of state killings in modern civilization.[133] It did not weaken his position, Reinach believed, to acknowledge the recent rise in manslaughter (*meurtre*), because this was the product of alcoholism, which created "impulsives" who are "less responsible" for their behavior.[134]

The liberal Catholic criminologist Henri Joly, who had supported a voluntarist position against Lombrosian determinism in the 1880s, was principal speaker for the retentionists.[135] Joly attempted to counter Reinach's principal points, but his chief argument was to allege a clear distinction between the "remediable" criminals and those "beyond the pale of humanity" for whom killing was "natural." For these individuals, capital punishment ought to operate as a kind of "selection," much approved, he asserted, by those knowledgeable in evolutionary science.[136] In light of the Christian redemptionism that infused his theory of punishment in the 1880s, this was tantamount to saying that Joly no longer believed that all men had souls. Joly also related a personal account of random apache violence, thereby legitimizing anecdote as a polemical instrument, and encouraging others to make the same point.[137]

Rather than follow the discussion in detail, I would like to try and find a structure of argument in the remarks of the legal professionals. There was first of all no consensus on the question of abolition itself. Opinion was split roughly in half, with perhaps a slight majority of the discussants favoring Reinach's motion. This may not be taken as a

[132] Participants in this debate included the elite of the French legal professorate and magistracy, and the country's most influential trial lawyers.

[133] Reinach, *Bulletin de la Société générale des prisons* 31, *séance* of February 27, 1907, pp. 300-305.

[134] Ibid., p. 307.

[135] Trained in philosophy, Joly rose to a deanship in Dijon in 1881 before anticlerical ministers short-circuited his career. Thereafter, apart from a few temporary assignments, he was only granted the right to teach a "cours libre" at the Paris law faculty, which he did after 1889. He was the brother-in-law of Louis Proal, the noted Catholic magistrate and "criminaliste." See his dossier, F17 21007, Archives nationales.

[136] Henri Joly, *Bulletin de la Société générale des prisons* 31, *séance* of March 20, 1907, pp. 310-312.

[137] Ibid. See also the anecdote by M. Brueyre about the "apaches" who had tied a little boy up and laid him on the railroad tracks, with no apparent motive. *Bulletin de la Société générale des prisons* 31, *séance* of March 20, 1907, p. 442.

favorable conclusion for abolitionism in any real sense, as we shall see, because of the nature of the reasoning that served as its foundation. However, two arguments emerged by the end of the debates on which there was significant agreement. One of these was on the nature of the "people we are all speaking about," to use Joly's phrase, and the other was on the general nature of the response society ought to make to capital criminals (leaving aside for the time being the specific pros and cons of the death penalty).

To take the first point, though it was not presented systematically or argued with evidence of any sort, there was a general agreement that there had been a rise recently in "serious crimes," attributable in large measure to the numerical growth of a certain kind of criminal. No one questioned at any point whether studies had been done to demonstrate this notion; it was simply affirmed without the least glimmer of sociological curiosity.

Some of the participants called the violent criminals apaches without further elaboration, as if their nature were known to all.[138] Others used more concrete language to describe the young men in question, whose murders qualified them for the death penalty. Raymond Saleilles, the internationally respected penologist and a formulator of the notion of "the individualization of punishment," called the authors of recent capital crimes "abnormal" and "impulsives" with "criminal temperaments and corrupt and perverse natures."[139] Rabbi Levy, the Jewish chaplain for Paris prisons, called assassins "wild beasts" with "nothing human about them when they kill."[140] René Demogue of the Lille law faculty called them physically and morally degraded, and Léon Granier, the inspector general of the Interior Ministry's Administrative Services, called them "impulsives" with no "self-control."[141]

In this discussion on the nature of the human material out of which

---

[138] Senator Bérenger argued that the contact of a young man with an "apache association" meant his certain doom. *Bulletin de la Société générale des prisons* 31, *séance* of February 27, 1907, p. 319. Senator de Lamarzelle connected "apaches" with "professional criminals." Ibid., p. 319. Paul Demange, a defense lawyer at the assizes courts mentioned that apaches were recruited in the *faubourgs* of Paris. Ibid., p. 335. Georges Honnorat used the term in reference to a necessary resuscitation of physical whipping. Ibid., *séance* of March 20, 1907, p. 446. Pasteur Arboux, the Protestant chaplain of Paris prisons, called apaches "these furious and violent beings who wield knives with a readiness and a skill everyone knows about." Ibid., p. 466. Ernest Cartier, an advocate at the court of appeal also used the term in his remarks. Ibid., *séance* of March 20, 1907, p. 476.

[139] *Bulletin de la Société générale des prisons* 31, *séance* of March 20, 1907, p. 430.

[140] Ibid., p. 468.

[141] Ibid., pp. 485, 499.

assassins are fashioned, one has the distinct feeling of overhearing a conversation between intimates who are describing a third person known to them in familiar terms. There was no need, therefore, for the members of the society to elaborate on the history of recent violent crime, or give the sources for their assertions. What is perhaps most extraordinary about the references to recent murders was that *both* pro- and antiabolitionists used this "nature" to justify their respective arguments. The classical abolitionist position had held that most men, being rational deliberators, were deterred from murder by fear of punishment. Life imprisonment (or some equivalent punishment) was exchangeable for the death penalty precisely because men did calculate the advantage of murder and found it wanting in the face of its severe consequences.[142] Those who murdered did so after considering the risk of punishment. There are still some vestiges of this notion of the rational deterrent effects of the death penalty in the arguments of the abolitionists, but they had become vague and confused.

Most abolitionists had moved around to the position that would-be murderers did *not* weigh the consequences of their acts in a manner one would call rational or deliberate. Either they supposed they would escape punishment altogether, which the abolitionists construed as an example of improper reasoning, or they had a *nature* so constituted that the normal deliberative processes were in some way impaired. Abolitionists were more likely to subscribe to some variation of the latter argument. We have already seen that alcoholism, apacheism, degeneracy, and depravity were favorite explanations of this *nature*. Another argument against the effectiveness of capital punishment as a deterrent was that the French, a brave race, did not fear death but prized their liberty and so were more likely to be deterred by threat of life imprisonment than the guillotine. All these arguments conceded the probably nonrational impulses of murder to an extent and in a range of particular instances that the classical abolitionist position had never admitted.

The problem now arose that, having argued the nondeterrent effects of the death penalty for murderers, abolitionists themselves helped undermine the general grounds of a rational deterrence theory of punishment. By extension, this limitation on deterrence theory also

---

[142] The original argument for this position, as stated by Beccaria in 1764, was even more positive in favor of the advantages of imprisonment: "Minds are less influenced by the rigor of punishments than by their duration . . . The most powerful disincentive to crime is not the terrible and rapid spectacle of death, but the hideous conception of a man deprived of his freedom." Chapter 16 of *Traité des délits et des peines*, as quoted in Savey-Casard, *La peine de mort*, p. 60.

applied to most violent assaults where death had *not* been the result, and, indeed, to nearly all crimes committed with a dangerous weapon. In addition, abolitionists had largely abandoned any purely ethical faulting of capital punishment on the grounds that it was morally wrong for the state to take a human life. This argument, of course, had been put in different ways, but it was generally stated in absolute terms. In its modern guise, however, this position was constituted in evolutionary naturalistic terms, as in the opening comments of Joseph Reinach that "customs" were changing, becoming "softer" and less tolerant of state-sanctioned killing. Both these retreats played into the hands of the antiabolitionists.

For their part, those who wished to retain the death penalty also based their positions on the natural depravity of murderers. The classical death penalty position had also been grounded in a theory of rational deterrence. Though adherents attempted to justify state executions on moral grounds, social contract theory, or the like, most of their strength derived from the proposition that the death penalty was by far the most effective form of deterrent. In view of the general agreement in 1907 on the nonrational impulsiveness of killers, antiabolitionists could only use the deterrence argument at risk of logical confusion. A few retentionists, therefore, simply invoked the principle that social defense demanded the elimination of defective beings without remorse. While this argument was at least consistent with the sort of criminal all imagined to be the "typical" assassin, it was too redolent of the kind of ironclad determinism that the penal-legal community had always shunned. Consequently, this position found only a few supporters among the penal professionals.[143] The more usual position was difficult to state without contradiction or confusion. It insisted on the violent and depraved natures of most murderers, but nonetheless held the death penalty to have a margin of deterrent effect.

One discussant, for example, spent much time describing the apaches and other violent criminals who were not susceptible to fear. But he still supported maintaining the death penalty for the residual deterrent effect it might have.[144] Paul Demange argued that depraved as they were, life was still meaningful for the apaches, and Alfred Le Poittevin

---

[143] In these debates, this position was defended outright only by Loys Brueyre and René Demogue, a law professor at Lille, and, with qualifications, by the Paris law professor Alfred Le Poittevin and Ernest Cartier, a lawyer. *Bulletin de la Société générale des prisons* 31, *séance* of February 27, 1907, p. 338 and ibid., *séance* of March 20, 1907, pp. 442, 475, 485.

[144] Senator de Lamarzelle, *Bulletin de la Société générale des prisons* 31, *séance* of February 27, 1907, p. 319.

said he would vote to retain the death penalty if it saved just one human life.[145] The prison pastor Arboux also argued that apaches were contemptuous of prison and feared only death. Arguments of this sort strongly evoke the unusual pressures working to retain a conception of the violent criminal as a thoroughly irredeemable being, despite the contradiction that position entailed for a deterrent theory of the death penalty.

This conclusion is encouraged by the general structure of the second major argument on which there was agreement among the penal professionals. This argument depended on a definite consensus that if the death penalty was to be abolished then whatever replaced it should be, in the words of Senator de Lamarzelle, "more horrible still." Thus much of the discussion of abolition was spent evaluating alternative modes of punishment. Emile Garçon liked life at hard labor in Guyana, citing its "devastating" reputation among criminals. René Bérenger wanted to replace the guillotine with a strictly isolated cellular imprisonment, and others wanted an initial period of cellular regime of silence followed by forced labor.[146]

Of course most of those who held for the intimidating effects of alternative punishments were abolitionists, but as they were a slight majority, their suggestions were seriously debated. There was in the reasoning supporting these alternative punishments a lingering concern for demonstrating their deterrent value, but more conspicuous was the concern for their reception by the public. Some, like Senator de Lamarzelle, believed public opinion would not stand for cellular imprisonment, with its appearance of a "comfortable and gay life." René Demogue seconded his point by saying that it would be necessary to convince the public that the replacement penalty was "worse than death itself."[147]

In his resumé of the debate, the president of the society, Albert Gigot, concluded that France was living through an era in which serious crime was on the rise, but said he was convinced that some punishment could be devised that was even more intimidating than death.[148] It was

---

[145] Bulletin de la Société générale des prisons 31, séance of February 27, 1907, pp. 335, 339.

[146] Ibid., pp. 320-333.

[147] Bulletin de la Société générale des prisons 31, séance of February 27 and March 20, 1907, pp. 135, 484-485. Paul Cuche, who taught law at Grenoble, argued that though capital punishment was no longer in the mores of the French, abolition would be a mistake as it would be interpreted as a sign of weakness and approval of crime, p. 437.

[148] Albert Gigot, Bulletin de la Société générale des prisons 31, séance of March 20, 1907, p. 486.

an odd kind of victory for the abolitionists. They had salvaged their point on the condition that they find an alternative punishment more brutal than death, and this with at least as much of an eye on public opinion as on the strictly philosophical needs of a deterrence theory of punishment. In addition they had, from inclination or out of a similar concern for public opinion, emphasized the unregenerate and bestial nature of the authors of recent capital crimes, thus further undercutting the rational and deterrent foundations of their outlook and putting in greater jeopardy than before any substitute punishment that justified itself simply on the grounds of its power to intimidate would-be murderers.

As reliance on classical deterrence theory declined, it was replaced by a theory of punishment based on the concept of social defense. Strictly speaking, the term was of criminological and legal provenance. It became popular during the 1880s and 1890s, the golden European era of legal agitation for revision of the classical codes. Generally, social defense was linked to the concept of the individualization of punishment; together they ordained a penal regime that adapted the punishment to the criminal, not his crime, and justified the appropriate punishment (or treatment) on the grounds of its *effectiveness* in protecting society against future transgressions. As we have seen, a related *political* theory of self-defense emerged in the late 1870s as a new "scientific" form of contract theory. As a theory of self-defense, this latter theory was in practice invoked only against extreme left- and right-wing *political* enemies; its most prominent value in the middle years of the Third Republic was as a component of the radical social philosophy named "solidarism," which emphasized positive aspects of the organic interdependency of society, not the negative quality of self-defense.[149]

Around the turn of the century, however, the notion of social defense was introduced into the political lexicon as a doctrine of defense of property by the nationalist politician Charles Benoist. Benoist and his Parisian political allies broadened the focus of social defense to include all forms of internal social disorder, and paired it explicitly with an equally strong bias toward "national defense."[150] Benoist and his move-

[149] On the development of solidarist social theory and its implications, see J.E.S. Hayward, "The Official Philosophy of the French Third Republic: Léon Bourgeois and Solidarism," *International Review of Social History* 6 (1961), pp. 20-32; Scott, *Republican Ideas and the Liberal Tradition*, pp. 157-186; Zeldin, *France, 1848-1945*, vol. 1, pp. 640-681.

[150] Watson, "The Nationalist Movement in Paris."

ment did not survive the 1906 elections intact, but the linkage of social and national defense was a political ideal whose time had come.

The extraordinary sensitivity of the criminological specialists to legal and public opinion has been demonstrated by their behavior during the Lombroso debates. The criminologists were no less sensitive in 1907-1908 to a new set of public attitudes, even though trying to reflect them in their work led them rather far afield from the doctrines they had enunciated in the 1880s. The national debate on capital punishment provided then an excellent opportunity to present a case for the social utility of criminological theory. In the 1880s their theories had articulated the optimistic environmentalism of the Republican legal-political regime of that era. In 1907-1908 they marshaled the forces of criminological knowledge to illustrate the great advantages of retaining the guillotine. In their zeal for this task, criminologists helped assemble a gridwork of ideas that significantly advanced the *political* resonance of a medical model of social defense.

It was Lombroso's Italian school that had made capital punishment a weapon in the arsenal of social defense by emphasizing its virtue as an eliminator of the biologically unfit. There was a split in the Italian school itself, however, Ferri maintaining the view that it made nonsense of any theory of punishment to execute the sane, the insane, and the biologically unfit under the same rubric. Despite the enthusiastic endorsement of Lombroso's views by Hippolyte Taine, [151] the international defeat of Lombroso's system weakened the popularity of this function of capital punishment in France for several years.

In 1907-1908 many of the figures who had won their spurs in the 1880s were still on the scene. Only Tarde was gone; his death left the criminological establishment largely in the hands of psychiatrists and doctors of legal medicine. Alexandre Lacassagne, the dean of French criminologists and the acknowledged leader of the French school, devoted an entire book in 1908 to capital punishment.

[151] In 1887 Taine wrote a letter to Lombroso which was published as a preface to the first French edition of *L'uomo criminale*: "If I were a jurist, a legislator, or a juror, I would have no pity for assassins, thieves, the 'born criminal,' or the 'moral idiot.' . . . if the criminal impulse is isolated, accidental, and probably transitory, one may, indeed ought to, pardon it; but the more closely that impulse is linked to the framework of ideas and sentiments of the individual, the more guilty' he is and the more he ought to be punished. You have shown us lubricious and ferocious orangutans with human faces; certainly, being such, they can act no other way; if they rape, steal, and kill, it is on account of their nature and their past. The more reason for us to destroy them when one is assured that they are and will remain orangutans. On this account I have no objection to the death penalty if society finds profit in it." Lombroso, *L'homme criminel* (Paris, 1887), pp. ii-iii.

Though he had questioned the value of the supreme penalty as recently as 1906, Lacassagne now found adequate reasons to support its retention. Some of these reasons, he argued, could be found in the recent growth of crimes of blood.[152] This point made, Lacassagne's arguments then became tortured and even contradictory. Recalling his role as a founder of the social interpretation of crime, he tried to pay homage to the criminogenic power of the social environment. But as he was also attempting to explain the greater depravity and monstrousness of contemporary violent crime, he resorted more to hereditarian arguments than he once had.[153] To underscore the naturalistic and "positive" origin of this new crime, Lacassagne remarked on the point that its evolution was independent of repression and penal law since repression had not been able to slow down its rapid increase. He also maintained in one place that these violent criminals "seem to fear nothing," while arguing elsewhere that "criminal natures dread death."[154]

The remainder of the book is simply a series of affirmations about the political advantages of retaining capital punishment. Prisons are expensive and overcrowded, juries are in favor of retention, and so is the public, if one can believe the *Petit Parisien*. He contended that 30,000 apaches plagued the capital, adding, for the benefit of "soft" magistrates: "After you, Messieurs, the apaches."[155] Beyond aphorisms and unsupported affirmations, Lacassagne made some points worth mentioning because they comprise the foundation for opposition to abolition stated by all the other criminologists. First is the notion that though the criminal is sick, he is still "guilty" and subject to "punishment" because he is also an "antisocial being." That is, he has offended the rules of a theory of social defense which has superseded the outmoded doctrine of individual criminal responsibility. As there was strong evidence of "moral imbecility" in the nature of violent criminals, the death penalty must be retained since "only physical pain will affect

[152] Alexandre Lacassagne, *Peine de mort et criminalité: L'accroissement de la criminalité et l'application de la peine capitale* (Paris: Maloine, 1908), pp. 30-31, 62, 70-75.

[153] Lacassagne refers to "monsters," "impulsives," "drunkard's sons," and "convulsive psychic degeneracy." He links these to other hereditary and abnormal traits manifested by these violent criminals. It is of course a matter of emphasis, but in this book Lacassagne's focus is seldom on the environment as the original source of crime, but on the degenerate or alcoholic criminal who is its product. It is a crucial emphasis, which, after all, was the basis of the difference between Lombroso and Lacassagne in 1885. See esp. pp. 96-120, *Peine de mort et criminalité*.

[154] Ibid., pp. 120-141. As proof of the latter contention in this standing contradiction he points to the "codes" of the "apaches" which punish informing by death, p. 141.

[155] Ibid., pp. 142-145, 151-152, 166, 178.

amoral beings." Second, Lacassagne also endorsed the corollary value of the guillotine's "surgical operation" as "preventive hygiene."[156] The logical incoherence of Lacassagne's book, its pleading and tendentious tone, is clear evidence of his difficulty in adapting his theoretical views to new ends.

Lacassagne's Lyon colleague Dr. Armand Corre confessed to having once been an abolitionist, but he could no longer support the "sentimental" pleadings of the abolitionists: "the arrogant intellectualists, rhetoricians of decadence, political intransigents. Mine is a protest against an excess of deplorable philanthropy, the mark of weakness."[157] In a more direct manner than his mentor Lacassagne had done, Corre divided the world into two categories: the moral, the just, and the honest, and the amoral, the unjust, and criminals. Life was a struggle between these two groups to which no weapon or tactic was forbidden. Among the honest men were the scientific realists; the misguided were cabinet intellectuals, and for honest men in general to triumph the realists must dictate policy.[158] On the whole, he continued, the determination of individual responsibility was difficult: the sanest in appearance are often the maddest, and the most disorderly are sometimes the most lucid. This fact, together with the rise in personal assaults, recommended to Corre a doctrine of punishment based on social defense, enforced by leaders like the admirable Committee of Public Safety, which spilled blood when necessary and did not worry about the inadvertent killing of a few innocents. Corre's cultural critique was more explicit than Lacassagne's. Criminals were lazy and "animalized" and seek prison like a "vile scum seeking shelter, bed, clothing, and food, conditions that are better than those available to humble workers employing great effort and trouble."[159] He also placed those who "deign to save money" in a binary opposition with the "apache," a "dishonest striker." Corre hinted darkly at the connection between criminals, the lazy and "antisocial," and the activities of contemporary labor as a kind

[156] Ibid., p. 161. Lacassagne wrote elsewhere in 1908 a definition of the criminal that lacks little in biological imagery: "a hereditary monster, something like a malignant tumor or a parasite." Preface to Emile Laurent, Le criminel aux points de vue anthropologique, psychologique et social (Paris: Vigot frères, 1908), p. x. What is more, he concluded, "in a society weakened and intoxicated by tuberculosis and alcohol, impulsives and criminals are more and more numerous. It is necessary that the signs that characterize antisocial beings be known to all those who operate the judicial administration," p. xiv.

[157] A. Corre, "A propos de la peine de mort," Archives d'anthropologie criminelle 23 (1908), p. 238.

[158] Ibid., pp. 230-234.

[159] Ibid., p. 231.

of "treasonous villainy" that only a Committee of Public Safety could deal with efficiently.

Henri Joly, for his part, also emphasized the general crisis of French culture in his article in the *Revue des deux mondes*. Until recently, he began, it was generally believed that the death penalty no longer served the aim it had in ancient times of protecting the collective integrity of societies. The dimensions of the current social crisis in France, however, have reintroduced this venerable sanction as the only possible basis for preventing a disaster of "anarchy and ruin."[160] Criminals, of course, are in the front rank of society's enemies, but these also include strikers, socialist levelers, egoists, and the income tax. Joly advanced the notion of collective and social defense against this host of enemies, choosing the supremely organic metaphor of a "lesion . . . pronounced enough that the social organism feels itself diseased in one of its limbs."[161] Grave harm to a *social* doctrine of repression has been done, he insisted, by the modern theory of the individualization of punishment, because it has been applied in the spirit of charity toward the criminal. The search for the motives of the individual criminal ought to illuminate "what makes the crime dangerous, especially the likelihood that the criminal will repeat his crime or suggest it to others; it matters, from the standpoint of social defense, to know in what measure that disposition exists."[162] From this principle, it followed that "we must no more discuss the responsibility of a guilty man than we would discuss the intelligence or the instinct of a dangerous animal that must be isolated or eliminated."[163]

Like the other writers discussed here, Joly found no contradiction in claiming that violent criminals were at once without human or moral qualities and yet respectful of the guillotine. Emile Laurent, the doctor of legal medicine who assumed leadership in the profession following Lacassagne's death in 1924, propounded similar views. In his encomium of the death penalty he wrote of the army of the sick besieging society: "Some are asocial, the insane; others, the extrasocial, are im-

---

[160] Henri Joly, "Le problème pénal au moment présent et la peine de mort," *Revue des deux mondes* (January 1, 1909), pp. 173-180.

[161] Ibid., p. 186.

[162] Ibid., p. 187. Joly was intent on linking the improper emphasis on adjusting the punishment to the crime to the general principle of assessing taxes and fines according to ability to pay. The effect of this policy would be to promote further social leveling.

[163] Ibid., p. 192. From having been certain of the social etiology of criminal acts, Joly has retreated to a position that holds crime to be "undecipherable." He justifies punishment on the grounds that the degree of social danger posed by an offender was relatively easy to ascertain, pp. 191-192.

beciles; others still, the antisocial, are criminal. In effect, crime, vice, imbecility, and madness are no different except in the eyes of society; their quality of utter determinism is what they share."[164] But, as determined as this statement suggests their acts to be, most of them, Laurent insists, can yet distinguish between "good and evil."[165] Only the "thought of the guillotine gives pause to criminals because they fear pain by nature. But if most of them accept their fate with a kind of 'calm cynicism' [a fact all parties seemed to agree upon], it was because they are the most 'unforeseeing of men.' "[166]

Shrugging off minor contradictions, Laurent constructed a foundation for effective punishment that was built of many parts, including severe corporal punishment and the death penalty. Thus in the narrow sense that they fear pain all the mentally ill and criminals, save the "delirious insane" and "epileptics," have "responsibility."[167] This was not responsibility in the limited individual sense, but one derived from the principle of "social defense and the conservation of humanity." Such a principle, Laurent asserted, excluded excessive pity and sentimentality in the name of preservation of the species and elimination of the weakest types. And since "one kills the ferocious beast that one is unable to muzzle, the legitimacy of the death penalty lies in that truth." Nature is humankind's best example: "Kill them! says nature to society. Kill them, says the past of humanity to its present with a hundred historical voices."[168]

Not all criminologists in 1907-1908 failed to realize the kind of compression of argument and the contradictions that were typical of their colleagues' support of capital punishment.[169] But those who spoke out were solidly behind retention of the guillotine. This fact was well enough known, as we shall see, that it was frequently remarked upon by the press. The criminologists clearly felt themselves to be under serious pressure to pronounce publicly against abolition; this is re-

[164] Laurent, *Le criminel*, p. 2.

[165] Ibid., p. 5.

[166] Ibid., p. 56.

[167] Ibid., pp. 236-240. See Max-Albert Legrand, "La peine de mort et les châtiments," *Archives d'anthropologie criminelle* 23 (1908), pp. 689-696.

[168] Laurent, *Le criminel*, pp. 240-242.

[169] Edmond Locard, Lacassagne's *préparateur* at Lyon, and the major figure in interwar criminalistics, reviewed a new edition of Lombroso's *Le crime* in 1907. He pointed out that Lombroso could not continue to argue for the hereditary predestination of murderers and the retention of the death penalty. Natural selection was an inadequate basis for a theory of punishment, and Locard felt Lombroso was in a profound contradiction. Edmond Locard, *Archives d'anthropologie criminelle* 22 (1907), pp. 271-285.

flected in the characteristic logical problems and the sort of confused pleading of their texts. In this it seems fair to conclude that these men believed themselves to be acting in the most reasonable interests of their discipline, perhaps in the same spirit as their actions of the late eighties and early nineties. In both cases they sought to present their positions in the way that would be most compatible with the public temper. Considerations of the same order worked on the psychiatrists in their efforts to adjust their conceptions of responsibility to these new expectations, as we shall see in the next chapter.

The ferocity of their views, however, and the effort to connect the threat of violent criminality with other internal problems feared by their fellow citizens, cannot be explained only by reference to the professional anxieties of the deviance specialists. Criminologists and psychiatrists may have believed they had special insights into the web of relations between different varieties of deviance, but they were as vulnerable to the pervasive *general* mood of cultural and social crisis as their fellow citizens. The doctrine of social defense neatly expressed the anxieties that underlay this mood of crisis. It articulated well with political and penal concepts of long standing in France; it spoke to the fears of several generations of French men and women about national decline and its geopolitical consequences; and it laid down a strategy for resolving or, at the very least, coping with these internal weaknesses. During the period of agitation about capital punishment, no public commentators, not even confirmed abolitionists, could resist the dominion of this concept.[170] A new mood of realism was settling in; it would not be quickly or easily dispersed.

[170] Paul Adam, a prominent anti-Dreyfusard and nationalist wrote an abolitionist argument in which he denied that the bestial instincts of apaches could be deterred by the death penalty, and recommended sending them to North Africa to fight the Arabs in the name of social defense. He was congratulated for this "realistic abolitionism" by an editor of the leftist *Revue du mois*, who concluded an abolitionist editorial with the words: "If a poet or a philosopher is able to take pity on the lot of our unfortunate apaches, society cannot afford to do so, for it must defend itself. The question is in knowing how it can do so most surely." See Paul Adam, "La peine de mort," *Revue hebdomadaire* (November 16, 1907), pp. 298-312; "La suppression de la peine de mort," *Revue du mois* 4 (December 10, 1907), p. 752.

CHAPTER VII

The Boundaries of Responsibility: Asylum Law and Legal Medicine in an Era of Social Defense

Two events spanning the years 1905-1909 provide exceptionally rich insights into the practical applications of the medical language of social defense. These events were the debate and passage of a bill revising the 1838 asylum law in the Chamber of Deputies, and the practically simultaneous existence of a crisis in public and judicial confidence in expert medical testimony. The principal figures in these events were doctors of legal medicine, asylum doctors, and psychiatric clinicians, specialists in the care of the mentally ill, and guardians of the state's *tutelle* over those who forfeited their civil status when they lost their reason. In the advocacy of their corporate interests during these years, experts in mental medicine were forced to chart a course that would yield a maximum degree of public support for their professional autonomy, with a minimum amount of compromise in the scientific status of their medical work. It is sometimes assumed that a firm scientific foundation has been historically the soundest, if not the sole, basis for launching claims for professional autonomy in scientific disciplines. The events of the period 1905-1909 reveal the limits of such claims and the considerable complexity of the task of psychiatric professionals in protecting their interests. There was, for instance, considerable disagreement among experts in mental medicine about the proper strategy to follow in this matter, which calls into question the monolithic character of the "disciplinary matrix" Michel Foucault has constructed for nineteenth-century medicine. In the end the medical professionals revealed themselves to be as sensitive to trends in public and political opinion as they had been in the "born criminal" debates, though they still sought to extend the scope of their technical competence as far as possible.

An analysis of these events can illuminate several aspects of the role medical discourse played in French culture in this crucial period. We can learn how experts in mental medicine sought to exercise their influence over the shape of the new asylum regime and how their formulas were appropriated by the legislative proponents of reform. We can show how the classic dialogue between civil libertarians and the defenders of public security on the issue of the rights of the mentally ill was resolved, despite appearances, in favor of the latter group. And we can follow the channels through which the question of the identification and treatment of the mentally ill became an issue of significant public debate in this period, linked by medical discourse to a host of pathologies threatening the nation. Above all, a detailed treatment of this period underscores the central role given to the concept of responsibility by all observers of these issues, both popular and professional.

I attempted to show in the preceding chapter that the way questions of responsibility were handled by commentators was deeply revealing of their general outlook on crime and criminals. In this chapter I wish to explore further the treatment of criminal responsibility by contemporaries, in this case in terms of the proposed creation of new facilities for the criminally insane. The tangle of issues relating to the circumstances in which social responsibility (*tutelle*) replaced individual penal responsibility is very important in itself; however, it will also recall the method of reasoning used by the penal and criminological professionals described in the preceding chapter, whereby redoutable individuals are held to be in the thrall of some overwhelming force and yet are judged to be responsible, in some measure, for their behavior. The sources and nature of this reasoning are an important part of this chapter. As we shall see, the medical community was deeply committed to an effort to find a formula that would replace the concept of individual responsibility, which was widely regarded as unreliable from the standpoint of public security, with a doctrine of social responsibility sufficiently broad to encompass most forms of deviance. The effort to redefine the meaning of responsibility for deviant acts was, to a significant extent, the way the French dealt with their fears of the irrational and disorderly behavior of criminals and the insane. It was an important mode of cultural self-assessment and a way of reestablishing order in an apparently chaotic and unpredictable social universe.

Before considering the effort to revise the 1838 law on the internment and release of the insane, it would be useful to bring the situation of French psychiatry up to date. As noted earlier, the organicist diagnostic "code" favored by Magnan's generation replaced the Pinelian "moral" model during the last quarter of the nineteenth century. The therapeutic model of Pinel's school persisted for a slightly longer time because of its residual optimism, but in the end psychiatrists could no longer retain the therapeutic strategy of "moral treatment" once they had effectively broken with Pinel's and Esquirol's diagnostic nosologies. The adoption, however, of a therapeutic code compatible with an "organic" analysis of the causes of mental illness posed some distinct problems for psychiatric specialists. How could they justify their existence as healers of the sick when their patients were firmly in the grip of biological forces that seemed too deeply rooted to oppose effectively? Did they not risk cutting themselves off from one of the traditional functions of the healer just as they were moving closer to mainstream medicine?

Several commentators have remarked on the therapeutic pessimism of this period and the growing percentages of the "incurables" housed in late nineteenth-century asylums. In Castel's words, "the prognosis of incurability came to replace the hope of leading the madman to reason by intervening actively to annul the pathogenic process."[1] It certainly was the case that by the 1870s psychiatrists had begun to doubt the uniform applicability of moral therapy to the inhabitants of France's overcrowded asylums. They apparently continued to mark time with a set of eclectic "physicalistic" treatments (massage, electrotherapy, and hydrotherapy) and unpredictable drugs. Progress was demonstrated by an ever-refined diagnostic virtuosity whose trademark was the differentiation of types of mental disorder. Valentin Magnan, whose *bureau de réception* at Saint Anne received most of the indigent and "dangerous" *placements d'office* in the Paris region, led the way in distinguishing idiots and imbeciles, alcoholics, epileptics, and the senile from other forms of insanity.

Gradually, movements were begun, often championed by psychiatrists with strong philanthropic sentiments, that argued in favor of different kinds of treatments for different kinds of mental illness. Rejecting the Pinelian notion that all forms of mental disorder were at base an alienation of reason which could be restored by a standard treatment, these specialists gradually developed therapies they believed were appropriate to the illness. By the turn of the century the chief demand of psychiatrists was for the creation of separate facilities, or at least quarters for various kinds of mental illnesses and an end to the "promiscuity" of the Pinelian asylum.[2] In the long run, this strategy,

[1] See Castel, *L'ordre psychiatrique*, pp. 279-282; see also Lamarche-Vadel and Preli, *L'asile*, p. 107; Baruk, *La psychiatrie française*, pp. 46-47.

[2] Lamarche-Vadel and Preli, *L'asile*, pp. 98-99 and Castel, *L'ordre Psychiatrique*, pp. 282-284.

which projected a progressive and vital image of the profession, had an undeniably positive influence; it resulted in a favorable press for psychiatry in a period of otherwise general pessimism.[3] As we shall see in Chapter Nine, much of the appeal of the sports movement in the *fin de siècle* lay in the "hygienic" and therapeutic effects promised by organized physical exercise.

In the short run, however, the effects for the inhabitants of French asylums were not so positive. As we shall see later in more detail, psychiatrists chose to argue a case for special quarters and new treatment facilities in the discourse of social order and public security, not in the language of healing and philanthropy. Even D. M. Bourneville, the enlightened exponent of education for idiots, couched his appeal for special education of idiots on the grounds of the "social danger" they posed when at liberty.[4] In general the movement to specialize within the asylum was merely an internal reordering of the disciplinary role thrust on asylums from their origins. In the words of Lamarche-Vadel and Preli: "The nosologies that permitted the separation of different sorts of mental illness had no other function than to replicate in the asylum a new system of order. . . . The moral and political order justified and guaranteed the scientific one. The progress of science was measured by the nature of the new equipment, in the progressive perfecting of the classification of the insane, and in the suitability of quarters adequate for their treatment."[5]

While making genuine efforts to distinguish between "curable" and "incurable" patients, psychiatrists still sought to retain their monopoly as the guardians of the mentally ill in all sorts of treatment, old and new. Their discourse thus stressed the "dangerousness" of most types of insanity or mental deficiency as the primary justification for the

---

[3] The most important permanent advances were in the education of the mentally deficient, particularly juveniles. Dumped into asylums indiscriminately throughout the nineteenth century, idiots were only recognized as educable near the end of the 1800s. The efforts and publicity of Dr. D. M. Bourneville finally released the first trickles of public finance for special schools. See Yves Pelicier and Guy Thullier, "Pour une histoire de l'éducation des enfants idiots en France," *Revue historique* 261 (January-March 1979), pp. 99-130. The "hypno-pédagogique" methods of Dr. Edgar Berillon for "degenerate" children also received attention at this time. Edgar Berillon, "Les applications de l'hypnotisme à l'éducation de enfants vicieux ou dégénérés," *Vᵉ Congrès international d'anthropologie criminelle* (Amsterdam, 1901), pp. 302-308. For an example of favorable public reception of these efforts see Jacques d'Arcy, "L'enfance dégénéré ou coupable," *La grande revue* 41 (February 16, 1907), pp. 390-395.

[4] Pelicier and Thullier, "Pour une histoire de l'éducation," p. 114.

[5] Lamarche-Vadel and Preli, *L'asile* pp. 98-99.

security of mental institutions. Though some incurables were admitted to be inoffensive (the senile, in particular), and could be released to low-security "nonmedical" institutions, many remained a grave danger to social order and could only be kept in high-security asylums. The greatest irony, noted by Lamarche-Vadel and Preli, was the emergence of a formula of "curability-dangerousness" which psychiatrists used to establish their continued supervision of the mentally ill.[6] The more likely it was that a certain patient could be cured, the more insistent were the claims of the asylum directors and the psychiatric professionals that they have immediate control of his destiny, in the interests of both the patient and the security of public order. In view of the general public conception of "degenerates" as violent and unpredictable sorts, and of madness as a species of degeneracy, it is not surprising that this mode of discourse gained a sympathetic hearing.

Psychiatrists did not rely exclusively, however, on the discourse of "curability-dangerousness" to enhance their social role as the technical interpreters of mental aberration. The reader may recall that in the prospectus of the *Annales d'hygiène publique et de médecine légale* in 1829, the new directors assured their readers that their aim was not solely to *cure*, but also to *prevent* illness by good social hygiene.[7] It is not a coincidence that B. A. Morel, the initial theoretician of degeneracy, became the chief exponent of this function of psychiatry. His prevailing pessimism about the effective treatment of illnesses that were at bottom biological and degenerative led him to stress a "preservative prophylaxy while trying to modify the intellectual, physical, and moral conditions of those who have been separated [by degeneracy] from the rest of mankind; it must, before returning them to the social environment, arm them, so to speak, against themselves with the aim of reducing the number of relapses." Medicine alone "is still able, in spite of the predominance of incurable cases, to be a precious means of self-preservation. It alone appreciates the nature of the causes that produce degenerescence in the human species, and to it alone belongs the right to indicate the positive remedies that may be employed against it."[8]

The change in the outlook of French psychiatry from Pinel's day to Magnan's is the best possible grounds for demonstrating the sensitivity of the profession to the deeper intellectual and cultural currents that affected the entire nation. Pinel's science of moral therapeutics faithfully reflected the rational individualism and the liberal philanthropy

---

[6] Ibid., pp. 106-107.

[7] See Castel, *L'ordre psychiatrique*, pp. 141-143.

[8] B. A. Morel, *Traité des dégénérescences*, p. 691, as quoted in Castel, *L'ordre psychiatrique* pp. 280-281.

of his generation. By the same token, the generation of psychiatry on which Magnan's synthesis put its stamp shared the deep anxieties of its contemporaries about the social effects of hereditary degeneration, the declining birthrate, the "intoxications" of alcohol, drugs, and syphilis, and other mainly biological problems. The shift in concern from the welfare and rehabilitation of the individual to the protection of the family and the social order was a trait that psychiatry had in common with scores of other professions and disciplines and with the French intellectual elite. In *fin-de-siècle* France there were no individual pathologies; there were social pathologies of which individuals were the signs.

The first serious efforts to revise the 1838 law were largely a product of the internal political dynamics of the Second Empire. Gambetta and Joseph Magnin, leaders of the Republican opposition, characterized the old law as capricious and authoritarian and proposed a new law in 1869 that gave juries the right to decide whether or not an individual was insane enough to qualify for internment. This bill failed to receive a serious hearing, as did a bill of 1872 proposed by Théophile Roussel. However, at Roussel's initiative, in 1887 the senate passed a comprehensive bill that was sent to the Chamber, but it failed even to make it to a first reading. This bill was revived in a slightly altered form by Joseph Reinach in the Chamber in 1893, but once again it failed to reach the floor. Both these bills embodied the major reforms demanded by both jurists and psychiatrists. They ended the administrative and medical monopoly of internment, providing for judicial review of committal and release processes. They both urged, in slightly different terms, the creation of "special quarters" for the isolation and treatment of particular categories of patients; both included provision for secure quarters for "insane" criminals. Each bill borrowed elements from the liberal penal reforms of those years, including a kind of provisional release (with medical veto) of "curable" patients. Finally, each bill increased surveillance of all asylums, Reinach's bill taking the extraordinary step of abolishing private asylums altogether.[9]

These bills failed owing to a combination of the indifference of the politicians and the apparent unwillingness of the permanent bureaucracy of the Interior Ministry to surrender any of its prerogatives. After the failure of Reinach's bill, psychiatrists began a systematic effort to educate public officials on the advantages of many of these reforms. Their strategy followed the general lines of the "curability-danger-

[9] For the details on these early bills the best account is Albert Mairet, *Le régime des aliénés: Révision de la loi de 1838* (Paris: Masson, 1914).

ousness" discourse noted by Robert Castel; that is, psychiatrists linked the discovery of treatments for new varieties of mental illness with findings about the unsuspected degree of danger these individuals posed to public security. Nor did they fail to exercise their claim as hygienic advisers, promoting themselves as the technicians par excellence of public health.

However, psychiatrists were also careful to lay stress on the civil rights of patients. The judicial liberals and reformers who had fought for civil liberties during the Dreyfus affair were their natural allies. In return for medical support for the rights of patients, psychiatrists could be sure of pleas by jurists in favor of special quarters and for the continued presence of the medical expert in the courts. In the campaign to educate the public, the lawyer and Radical deputy Jean Cruppi used language that nicely illustrates the mixed discourse adopted by the reform coalition of medicine and law. Writing to the readers of *Le matin* in 1901, Cruppi spoke of the need for psychiatric experts and magistrates to work together to identify and institutionalize the criminally insane in special quarters designed for them alone. He wanted to short-circuit the current two-step process wherein after the acquittal of a nonresponsible suspect, or the delivery of a verdict of *non-lieu*, an administrative decree on the dangers of the individual to public security had to be reached separately (under the 1838 law) before a *placement d'office* could put the lunatic into an asylum. But the effect of this "reform" had little to do with the safeguarding of individual rights; it was in fact designed to streamline the process of internment and avoid the likelihood that, in the absence of clear proof of dangerousness, the prefectural administration would fail to take the proper initiatives. Nonetheless, Cruppi chose to express himself in the mixed discourse of the period, arguing that this measure was needed to "prevent terrible crimes, monstrous convictions, or equally ludicrous acquittals" and that it would satify the needs of both "individual liberty and social defense."[10]

Councilor of State Henry Monod, permanent director of the Conseil supérieur de l'assistance et de l'hygiène publique, also supported a measure that would increase the diagnostic role of mental medicine in the courts. His findings put the annual number of individuals who were first sentenced to prison terms in French courts but were later transferred to asylums as manifestly insane at 1,000. Though his pri-

[10] *Le matin*, October 19, 1901. See also the support for this measure by the jurist Raphael Fontanille, in *Aliénation mentale et criminalité: Historique expertise médico-légale, Internement* (Grenoble: Allier, 1902), pp. 59-63.

mary message was indignation over the injustice done to the irresponsible, Monod's case depended heavily on the argument that cures of the mentally ill were dangerously delayed in these judicial errors, and that medical expertise should be required at the level of *instruction* and on a permanent basis in penitentiaries.[11]

From the late 1890s Monod's Conseil de l'assistance publique held an important series of hearings on the reform of the asylum system. In 1902 Monod pointed out that a serious lacuna of the 1838 law was its criterion that an individual must threaten public security before he qualified for state-supported asylum treatment. This law, Monod argued, discriminated against nondangerous indigent lunatics by depriving them of the benefits of the 1893 law on medical assistance. They could not be formally labeled in need of medical care unless they committed a crime; the authorities took no notice, he complained, of the mentally ill who were not an immediate threat to society. In support of Monod's position, however, Dr. Marcel Briand held that the early identification and treatment of the "nondangerous curable" were necessary because delaying treatment would be likely to convert these individuals into "incurable" and "dangerous" ones.[12] The argument for early treatment was a standard part of the psychiatric lexicon in the nineteenth century; it both justified the expansion of the domain of mental medicine, and "explained" the low rates of cure in the asylum system.[13]

Strong arguments were also made in favor of special asylums (or

[11] Henry Monod, "Deuxième note sur les aliénés méconnus et condamnés," Conseil supérieur de l'assistance publique, fasc. 50 (1899), pp. 1-109. In his survey of the public asylums Monod fully accepted the huge range of esoteric classifications used by the asylum directors to describe the illnesses of these "méconnus"; they are a curious mixture of organicist classification (*dégénérescence mentale*) and hangovers from the Esquirolian nosologies (*lypémanie, délire des persécutions*). See complete listing on pp. 108-109.

[12] "L'assistance médicale aux aliénés curables," Conseil supérieur de l'assistance publique, fasc. 92 (November 1902). Monod's remarks may be found on pp. 1-4, Briand's on pp. 17-19. Another defect of the financing of the 1838 law was pointed out by two other jurists, Henri Segnitz and Adrien Lesueur. When an indigent criminal was discovered to be insane, he was usually transferred to an asylum, where the penitentiary administration paid his expenses until the expiration of his punishment. However, cured or not, the patient was often released when the funds ceased coming in if he was not considered dangerous by the *médecin-directeur*. The potential danger of these individuals, these authors argued, and their poor behavior when mixed together with other patients were a grave cause of concern. "La réforme du régime des aliénés," *Revue politique et parlementaire* 57 (September 1908), pp. 488-489.

[13] For the British example see Scull, *Museums of Madness*, pp. 190-191.

quarters) for both alcoholics and the criminally insane at other hearings of the council. Valentin Magnan testified in the strongest possible terms in favor of the need for isolation and a special regime for "habitual drinkers." Alcoholics were not only an immediate danger to those around them, owing to their "violent natures," but they were also a danger "for the race, which they can infect with the terrible stigmata of degeneracy," producing "unstable or feeble individuals, idiots, epileptics, and the tubercular."[14] Magnan's supporters on the council endorsed his position with strong language about "social preservation," and approved the notion that an alcoholic ought to receive an indeterminate sentence until cured.[15] But skeptics, led by the reforming psychiatrist Dr. D. M. Bourneville, questioned the conflation of madness and alcohol. What, asked another interlocutor, would have been the consequence for French letters if Musset or Nerval had been given an indeterminate sentence for drunkenness?[16] Still, in his summary to the Ministry of the Interior, Monod stressed the general agreement of the group on the "growing progress" of alcoholism, adding that it doubtless complicated the population problem by raising mortality and lowering the birthrate.[17]

Another important debate at the council in 1901 concerned the creation of asylums for insane criminals. The measures supported in this session would provide magistrates with the authority, after "contradictory" psychiatric testimony (the defendant's mental expert), to send an insane individual accused of a crime to an extrasecure asylum. There was little discussion here of therapy for these individuals. In his remarks in support of this proposal the rapporteur Dr. Félix Regnault made an extraordinary statement on the danger of insane criminals, mixing the language of the street and the clinic.[18] These beings, he asserted, were afflicted with a "degeneracy of the affective and moral centers, so that their greatest desire is to plant a knife in your belly or burn down houses or harvests."[19]

[14] "Création d'asiles spéciaux pour les aliénés alcooliques," Conseil supérieur de l'assistance publique, fasc. 52 (1899), pp. 2-3, 11.

[15] See the remarks of Senator Théophile Roussell, Emile Cheysson, and Dr. Marcel Briand, in ibid., pp. 14, 26, 27.

[16] These are the remarks of Loys Brueyre in ibid., p. 12.

[17] The summary of Henry Monod's support for the creation of separate asylums is in ibid., pp. 31-33.

[18] On the whole, distinctions between *aliénés-criminels* and *criminels-aliénés* were not observed in these discussions.

[19] "Creation d'asiles spéciaux pour les aliénés criminels," Conseil supérieur de l'assistance publique, fasc. 83 (1901), pp. 6-8. Another of Regnault's reasons for these special asylums was the need to sequester the "vicious" insane from the non-

Two other psychiatrists, Magnan and Briand, spoke of their confidence in diagnosing the "dangerousness" of these "thoroughly harmful cases."[20] The veteran court observer Jean Cruppi insisted that such a reform would contribute to both "individual rights" and "social defense." The former, he assured his listeners, would be guaranteed by the "contradictory psychiatric testimony" in the tribunal.[21] Despite such assurances, the discussants overwhelmingly agreed that the advantage of such a measure lay in protecting society against the sort of degenerate described in Regnault's opening remarks. Only the dogged Dr. Bourneville characterized the measure as a pathetic return to the "*grilles*" and "*cachots*" of the middle ages. It seems fair to argue that in the agitation for revision of the 1838 law, while concern for individual rights was included, far more concern was expressed for the grave risk represented by the untreated and unrestrained madman.

The Dubief project, debated in the Chamber in early 1907, was the most comprehensive of all the pre-World War II efforts to reform the law of 1838, and the one that came closest to success.[22] Passed without opposition by the Chamber, it languished in the Senate. Revived in amended form by Paul Strauss, it seemed certain of passage on the eve of the war, until dying in the upheaval of 1914. In 1907 the project attracted an unusual amount of public and political attention and was widely supported by nearly all interested parties. It redistributed responsibilities and prerogatives among the administration, the magistracy, and mental medicine in such a way that none of these groups felt that its interests were harmed; thus, though some were not openly enthusiastic, at least no group made serious efforts at sabotage. Though not a government-sponsored bill, Fernand Dubief's reform had the blessing of Clemenceau's government, and Jean Cruppi, Joseph Reinach, and Dubief, its chief spokesmen in the Chamber, made every effort to incorporate the legal refinements suggested by the government's experts.

---

violent patients in asylums. See also Henry Colin, *Les aliénés vicieux dans les asiles* (Paris, 1900).

[20] "Création d'asiles spéciaux pour les aliénés criminels," pp. 39-41. Dr. Albert Mairet argued that only psychiatrists could judge this dangerousness, and that it was not always apparent to the untrained eye, especially in the organized world of the asylum. Mairet employed this "larval" theory to explain that "their present inoffensiveness is attributable exclusively to the condition of the environment in which they live; it is more apparent than real. When conditions change their offensiveness will not delay in reappearing." *Le régime des aliénés*, p. 224.

[21] "Création d'asiles spéciaux pour les aliénés" pp. 36-39.

[22] On the legislative details of the project see Mairet, *Le régime des aliénés*, pp. 93-101.

But the high degree of general interest in the bill was to a great extent an expression of the cultural fascination with pathology and things medical. An additional portion of drama was added to this debate by a circular distributed the previous year by Clemenceau, then interior minister in Sarrien's cabinet, to the prefectures. Seeking to establish firmly his claim as the future leader of Sarrien's left-of-center coalition, Clemenceau mentioned several recent instances of unjustified internment and reminded his prefects that they had the right to intervene in behalf of individuals they believed to be wrongly confined to asylums.[23] Though he chose his words with great care, many psychiatrists interpreted his remarks as an admonition and reacted indignantly. Clemenceau's actions were ostensibly taken in response to certain scandals reported in the left-wing press. However, the charge of improper internship was a venerable one, and Clemenceau's circular was not an unusual action. No wave of releases followed the distribution of the circular.

A major object of the Dubief bill was to break the administrative and medical monopoly on the internment and release of the insane.[24] A longer and more medically precise report than the one required under the 1838 law was demanded under the new bill. It was to be done within twenty-four hours of the admission of the patient, and a copy was to be sent to the district prosecutor.[25] Within fifteen days a definitive medical report was to be filed with the prefect and with the district tribunal. Internment could then only become definitive if the district magistrate, with the patient's full medical dossier at his disposal, so ordered. At this stage a challenge to the internment could be made by the guardian of the patient or by the district prosecutor. In such cases the magistrates had to meet in *conseil* (three judges, a majority deciding) and a "contradictory" medical opinion had to be solicited. Following definitive internment, the prosecutor gained the right to order new hearings on his own initiative. The new bill also attempted to plug the notorious lacuna of the old procedure whereby a verdict of *non-lieu* or acquittal for criminal nonresponsibility ended the court's role in the fate of the former suspect, leaving the initiative for intern-

[23] The circular was widely reprinted. See *Annales médico-psychologiques* (June 1906), pp. 150-153.

[24] Fernand Dubief, a veteran Radical legislator, was a former civil servant and had once been the chief administrator of a major provincial asylum. He appears to have had strong ties with the psychiatric community and had long been a supporter of reform legislation.

[25] In the case of a private asylum the prefect was required to obtain an independent medical judgment within three days.

ment to the police and the prefecture. Under the new procedure the suspect was returned to the original tribunal of jurisdiction for a hearing on his internment. After new and "contradictory" medical testimony he could be interned if it was thought he was a danger to public security. However, these were in effect the same grounds on which the prefectural *placements d'office* had taken place under the old law.[26] Indeed, it could be argued that, apart from the required "contradictory" expertise, the new law merely substituted the tribunal for the prefect in what was essentially a measure of public security, indeed a more effective one than under the old law.

A feature of the bill that seems indisputably to have had the interests of the patients at heart were the articles protecting their financial holdings. Designed to forestall the rapacious legal maneuvers of greedy relatives, the Dubief bill required that the property of interned individuals be held in trust and administered by a committee of local notables until final legal disposition could be made. These provisions of the bill were certainly the heart of the "patient's rights" section of the bill and were passed without any opposition in the Chamber; but their passage in no way compromised the deeply felt priority of social defense.

It would be inaccurate to conclude from the foregoing that the new bill proposed a diminution of the role of the doctor in the new regime. Dubief went out of his way to assure the Chamber that the more precise medical reports and "contradictory" expertise required in his bill meant no disparagement of the medical profession.[27] Indeed, it appears that in the provisions touching on medical reorganization the bill evinced great faith in the aims and abilities of mental medicine. It explicitly ordered the creation of the special quarters for idiots, epileptics, alcoholics, and the criminally insane for which psychiatrists had been vigorously lobbying. Departments were given ten years to build these institutions, a clear intrusion of the power of the state into the domain of private asylum care. During the debates it became clear that most of the indignation of the civil-rights militants was directed against the private asylums and the great number of new clinics advertising cures

[26] The Senate version of Paul Strauss was amended to add to the public security clause, which was a legal concept, a medical one which also allowed internment for those, public danger aside, "possessed of mental disease." See Mairet, *Le régime des aliénés*, p. 100. It is practically unnecessary to remark on the great importance of this sort of innovation: public danger and mental illness were regarded as synonymous.

[27] Fernand Dubief, *Journal officiel*, "Chambre des députés," January 14, 1907, p. 20.

for the ravages of neurasthenia.[28] Government surveillance, a feature of the new bill, was extended to private institutions despite some objections to the assault on "liberties." Joseph Reinach unsuccessfully attempted to have private institutions abolished altogether. None of these measures was unwelcome to the psychiatrists. Nearly all psychiatric interning and full-time placement took place within the network of the state-supported asylum system. Few specialists trained at the Bicêtre or the Salpêtrière by the acknowledged European masters in mental medicine left the public asylum system, with the consequence that private institutions were usually guided by medical generalists.

In his opening remarks Dubief set the tone for the entire debate by stressing that a major aim of the new bill was to incorporate the treatment of the insane into the structure of public assistance. He attacked the old law for laying undue emphasis on public security and neglecting treatment. My bill, he declared to general enthusiasm, "is not a simple law of security, but a medical law, a law of healing."[29] Dubief proceeded to explain that much had changed within mental medicine since 1838. One used to believe, he said, that only "acute and accidental psychoses" could be cured, but now it is known that even the long-term mentally ill could be cured, and these in ever-increasing numbers. He referred to the mentally ill as "sick" and called for an alliance between the "hospitalization applied to those afflicted with mental disease" and the "hospitalization that is applied to all other illnesses."[30] But what did Dubief mean by calling for this new "regime worthy of our century and of the Republic"?

If one follows Dubief's justifications for separate quarters and special treatments, one finds a message different from the humane welfare-state rhetoric of the preceding passages, something much closer to the medical model I have been at pains to elaborate. According to Dubief, epileptics needed special quarters not only because of the danger of their injuring themselves, but because their "crises" could engender

---

[28] See the remarks of Victor Fort and Jean Cruppi, *Journal officiel*, "Chambre des députés," January 14, 1907, p. 28; and Cruppi, ibid., January 17, 1907, p. 53. The argument was successfully made here to extend surveillance to all institutions of any sort purporting to treat "nervous" illnesses.

[29] Dubief, *Journal officiel*, "Chambre des députés," January 14, 1907, p. 21.

[30] Ibid. This language did not appear, however, anywhere in the text of the bill itself; that document was content to speak of the state's obligation to "care" (*soigner*) for the mentally ill. When later in the debate Edouard Vaillant insisted on inserting the declaration, "The asylum is assimilated in all measure possible into the hospital," he met with considerable resistance from the government and the bill's sponsors, indicating the limits to which their rhetoric could be pushed. See this discussion, *Journal officiel*, "Chambre des députés," January 21, 1907, pp. 102-103.

epileptic contagion affecting the "predisposed" individuals among the general asylum population. The education of idiots and cretins would permit the replacement of "exterior" disciplines by interior "safe-guards" and would make them useful citizens and deliver them from the "bad instincts" that too often rule them "—and you know that the instincts of idiots and cretins are among the worst."[31] Finally, Dubief justified special quarters for alcoholics (*buveurs*) afflicted with this "dis-ease of the will" on the grounds that their drunken ravings were usually diagnosed as only temporary in nature, and this was inadequate grounds for the permanent internment they often required. Thus, individuals with severely damaged "cerebral centers" were released to steal and perhaps kill to support their "fatal" need for drink. The newspaper accounts of "fathers cutting the throats of their wives and children," setting fire to their own or neighbors' houses, or committing other "terrible" crimes would cease once one recognized alcoholism as a species of madness that required long and systematic treatment.[32]

The sections of the bill that dealt with the establishment of special quarters for "insane criminals" constituted by far the greatest break with past practice, in part because they rewrote the code of criminal procedure. The bill required that criminal juries (or magistrates in the correctional courts) address not only the question of the defendant's *culpability* but also that of his *responsibility* for his criminal act and decide this issue by a majority vote. The advantage of this "innovation" and "guarantee," as Dubief called it, was the protection it offered to the insane defendant against the danger of being condemned to a peni-tentiary where he would receive no treatment for his illness and undergo a punishment he did not deserve.[33]

[31] Dubief, *Journal officiel*, "Chambre des députés," January 14, 1907, p. 21.

[32] Ibid.

[33] Both the principal speakers on the measure, Reinach and Dubief, stressed the horrors of false condemnation for the insane. This provision was also aimed at ameliorating a situation in assizes procedures that many observers had deplored. When a jury was confronted with a case where it feared that the magistrate would reverse the sense of its decision in his pronouncement of the sentence, it often attempted to anticipate him by changing its verdict. For example, the formal penalty for infanticide was death, but it was seldom pronounced. If a jury feared the magistrate might pronounce that sentence against its better judgment, it might choose to acquit. On the other hand, the jury, fearing too great a reduction of the penalty by a judge, might refuse to find for extenuating circumstances despite clear evidence that they existed. This standoff sometimes resulted in what Jean Cruppi called "a bastard regime of reciprocal concessions," in which a compromise was worked out between judge and jury in negotiations. By deciding both culpability and responsibility, the acquittals and *non-lieus* delivered by juries and magistrates attempting to redress one another's exaggerations would not result in potentially

However, judging from the presentation and debate in the Chamber, one might conclude that a more important aim of this provision was to vigorously tighten public security. These special quarters were designed to hold the individuals judged nonresponsible in criminal trials, as well as those who committed "crimes" in asylums or went mad while in prison. Joseph Reinach, who had made a reputation for himself as a reformer *au courant* of science and medicine, took it upon himself to describe the nature of these "insane criminals." Using the outmoded terminology of Esquirol, Reinach referred to the "monomanias" of homicide, theft, and arson, asserting that these "illnesses" were the product of organic lesions. Despite the unlikelihood of cure, the asylum is the best place for these beings because "if the insane are sick, the insane criminals are the sickest of the sick."[34] Reinach mocked the jurists who resisted the jury's pronouncement of irresponsibility; he was entirely satisfied that this measure "is in perfect accord with the most reliable theories of modern science and of the modern idea of justice."[35] It was the psychiatrist who would realize this "modern" rapprochement of science and justice and who was to be the key to this system of social defense.

According to the bill, no one could be released from an asylum for insane criminals unless the responsible doctor declared him not only "cured" and unlikely to disturb public "decency and tranquillity," but also not "susceptible to relapse." These pronouncements were to be delivered in full tribunal where the role of the court could be as much to check hasty releases of asylum patients as to guarantee their rights. Finally, the law provided for strict surveillance of former insane criminals and waived the usual hearing and detailed medical report on the reinternment of anyone suspected of a relapse.

Once interned in these special asylums, Reinach argued, the patient, "you may be assured, will get out no more easily than from a prison or a convict colony [*bagne*]."[36] Quite simply, in Reinach's view, no doctor would release a patient who was likely to have a relapse. "I believe, and I am seconded in this by nearly all men of science, that the doctor will make such a declaration very rarely. Esquirol long ago affirmed

---

dangerous individuals being left at liberty. On this reform see Jean Cruppi, *La cour d'assises* (Paris: Calmann-Levy, 1898), p. 100, and Henry Berr, "Ce qu'est le jury criminel: Ce qu'il devrait être," *Revue politique et parlementaire* 53 (September 1907), pp. 499-501.

[34] Joseph Reinach, *Journal officiel*, "Chambre des députés," January 14, 1907, p. 26.

[35] Ibid., p. 26.

[36] Ibid.

that homicidal mania was incurable, and there is overwhelming proof that this is still the case. The proposition, in any event, is taken for granted by the English legislator that the individual afflicted with homicidal or incendiary monomania is in fact interned for life."[37]

Reinach mixed the discourse of individual rights and social defense while castigating his fellow deputies for not being as progressive in defending individual liberties as the English, who, he asserted, had possessed asylums for the criminally insane since 1860. He concluded by saying: "In fact, however, the text before you at this moment proposes nothing less than perpetual internment in a special asylum. If you adopt this measure we may acquit without fear those who are [penally] irresponsible or mad."[38]

Despite the humanitarian rhetorical flourishes, there seems little doubt that the great majority of the deputies knew they were making a law of social defense, one that enhanced security and promoted public hygiene against a growing tide of insanity. Many remarks were made concerning the rising rates of alcoholism and the relations between crime, madness, and alcoholism which the new bill addressed.[39] There seemed to be a consensus that, despite disputes over the number of asylum patients, insanity was on the increase and asylums grossly overcrowded, leaving little realistic chance for overburdened doctors to effect cures.[40] Yet a proposal by a government administrator to increase dramatically the number of doctors in asylums failed because agreement could not be reached about who would bear the cost of this expensive work force. Indeed, the most intense debates throughout the four days of discussion were over matters of financing. It even appears as if the apparently progressive measure providing for conditional release was a stopgap device allowing asylum doctors to eliminate from public asylums the mentally deficient who were there because they lacked private means or willing families. The measure's chances of success were no doubt enhanced by the statistics that were

[37] Ibid. It appears that Dubief had no more real faith in the wholesale curability of the insane than Reinach. P. A. Lefort maliciously teased Dubief by quoting from a private conversation with him in which Dubief claimed that psychiatry was closely linked to medicine now since "all brain illnesses have a lesion as a physical cause." *Journal officiel*, "Chambre des députés," January 17, 1907, p. 59.

[38] Ibid., p. 26.

[39] See especially the debate on January 14, 1907, in the *Journal officiel*, "Chambre des députés," pp. 27-31 and January 21, 1907, ibid., p. 106.

[40] Léon Mirman, the government expert on mental illness, gave the following statistics: in Germany there was one doctor for every 107 *aliénés*; in the Paris region one for every 240; and in provincial asylums only one for every 445. *Journal officiel*, "Chambre des députés," January 14, 1907, p. 32.

presented alleging the French to be far behind other European countries in the annual percentage of "cures" of lunatics.[41] In his concluding remarks Dubief invited the Chamber to continue its work of social assistance: "There still remains much to be done to relieve all the misery from which humanity suffers."[42] Despite the humane rhetoric the bill was very much a "disciplinary" measure of public security on the medical model of social defense that had so much currency in the first decade of the twentieth century. The final vote was a voice vote without apparent demurral.

On the whole, reaction within the psychiatric and legal-medical communities was favorable to the new project. Some commentators objected to the new practice of "contradictory expertise," arguing that it compromised the scientific basis of expert testimony and was a "contradiction in terms."[43] Others, however, freely welcomed the innovation, holding that it would ultimately strengthen the hand of mental medicine and avoid embarrassing disasters like the Jeanne Weber case.[44] There was the anticipated amount of carping about the large new role played by the judiciary in internment, and some spirited defenses of the past record of collaboration between the prefects and the doctors,[45] but most doctors regarded the provisions on patients' legal and financial rights as manifest advances and the new legal safeguards as harmless to their work.[46]

The verdict was practically unanimous on the advantages of the new bill for the organization of psychiatric medicine. The bill put no serious

[41] A deputy from the Nord, Gustave Dron presented figures showing that in France only 6.26 per 100 of the mentally ill were "cured." Villejuif, in the Paris region, had the best rate at 12 per 100, while German asylums regularly achieved rates of 18 and 20 per 100. *Journal officiel*, "Chambre des députés," January 22, 1907, p. 125.

[42] Dubief, *Journal officiel*, "Chambre des députés," January 22, 1907, p. 142.

[43] Victor Parent, "La désignation contradictoire des experts devant les tribuneaux," *Bulletin de la Société générale des prisons* 31 (February 1907), p. 345. See also Charles Constant, "Rapport," *Bulletin de la Société de médecine légale* (April 1908), pp. 187-193; Gustave Drouineau, "La nouvelle loi sur les aliénés," *Revue philanthropique* 20 (February 1907), pp. 403-420.

[44] Raoul LeRoy, "La responsabilité et l'hystérie," *Annales d'hygiène publique*, 4th ser. 9 (June 1908), pp. 411-412.

[45] Dr. Albert Giraud wondered what competence a magistrate could have on internment "situated as he is in his office, without having seen the sick person." See "Chronique," *Annales médico-psychologiques* (March 1907), p. 183.

[46] For example, Antony Rodiet, "Sur la réforme de la loi de 1838," *Revue de l'hypnotisme et de psychologie physiologique* 21 (October 1906), pp. 123-126; they were also grateful for the numerous references in the project to medical expertise, a formal acknowledgment of their integral part in the criminal justice system.

obstacles in the way of the guarantees of a rapid treatment, and psychiatrists and doctors of legal medicine were especially delighted at the creation of the new special quarters.[47] These quarters ensured a new flow of public appropriations and the subsidizing of the latest technology for the treatment of the mentally ill. When it became clear that the Senate would delay final passage of the bill, it was the special quarters, in particular those for criminals and alcoholics, that received most of the attention in the professional press. From 1907 until 1914 psychiatrists and doctors of legal medicine kept up a steady drumfire of propaganda that they hoped would arouse public support for their cause. They demonstrated thereby not only their belief that these new institutions were crucial to the "progress" of mental medicine, but a clear willingness to serve as the police of moral discipline in the *belle époque*.

Beginning in early 1903, Dr. Antoine Ritti, editor of the venerable *Annales médico-psychologiques*, had begun publishing a regular column entitled "Les aliénés en liberté." Ritti listed all the crimes culled from the Paris and provincial press allegedly committed by mentally disturbed individuals. According to Ritti, between 1903 and 1908, 455 crimes ranging from homicide and death threats to arson were committed by individuals later judged to be insane. No fact, he asserted, could more eloquently defend the useful social role of psychiatrists than these "hecatombs," these "massacres of innocents, victims of delirious individuals that indifference, fear, and ignorance permit to wander without care or surveillance in our towns and countryside."[48]

Ritti had been clearly stung by the brief press campaign in some of the left-of-center press in support of Clemenceau's charge of medical cooperation in unjust internments. In the following years, during the concerted effort to have the Dubief bill made law, the notions "public security" and "individual liberty" became increasingly incompatible in psychiatric discourse. Many testily denied that arbitrary sequestrations were frequent occurrences, and argued that when these did occur they were blown out of proportion by the "political" (left-wing) press.[49] Dr. Albert Mairet claimed that in his twenty-three years of practice no more than 2.08 percent of the internees in his asylum in Montpellier

[47] Victor Parent, "Les garanties d'un traitement rapide," *Annales médico-psychologiques* (May 1907), pp. 401-413.

[48] Antoine Ritti, "Les aliénés en liberté," *Annales médico-psychologiques* (January 1908), pp. 5-6.

[49] Ibid., p. 5; Gustave Drouineau, "Compte-rendu du XVIᵉ congrès des médecins aliénistes," *Annales médico-psychologiques* (July 1906), p. 228.

turned out to have been wrongly admitted.[50] Many commentators darkly warned that by far the greater danger was in the general failure to recognize the widespread and threatening presence of the insane throughout society and in other public institutions.

Psychiatric commentators spiced their demands for special asylums—in particular criminal asylums—by figures showing the high percentage (one claimed 60) of insane in the penitentiaries,[51] and by emphasizing the great threat of these "dangerous psychopaths" to the regular prison population.[52] A major study of asylum escapees promoted the view that these individuals were "degenerate and morally perverse," requiring special security measures and a "disciplinary surveillance."[53] Others suggested that many of the violent and "passionate crimes" were committed by "alcoholics, the unstable, and degenerates," some of whom had been prematurely released from asylums by well-meaning prefects.[54] The widespread claims that violent individuals were at large were invariably coupled with appeals for placing even more discretionary power for internment in the hands of psychiatrists. Dr. Paul Sérieux, the protégé of Valentin Magnan, called for the return of psychiatric *lettres de cachet* and Magnan's coauthor, Dr. Paul-Marie LeGrain, assured readers that "we are desirous that society be freed of these noxious elements."[55] The general turn to a new "protective and preservative regime," in LeGrain's words, fully squares with Robert Castel's observations about the renewed emphasis on the public hygiene component in mental medicine.[56] Mairet articulated perfectly this imperial aspect of psychiatry in his book on asylum reform: "The field

[50] Mairet, *Le régime des aliénés*, p. 180.

[51] F. Poctet, "Enquête internationale sur l'aliénation mentale dans les prisons," *Revue de psychiatrie* 12 (February 1908), pp. 44-46.

[52] Paul Sérieux and Lucien Libert, "De l'internement des anormaux constitutionnels: Asiles de sûreté et prisons d'état," *Archives d'anthropologie criminelle* 27 (1912), pp. 342-343. Mairet called them "revolutionaries" and "wicked and violent" in *Le régime des aliénés*, p. 129.

[53] Georges Collet, *Sur les évasions des aliénés* (Lyon: Delaroche, 1907), pp. 57-60.

[54] Henri Charuel and Gaston Haury, "Un aliéné en liberté: Un persécuté reconnu tel par toutes les autorités pendant plusieurs années et non interné," *Archives d'anthropologie criminelle* 27 (1912), pp. 191, 202. Henry Huchard, "Les aliénés en liberté," *Revue de l'hypnotisme* 22 (May 1908), pp. 321-323. Huchard approved of Ritti's publication of the crimes of the insane in the *Annales médico-psychologiques*. See also Félix Regnault, "A propos du crime de Soleilland," *Revue de l'hypnotisme* 21 (March 1907), pp. 281-282.

[55] Sérieux and Libert, "De l'internement des anormaux constitutionnels," pp. 348-349; Paul-Marie LeGrain, "L'expertise médico-légale et la question de la responsabilité," *Revue de l'hypnotisme* 22 (November 1907), p. 251.

[56] LeGrain, "L'expertise médico-légale," p. 252.

of action of medicine extends over the whole range of public assistance, treatment, hygiene, and the well-being of the sick. Treatment and hygiene must be placed under [medicine's] direction and inspection."[57]

At the same time as psychiatrists, government officials and magistrates slowly began to embrace policies affirming the sure evolution toward doctrines of social defense. Shocked into action by revelations on the links between mental illness and alcohol, the Clemenceau ministry sent a circular to the state asylums requesting information on alcoholic patients.[58] Since professional psychiatric journals had lamented the lax enforcement of the public drunkenness laws and given maximum publicity to the crime-madness-alcohol connection,[59] it is not surprising that the survey of alcoholics in asylums revealed increases in their numbers since 1897; it stated a provisional figure of 13 for the percentage of insanity caused in some degree by alcoholism.[60] *Juges*

[57] Mairet, *Le régime des aliénés*, p. 151. This control, in Mairet's opinion, ought to extend to all aspects of asylum life, including the recruitment and administration of asylum guardians and personnel. He favored the recruitment of local people, which offered great advantages "by way of discipline [and] attachment to service, and as a means of realizing such improvements as the elimination of all signs of contention," p. 155.

[58] The circular itself was the very model of *fin-de-siècle* nosology. The government requested the listing of alcoholics in one of three classes depending on the extent of the alcoholism:

A. Simple alcoholism: hallucinatory delirium, weakening of the faculties, etc., or where alcohol is the exclusive cause of mental troubles.

B. Alcoholism complicated by degenerescence or mental debility "or where there is alcoholism among the ascendants."

C. Mental illnesses in which alcoholism figures among the determining causes. See the reprint of the ministerial circular in *Annales médico-psychologiques* (March 1907), pp. 345-346. See also the letter sent to Clemenceau by Charles Dupuy of the Senate and Alexandre Ribot of the Chamber begging his action on alcohol as a source of "moral and physical disorders." *Bulletin de la Société générale des prisons* 31 (February 1907), pp. 285-286.

[59] See the editorial "L'application de la loi du 23 Janvier 1873, tendant à réprimer l'ivresse publique," *Revue de médecine légale* 1 (February 25, 1906), pp. 287-289. According to statistics compiled by the head of government judicial statistics, Maurice Yvernès, the government put enormous pressure on the police to increase arrests under the 1873 law. Convictions in all tribunals jumped dramatically from 1906 to 1907, clearly indicating the new degree of official consciousness about the dangers of drink. In 1906 judgments by simple police and correctional tribunals rose respectively from 43,152 to 62,965 and 6,913 to 10,065. Maurice Yvernès, "L'alcoolisme et la criminalité," *Journal de la Société de statistique de Paris* 49 (November 1908), pp. 375-377. Yvernès insisted that the problem now went beyond the danger to individuals and posed a threat to the "social organism." Yvernès also explicitly linked alcoholism with madness, crime and suicides. "L'alcoolisme et la criminalité," pt. 2, p. 401.

[60] These figures were reprinted in "Les alcooliques dans les asiles d'aliénés," *Revue*

d'instruction were also asked to address two new questions in the standard form sent on to the correctional and assizes magistrates: was the infraction committed under the influence of alcohol, and was the accused an "inveterate alcoholic"?[61]

The effect of the campaign to reform the 1838 law on the asylum regime was to further tighten links that were already present in the medical model of deviance between insanity, dangerousness, and constitutional "perversity." Despite the presence of a clear sympathy for the civil and financial rights of the mentally ill, the overwhelming emphasis in the reformist agenda was placed on the location and control of the most threatening manifestations of insanity. Historically, madness has probably never had a wholly transparent social identity; it has assumed the mantle of divine inspiration, of prophetic genius, and, in the eighteenth century, of deluded reason. But it is unlikely that the *social* image of madness was ever before so closely aligned with moral disorder and common deviance as it was in this era. As we shall see, the collapse of the distinctions between crime, alcohol, madness, and other deviant behavior provoked some unusually harsh suggestions on treatment and moral responsibility by both medical professionals and concerned intellectuals.

While psychiatrists were organizing their campaign for asylum reform, trouble was brewing on another front. As we have seen, the 1907 bill contained a provision that allowed the courts, after medical advice, to pronounce on both the guilt *and* the responsibility of a criminal defendant, making it unlikely that a nonresponsible criminal would escape some form of close confinement. Before this alternative surfaced, however, a different approach was attempted that plunged the community of experts on mental medicine into a crisis. In 1905 Joseph

---

philanthropique 22 (February 1908), p. 329. In his own study of alcoholism at the huge Ville-Evrard asylum, Dr. R. Benon found that of the alcoholics there, 95 percent were "potential" criminals and 51 percent "actual" criminals. Eighty-four percent of these insane alcoholics had pathological exterior defects and were "automatons" without the slightest degree of individual responsibility. "L'alcoolisme et criminalité," *Bulletin de la Société de médecine légale* (May 1907), pp. 99-103. A later, more elaborate study was done at the Saint Anne asylum by Magnan and Fillasier. They revealed that alcoholism had increased dramatically since 1868. Even worse, the number of insane at Saint Anne who had an alcoholic among their immediate ascendants had gone from 35 per 100 to 37 per 100 for men and from 16 per 100 to 20 per 100 for women. Figures on women's alcoholism were increasing especially fast, and fully three-quarters of all male inmates at Saint Anne's were either alcoholics or the descendants of alcoholics. "L'alcool et la folie à l'asile St. Anne," *Archives d'anthropologie criminelle* 28 (1913), pp. 159-160.

[61] Quoted in Yvernès, "L'alcoolisme et la criminalité," p. 404.

Chaumié, the Minister of Justice in the Rouvier ministry, sent a circular to the district prosecutors concerning criminal responsibility. The "Chaumié circular" required two new questions to be asked of the expert medical witnesses in criminal cases. Whereas the medical expert had been previously asked only to pronounce on whether the accused was "demented" at the time of his crime, he was now asked, first, whether the accused had "mental anomalies," and, second, whether these anomalies were of such a nature that they qualified him for the dementia provision of article 64 or, in the case of a less serious illness, "in what measure was the defendant, at the moment of the infraction, responsible for the act with which he is charged?"[62]

The immediate reason offered by the minister for these new questions was that he was responding to the repeated requests of magistrates and penologists for more help from medical witnesses in passing appropriate sentences. According to Chaumié, the general response of "reduced" or "limited" responsibility was not particularly helpful and a more precise estimate of criminal responsibility was necessary. The circular also referred to the bewildering variety of "intermediate" stages of mental illness such as "degeneracy" and "morbid impulsion" requiring translation into the language of penal responsibility.[63]

The publication of the circular marked the beginning of a new crisis in the relations between jurists and doctors, which, as we have already seen, had not always been smooth. But it also precipitated a profound division within the medical community about how best to respond to this request. Many psychiatric experts were reluctant to pronounce on degrees of responsibility, believing that this did not lie within their sphere of competence. After pressing for generations for an expanded role for medical expertise in the judicial system, many doctors now appeared to be unwilling to assume the new tasks of social defense alongside jurists. Is this a contradiction of the imperialistic ambitions often attributed to French psychiatry, or is it rather, as I shall argue, a reflection of the complexity of the choices involved and of divisions within the medical community itself?

To a very great extent the psychiatrists of the post-1905 period were simply feeling the fallout from the historical ambitions and presumptions of mental medicine. Article 64 of the penal code, by making dementia the criterion of judicial irresponsibility, had made it possible for jurists to rule on the basis of common sense and with a minimum

[62] From the Chaumié circular, quoted in *Revue de médecine légale* 1, no. 1 (1906), pp. 46-47. See also Lamarche-Vadel and Preli, *L'asile*, pp. 21-22.
[63] "Chaumié circular," *Revue de médecine légale* 1, no. 1 (1906), pp. 46-47.

of medical intervention. By the 1820s, however, psychiatrists had already "begun to discern mental syndromes that were expressed in particular obsessive compulsions and that were not characterized by any general debilitating dementia." These "involuntary acts without delirium," as Castel has called them, were embodied in the celebrated group of monomanias of Esquirol and his disciples, who thus "pathologized a whole new sector of comportment."[64] However, as the generation of the 1850s discovered, medicolegal testimony had to tread a thin line. Psychiatrists could not take refuge in medical arcana because decisions of responsibility would be made anyway, in the words of J. P. Falret, "without us, in spite of us, against us."[65]

However, in expanding the horizons of madness, as in fact was done in the group of monomanias, psychiatrists could not risk the fearsome charge of seeing madmen everywhere, thus inhibiting the "proper" function of penal repression. What is more, the nature of the psychiatric diagnosis was critical; if it failed to be empirically convincing to jurists and jurors, it invited skepticism and incredulity. It was precisely this test that monomanias failed. Defects of the reasoning apparatus were not, in the absence of other external signs, convincing to the lay observer, and this fact in itself was in part responsible for the gradual abandonment of monomanias and the victory of the "organic" hypothesis over the moral one.[66]

From the 1840s on, psychiatrists experimented with various descriptions of intermediate stages, including *folie raisonnante* (Marc), *folie lucide* (Trélat), or *folie périodique* (Bigot), in an effort to find a formula that would accommodate the traditional basis of penal responsibility and the observations of the clinic. While not taking the right to punish out of the hands of jurists altogether, these intermediate categories usually permitted doctors to fulfill their professional and legal obligations, even if they did not always satisfy the requirements of magistrates and juries. During the 1860s, psychiatric militants like Eugène Dally advanced the argument that the new materialistic medicine was scientific enough to treat the issue of penal responsibility under its own rubric, thus making the choice between prison or the asylum a question of heredity and cranial anatomy. The controversy over this early "organic" thesis simmered throughout the 1860s and 1870s, but divisions between the medical experts and the penologists were never unbridgeable. For their part the psychiatrists resisted the extreme anatomical

[64] Castel, *L'ordre psychiatrique*, p. 175.
[65] Quoted in ibid., p. 180.
[66] Ibid., pp. 180-182.

determinism of Dally; they concentrated in practice on making the most convincing case for insanity under the terms of article 64.[67] Penologists, as we have seen, were willing to meet the doctors partway, admitting some of the biological and medical limitations on free will and absolute responsibility.[68]

Following the defeat of the Lombrosian heresy, organicist nosology became increasingly complicated. By 1900, like a giant whirlpool, degeneracy theory had pulled into its vortex a huge area of individual and social behavior, and new terminology was invented to accommodate these efforts to extend the boundaries of mental pathology. By the eve of the drafting of the Chaumié circular, jurors in assizes trials and magistrates throughout the criminal justice system had become dependent on medical expertise to help them through this terminological maze. The extent of this growing dependence can be clearly observed in the judicial calendars of the newspapers and in the technical reports of psychiatrists reprinted in the professional journals, yet this dependence still had, in the words of one sympathetic observer, "the force of a professional secret."[69] How did one judge, for example, the relative weight of heredity and environment, weigh the influence of alcoholic parents or a deprived childhood, and settle finally on the degree of penal responsibility possessed by the accused as required by law?

The historian Henri Berr, who served on a Paris assizes jury in 1907, has left us an account of how complicated this process actually was. According to Berr, each case finally resolved itself into a difficult decision about penal responsibility for which some knowledge of "moral

---

[67] See, in general, Castel, "Des experts providentiels," in *L'ordre psychiatrique*, pp. 153-190; an excellent example of this strategy is E. LeLorraine, *De l'aliéné au point de vue de la responsabilité pénale* (Paris, 1882).

[68] Elme Caro, "La responsabilité morale et le droit de punir dans les nouvelles écoles philosophiques," *Revue des deux mondes* (August 1, 1873), pp. 531-564. See also Ludovic Carrau, "La folie au point de vue psychologique," pt. 2, ibid. (October 15, 1876), p. 858. Carrau accepted much of the work of Despine, Maudsley, B. A. Morel, and Théodule Ribot, acknowledging the clear evidence that heredity and environment shaped the nature of moral judgments. He was even willing to concede that there was a larger proportion of the insane among criminals than among the rest of the population, p. 856. See also part 1 of the same article, ibid. (November 16, 1876), pp. 348-372.

[69] Edmond Locard, *Archives d'anthropologie criminelle* 22 (1907), pp. 60-61. For a summary of the major criminal trials of the years 1904-1905 see the collected writings of Edgard Troimaux, the popular court reporter for the *Echo de Paris*. *Les procès célèbres de l'année 1904-1905* (Paris: Librairie Universelle, 1905). Some typical medical testimony stressing the heredity and degeneration of criminals appears on pp. 150, 267-270.

and especially pathological psychology" as well as information from sociology was necessary to make intelligent judgments.[70] One trial in particular was an excellent example of the problems involved in expert testimony. The medical expert, Dr. Brissaud, pronounced the defendant to be "a perfect specimen of degenerate moral insanity," and concluded his testimony with a pitch for "prison-hospitals." But what help was this testimony to jurors trying to decide on the defendant's responsibility for his crime and the appropriate punishment or treatment? Berr was amazed to find that at least one of his fellow jurors concluded that the defendant in question was innocent and so voted.[71] It is no wonder that, required to make practical decisions with only esoteric expert testimony at their disposal, magistrates out of desperation importuned the justice minister to ask psychiatrists to pronounce directly on the question of responsibility. The psychiatrist Charles Blondel reminded his colleagues that for magistrates and the general public, the problem of responsibility resolved itself into a matter of repression and self-protection: "If their good will toward science is not returned in kind, they are hindered without being enlightened, and frustrated rather than led."[72]

The response of the psychiatric community in France to the Chaumié circular was largely to refuse to pronounce on the required second question dealing with responsibility. The majority of the community clearly preferred to maintain the practice of pronouncing only on the nature of the mental illness itself. This essentially defensive posture reached its clearest public expression at the 1907 summer congress of the "alienists and neurologists of the French-speaking world" held in Geneva. By a clear majority the congress passed two resolutions proposed by the distinguished psychiatrist and medical professor Gilbert Ballet. One stated that questions of moral responsibility were "entirely of a metaphysical, not a medical order." The other held that as a general principle expert medical witnesses ought to confine their testimony to the "reality and the nature of mental troubles."[73] Members of the minority, led by the clinician Joseph Grasset, had vigorously defended the notion that psychiatry was now perfectly able to decide questions of responsibility, but the greater sympathy still lay with the

[70] Berr, "Ce qu'est le jury criminel," p. 493. Jean Cruppi makes the same point in *La cour d'assises*, pp. 60-61.

[71] Berr "Ce qu'est le jury criminel," p. 494.

[72] Charles Blondel, "Les médecins et la responsabilité," *Revue de Paris* 15 (July 15, 1908), p. 365.

[73] Reprinted in *Bulletin de la Société de médecine légale* (July 1907), p. 168.

conventional wisdom that medicine and justice dealt with different matters.

Under normal circumstances this reaction of the psychiatrists would have gone entirely unnoticed. Unfortunately for the profession, however, this gesture was made in the midst of a major crisis of public confidence in the ability of public officials to protect people from what was perceived as a rising tide of crime and violence. Ironically, as we have seen, psychiatrists themselves had contributed to this public mood by virtue of their long campaign to educate the public about the dangers of alcoholics, degenerates, and the criminally insane and by their reminders of the great numbers of potentially violent "madmen at large." When the results of the Geneva congress became known, the big Paris daily *Le matin* announced with bold headlines: "The bankruptcy of scientific justice; doctors affirm that they cannot tell whether criminals are responsible or not."[74]

The mass press, forever trusting the orderly instincts of its bourgeois subscribers, had always been rough on expert testimony when it had the effect of saving a favorite villain from the guillotine.[75] It found an easy target in the hubris of "scientific" testimony. A mocking article announcing the formation of a new society for medical-historical studies held that "we certainly stand to be amused if the findings of medical history have the same worth as those of legal medicine, at whose expense public opinion has been recently much diverted."[76] Indeed, in 1908 Jeanne Weber was in the news again after her third killing, providing new grounds for the abuse of expert testimony. Weber's perennial homicidal tendencies, which had already brought her to trial in 1905 and again in 1906, provided occasions for the humiliation of legal medicine. She was acquitted each time of the charge of strangling children (five altogether) while taking care of them for their working mothers, largely on the strength of testimony by the capital's most eminent medical legists, Brouardel and Thoinot. Apparently, though the children had died of suffocation, there was no anatomical evidence

---

[74] *Le matin*, August 20, 1907. See the equally mocking outburst in *Le soleil*, August 24, 1907.

[75] During the Soleilland trial, the press openly anticipated a testimony of insanity, though the doctor later proved to be cooperative in pronouncing Soleilland sane. Maurice de Fleury in *Le Figaro* wrote that we must "demonstrate to future degenerates that allowing free reign to one's impulses will not be without some serious inconveniences." "L'état mental de Soleilland," *Le Figaro*, February 26, 1907.

[76] Lucien Descaves, "La nouvelle histoire," *Le Figaro*, May 27, 1908. See Léon Daudet's attacks on alienists' tendency to see the insane everywhere in *L'action française*, July 25, 1908; and "Experts en folie," July 31, 1908.

to suggest that they had died from forceful or violent strangulation.[77] Weber denied the killings on each occasion, and, in the absence of witnesses and the usual bruises and signs of violence, she was acquitted, though no one had shown convincingly how the deaths actually occurred. Though it seemed as incredible to contemporaries as it does to us, no grounds for either a conviction or internment in an asylum could be found.

Accordingly, in the spring of 1908, when Weber was found attempting to suffocate another child with a pillow, in circumstances that left no doubt about her intentions, there was a great chorus of publicity. Much of the venom of the press was directed against the inadequacy and tentativeness of the expert medical testimony. Dr. Thoinot himself, who had replaced Brouardel as professor of legal medicine at the Paris Medical School, did little to rehabilitate the reputation of his profession by insisting on the accuracy of his earlier diagnoses and explaining Weber's most recent actions as a consequence of an obsession with strangulation embedded in her mind from the first two trials.[78]

Public outcry was intense. Paul Bourget took the opportunity to argue that the courts should consult medical experts less often and admit "pathological extenuations" as grounds for nonresponsibility less frequently: "Today our fear of compromising ourselves in denouncing or repressing evil reigns supreme. We no longer dare to punish. We no longer dare to defend ourselves. We are like oversensitive philanthropists frightened by the idea of harsh repression."[79] Following her internment at a November trial, Jean Le Coq predicted Weber would be released to kill again. Openly doubting the effectiveness of psychiatric medicine, he insisted that the magistracy of 1825 had not sacrificed "social interest" to such "filthy theories."[80] The Weber case also provoked the longstanding prejudices of some jurists. In "all slightly complicated affairs," complained H. Stagiaire in *La revue judiciaire*, medical experts demonstrate their "absolute incapacity." Simply by "calling an honest man an expert, you will make of him an imbecile or a pontiff, which amounts to the same thing. He will believe himself suddenly to possess omniscience."[81]

[77] For a summary of the case see Rayner Heppenstall, *Little Patterns of French Crime* (London: Hamish Hamilton, 1969), pp. 54-57.

[78] Ibid., p. 57.

[79] Emile Berr, "Le cas de Jeanne Weber: L'opinion de M. Paul Bourget," *Le Figaro*, May 16, 1908. See also Georges Grison, "Jeanne Weber," in ibid.

[80] Jean Le Coq, "Les incohérences de la médecine légale," *Le petit journal*, November 28, 1908.

[81] H. Stagiaire, "Variations sur Jeanne Weber," *La revue judiciaire* 1 (June 25, 1908), p. 184.

There was never really any likelihood, however, despite the storm of criticism over expert testimony, that magistrates would take Bourget's advice and stop consulting medical experts in criminal trials. A year after the Congress of Geneva, Dr. A. Giraud of the *Annales médico-psychologiques* noted no dropping off in the usual rate of demand for psychiatric testimony, and predicted that the crisis would soon pass.[82] This opinion was shared by some observers in the press, and by members of the intellectual community who firmly evinced their faith in psychiatric diagnosis.[83]

However little it may have changed the way in which day-to-day legal-medical relations operated in the courts, the "crisis" in expert medical testimony had other effects of far greater significance. It was, as I have suggested, part of a general "crisis of repression" that was deeply felt by the French public and by the nation's intellectual elite. The apparent feeling of helplessness in the face of the alarming trends of pathologies in French national life provoked some dramatic reassessments in the traditional views of individual responsibility and an upsurge in the popularity of ideas of social defense. Concomitantly, there was a notable weakening of sympathy for the legal or human rights of individuals unlucky enough to be labeled dangerous or antisocial, and a general ebb in the high tide of humanitarian and libertarian trends that had crested only scant years earlier in the Dreyfus affair.

The "crisis" in medical testimony lent considerable encouragement to the militants within the medical community who were agitating for a new "scientific" definition of criminal responsibility. Provoked by the timorous stand articulated at the Geneva congress—which they regarded as disastrous for the public image of mental medicine—the militants vigorously defended a larger rather than a smaller role for

[82] Albert Giraud, "Revue de médecine légale," *Annales médico-psychologiques* (July 1908), pp. 15-20.

[83] See Griff, "A vous, père conscrits," *Dépêche de Toulouse*, August 3, 1908, who affirmed that there are many "dangerous" individuals not "swarming with the signs of madness." Paul Fauconnet, the juridical expert among Durkheim's young disciples, argued in a review of one of Joseph Grasset's books that "the progress of psychiatry and criminal anthropology has had the consequence that cultivated people today realize many individuals of normal appearance, are, in reality, abnormal, that the domain of psychoses and neuroses is much greater than is commonly appreciated, and that a great deal of experience is necessary before one can diagnose or even suspect the existence of perfectly pathological states of mind." *L'année sociologique* 11 (1910), p. 457. Fauconnet later composed the definitive "Durkheimian" account of responsibility, into which he put these views. *La responsabilité: Etude de sociologie* (Paris: Alcan, 1919).

psychiatry in the defense of society against the whole spectrum of deviance. They took their lead in great measure from public opinion, and were above all anxious to demonstrate that psychiatry was a valuable weapon in the struggle against crime and disorder. The militants had the advantage of both the historical moment and the logic of the recent evolution of mental medicine, which had synthesized, as we have seen, a biological theory of mental disorder that had set its stamp on popular culture. In their capacity as the technical intermediaries between madness and general culture, psychiatric militants helped construct a new vocabulary of responsibility and a rigorous doctrine of social defense that paralleled the efforts of the criminologists. There was considerable public support for a new theory of scientific responsibility.

Though there were some notable exceptions among the left-wing "opinion" newspapers (*L'humanité, La justice*), the press in general seems to have favored the view that legal decisions of irresponsibility weakened social defense. Asylums were not believed to be as "secure" as prisons; escapes were frequent, and cures often "premature," views promoted, as we have seen, by psychiatrists themselves. A favorite solution to this problem was to deny the significance of penal responsibility and punish all convicted criminals regardless of the claims made for their mental state.[84] In the words of Pierre Baudin, writing in *Le journal*, "what does it matter to us if a crime is committed by someone who has diminished responsibility? It must be punished even so, and society has no need to know the interior combat in the criminal's mind at the moment his crime is conceived."[85]

Some journalists developed arguments designed to show that some forms of mental disorder (alcoholism, *perversion raisonée*) were still rational enough that the individuals afflicted with them nonetheless deserved punishment.[86] Arthur Huc and Leon Millot, writing in the *Dé-*

[84] "Man has much more self-control than modern science believes him to have." Léon Daudet, "La peine de mort," *L'action française*, July 5, 1908. See also Berr, "Le cas de Jeanne Weber." Another "psychological" novelist, Henry Bourdeaux, wrote the psychiatrist Jules Grasset on the "entirely natural reaction against the mania of irresponsibility that has seized us and against a humanitarianism and a sensibility that profit only the criminals and never their victims." Quoted in Jules Grasset, "La responsabilité des criminels devant le congrès des aliénistes et neurologistes de Genève," *Journal de psychologie* 4 (1907), p. 509n.

[85] Pierre Baudin, "Les demi-fous," *Le journal*, February 17, 1907.

[86] See Adrien Vély, "Guerre à l'alcool," *Le Gaulois*, July 8, 1908; "L'Affaire" [on Mme. Steinheil], *L'intransigéant*, December 1, 1908. Maurice LeClerc argued that despite Mme. Steinheil's "moral perversion" she was responsible before the law. "Suggestion? Non. Mensonge? Oui," *L'éclair*, November 28, 1908. Edgard Troi-

pêche de Toulouse expressed a position that seems to have been in some favor on the Republican left, namely that many of those with mental troubles, whether they could reason clearly or not, were sensible to pain and to fear on a brute animal level and so could in good conscience be punished when they committed a crime.[87] These positions were of a moderate sort; they did not deny the existence of penal nonresponsibility, but attempted to extend the realm of individual responsibility as far as possible.

The most common justification for punishing insane criminals rather than attempting to cure them in asylums was the vague invocation of the term social defense. The origins or meaning of the term were never explained in a thorough way; the phrase "social defense" or "social preservation" was deemed sufficient justification in itself.[88] Thus Achille Buimard argued that even "incurables" should be eliminated "simply out of the spirit of social preservation and with as little anger as when we are killing a rabid dog."[89] Lucien Corpechot argued straightforwardly that even apparently insane criminals should be punished because "the first crime of a citizen is the one of losing control over himself and the *policing of his instincts*. That done, no matter what actions flow from it, his responsibility should not be regarded as diminished in any way."[90]

The commentators who wrote in highbrow reviews and learned periodicals treated the crisis of repression in a more complex way, but they were not immune to the temptation to coin a telling aphorism. Thus, in the words of Marcel Réja, "those criminals who are able to establish that a great aunt suffered some sort of cerebral disorder may practice their profession with the most complete impunity."[91] At this more sophisticated level of argument, there was no effort to deny that lawbreakers were occasionally insane; a century of psychiatric progress

---

maux, noting that juries in 1908 were less likely than usual to excuse responsibility for "crimes of passion" employed the curious phrase "ferocious egotist" to label an individual for whom the usual defense failed. Edgard Troimaux, "Le drame de Stains," *Echo de Paris*, November 13, 1908.

[87] Arthur Huc, "Contre l'apachisme," *Dépêche de Toulouse*, July 10, 1908. Huc blamed both jurists and doctors for wanting, respectively, to moralize and cure criminals who are able to understand only pain. See also Léon Millot's praise of corporal punishment, "Le fouet aux apaches," in ibid., August 8, 1908.

[88] Ernest Judet, "La presse et le crime," *L'éclair*, July 4, 1908; Georges Bonnamour, ibid., November 5, 1908; Maurice de Fleury, *Le Figaro*, August 25, 1907.

[89] Achille Buimard, "Supprimons les scélérats quand ils sont inguérissables," *Echo de Paris*, November 10, 1908.

[90] Lucien Corpechot, "Le mobile du crime," *L'intransigéant*, July 9, 1908. My emphasis.

[91] Marcel Réja, "La responsabilité criminelle," *Mercure de France* 71 (January 1908), p. 57.

was impossible to repudiate. Instead, it was often acknowledged that nearly all criminals *were insane* in some degree or another. Rémy de Gourmont and Emile Faguet used practically the same words to justify putting all criminals permanently "out of harm's way":

> But are not all asylums prisons, and are not all prisons asylums? [de Gourmont][92]

> I am for making all prisons into asylums and all asylums into prisons (which they are already). [Faguet][93]

The criterion for incarceration or internment ought no longer to be responsibility but "dangerousness."[94] Faguet complained that under the present system of criminal justice, "dangerousness is inversely related to culpability." Thus, he, Faguet, is morally blamable for his actions; but "is Soleilland morally responsible? Not at all, no more than a dog, although he is violently dangerous."[95] In de Gourmont's words, "the mad and the half-mad must be equally condemned if they have been found guilty of crimes."[96] A more moderate view, advanced by Philippe Chaslin in the *Revue philosophique*, attempted to define separate grounds for sending criminals to asylums or prisons, but acknowledged that the practical basis for putting lawbreakers one place or another must be the security of society.

In 1907-1908, all commentators on the issue of insane criminals clearly inclined toward basing punishment in some way on social defense or social, rather than individual, responsibility. Chaslin, for his part, did not think that Eugène Dally's 1863 argument for social defense had ever been improved upon.[97] Réja called the whole notion of justice into question as a luxury for the national organism: "Any living thing, whether a society or an individual, cannot sustain life except by a fundamental egotism that repudiates the notion of equity: any living being must commit itself to the violation of metaphysical justice or resolve on its own suicide."[98]

This crisis of public faith in the salutary effects of expert psychiatric

[92] Rémy de Gourmont, "Sur la responsabilité des criminels," *Revue des idées* 5 (March 15, 1908), p. 289.

[93] Emile Faguet, "La responsabilité des criminels," *Revue latine* 7 (July 25, 1908), p. 403.

[94] Réja, "La responsabilité criminelle," p. 62; Faguet, "La responsabilité des criminels," p. 396; de Gourmont, "Sur la responsabilité des criminels," p. 288.

[95] Faguet, "La responsabilité des criminels," pp. 296-297.

[96] de Gourmont, "Sur la responsabilité des criminels," p. 289.

[97] Philippe Chaslin, "Sur la responsabilité des fous et des criminels," *Revue philosophique* 66 (1908), pp. 305-306.

[98] Réja, "La responsabilité criminelle," p. 60. See, in addition, G. L. Duprat, "Psycho-sociologie juridique," *Revue philosophique* 65 (1908), pp. 286-292.

testimony thus presented the medical community with the challenge of justifying the traditional role it had played in criminal justice. The resolution taken at the Geneva congress of 1907 was an effort to reclaim that traditional function.[99] But it met, as we have seen, with skepticism from those who believed that function to be an ineffective part of the judicial system of social defense. On the other hand, medical experts continued to meet resistance from the defenders of the classical model of absolute responsibility who, as Charles Renouvier had once written, disapproved of justice" passing into the hands of men who call themselves reasonable in order to pass on the conduct of those who are without it."[100]

The response of the psychiatric community as to the proper strategy to follow in the face of this challenge was not, as we have seen, completely unified. However, the main disagreement was confined largely to the issue of the proper short-term policy to be followed vis-à-vis the Chaumié policy. Beyond this knotty issue of medical politics, psychiatrists, doctors of legal medicine, and criminologists shared remarkably similar views on the long-term prospects and needs of medical expertise. Most professionals were buoyant about the growing role for psychiatry in a new system of "social defense" that stressed the role of doctors as specialists in social and biological hygiene. Most were bitterly opposed to the classical legal concept of responsibility and wanted to replace it with a more "scientific" or "medical" one; and virtually all these professionals believed that the absolute distinction between sanity and dementia observed in the criminal code was as hopelessly unrealistic as the absolute distinction between prison and asylum.

Where they differed among themselves was on the readiness of the public to accept a scientific definition of responsibility and how far, under the present system, they ought to mix medical diagnosis and judgments on (penal) responsibility as demanded by the Chaumié instructions. The great danger, and all of them agreed on this, was the likelihood that any present attempt to distinguish intermediate states of responsibility in a suspect was likely to lead to a judgment of ex-

[99] Gilbert Ballet had earlier given a clear indication of his intentions by founding a new journal devoted to establishing a friendly accord between jurists and "alienists." See "Aux lecteurs," *Revue de médecine légale psychiatrique et d'anthropologie criminelle* 1 (February 25, 1906), p. 1.

[100] Quoted in Picard, *La philosophie sociale de Renouvier*, p. 163. As we have seen, psychiatric medicine had made inroads into traditional philosophy. V. Egger's 1908 Sorbonne course on "morality" acknowledged the existence of lower degrees of consciousness in degenerates and the unstable, concluding that "it is more useful to speak of *normal* responsibility than of absolute responsibility." "La morale," *Revue des cours et conférences 1908* (November 26, 1908), pp. 110-111.

tenuating circumstances, requiring a reduced prison term, thereby producing the worst possible situation: an individual is punished in prison though possessing clear symptoms of mental disorder, but he receives a relatively shorter sentence than is required to meet the needs of an orderly social defense.[101]

By 1906 all specialists in mental medicine subscribed to the view that there were multiple intermediate states between complete mental equilibrium and insanity. Most psychiatrists were perfectly willing to say that, in fact, one individual was more mad than another, but it was not common to calibrate degrees of madness in terms of intelligence or rationality. Since the decline of Pinel's system it was regarded as much more sound to base a diagnosis on a *biological* foundation, usually related to degeneration theory. "Troubles of the understanding," as they were called, were thus not the stuff of madness itself, as they were for Pinel, but merely part of a range of *symptoms* related to an underlying biological syndrome. Thus, to a certain extent the seriousness of the madness depended on the degree to which it was a hereditary problem, and especially on the place of the victim's generation in the descending order of infected generations. A sampling of the major handbooks of legal medicine from the 1880s to the war reveals that medical experts were invariably counseled to obtain not just the defendant's own life history, but precise biological information on previous generations as well.[102]

The theoretical proponent of these intermediate states of madness in the period of this crisis was Dr. Joseph Grasset. Grasset hoped to bring some order into the nosological complexity of degenerate mental disease by coining the term "half-mad" (*demi-fou*) to cover all these inter-

[101] See Gilbert Ballet's separately printed remarks at the Geneva conference to this effect. *L'expertise médico-légale et la question de responsabilité* (Geneva, 1907); see also the remarks of Dr. Ernest Lallemant in introducing the transcript of the congress in *Annales médico-psychologiques* (July 1907), p. 182.

[102] See, for example, Henri LeGrand du Saulle, Georges Berryer, and Gabriel Pouchet, *Traité de médecine légale de jurisprudence médicale et de toxicologie* (Paris: Delahaye, 1886), pp. 760-785. Henry Coutagne, *Précis de médecine légale* (Paris: Masson, 1896), pp. 109-120; Alexandre Lacassagne, *Précis de médecine légale* (Paris: Masson, 1906), pp. 781-782; Alexandre Lacassagne and Louis Thoinot, *Le vade-mecum du médecin-expert*, 3d ed. (Paris: Masson, 1911), pp. 141-145; Charles Vibert, *Précis de médecine légale*, 7th ed. (Paris: Baillière, 1908), pp. 682-730. The diagnostic section of these books recommended the identification of telltale physical "defects" typical of degeneracy. Paul Farez, otherwise a supporter of Ballet's resolution, resolutely stated that "an infinity of degrees" of illness existed between sick and healthy. "L'expertise médico-légale et la question de la responsabilité," *Revue de l'hypnotisme* 22 (October 1907), p. 133.

mediate states.[103] The term achieved a certain currency in the press but failed utterly to win the approval of Grasset's colleagues. As the most vigorous opponent of Ballet's Geneva resolution, Grasset argued that *demi-fou* would not confuse magistrates and juries but would provide a basis for medical experts to claim diminished medical responsibility for criminal defendants so they could be interned in asylums or special quarters for the criminally insane. It is clear from the numerous popular articles Grasset wrote in behalf of his hybrid concept that for him a *demi-fou* was a hereditary degenerate par excellence with troubles of both moral sense and the understanding.[104]

Most of Grasset's colleagues believed that his efforts to force the magistracy to recognize a new version of penal responsibility were impolitic, and the internment of *demi-fous* an utter impracticality under 1907-1908 conditions. But the great majority of them nonetheless fully agreed with the need to refine a more "scientific" criterion of responsibility, however premature its present implementation might appear to be. The psychiatrist Marandon de Montyel had already written in 1891 that "for a metaphysical criterion, which any man who has read Jean-Jacques or Auguste Comte believes himself qualified to discuss, you will have substituted an experimental criterion, accessible only to psychiatrists."[105] What was remarkable about the period between 1906 and 1910 or so was not the mere existence of this sentiment, an enduring aspect of positivistic medicine, but the great number of serious efforts to define serious scientific criteria of responsibility.

Some authors worked more or less within the traditional medicolegal structure, confining their efforts to an exhaustive listing, in order of their seriousness, of the various mental problems that might limit responsibility. This approach was also popular with the authors of legal-medical handbooks.[106] Others made more serious attempts to work out a theory based on internal physiological functions, as had Grasset. Marandon de Montyel, long a proponent of such measures, postulated the existence of "powers of inhibition," basing his ideas on

[103] Grasset's principal work in this period was *Demi-fous et demi-responsables* (Paris: Alcan, 1907).

[104] See, in particular, "Le problème physiopathologique de la responsabilité," *Journal de psychologie* 2 (1905), pp. 97-114; "La responsabilité des criminels devant le congrès des aliénistes et neurologistes de Genève," *Journal de psychologie* 4 (1907), pp. 481-516; "L'internement obligatoire des demi-fous," *La nouvelle revue* 3d ser. 4 (July 1, 1908), pp. 19-28.

[105] de Montyel, "Les aliénés dits criminels," p. 438.

[106] Georges Morache, *La responsabilité* (Paris: Alcan, 1906); also Vibert, *Précis de médecine légale* and the earlier work of Henry Coutagne, *La folie au point de vue judiciaire et administratif* (Lyon: Storck, 1889).

the experimental work of Charcot and Rouget. Certain nerve ganglia, strategically located on the linking pathways between all the higher brain functions, had the power, at the command of the will, to inhibit nerve impulses. Certain hereditary nervous illnesses weakened or destroyed the ability of these ganglia to function properly, thereby damaging the ability of the will to resist the power of certain "impulses." All persons, normal and pathological, felt, according to Montyel, equally strong impulses, but the ability to resist was based on the progress of degeneration and was thus "variable with the degree to which the power of inhibition is weakened or even absent, constituting what Ribot has imaginatively called 'idiots of the will,' and Pierre Janet has labeled 'abouliques.' "[107]

In his more ambitious study Dr. Albert Mairet, who shared Montyel's view that the assessment of responsibility depended to a large degree on the physiological integrity of the will, assumed that all individuals were occasionally swept by primal emotions such as sexual lust, hate, anger, and jealousy, but that, on account of physiological organization, "normal" individuals were better equipped to resist them. Mairet was persuaded by the James-Lange "law" that emotional states were merely the secondary signs of physiological forces already in motion; thus the real interior struggle was largely an unconscious one between forces whose relative strengths were predetermined. The elements on the resistive side, "sentiments," "moral sensibility," "fear of punishment," "will," and "intelligence," were the joint products of heredity and education. However, in the classic Lamarckian manner, Mairet claimed that moral sensibility, sentiments, and fear of punishment, though learned, had been converted in the organism into unconscious reflexes, so that, for analytical purposes, "moral sensibility is nothing more than the transformed identity of physical sensibility."[108]

In "normal" individuals the "struggle" between "impulses," "emotions," and these resistive forces regularly ended in a "victory" for the defensive faculties. In damaged individuals, however, one or more of these physiological resistances was limited or nonexistent, permitting unruly primal drives to dominate the organism. Mairet wanted to assess responsibility in terms of the degree of "physiological" impairment of these faculties. Mairet also had a complicated scheme for gauging the

[107] Marandon de Montyel, "Contribution à l'étude clinique et médico-légale de l'imitation involontaire," *Archives d'anthropologie criminelle* 21 (1906), p. 29.

[108] Albert Mairet, *La responsabilité: Etude psycho-physiologique* (Paris: Masson, 1907), p. 50. See esp. pp. 47-50.

force of the "impulse," which depended on its "pathological" nature.[109] His system of responsibility is perfectly isomorphic with organicist psychiatry in regarding the human subject as torn between the countervailing influences of good and bad heredity. It was Mairet's notable conceit that one could assign precise values to these forces and award to each individual his proper degree of "responsibility."

The key issue for Mairet as for all those within organicist psychiatry was the health and resistance of the will. Will pathology also figured in the system of Dr. L. Mathé, whose book on the physiological basis of responsibility won the enthusiastic plaudits of that inveterate enemy of alcoholism, Joseph Reinach.[110] Mathé made the parallel between organic disease and mental illness as explicit as possible, making specific analogies between illnesses such as gastric difficulties and "alcoholic degeneration."[111]

In all these systems, despite some rhetoric to the contrary, the basis for assessing responsibility had a different aim than it had under the regular system of criminal justice. Instead of seeking to determine simply whether an individual deserved punishment for his crime or cure for his illness, the entire focus was on another question, namely the degree of danger or threat posed by an individual to society, who, sane or not, needed to be put safely out of harm's way. The finding that an individual was indeed dangerous and also mentally ill thus made him a greater danger than if he had been possessed of his faculties when committing a crime.

The psychiatrist Dr. V. Laupts outlined the medical basis for a theory of *social* responsibility on the same *physiological* terrain as the systems of individual responsibility just examined: "Every organism has defensive reactions that are fully consonant with its need for self-protection and survival. Society is an organism like any other; like other organisms the social organism reacts when it is wounded; it suppresses or disarms the noxious agents and puts itself on guard against future assaults."[112]

In view of the popularity of such criteria for assessing "responsibility," it is not surprising that the question of the appropriateness of the prison or the asylum became as much a practical matter of social

[109] For instance, only a "normal" physiological organization had a chance of resisting "pathological" impulses, while the impaired faculties would have difficulty resisting even the "normal" impulses. Ibid., pp. 121-122.

[110] See the preface by Joseph Reinach to L. Mathé, *La responsabilité atténuée* (Paris: Vigot frères, 1911), pp. v-x. See Mathé on the centrality of will, p. 5.

[111] Ibid., pp. 25-31.

[112] V. Laupts, "Responsabilité ou réactivité?," *Revue philosophique* 65 (1908), p. 616.

defense as one of diagnostic accuracy.[113] This in turn encouraged the notion that "prison is merely a word, asylum is another; in practice one may make prisons into asylums and asylums into prisons."[114] The conflation of crime and madness that was the consequence of these developments simply heightened the anxieties of the general public by associating unpredictability and violence so intimately with criminal activity.[115] It was a logical step for medical experts to recommend a series of eugenical strategies to deal with this problem. Among the recommended measures were sterilization and vasectomies for the criminal and the madman, the prohibition of marriage to degenerates, and rigorous medical and "hereditary" premarital exams to forestall, in Joseph Grasset's words, "conjugal hells."[116] In this, its most extreme form, the medicalization of the problem of responsibility demanded a social prophylaxis presided over by doctors, and reduced all questions of responsibility to biological ones.

In the period 1906-1908 many experts in mental medicine were afraid of damage to their professional stature and prestige; they were impatient with a judicial process and a basis of deciding penal responsibility that often made them appear to be the weak link in the system of repression. Many doctors thus willingly embraced a theory of social defense in which they were no longer mere accessories to the process of deciding mental responsibility, but its sole determinants. In this new system the question of individual responsibility became irrelevant; whether one favored making all criminals responsible for their acts no matter what their mental condition, or decided that there was some madness, and therefore some irresponsibility, in all criminal acts made no difference at all. In each category, *criminel-aliéné* and *aliéné-criminel*,

[113] Vibert, *Précis de médecine légale*, p. 681. See also de Montyel, "Contribution à l'étude clinique," p. 8; Mathé, *La responsabilité atténuée*, p. xiii; Mairet, *La responsabilité*, pp. vi-x.

[114] Laupts, "Responsabilité ou réactivité?" p. 617.

[115] The images used by legal-medical commentators invariably encouraged the notion that the threat of violence lay just beneath the surface in any criminel-aliéné. Only the trained eye of the mental clinician could discern it. Lacassagne's disciple Henry Coutagne wrote in 1889 that madness hid "under an apparent mask of mental integrity, until the progress of the delirium leads to an unexpected explosion in the form of vicious or criminal acts that an opportune and competent examination would have prevented." *La folie au point de vue judiciaire et administratif*, p. 5.

[116] See Joseph Grasset, "Défense sociale contre les maladies nerveuses," *Revue des idées* 3 (March 15, 1906), p. 164; see also Thulié, *La lutte contre la dégénérescence*, pp. 1-15; Henry Cazalis, *Science et marriage* (Paris: Doin, 1900); Fernand de Lavergne, "Marriage et psychopathes," *Archives d'anthropologie criminelle* 27 (1912), pp. 616-629. See also Schneider, "Toward the Improvement of the Human Race," pp. 268-291.

there was but one basis for determining the "responsibility" of its members: their "dangerousness" to the social order. Would not the freewill philosopher Elme Caro have asked of this generation as he had of an earlier one in 1873: "Isn't there something even more inhuman about conserving the blame when there is no fault?"[117]

[117] Caro, "Le droit de punir," p. 536.

CHAPTER VIII

1908: The Capital-Punishment Debate in the Chamber of Deputies

In the political life of the Third Republic the Chamber of Deputies was all-powerful. Though the constitutional arrangements written by the conservatives in 1875 were meant to build dikes around the exercise of unlimited power by a radical lower house, these efforts were thwarted by the overwhelming electoral success of Republicans in the 1880s. The presidency and the Senate, designed as checks to popular sovereignty, became nothing more in practice than echoes of the Chamber itself. By 1900 the Senate had become a polite debating society and a fact-gathering agency for legislative proposals of relative insignificance. All important legislation was initiated in the lower house, and it was there the votes were taken that determined the existence of each of the regime's many governments. After the election of Jules Grévy in 1879, the President of the Republic was expected routinely to countersign all ministerial circulars and approve all legislation sent him by the Parliament. As an executive elected by Parliament itself, the President was expected to be the docile servant of legislative will. Practically the sole initiative that remained totally in the hands of the chief executive was the right to pardon.

It became fashionable even before the turn of the century for critics to refer to the Chamber of Deputies as the spokesman of the "legal country" and to characterize it, according to political bias, as out of touch with the genuine sentiments of the "real country." This accusation, however, was most often leveled by intellectual spokesmen for the country's most extreme political parties, and reflected the antibourgeois sentiment at both extremes of an overwhelmingly bourgeoisified (if not bourgeois) society. Part of the basis for the charge that the Chamber was nonrepresentative was its overwhelming dominance during the lifetime of the Third Republic by members of the liberal professions. Jurists, doctors, and educators comprised nearly half of all the chambers of the early Third Republic, losing their clear preponderance only in the interwar years. Of this number, by far the best-represented group was the jurists, who made up fully 37 percent of the chamber of 1906, or 217 of the 580 seats.[1]

But it would be absurd to conclude from these occupational differences that parliamentary jurists were truly unrepresentative of their constituents, who, in a society still half-rural, exercised more humble trades. Jurists were, after all, the masters of the legal mysteries undergirding the system of rights and property so crucial to Third Republic civic life. And, "counselors of the 'real country,' jurists were naturally called to become its representatives."[2] Jurists were manipulators of language par excellence, well schooled in the techniques of debate, and usually well informed on contemporary affairs. The electoral system in the Third Republic ensured their sensitivity to the opinion of their constituents. Legally educated men also made up the overwhelming majority of those entrusted with key ministries, the executive offices in both houses, and the presidency of the Republic itself. In the spectrum of Republican politics, jurists were decidedly men of the center and left-center. Thus 65 percent of the Radicals were jurists in the 1906 Chamber. The lowest percentages came at both extremes: the Socialists had but 14 percent and the extreme right 26 percent.[3] Far from speaking in the name of some abstract corporate intellectual interest, parliamentary jurists stayed well within the confines of the *juste milieu* that dominated late nineteenth-century political life.

Was there an "*esprit juriste*"? Alain's phrase for a Radical might suffice for the parliamentary jurist—"A Radical is a man who loves the law and equality"[4]—but it makes more sense to speak of this quality in terms that help us to understand the nature of its appeal to nineteenth- and early twentieth-century electors. Thus,

> this spirit . . . enjoys a privileged role in the definition and practice of political life; having as its active principle a synthetic approach to the problems it examines, it permits, through the play of successive distinctions in which the jurist excels, the representation of multiple realities and generally satisfactory conclusions. That method gives the impression of great authoritativeness, a sort of mathematical politics, with its mechanisms of deduction, induction, analogy, whose

[1] Jurists include all those who were *docteur en droit* and who exercised a juridical profession (*avocats, avocats aux conseils, magistrats, professeurs des facultés de droit*) before, or during, their political careers. Yves-Henri Gaudemet, *Les juristes et la vie politique de la IIIᵉ République* (Paris: Presses Universitaires de France, 1970), p. 18.

[2] Ibid., p. 33.

[3] See appendix I-B in ibid., p. 96.

[4] Quoted in ibid., p. 38.

relatively hermetic character seems to the uninitiated a supplementary proof of effectiveness and infallibility. Magi of the word, jurists were more likely to be chosen to conduct the business of a country which, barely awakened to the realities of political life, continued to consider it a form of magic, indeed a black magic, in which only the initiated could participate . . . they are the ones who know, who explain, who foresee.[5]

In the debate over capital punishment in 1908 it was, quite naturally, the jurists among the parliamentarians whose words carried extra weight. Crime and punishment were, after all, within their domain of "black magic," and the discussion of the supreme punishment was often learned and legally technical. But, as we shall see, they used their knowledge of legal discourse as much to camouflage as to reveal, and were at bottom as much moved by political as by legal considerations. This flexibility will help to explain how a government of jurists could introduce a bill that was justified in largely legal discourse, and have it decisively defeated by a jurist-dominated Chamber whose discourse was practically identical.

The legislative history of the abolition effort in 1906-1908 is an interesting one; it helps to clarify appreciably the extraordinary reversal of opinion that occurred in those years. The Sarrien ministry, which preceded Clemenceau's in 1906, passed on its budget proposals to the new ministry in October. Included in the new budget was a measure offered by the Budget Commission of the Chamber which would have cut off the funds for capital executions by the Interior Ministry. The intention of the Budget Commission was quite clear: by cutting off the salary of the state executioner, M. Daimler, and his assistants, they were in effect abolishing capital punishment by the back door. When the measure reached the floor, Jean Guyot-Dessaigne, Clemenceau's new justice minister, argued that it was dishonorable to resolve so important a matter in this indirect fashion. He moved to have the funds for capital executions restored, and promised to introduce an abolition bill in the government's legislative program of November.

Guyot-Dessaigne was seconded in his proposal by Joseph Reinach, a long-time opponent of capital punishment, who argued forcefully for the reinstatement of the appropriation and a full-scale debate on the supreme punishment at an appropriate parliamentary occasion. Accordingly Reinach and many of his political associates, together with

[5] Ibid., pp. 34-35.

all those who presumably wanted to retain capital punishment on principle, voted to restore the appropriation. Astonishingly, the measure succeeded by only 12 votes, 247 to 235. Without the support of some convinced abolitionists, it would have failed, and capital executions would have come to an end in France. In the debate of November 11, 1908, a beleaguered Aristide Briand rightfully reminded the Chamber that it had clearly indicated its abolitionist sentiments in that vote; he had the temerity to add that a good many of his colleagues who had voted to abolish funding in 1906 were now among the most passionate retentionists.[6]

The new abolition proposal was sent along the regular legislative channels to the Chamber's Commission on Judicial Reform where it was put into the hands of Jean Cruppi, a well-known abolitionist who had agreed to become the bill's reporter. The commission itself was headed by Louis Puech, a veteran Radical politician from Paris and among those who had voted to abolish funding in October 1906. His abolitionist credentials were beyond reproach. As a member of the Paris Municipal Council in 1898, Puech had voted with a majority that had prohibited public executions in the city, thereby ending guillotining in the capital, since executions in camera were prohibited by law. Cruppi's favorable report, which was released in October 1907 shortly after the infamous Soleilland killing, received the support of the commission, and was put on the legislative calendar for the following year. By mid-1908, however, several new factors had intervened to partly confound the hopes of the abolitionists.

The new course of events began with the death of Justice Minister Guyot-Dessaigne in late 1907. He was replaced by Commerce Minister Briand, a firm supporter of abolition, and Briand was replaced at Commerce by Cruppi. The retentionist campaign was well underway in the press by the time these events had taken place, and a growing number of jury petitions supporting retention and antiabolitionist resolutions by departmental councils had appeared. Late in the spring the Commission for Judicial Reform was required to give a final report on the bill. The abolitionist Raoul Peret, Cruppi's successor as the bill's reporter, suddenly resigned and was replaced by Rémy Castillard, a Radical from the Aube, who promptly issued a negative report on the bill. The commission, apparently convinced that the tide of opinion was running against it, had changed its mind. Interviewed by the *Petit Parisien* in late June, the new reporter explained the commission's actions as a response to the huge growth of crimes in Paris and the

[6] *Journal officiel*, "Chambre des députés," November 11, 1908, p. 2210.

provinces, assuring the paper that retention was the only way to give "a bit of salutary terror to criminals."[7]

Unfortunately for the abolitionists, public consciousness of violent crime was at an unusually high point. Since the conviction of Soleilland and the opinion "survey" of the *Petit Parisien*, crime news had enjoyed particularly strong popularity. Paris newspapers cited the events of "recent months" and proclaimed that a "crisis of repression" existed that threatened to enlarge the "army of crime" and increase the danger to the property and persons of "honest folk."[8]

Coincidentally, the Parisian bourgeoisie lost three of its best-placed members in the month just preceding the opening of the debate. Adolphe Steinheil, the society painter, was murdered in his townhouse in the impasse Ronsin on May 31. The circumstances of the murder were exceptionally bizarre. The testimony of his wife Marguerite, whose elderly mother had also been killed, blamed intruders in strange costumes speaking some undecipherable tongue. The case, which continued under investigation until December, supplied a special *frisson* to the Paris press in that Marguerite Steinheil was understood to have been the mistress of President Félix Faure; her tender caresses, what is more, were widely regarded to have been the immediate cause of his death in 1899. The contemporary celebrity of Faure's death, its entwinement with the Dreyfus affair (Dreyfus was pardoned by Faure's successor, Loubet), guaranteed an instant press sensation.[9]

When, three days later, a wealthy *rentier*, Auguste Rémy, was assassinated in the rue Pépinière, *Figaro's* headlines announced "It's Too Much," and "Yet Another Murder!"[10] The investigation for this case was conducted in a particularly outrageous manner. The *juge d'instruction* used all the standard ploys for extracting confessions from the prime suspects: dramatic returns to the scene of the crime, the sudden

---

[7] Rémy Castillard, *Petit Parisien*, June 26, 1908.

[8] See in particular the considerable space given to the "crisis" of repression in the Sunday illustrated supplement of the *Petit journal*, November 17, 1907. See also *La patrie*, February 19, 1908; and "Trop de criminels: Il faut les pendre," *Le matin*, February 18, 1908. An example of how the newspapers promoted their views on crime is a letter to the criminologist Alexandre Lacassagne from the director of the *Echo de Paris*, Henri de Noussanne, requesting an article on the death penalty. A leading article of 180-200 words would have, Noussanne suggested, a "much more striking effect on public opinion" than a simple review of Lacassagne's book on the same subject. Letter of February 28, 1908, Ln5.5174, Fonds Lacassagne, Bibliothèque municipale de Lyon.

[9] Marguerite Steinheil, acquitted, had her own version of these events. See *My Memoirs* (London: E. Nash, 1912).

[10] *Le Figaro*, June 3, 1908.

"My dear sir, for me there is but one way to live: follow Nietzsche's advice and *live dangerously!*"

"But that is just what I am doing, my good woman! I live in a private apartment in Paris . . ."   by Albert Guillaume, *Le Figaro*, June 26, 1908

appearance of the murder weapon, the personal confrontation of two antagonistic witnesses. The press, liberally supplied with a steady flow of information by the judge and his assistant, was omnipresent, even, it appears, in the investigator's chamber itself, a situation that gave rise to a ministerial interpellation later in the month. The fact that the two prime suspects (one of whom later confessed) were Rémy's personal manservants seems to have created a wave of anxiety about the security of the bourgeois household, providing an occasion for the reexamination of the future of the class hierarchy.[11]

---

[11] Apropos of the Rémy killing, Ernest La Jeunesse complained that it was par-

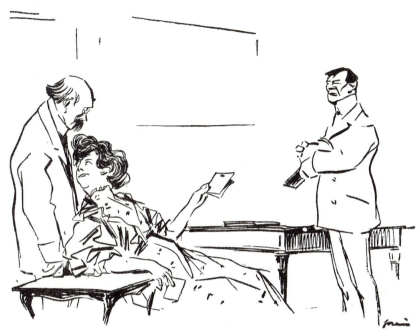

"He is a domestic recommended to us by the duchess."
"Then of course we must take him . . . but he frightens me!"
by Jean-Louis Forain, *Le Figaro*, September 7, 1908

When a third assassination occurred in June (Mme. Sauvezon, a dealer in jewelry) the first two killings had not yet been solved, prompting the *Petit Parisien* to remark that this new crime equaled the first two "in mystery."[12] The papers knew they had an attention-getting

---

ticularly unsettling when those who "ought to protect you, serve you, save you from pain and material fatigue" ended by stealing and murdering. *Le journal*, July 30, 1908. The *Dépêche de Toulouse* suggested that one ought to learn to suspect everyone, July 25, 1908; Léon Daudet wrote an emotional article in *L'action française* deploring the social upheavals that were destroying the old honest "race" of domestics. In their place there had emerged a new breed of servant closely linked to the criminal class, and full of hate for its superiors. How are they made? "It is a dark sorcerer who combines two or three instincts in a rude cauldron, concentrates them, and, after a few minutes adds serpents, toads, larva, and a whole filthy and swarming menagerie." "Gens de maison," July 24, 1908. A criminological monograph that appeared in 1908 testified to the interest of the professionals in the matter of servants and crime. See Raymond de Ryckère, *La servante criminelle: Etude de criminologie professionelle* (Paris, 1908).
[12] *Petit Parisien*, June 25, 1908.

theme. The day after this latest killing *Figaro* printed a cartoon captioned in mock Nietzschean language, "The Partisans of Energy." A man who has been counseled to "live dangerously" replies: "But that is just what I am doing, my good woman. I live in a private apartment in Paris."[13]

In the spring the grisly deeds of Jeanne Weber provided excellent copy, but the frenetic press campaign to attract attention to the threat of violent crime continued up to the beginnings of the debate itself in early July. When there were no crimes in Paris, provincial violence was reported in front-page space usually reserved for the capital. "Yet More Blood" bleated *La presse* on July 2 and "Another Satyr" on the fifth;[14] also on the second *Le journal* announced: "A Courtesan Strangled by a Satyr."[15] A more sinister chord was struck—and frequently repeated in the coming months across the whole spectrum of the press—by the account in the *Petit Parisien* of a lynching of blacks in New York State.[16] It was the first sign of the willingness of the mass press to allude to vigilante activity as a remedy for the insufficiencies of "official" justice.

On the eve of the debate itself, press opinion was uncertain about the legislative outcome of the abolition movement. However, the vast bulk of editorial opinion was firmly in favor of retention of the guillotine, expressing fear at rising rates of violent crime and the virtual disappearance of capital executions under "father pardon" Fallières. Though papers could cite jury attitudes and "public opinion" strongly hostile to abolition, many acknowledged this trend was of recent origin and was not yet adequately established.[17] Many retentionists openly wondered if the politicians would take notice of this popular movement, and some, like *La liberté* and *Le petit Marseillais* feared, with great outrage, that abolition might succeed.[18] Only the *Petit Parisien* in its typically buoyant way, was certain abolition would fail.[19]

[13] Gilbert Guillaume, "Les professeurs d'énergie," *Le Figaro*, June 26, 1908.

[14] *La presse*, July 2, 5, 1908.

[15] Arthur Dupin, "Une femme galante étranglée par un satyre," *Le journal*, July 2, 1908.

[16] *Petit Parisien*, June 29, 1908.

[17] Many retentionist papers took heart at the Commission on Judicial Reform's reversal of its stand on abolition. Louis Puech, "La peine de mort," *Le matin*, July 3, 1908; *Le petit journal*, July 4, 1908. Other retentionist papers citing the surge of public opinion as justification for retention were Pas Perdus, "La peine de mort," *Le Figaro*, July 4, 1908; *Le Gaulois*, July 2, 1908; Albert Robert, "Lettres parisiennes," *La petite Gironde*, July 2, 1908; *Le progrès de Lyon*, July 2, 1908; *Lyon république*, July 3, 1908.

[18] Léon Daudet, "Le règne de l'opinion," *L'action française*, July 1, 1908; *La liberté*, July 3, 1908; *Le petit Marseillais*, July 1, 1908; Georges Bonnamour, "La Chambre et la peine de mort," *L'éclair*, July 4, 1908.

[19] Lucien Vrily, "La peine de mort sera maintenue," *Petit Parisien*, July 4, 1908.

"You will copy for me three times the phrase, 'I have killed Mme. Lebon and her two daughters.' " by Abel Faivre, *Le Figaro*, July 8, 1908

On the eve of the debate all the Paris *journaux d'information* were solidly behind retention. All right-wing and center Republican papers and one or two Socialist organs[20] lined up in favor of retention as well. Though some expressed support at later dates, the only papers taking a stand in favor of abolition in the days before the debates were of Socialist or center-left conviction. These showed their grave concern at, in Jaurès's words, the "ground lost" by abolitionist sentiment in the past months.[21] Gaston Desmons, writing in the *Reveil du nord*, blamed the turnaround on the press publicity given to the Soleilland murder,[22] but Jaurès, and especially Paul Margueritte in the *Dépêche de Toulouse*, blamed the press coverage of crime, especially the sensational treatment of the previous month's murders. The reversal of the commission's stand on abolition, explained Margueritte, was attributable to "the yellow press, with its enormous headlines and its portraits of killers, the press blaring the most recent crimes to the four corners of the world in the voices of a thousand trumpets, the press crammed with revolting details, cynical, obscene, sticky with mire and blood; the

---

[20] Notably *Le petit Provençal*, July 2, 1908.
[21] Jean Jaurès, "Bonne journée," *L'humanité*, July 4, 1908.
[22] G. Desmons, "La peine de mort," *Reveil du nord*, July 1, 1908.

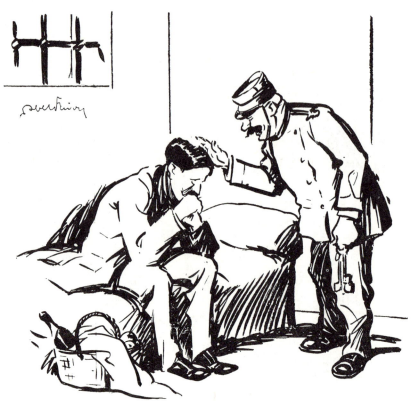

"Rest assured, you will never have anything cut but your hair."
by Abel Faivre, *Le Figaro*, August 29, 1907

press, I tell you, has inflamed public opinion and burdened the thoughts of our legislators."[23]

At the time the debate began the number of crimes in common law that required capital punishment was thirteen (ten in the penal code and three in special law). This number is deceiving, however, since a good many merely preserved archaic distinctions within the general category of voluntary homicide (assassination, infanticide, poisoning, parricide), while others were of ad hoc historical origin and were rarely applied (the law of 1845 on railway accidents, the law of 1892 on *engins explosifs*). There was, however, an article of the code that punished with death any murder committed in the course of another crime (usually

[23] Paul Margueritte, "Tombera, tombera pas?" *Dépêche de Toulouse*, July 3, 1908.

"You are arresting me! . . . Very well, I'm going to write my deputy."
by Abel Faivre, *Le Figaro*, September 19, 1907

armed robbery) with the intention of facilitating flight or eliminating witnesses.[24] The most all-embracing of these crimes was "assassination," characterized as "murder committed with premeditation or in ambush"; in practice premeditation and full mental capacity were required for conviction in all capital crimes.

Also included within the category of voluntary homicide was *meurtre*, defined as "intentional homicide," but applied to those cases in which there was no clear evidence of considerable premeditation. Under the penal code this crime was punished by life imprisonment or life at

[24] The whole list may be found in Levasseur and Doucet, *Le droit pénal appliqué*, pp. 285-287.

forced labor, not the death penalty. Finally, completing the list of "crimes of blood," was personal assault, which resulted in death without that having been the intention. Like *meurtre* this category did not fall within the domain of capital crimes. It is important to understand these distinctions; their importance for the abolition debate was enormous, both when they were being correctly made or when, significantly, they were ignored.

For the purist in legislative matters, the 1908 debate was by no means a simple case of yes or no on abolition. Guyot-Dessaigne's original bill had abolished the death penalty, replacing it by life "internment" (imprisonment, transportation) preceded by six years in a cell. The Radical Joseph Reinach had also written an abolition bill at the beginning of the legislative session, cosigned by seventy-five colleagues, so that there were, in effect, two abolition bills, one official and one complementary. However, in the shake-up that took place in the Commission for Judicial Reform, two new bills emerged, both in the name of the reporter Rémy Castillard. One simply maintained the death penalty; the other added to the scale of punishments life "internment" preceded by six years of cellular confinement to apply to capital criminals who had benefited from extenuating circumstances or who had had their crime commuted by the president. The new element in this punishment was the six years of cellular confinement.

There were also two counterprojects. One of these written by Pierre Ajam, would have retained capital punishment, but also given juries the chance to sentence capital criminals to life internment, an alternative not allowed by Castillard's bill. The other, proposed by Paul-Meunier abolished capital punishment but substituted for it life at forced labor. Finally, in an earlier related proposal Castillard had introduced a bill to abolish public executions, apparently in the hope this would satisfy some abolitionists and allow the death penalty to survive. As it turned out, this diversionary measure was not necessary.

Before the debate ceased in December some of these projects had been abandoned and some amended or amalgamated with others. The net effect of having all these proposals before the Chamber at once was to produce, to be sure, a certain amount of confusion, but also, in the interests of comprehensiveness, the most wide-ranging format possible for such a debate within the framework of French penal law. In the end, though they spoke in favor of or against one or another of these measures, all the participants made the question of capital punishment their central concern.

The parliamentary debate took place over five sessions between July 3, 1908, and December 7, the last four bunched after November 4.

The long delay between the July and November debates resulted from the successful efforts of left and left-center deputies to postpone debate until the fall session because of the emotional state of public opinion. Even so, a measure by hard-core retentionists to end debate and vote before the summer recess fell short by only 6 votes, 260 to 254. Despite the extended period of debate, and the occurrence of events during that time to which I refer later, the debates may be usefully treated as a unit. There were inevitable repetitions and summaries and some obvious efforts to obfuscate issues, but in the end some readily identifiable themes emerged around which open debate clustered. These themes may be roughly grouped at four levels: the most visible level of classic arguments (vintage 1908) for and against capital punishment; a level of arguments addressing French criminal statistics and penal institutions; a level of political discourse that was both practical and rhetorical; the deepest and perhaps most important level, at which the deputies discussed the health and prospects of the French national organism. I examine each of these levels in turn.

The classical arguments for and against the death penalty—its efficacy, its moral legitimacy, its place in social evolution—have been repeated in debates in other times and places. But the resonance of specific arguments has certainly varied from setting to setting, and the French debate of 1908 may be readily placed in its historical habitat. What did the deputies think was the state of French and European customs in 1908? Had European civilization reached a stage of moral evolution that was incompatible with the barbarism of capital punishment? "The question," argued the abolitionist Abbé Lemire, "is not in knowing whether the Socialists are the comrades of assassins, or if Conservatives are the brothers of the executioners. . . . The question is to determine if France has arrived at the precise point that it is able, in accord with the true principles of a generous and humane nation, to abolish the death penalty."[25]

For Lemire, Jaurès, and many other abolitionists, it was the historic mission of France to spread the noble fruits of civilization to the rest of the world: a growing recognition of human dignity in which violence and force have been replaced by consent or agreement, by the vote, by legislated taxation, and by collective contracts for wages and working conditions. As the lone cleric to speak for abolition, Lemire was insistent that the church be squarely in the camp of "pity and human sentiment."

[25] Abbé Lemire, *Journal officiel*, "Chambre des députés," November 18, 1908, p. 2394.

"My religion," he declared, "demands that I be of my century and my time, and I rejoice in that."[26]

For his part, the Socialist leader Jean Jaurès agreed with Lemire's assessment of the evangel's message of compassion and pity, and chided the right: "Between justice, such as you practice it, and Christianity, such as you profess it, there is an irresolvable contradiction."[27] Jaurès preferred to depict the evolution of human sensibility naturalistically, reproving in turn the retentionists among his anticlerical colleagues: "And you, Messieurs, who, whatever else you believe, do not admit of miracles in the general scheme of things, you who explain the nature of man as an immense and painful ascension of life toward higher forms, you who hold that the human race has emerged by degrees from a transformed primitive animality, how, and by what right can you pronounce, against an isolated human being, a definitive sentence of exclusion and of extermination?"[28]

Joseph Reinach read a letter from the Italian partisan of capital punishment, Cesare Lombroso, to prove his own point about the level of his nation's sensibility: "To be efficacious, the death penalty must be frequently carried out; but then it is barbarous; and if it is done but rarely, it becomes useless."[29] Reinach doubted the country's will to return to frequent executions, and implored his colleagues to accomplish an act of "statesmanship" by taking "but one more step, the last step in a path we began with the Encylopedia."[30]

The most convincing proofs the abolitionists used to demonstrate how repugnant capital punishment was to contemporary sensibilities were those that reminded the deputies that many particularly savage punishments, including torture and dismemberment, had disappeared from the penal code, and that the number of capital crimes, which had stood at over one hundred in the old regime, had been systematically reduced to only a handful during the nineteenth century. Paul-Meunier attempted to make a case that juries, since the option of granting extenuating circumstances was given them in 1832, had displayed a growing reluctance to condemn killers to death. In 1825 juries had pronounced 134 death penalties, but in 1833 only 33; indeed, between 1871 and 1896 the number exceeded 35 only three times, and from 1897 to 1905 was never above 20.[31]

[26] Ibid., p. 2400.
[27] Jean Jaurès, *Journal officiel*, "Chambre des députés," November 18, 1908, p. 2394.
[28] Ibid.
[29] Joseph Reinach, *Journal officiel*, "Chambre des députés," July 3, 1908, p. 1538.
[30] Ibid., p. 1539.
[31] Paul-Meunier, *Journal officiel*, "Chambre des députés," November 4, 1908, p.

In 1908, however, building a case on jury behavior or on public sentiment more or less played into the hands of the retentionists. Arguments about the amelioration of official punishments and the softening of customs were useful only in the long run. Nearly all retentionist speakers referred at some point to the number of jury petitions and the plethora of resolutions voted by departmental and municipal councils in opposition to abolition; to their credit, however, none made any effort to claim the howling of the mass press as a proof of public sentiment in support of retention.

In the matter of jury opinion, Louis Puech of the Commission for Judicial Reform had the recent figures at hand for death condemnations. Never above twenty per year between 1897 and 1905, the number climbed to twenty-nine in 1906 and forty-one in 1907; it stood at thirty-nine after the first three-quarters of 1908 (and reached forty-nine by the year's end).[32] Retentionists repeatedly claimed that the "recrudescence" of crimes of blood was ample proof that "customs" had not advanced to the stage at which violence could cease to operate in human affairs, and more than one repeated the bon mot of Alphonse Karr, voiced in an earlier abolition debate: "Abolish the scaffold? So that messieurs the assassins may begin!" In response to the challenge of Albert Willm to promote justice, liberty, and humanity by abolishing the "law of blood," the Radical Georges Berry rejoined: "I am altogether disposed to work with [M. Willm] for social amelioration. But at the present moment, dear colleague, that perfect social state desired by you does not yet exist; not having yet arrived at the happy condition that you wish for all citizens, we are not yet ready to eliminate the punishments that are aimed at thieves and killers."[33]

In one very revealing aspect of the debate, however, the retentionists may have inadvertently conceded the abolitionist argument. As will be recalled, the elimination of public executions was on the Chamber's agenda; many retentionists alluded to the need to end the grisly spectacle of public killing. Some cited the evidence of public opinion, referring to the Paris Municipal Council's decision to prohibit the spectacle within the city. Others admitted that, far from having a moralizing

---

2035. For the figures from 1871 to 1913, see Savey-Casard, *La peine de mort*, pp. 122-123.

[32] Louis Puech, *Journal officiel*, "Chambre des députés," November 4, 1908, p. 2042. Puech concluded that in the face of the growth of crime, "to accuse juries of condemning men to death for the pleasure of it, or out of a spirit of opposition, is childish and unjust. If a jury has made such pronouncements it is because it finds itself in the presence of vicious crimes of brigandage."

[33] Georges Berry, *Journal officiel*, "Chambre des députés," November 4, 1908, p. 2027.

influence, public executions probably contributed to subsequent crimes of blood. In the words of the retentionist Gabriel Faillot, capital punishment was "necessary and just; what must be eliminated is unhealthy publicity; we must avoid manifestations that diminish its preventive character and act as excitants for certain perverse types."[34]

A colorful part of the lore and legend of public slayings were the stories of English pickpockets working the Highgate Prison hanging crowd while a colleague was being hung for the same crime.[35] The French versions of this lore were rather more inclined to follow the "perverse nature" argument of Faillot and emphasize the argument of incitement to kill followed by heroic death. This reasoning was apparently regarded by retentionists as among the most potent weapons in their enemies' arsenal, and many attempted to defuse it by conceding the point straightaway. This did not prevent the abolitionists from hauling out several graphic anecdotes anyway.[36]

The problem for the retentionists was to demonstrate how the guillotine, a demoralizing agent when viewed in operation, became a moralizing one in secret. Maurice Barrès, who had himself witnessed a beheading, offered this formula: "I believe that the example is more striking when it takes place, as it does in England, in secret and behind high walls, indeed much more terrifying than the manner of vulgar apotheosis that we trot out in public places."[37]

Aristide Briand demonstrated his formidable debating skills by turning this concession to his advantage. Reminding the deputies that few of them supported the edifying or moralizing force of public execution, he equated their sentiments to those of a common murderer: "Just as the individual murderer hides his act out of fear, you are asking social murder to hide itself out of shame."[38] No one felt for the actions and appearance of the executioner and his assistants anything but repugnance, but is this not the worst form of hypocrisy, asked Briand: "The executioner and his aides . . . are surrounded by an atmosphere of reprobation. These men, charged with a social act of the highest solemnity, of which society ought to be proud, are isolated! But in that

[34] Gabriel Faillot, *Journal officiel*, "Chambre des députés," July 3, 1908, p. 1534.

[35] On the debates that ended public executions in Britain in 1868 (not abolished in France until 1939), see the excellent study of David Cooper, *The Lesson of the Scaffold* (London: Allen Lane, 1974).

[36] See in particular the examples offered by Albert Willm, *Journal officiel*, "Chambre des députés," November 4, 1908, pp. 2021-2022.

[37] Maurice Barrès, *Journal officiel*, "Chambre des députés," July 3, 1908, p. 1539.

[38] Aristide Briand, *Journal officiel*, "Chambre des députés," November 4, 1908, p. 2211.

circumstance society is personified by the executioner and his assistants; they are its representatives; their operations, and their gestures are those of society itself. I shall not insist on the moralizing point of view as we are all in agreement. The honorable M. Barrès has justly condemned these spectacles. And so, here is a punishment already deprived of an essential quality."[39]

Jaurès made a similar point in brilliant fashion. Partisans of the guillotine did not truly possess the courage of their convictions: "Ah, if only one had the courage to say openly: the scaffold must function frequently, vigorously! This would be a detestable, but a logical doctrine; but you do not dare do so and thus compromise in advance the vote you are asking the Chamber to make. Is there any among you, Messieurs, who imagines that after this virtual interregnum of the guillotine, it will suddenly reappear in a frequent and triumphant guise?"[40]

What of other nations? What was the scoreboard for abolition in 1908? Abolitionists made much of the fact that many progressive states had eliminated capital punishment, among them Norway, Holland, Italy, Belgium (the law was still on the books, but there had been no executions since 1863), and Switzerland. Portugal and Romania, some South American countries, and several American states had also voted for abolition. Retentionists countered that several states that had been at one time in the abolitionist camp (Austria-Hungary, Finland, Tuscany) had eventually reversed themselves, and that several of the Swiss cantons had taken advantage of a federal option of 1879 to reestablish the punishment abolished in 1874. Retentionists also had their "progressive" states: Denmark, Sweden, and England, and made frequent reference to the fact that none of the "great" world powers—England, Germany, the United States, Austria-Hungary, Russia, or Spain—had abolished capital punishment.[41] The implications of this argument for the global status of the French nation were made absolutely clear.

[39] Ibid.

[40] Jaurès, *Journal officiel*, "Chambre des députés," November 18, 1908, p. 2398. Jaurès was, of course, correct in this prediction. With the exception of one year, 1912, the number of executions never exceeded twenty again in this century. See Savey-Casard, *La peine de mort*, pp. 123, 144.

[41] See the summary of Berry, *Journal officiel*, "Chambre des députés," November 4, 1908, p. 2035. Berry's argument owes something to the geographical determinism of Montesquieu: "It is my understanding that in a small state or kingdom one may eliminate the death penalty because it is easier to ensure the security of citizens, but that in large nations security is impossible without the death penalty." It was Jean Jaurès who later exploded this absurd argument, saying, "We have been chided for using the examples of Belgium, Holland, and Norway, but I rather imagine

Retentionists were by no means insensitive to charges that their endorsement of the guillotine harked back to a medieval or barbaric conception of punishment as vengeance. Paul-Meunier's charge that whatever the justification offered, capital punishment was nothing more than primitive vengeance, must have vexed several of his anticlerical and "progressive" colleagues.[42] Yet a reading of the debates produces the clear impression that the *état des moeurs* question was largely rhetorical, and, as we shall see, political. Neither side could adduce convincing empirical proofs on the issue, for the nub of the factual basis lay elsewhere. Louis Gérard-Varet developed this point clearly by addressing the borderline retentionists who had expressed their theoretical approval of abolition but who felt that the present moral atmosphere made immediate abolition unpropitious: "You who are convinced that you are having recourse to a temporary institution, you who nurture the hope that this measure will be short-lived; you are enclosing yourselves inside your own formula, you have become the prisoner of your text; you, theoretically an adversary of the scaffold, are helping to reestablish it on an unshakable foundation."[43]

Capital punishment was either a deterrent or it was not, he argued, and those who conceded its ability to paralyze the arm of the would-be assassin at this moment would have to concede its continued ability to do so in the future. Deterrence was the only basis for admitting the supreme punishment; all else flowed from that.

In 1908 the classical deterrent argument was not one the parliamentary retentionists used either exclusively or systematically. As we have seen in the debates at the Penitentiary Society, the standard deterrent argument was combined with other arguments within a general strategy of social defense. Though it did not invariably square with the other arguments in the strategy, many of the retentionists still endorsed the exemplary virtues of the death penalty. The argument took its characteristic form in the words of Georges Berry: the potential assassin "at the moment he is on the point of committing his crime, sees before him the silhouette of the guillotine, and there lies the whole question. No one doubts that a condemned man is afraid of the guil-

---

that the instinct of self-preservation of men in small countries is as developed as it is everywhere else. So if the scaffold is necessary to prevent crimes in the Departments of the Nord and Pas-de-Calais in France, it would seem to be necessary at Namur, Liège, Mons, and Brussels as well." Jaurès, ibid., p. 2396.

[42] Paul-Meunier, *Journal officiel*, "Chambre des députés," November 4, 1908, p. 2038.

[43] Louis Gérard-Varet, *Journal officiel*, "Chambre des députés," December 7, 1908, p. 2776.

"This is how we get ready for a happy old age!"

by Jean-Louis Forain, *Le Figaro*, October 7, 1907

lotine just before he is executed. But at the moment he is about to commit his crime, may he not be halted then by the fear of death?"[44]

Berry's proofs for the exemplarity of the "silhouette" of the guillotine come largely from anecdotes from his courtroom experience, police officials, and others. Hardened thieves, confronted in their work by unexpected witnesses or captors whom they might have killed, chose arrest or exposure in preference to a charge of first-degree murder.[45] Indeed, a corollary of this position was one of the retentionists' most effective and popular arguments. What, they asked, is to prevent any armed thief from killing a witness to his crime if the penalty for doing so is not qualitatively different (i.e., death) from the punishment he would receive for his theft alone (i.e., additional years of detention)? The supplementary intimidational power of death for armed robbers, argued many, is in itself a sufficient justification for retention.[46]

The indispensable cognitive basis for these arguments was the presumption of calculation by would-be killers: their ability to weigh the consequences of an act, to consider the weight of capital punishment

[44] Berry, *Journal officiel*, "Chambre des députés," November 4, 1908, p. 2027.

[45] Ibid., p. 2028.

[46] See, for instance, the example of Faillot, *Journal officiel*, "Chambre des députés," July 3, 1908, p. 1533; Puech, ibid., November 4, 1908, p. 2041; Louis de Folleville, ibid., December 17, 1908, p. 2779.

in the scales against the advantages to be gained by committing a capital crime. But the hyperrationalist bias in the classical argument was no longer in fashion, and none of the legally astute debaters in 1908 tried to make a case for the universal intimidating power of the guillotine. Indeed, those debaters who had recourse to the argument at all were careful to specify the circumstances in which it applied. For Georges Berry, it applied certainly to "thieves and professional robbers" who were by nature "calculators" and who were restrained from killing in the course of their work by the ubiquitous silhouette. He also stretched the argument to include certain "assassins" who, according to former Sûreté chief Goron, had "some" calculation in their minds.[47]

Louis Puech also quoted experts to make the point that capital punishment effectively deterred certain categories of criminals, recalling Henri Joly's words that if the death penalty were abolished, "burglars . . . when they may steal and kill without risk, will not shrink from committing murder."[48] The punishment, he explained, was not meant for "passionate" crimes or crimes committed under the influence of "a more or less morbid impulse," but rather for crimes "scrupulously prepared, for crimes committed by these criminal groups that operate in the manner of industrial associations and terrorize certain departments."[49] Fernand Labori made a similar distinction between "responsible assassins" and those "degenerates who are entirely irresponsible."[50] Moreover, he argued that the best proof that criminals respected the intimidational force of death was the well-known fact that in their own organizations they recognized but one penalty for transgressions against the laws of the group, namely death.[51] Briand later made short work of this rather absurd argument; it is included here as an example of the style of "realism" often favored by the retentionists.[52]

The question, Do criminals calculate the consequences of their crimes? was not, strictly speaking, amenable to any kind of convincing empirical proof, and the abolitionist arguments in this domain are similarly appeals to common sense or the folklore of crime and punishment. The

---

[47] Berry, *Journal officiel*, "Chambre des députés," November 4, 1908, p. 2028.

[48] Puech, *Journal officiel*, "Chambre des députés," November 4, 1908, p. 2041.

[49] Ibid.

[50] Fernand Labori, *Journal officiel*, "Chambre des députés," November 4, 1908, p. 2046.

[51] Ibid., p. 2047.

[52] Briand, *Journal officiel*, "Chambre des députés," November 11, 1908, p. 2212. Arguing that there was something "humiliating about putting bandit groups and society on the same footing, Briand also pointed out that death was the only sanction available to bandits, there being a distressing shortage of jails in the criminal underworld.

retentionists were able to produce only one undisputed morsel of statistical evidence, but that did not involve a crime of violence. Counterfeiting, which had been punished everywhere in the old regime by death, was only removed from the list of capital offenses in France in 1832. As Louis Puech pointed out, the rise of accusations of and condemnations for this crime promptly rose, constituting, he alleged, conclusive proof for the deterrent power of death.[53]

In the end the retentionists' use of deterrence theory can be reduced to assertions such as the one that assassins had an "instinct of conservation" or to the plea uttered by Fernand Labori to his fellow deputies: "If you look into your hearts, is there one among you who is able to say in all sincerity that he believes the fear of the death penalty has never prevented a single crime?"[54] To Labori's evident displeasure, Louis Lagasse, a former Communard who had logged his time in the penal colonies, refused to concede even this minimal point, replying: "never, never, never."[55]

The abolitionists attempted to refute the deterrence argument for capital punishment by two principal lines of reasoning. One made the effort to review the statistics on blood crimes in countries that had abolished the death penalty to determine whether these figures decided the question of its intimidational force. The other line challenged directly the cognitive foundations of deterrence by arguing that would-be assassins were in no sense guided by the rationalist calculus of the classical theory during the mental operations that preceded homicide.

The Minister of Justice presented the case for the first point in a long speech on November 11. If the death penalty has a power of intimidation, he began, "its abolition should lead immediately to an increase in crimes; if that increase does not occur it is because the abolition was without effect."[56] He then reviewed the figures for the principal abolitionist nations. He presented figures showing that in Belgium capital crimes had been fewer from 1830 to 1895, when the penalty was not used, than in an earlier period when it was. He also showed that within the regional jurisdictions of France there was a

[53] Puech, *Journal officiel*, "Chambre des députés," November 4, 1908, p. 2041. But even this argument can be disputed on the grounds that police officials and prosecutors became more zealous in their enforcement of the law after 1832, when the punishment no longer seemed to them an extreme one for the crime.

[54] Labori, *Journal officiel*, "Chambre des députés," November 4, 1908, p. 2045.

[55] Louis Lagasse, *Journal officiel*, "Chambre des députés," November 4, 1908, p. 2045.

[56] Briand, *Journal officiel*, "Chambre des députés," November 11, 1908, p. 2212.

relationship between the number executed and the number of murders, with fewer murders in the places that executed fewer criminals.[57]

In Italy, since abolition in 1889, crimes formerly punished by death had fallen from 4,089 to 3,106 in 1903. In Holland, from an average of 78 condemnations for capital crimes in the decade prior to abolition (1870), the number fell in later decades to 30 or less for the same crimes. Paul-Meunier had argued earlier that the seventeen Swiss cantons that remained abolitionist after 1879 experienced a regular drop in blood crimes after that date.[58] Such statistics were, or course, easy to come by. First- or second-degree murders were in decline throughout nineteenth-century Europe, within abolitionist and retentionist countries alike. The retentionists in the debate tried to argue that this diminution in retentionist countries was caused by the intimidational power of death, and in general showed a certain reluctance to avail themselves of long-term statistics of any sort, surrendering this field altogether to the abolitionists. It might be concluded from the above statistics that capital punishment and killings are independent variables, but no one tried to argue this case directly. Retentionists were too deeply committed to the intimidational component of their argument to admit such a relationship; abolitionists may have avoided stressing this point because it ran too clearly against the tide of their own welfare-state interventionism. It would be a dangerous precedent to build a case on the premise that man was powerless to change the course of human behavior.

In attacking the rationalist foundations of deterrence theory, abolitionists concentrated on two points. These points were different enough to involve a mild contradiction, though it went unperceived by the retentionists. Briand stated one of them on November 11: "The criminal commits his crime with the conviction, indeed the certitude, that he will not be apprehended; that is the truth of the matter."[59] Briand and the others who used this argument relied on the testimony of criminals of all sorts, not just murderers, and on a conception of criminals as professional risk takers who weighed the likelihood of apprehension, not the severity of the punishment. Completing his line of

[57] Ibid. In the earlier report, Paul-Meunier had presented the long-term figures for Belgium, showing that in 1860, prior to abolition, Belgium condemned thirty-eight people to death and in 1903 had condemned only twenty-five for similar crimes, despite a population growth from 4,500,000 to 6,600,000, *Journal officiel*, "Chambre des députés," November 4, 1908, p. 2036.

[58] Paul-Meunier, *Journal officiel*, "Chambre des députés," November 4, 1908, p. 2036.

[59] Briand, *Journal officiel*, "Chambre des députés," November 11, 1908, p. 2215.

reasoning, Briand said that it was certainly the case that, once captured, the criminal regained the fear of death as the certainty of punishment increased, but nothing could be further from his mind as he contemplated his crime.[60]

Briand also articulated the second point: "It is true that blood and the thought of blood breathe out a kind of intoxication which works on all men. The will to act has never been paralyzed by the fear of death, and in certain historical periods, a sort of mysticism envelops death which frees it altogether from fear."[61]

By far the more popular attack on rationalist deterrence was to argue purely and simply that most killings were accomplished by men whose reason was diminished or who were in the grip of emotional states they could not control. Reinach called most killers, the infamous Soleilland among them, "refuse" and "degenerates." The most rabid partisans of capital punishment, he said, even those who can approve the execution of "brutes of that sort," are not able "to pretend that the execution of Soleilland would have prevented future crimes such as the one he committed."[62] Even the leftists most inclined to explain crime in terms of sociological determinism emphasized the individual and biological causes that led individuals to kill. Jaurès referred to a "hereditary taint," and Marcel Sembat stated that "there are madmen and passionate individuals who will always kill, under any kind of regime or social environment."[63]

It followed from these widespread characterizations of killers as "madmen" that abolitionists believed the guillotining of an insane killer to be a particularly heinous crime. Many of them argued that it occurred frequently and Briand referred to clear evidence in Soleilland's dossier testifying to his incontrovertible insanity.[64] The evidence for these acts of apparent injustice was part of the folklore of nineteenth-century crime. A cardinal point of the medicine of the day, as we already know, was that serious mental problems were invariably associated with pathological brain formations, and it was consequently widely taken as proof of insanity when autopsies revealed cerebral abnormalities. That this belief was deeply rooted in popular attitudes toward crime and insanity can be demonstrated by the widespread contemporary interest in the results of the official autopsies of victims

[60] Ibid.

[61] Ibid.

[62] Reinach, *Journal officiel*, "Chambre des députés," July 3, 1908, p. 1536.

[63] Jaurès, *Journal officiel*, "Chambre des députés," November 18, 1908, p. 2397; Marcel Sembat, ibid., November 4, 1908, p. 2048.

[64] Briand, *Journal officiel* "Chambre des députés," November 18, 1908, p. 2216.

of the guillotine.[65] For Albert Willm it was sufficient to show that one madman had been guillotined to justify the abolition of the death penalty.[66]

One response the retentionists made to this argument was not to dispute the accuracy of the claim that madmen were among the guillotined, but to argue, as did Fernand Labori, that "if one condemned a madman to death who had killed a dozen persons I would not be in the least sympathetic; because if, by chance, a mad criminal was released from an asylum—and I know there are madmen who have left the asylum only to commit new crimes—the evil would be much greater than an execution committed in error."[67]

Nearly all the major abolitionist speakers included some reference to the irreparability argument in their presentations; some built their entire argument against the guillotine on the grounds of judicial fallibility. One suspects that the great appeal of the argument lay in its nonideological nature; it did not inevitably commit the speaker to any of the left-wing or socialist baggage about the origins of crime or lay him open to the charge that by defending abolition he was defending assassins against "honest" men. Who is more "honest" than an innocent wrongly condemned? This was certainly the argument that appealed to Paul Deschanel, who made a magisterial speech to the Chamber on November 4, holding that he had always opposed capital punishment on the grounds of judicial error, a basis that "invalidated" all other

[65] Beginning in the 1880s, it was fairly common for postexecution autopsies to be performed on capital criminals. The results of the Parisian autopsies were widely reported in the press. The pathologists who performed these operations were often the most skilled doctors available. For a particularly important guillotining, the postmortem might be conducted by the professor of legal medicine at the University of Paris, or by his counterpart at the Ecole d'anthropologie. Throughout the 1880s and 1890s, influenced by the craniometrical trends in physical anthropology, doctors attempted to locate lesions in the brain that might "prove" that an "innocent" madman had been executed. The press followed the outcome of these little dramas with the breathlessness typical of all crime reporting of the era. An excellent example of this phenomenon was the execution of the multiple murderer, Pranzini, at the end of August 1887. Nothing unusual was found, to the astonishment of some crime reporters, who expected this cold-blooded killer to have a brain riddled with lesions. In compensation, certain anatomical sexual peculiarities in this "beautiful human animal" were hinted at. See Hughes Le Roux, "L'exécution de Pranzini," *Le temps*, September 3, 1887; C. Chincholle, "L'autopsie de Pranzini," *Le Figaro*, September 3, 1887.

[66] In the debate of 1908, see the remarks of Albert Willm, and his many examples of this sort, *Journal officiel*, "Chambre des députés," November 4, 1908, pp. 2021-2023.

[67] Labori, *Journal officiel*, "Chambre des députés," November 4, 1908, p. 2045.

arguments to the contrary: "It suffices," he said, "for . . . a single man to have been condemned unjustly to death to dishonor capital punishment forever."[68]

Jean-Marie Magnaud, an assizes magistrate who had gained a certain celebrity by refusing to deliver a death sentence in his tenure on the bench, appealed to the Catholic dogma of human imperfection and fallibility that he knew to be in favor among many of the retentionists of the right. As a judge, he explained, he often agonized over decisions where guilt seemed clear-cut, but in complex cases "through what qualms of conscience have I not passed, what hesitations have I not felt in considering the cunning of testimony and the pitfalls of circumstances and appearances."[69]

Joseph Reinach quoted statistics that purported to demonstrate that there was 1 innocent included in every 257 condemnations. Other figures showed clearly, said Reinach, that the French criminal jury, which decided even capital crimes by *majority* vote, was the more likely to err where its majorities were more slender. Underscoring his point, Reinach admitted that if France opted for the English system of unanimous votes, it would do much to convince him, a lifelong abolitionist, to reconsider his position.[70]

To these arguments the retentionists had two replies. One, articulated by Rémy Castillard, held that if irreparability was a special problem in cases involving capital punishment, then one ought only to condemn when there was not a shadow of a doubt. In the face of the loudly voiced objections of the left-wing deputies, Castillard professed a complete faith in the judicial process, ticking off the various individuals and groups who review the criminal's case at each stage, which offered "all the guarantees one could humanly desire."[71]

Fernand Labori replied in the "realistic" manner so much favored by the retentionists in this debate. Error, he said, was all around us; to view death as a special type of irreparability was unjustified. Irreparability occurred in all sorts of human affairs, and few of the wrongs

[68] Paul Deschanel, *Journal officiel*, "Chambre des députés," November 4, 1908, p. 2042.

[69] Jean-Marie Magnaud, *Journal officiel*, "Chambre des députés," December 7, 1908, p. 2780. Briand, from his position at the ministry, claimed to see regular cases of judicial error at all levels of the system, and gave several appalling examples of recent incidents. Albert Willm also read graphic testimony of cases of capital punishment in which the subsequent innocence of the victim was discovered. Briand, ibid., November 11, 1908, p. 2216; Willm, ibid., November 4, 1908, pp. 2021-2023.

[70] Reinach, *Journal officiel*, "Chambre des députés," July 3, 1908, p. 1538.

[71] Rémy Castillard, *Journal officiel*, "Chambre des députés," November 11, 1908, p. 2209.

in this world were of a nature that the status quo could be entirely restored. Labori was reminded by hostile deputies that his own defense of Dreyfus had been a struggle for reparability; and what if Dreyfus had been shot? "If he had been shot, there would have remained to you the duty of defending his memory, which, I imagine, would not have been an indifferent satisfaction to his family."[72] This remark, followed by "ironic exclamations from the extreme left" suggests that either much had changed between the great years of the affair and 1908, or that the abstract desire for justice had played a minor role in the motivations of the Dreyfusards. Labori, the redresser of judicial fallibility of 1899, was a "realist" and fatalist in 1908, baiting the left with charges of pacifism and "sentimentality."

The prevailing mood of realism in the Chamber was such that none of the abolitionists made a systematic effort to argue that capital punishment was utterly unjustified in itself; rather, they raised objections to practical procedural problems or questioned its deterrent value. Thus abolitionists reasoned that effective deterrence had never rested and never would rest on the state having the most ferocious weapons in the balance of terror. In the past, when punishment had been most savage, it had not prevented unspeakably brutal crimes. Abolitionists posed Montesquieu's doctrine on classical penal theory as an alternative: "It is not the atrocity of torture that terrifies the criminal, but the certainty of the application of a punishment."[73] Deschanel and others argued that if the defense of society was the fundamental object of punishment, then a prison cell or some other system of internment was equally redoutable.[74] The certainty and the equality of punishment, they argued, were the greatest guarantee of a citizen's security.

There were two other major arguments popular among the retentionists. One of these was stated by Georges Berry: "If I find myself in the presence of an apache or an assassin who wishes to kill me, do I not have the right to try to kill him first, and does not society have the right to defend itself like a simple citizen?"[75]

The notion of legitimate defense, an important component of old regime criminal law, figured in the Napoleonic Code as a basis for justifiable individual reaction against the "present danger" of aggression. Providing self-defense was proportionate to the aggression, the defender was formally blameless even if the aggressor was "not pun-

[72] Labori, *Journal officiel*, "Chambre des députés," November 4, 1908, p. 2044.
[73] Reinach, *Journal officiel*, "Chambre des députés," July 3, 1908, p. 1534.
[74] Deschanel, *Journal officiel*, "Chambre des députés," November 4, 1908, p. 2043.
[75] Berry, *Journal officiel*, "Chambre des députés," November 4, 1908, p. 2033.

ishable on account of penal irresponsibility (child, madman, animal)."[76] Retentionists elevated this essentially individual notion of defense into a social one, claiming they were guided not by vengeance but by a desire to defend society. Yet by placing the conditions for the use of this defense on a footing of immediate or present threat they also justified reflexive "punishments" that did not consider the nature of the aggressor or his degree of moral responsibility to be questions worthy of concern.

The second argument cannot be restated simply. It is perhaps best to reproduce it in the actual words of its proponents. Louis Puech held that in the face of the "recrudescence" of "blood crimes" he did not believe that

> the hour is appropriate to weaken our system of repression in any measure; we do not think the moment has arrived to abolish the keystone of our penal edifice, the pain of death to which our adversaries deny all intimidational force and exemplariness, but which in the end, in the absence of any proven substitute punishment, remains the only barrier that one can use against the rising tide of these crimes of brigandage and the repeated attacks of a veritable army of criminals who are admirably organized, and whose exploits each day increase the threats to both public and private security.[77]

Later, Jules Dansette complained that in the face of the current crisis of repression, it would not do to dispose with the "keystone" of the penal organization: "I limit myself to considering the general progression of criminality of all sorts, a progression we are aware of even before we learn of the testimony of the statistics, and in the face of that evident, tangible, and indisputably worrisome progression, I grieve over the consequences of a legislative gesture that would remove the supreme rung from our present state of penalties."[78]

The retentionists were profoundly attracted to the notion that the guillotine acted in some unspecified way to provide a latent intimidational force to all punishments, whether or not the crimes that earned them were themselves deserving of death. As the last and highest weapon in the armory of repression, the death penalty somehow guaranteed a greater measure of security to potential victims of lesser crimes

---

[76] Jean Larguier, *Le droit pénal*, 3d ed. (Paris: Presses Universitaires de France, 1969), p. 48. For the historical origins of legitimate defense see Raymond Charles, *Histoire du droit pénal* 3d ed. (Paris: Presses Universitaires de France, 1969), p. 55.

[77] Puech, *Journal officiel*, "Chambre des députés," November 4, 1908, p. 2039.

[78] Jules Dansette, *Journal officiel*, "Chambre des députés," November 11, 1908, p. 2217.

by indicating to their authors the determination of the state to respond to ascending levels of criminal action with ascending degrees of punishment. In this view, if the state was deprived of the death penalty, there would be an instantaneous disequilibrium in the fragile balance of power which would give an immediate advantage to the enemies of law and order. The existence of the death penalty was testimony to the state's will to defend itself.

The abolitionist's rebuttal to this argument has already been revealed in part. It consisted in showing that capital punishment has never demonstrated an ability to deter would-be assassins, and that the incidence of crimes meriting capital punishment had been constantly declining both in countries possessing it and in those without. Many of the abolitionist speakers, Briand chief among them, demonstrated the retentionist speakers were introducing a red herring by using the rise in "blood crimes" in the last few years as an excuse for retention, because the majority of these crimes were murders, not assassinations, and therefore outside the jurisdiction of the guillotine. Abolitionists reminded their foes that they would have to somehow show that assassinations had increased as a consequence of the recently relaxed regime of capital executions, and that even then their figures would be suspect owing to the short length of time of the sample.

This dispute produced the only real flurry over statistics in the whole debate. Obviously statistics are not a congenial subject in standard legislative discourse. Each speaker embarking on a journey of numbers begged the forbearance of his audience, or covered himself by saying he was not so naive as not to realize that with numbers one could prove anything, however. . . . Several retentionists produced figures showing that "blood crimes" or "murders" or "crimes against persons" had augmented.[79] Some quoted to great effect the prefaces to the annual figures written in 1905 and 1906 by officials at the ministry expressing worry at the "alarming" increase in these rates. Puech managed to produce the figures for the years 1907 and part of 1908 from some private source at the Justice Ministry, which he used to show that the number of blood crimes tried in court had risen from 458 in 1905 to 514 in 1907, while those that did not come to trial rose from 1,313 to 1,434. These figures, he contended, were 25 to 30 percent higher than the same categories in 1901. Briand's statistics, he alleged, were misleading because the minister had contented himself with averages drawn

[79] Among the speakers arguing in this vein were Pierre Ajam, Georges Berry, Rémy Castillard, and Louis de Folleville. *Journal officiel,* "Chambre des députés," July 3, November 4, and December 7, 1908, pp. 1540, 2028-2029, 2205, 2779.

from decade-long periods. This tactic allowed him to cover up the alarming increase since 1905 by averaging that year's figures with the lower ones from the previous seven years.[80] These last years, during which no executions had taken place, were the best proof, argued Puech, that blood crimes will rise when capital punishment is no longer in force.

In his response, Briand simply repeated the figures he had stated earlier in the debate. From 1871 to 1880 there were 6,101 serious crimes which formally carried the death penalty; during that period there were 107 executions. For the ten-year period from 1898 to 1907 there were 4,901 such crimes and only 28 executions. How, asked Briand, could one use this to argue that fewer executions lead to higher rates of assassinations? The numbers Puech and his colleagues produced mixed simple murders with first-degree crimes punishable by death, and this, Briand repeated, was an utterly illegitimate way of proceeding. No one denies, he admitted, that simple murders (second-degree homicide) have augmented seriously, but as they are not punishable by death, one cannot use their increase as an excuse to keep the guillotine. One must show a consistent increase in assassinations, and this had not been successfully done.[81]

It seems clear that in this apparently important statistical argument, the abolitionists had much the better position. Not only did the long-run statistics show a steady diminution in capital crimes, they also revealed that executions had fallen at an even faster rate, clearly illustrating that the relationship between the intimidating effects of the guillotine and murder rates claimed by retentionists could not be proven. Retentionists were forced, as we have seen, to resort to mixing murders and assassination together to make any case for a rise in violent crime, and were able to use only the few years prior to 1908 to establish their "trend." And even here their logic did not go uncontradicted.[82]

[80] Puech, *Journal officiel*, "Chambre des députés," November 18, 1908, pp. 2391-2392.

[81] Briand, *Journal officiel*, "Chambre des députés," November 4 and 18, 1908, pp. 2040-2041, 2393. Other abolitionists also found it necessary to repeat this apparently elementary point on several occasions. See Joseph Reinach, Albert Willm, Marcel Sembat, and Victor Déjéante, ibid., July 3, November 4 and 11, 1908, pp. 1534, 1543, 2047-2048, 2207.

[82] Puech had argued that the rise of blood crimes after 1900 was "certain, incessant, regular." But Briand pointed out that this was by no means the case. How, he asked, did Puech explain the fact that there were 1,313 blood crimes in 1905, the last year of executions, and only 1,271 in 1906 when no one was executed at all? What sort of trend was this, he asked. See *Journal officiel*, "Chambre des députés," November 4, 1908, pp. 2040-2041.

The terrain on which the retentionists stood owed more to the logic of expediency than to any other kind. Rémy Castillard directed the attention of his colleagues to "the world" where "for the mass of the French people, what deserves capital punishment is the killing of one's fellow man, the fact of using a knife or a revolver, of committing, in short, a voluntary homicide. They do not bother with the question of knowing—because there are no jurists out there—if that homicide was accomplished in the course of another crime, whether it must precede or accompany that crime to merit the death penalty . . . Once more, the people see but one thing, that willful killing, no matter what kind, must be punished by death."[83]

Louis de Folleville made a similar point on behalf of victims. No doubt, he said, "one must not confound simple murder with premeditated assassination. Yes, the distinction is true in law and exact in theory; but in practice, for the unfortunate victim who is stabbed or shot to death, there is scarcely any difference between premeditated murder and a killing that has been the result of a sudden impulse."[84]

On the first day of the debate Pierre Ajam had warned his colleagues that they ought not to forget they were "making laws for the crowd," not for "the elite" or "educated people": "In effect, crime, or blood crimes as the specialists call them, do not always find their victims in the most elevated classes of society. It is in the suburbs and in rural areas that killers are the most dangerous. It is not always M. de Rothschild who is killed, but more often Jacques Bonhomme! That is why, from a democratic point of view, we are forced to take this fact into consideration."[85]

Georges Berry put it even more bluntly. Forget, he said, the distinction between murders and assassinations. Murders by "apaches" are "equal in value to assassinations" and ought to be put in the same category. "All I know," he said, "is that there are now more victims and more criminals. That is the whole of it. You may make all the fine distinctions you wish without proving that there are not more dishonest men and criminals."[86]

Whatever other arguments they made in the course of their remarks, none of the retentionists failed to acknowledge at some point the general orientation of public opinion. Many were blunt about the dangers

---

[83] Castillard, *Journal officiel*, "Chambre des députés," November 11, 1908, p. 2214. To this point, Briand could only reply, "We are not in the streets here, M. Castillard; we have other duties than the crowd."

[84] de Folleville, *Journal officiel*, "Chambre des députés," December 7, 1908, p. 2779.

[85] Pierre Ajam, *Journal officiel*, "Chambre des députés," July 3, 1908, p. 1540.

[86] Berry, *Journal officiel*, "Chambre des députés," November 4, 1908, p. 2029.

of contradicting the apparent evidence of this sentiment. The Radical Louis Puech warned of a "grave political mistake." Many worried, as did Puech, that abolition would stimulate "in the immense majority of the *healthy*, working population . . . the impression of insecurity which we now see all around us."[87] As if the argument from the "impression" of insecurity were not enough, the retentionists added a more practical point. "In the current state of our penal legislation," said Puech, "there is no substitute punishment for capital punishment that could approach the intimidational force of the guillotine." Forced labor in the colonies was viewed as light punishment by criminals and the public, and the cellular regime ordered in 1875 had never been built.

To make this point clearly Fernand Labori needed only to resort to the ill-fated abolitionist report of Jean Cruppi, issued in the name of the Committee on Judicial Reform in 1907. Together with the demand for abolition, Cruppi's report had identified a whole range of short-comings in the French penal system that needed reform and vast expenditures. Labori read sections of the report aloud, concentrating on Cruppi's devastating attack on prisons: "Our prision colonies are putrid cesspools, and our departmental prisons are centers of corruption."[88] Labori's remarks were calculated to place the costs of the vast and expensive reforms outlined by Cruppi in the scales with the guillotine. In the absence of a modern prison system, he argued, the abolition of the guillotine must remain a "formula of the future." Deputies who may have thought that the only question before them was whether or not to abolish were faced with the need, on the authority of one of the chiefs of the abolitionist camp, to choose between retention on the one hand and massive outlays for institutional reforms on the other, a choice similar to that faced by the Chamber in 1885. "Labori's razor," together with the great fear of offending public opinion, may have been among the most decisive factors in the entire debate.

If we turn now to an analysis of the political context of the debate, we find ourselves leaving the classical arguments to kill or not to kill behind, and approaching more closely the fine grain of French life in the late *belle époque*. A cross-section of political conflict in 1908 reveals with remarkable clarity the situation of Republican ideology. Republicans constituted a satisfied and conservative majority in 1900, more often divided among themselves than united against their traditional enemies. However, under duress, as in the Boulangist years and during

[87] Puech, *Journal officiel*, "Chambre des députés," November 18, 1908, pp. 2391-2393. My emphasis.

[88] Labori, *Journal officiel*, "Chambre des députés," November 4, 1908, p. 2046.

the Dreyfus affair, the old ideological core of the tradition served for all Republicans as a basis of solidarity against political and military adventurers on both ends of the spectrum. The Republican coalition constructed in 1899 by Waldeck-Rousseau was the first to readmit the left republicanism which had been banished after 1870-1871; the Cartel des gauches completed the political program of the Opportunists and moved tentatively toward the implementation of some modest social legislation.

The program of the Clemenceau ministry in 1906 seemed to promise the fulfillment of the century-old ideal of Republican egalitarianism. However, by the fall of 1908, only the nationalization of the bankrupt Western Railway had been accomplished. Some of the other progressive measures had failed to receive legislative approval, and, as we have seen, the government became increasingly preoccupied with a combination of internal labor unrest and growing diplomatic tension with Germany in the wake of the "coup" of Tangiers. The debate over capital punishment provides an opportunity to examine the state of Republican solidarity in this ambiguous atmosphere and to sample the mood of the political class on a question that seemed nonpartisan on the surface but in fact encouraged open discussion of the most divisive political issues of the era. The appeal to Republican unity did not have as profound a meaning as it once possessed, but in 1908 the stakes for a common front against deviance seemed high and the costs of disunity terrible to contemplate.

It was clear from the outset of the debate that the abolitionists would appeal to the progressive aspects of Republican ideals to establish their case against the "medieval" guillotine. Joseph Reinach appealed to this tradition in his remarks in favor of a substitute punishment, and ensuing speakers for abolition routinely invoked the time-honored vision of human perfectibility.[89] Albert Willm quoted Robespierre on the "sad testimony of barbarism in our penal laws." He recalled the heroic days when Republican journalists, philosophers, and politicians were "in accord in demanding the abolition of capital punishment."[90] Paul-Meunier supplied the names of many of the Republican heroes—Hugo, Lamartine, Ledru-Rollin, Carnot—who had voted in the minority for the abolition bill of 1848. The list that supported Jules Simon's bill in the last year of the Second Empire was also composed of men with impeccable Republican credentials: Garnier-Pagès, Favre, Arago, Ferry,

[89] Reinach, *Journal officiel*, "Chambre des députés," July 3, 1908, p. 1539.
[90] Willm, *Journal officiel*, "Chambre des députés," July 3, 1908, p. 1545.

and Gambetta.[91] For the most recent generation of Republicans, Willm contented himself with quoting abolitionist sentiments from Clemenceau's *La mêlée sociale* and *Grand Pan* and from venerable Republican papers like *Le radical* and *La lanterne*, which were firmly in the abolitionist camp.[92]

The political aims in recollecting the heroes of the Republican pantheon were transparent. Socialists and members of the radical left wanted to remind Republican centrists of their common ground in the old struggle against obscurantism and superstition. They hoped their eloquence would draw a circle wide enough to include all Republicans. In the language of Louis Gérard-Varet: "After twenty-five years of laic education, thirty-eight years of the Republic, sixty years of universal suffrage, and eighty years of noble and ardent discussions . . . which have set forth the reasons, the arguments, and the objections [to the death penalty], you wish to turn back the clock an entire century and embrace a formula that flourished at the beginning of the nineteenth century."[93]

Other leftist speakers reminded Republicans that their historical enemies were engaged in a common effort to bring the regime to its knees. Louis Lagasse spoke of the "campaign" against the Republic, and Jean Allemane sketched the outlines of a grim plot led by the "caesarist" right, plutocrats, and the lackey press. They have no supple Boulanger at their disposal now, he cried with obvious emotion, but "there are still men—oh! too numerous still—who fear for their privileges and who wish to divert public attention with such sad trifles as the death penalty. And you have seen the delectable morsels one feeds society nowadays! The heroine of the impasse Ronsin! [Mme. Steinheil]."[94]

The "solidarity" Allemane demanded was a clarion call to which Republicans had rallied many times before. It was the brilliant Socialist orator Jaurès who warned loyal Republicans about their present bedfellows, while invoking the memory of Alfred Dreyfus.

> Messieurs, it is just as we experienced in that earlier drama. Today as then, the true interest of the Republican party is to warn the country in good time. If matters go on in this way, and if you help cultivate in the nation an appetite for murder and a hungering after

[91] Paul-Meunier, *Journal officiel*, "Chambre des députés," November 4, 1908, p. 2037.

[92] Willm, *Journal officiel*, "Chambre des députés," November 4, 1908, p. 2026.

[93] Gérard-Varet, *Journal officiel*, "Chambre des députés," December 7, 1908, p. 2776.

[94] Lagasse and Jean Allemane, *Journal officiel*, "Chambre des députés," December 7, 1908, p. 2788.

reprisals, you will find that you are unable to follow the path you are traveling as far as those who are leading you down it. You will be hesitant and unsure, you will become suspect, and your uncertain words will be readily concealed and swept off in the violent diatribes of those who, in the name of the principle of eternal authority, have proudly created the scaffold. You cannot become, you Republicans, the party of capital execution; you cannot do so without hesitating, trembling, and covering yourselves in equivocation. The surest and the most prudent position to take from today is to vow to a deceived nation: here is the error! It is to distract us from our social responsibilities that one wishes to set up the scaffold; while we, to help bring about social solidarity, wish a justice in peace.[95]

A parliamentary incident that occurred on the first day of the debate is worth reproducing in full because it dramatically illustrates the powerful influence the Dreyfus affair still had on French political life; for a moment at least, the fires of the case were relit with all their brilliance. Joseph Reinach had remarked that the true enemy of "the race" was alcohol:

M. Maurice Barrès: Don't you dare speak of race! (exclamations on the extreme left and on the left—applause on the right).

M. Joseph Reinach: I am, in fact, a member of the race to which belongs the victim of the judicial error M. Lasies was just speaking about. And the difference between you and me, Monsieur Barrès, is that at the risk of temporary unpopularity, I am willing to defend the interests of the French race in which you apparently set little store, preferring to yield to the entreaties of the sellers of absinthe and alcohol or the distilling lobby (applause on the left and on the extreme left).

M. Maurice Barrès: Will you permit me a word of reply?

M. Joseph Reinach: If you wish.

M. Maurice Barrès: I am not astonished for a moment that Joseph Reinach defends the interest of his race, it is altogether natural; on that point there is no dispute (loud protests on the left and extreme left—noise).

M. le president (Brisson): Here, Monsieur Barrès, we know no races (loud applause on the left, extreme left, and center). There are only, in this assembly, representatives of the French nation; and I will not permit you or anyone, to make distinctions on this matter among our colleagues (repeated applause).

[95] Jaurès, *Journal officiel*, "Chambre des députés," November 18, 1908, p. 2397.

M. Lagasse: After this incident, there will not be a single Republican who will vote for the retention of the death penalty (applause on the extreme left).[96]

This brief interchange yields some interesting insights. The old Radical Brisson reacted sharply to the anti-Semitism of Barrès and argued for a higher principle of justice; in this he was seconded, if we can believe the observations of the Chamber clerk, by all the center and left. But Reinach himself acknowledged his membership in the Jewish "race," and in his response to Barrès clearly indicated that his own concern for the French "race" was not that justice be done to it, but that its health be preserved. And finally, Lagasse's hopeful comment on Republican solidarity was applauded by the left alone, indicating, it would seem, that even the most gratuitous anti-Dreyfusard insolence could not provoke unity along a Republican front on this issue.

The break in Republican unity feared by the abolitionists was not only immediately evident, but retentionists even managed to find support for their claims in the same pantheon of Republican heroes as their opponents. Georges Berry cited Mably and Rousseau as "Republican" writers who supported the death penalty. Quoting from the *Social Contract*, Berry demonstrated that in Rousseau's political utopia, homicide was treated as a breach of the social contract and rewarded in kind.[97] Louis Puech also referred to Rousseau, adding for good measure Jean-Paul Marat and Montesquieu. Both Berry and Puech also sought to indicate that divisions on the matter between Republicans continued down to the present moment. Puech pointed out that even Republicans respected political contingencies: Jules Simon, a vociferous opponent of capital punishment when he was in the opposition, never introduced an abolitionist bill when he was later a minister.[98] Labori, the defender of Dreyfus, disposed of the appeal to the Dreyfusard alliance by making a hard distinction between the issues underlying each cause: "I always considered his case [Dreyfus's] a matter of justice and not of sensibility."[99]

In this end, the final vote, which solved the dilemma of the myriad proposals before the chamber by voting to retain the status quo ante 330-201, best displays the political divisions in the issue. The reten-

---

[96] *Journal officiel*, "Chambre des députés," July 3, 1908, pp. 1537-1538.

[97] Berry, *Journal officiel*, "Chambre des députés," November 4, 1908, pp. 2033-2034.

[98] Puech, *Journal officiel*, "Chambre des députés," November 4, 1908, pp. 2039-2040.

[99] Labori, *Journal officiel*, "Chambre des députés," November 4, 1908, p. 2044.

tionists included the right en bloc, minus only the renegade Abbé Lemire, nearly all the Radical and centrist Republicans, and a number of the Radical Socialists. Only the Socialists voted unanimously against retention, and their numbers were probably augmented by the votes of some fence sitters who voted their hearts once their heads saw the way the vote would go. With the exception of Briand himself, none of the government ministers spoke in the cause of abolition. Even the Prime Minister, whose own abolitionist sentiments were widely praised, limited his participation in the debate to a single sentence. Because the original government bill reported out in 1907 had been essentially reversed in the Commission for Judicial Reform, it was no longer a matter on which the government had to risk interpellation and possible defeat; this may in part explain the grateful silence of the ministerial benches throughout.

The debate of 1908 was much more, however, than a transitional political struggle between an old set of political enemies and new ones, or, for that matter, an airing of the arguments, vintage 1908, pro and con the death penalty. There was a deeper structure to the debate that expresses with great force the anxieties of the political class, regardless of party conviction, about the vital trends in French life. On these trends there was nearly total agreement. The suggested solutions to these problems provoked the usual discord, but even this discussion was rife with pessimism and a gloomy foreboding that the patient would worsen before it improved. The symptoms of the problems were biological in nature, and the suggested cures were expressed in the usual organic metaphors. The choice of a proper therapy for the patient determined the course of the years before the war.

The most conspicuous loser in the entire debate was the intellectual tradition of humanitarian ideas. What seems clear enough is that the Republican opposition in France had the most powerful claim on the use of these ideals in the political arena from 1848 through the first decade of the Third Republic. Though the use of humanitarian ideals was somewhat less attractive to the Opportunists who governed the nation after 1880, the secular humanist ethos remained the ideological underpinning in the party's continual war with the Catholic church. An eclectic ethical naturalism was indispensable to Jules Ferry, Paul Bert, Ferdinand Buisson, and the moderate Republicans who sought to disseminate a secular moral system in the public schools. However, by 1905 the church had been substantially weakened as either a political or educational rival to the Republican establishment; the party ideology, which for some years had shown something less than the unifying force it once possessed, developed an increasingly ad hoc nature. Republican festivals commanded less and less public support after the great enthusiasm of the 1889 centennial.[100] The vision of a secular human perfectibility that Republican orators had traditionally traced to Enlightenment ancestors was no longer a sacred cow.

In 1908 Republican retentionists felt free to attack this once proud tradition in a savage and unrelenting manner so as to highlight the practical and "realistic" nature of their own position. Speakers called for an end to "false sensibility," or the "humanitarian ideas" that they believed lay at the foundation of the abolitionist philosophy.[101] Rémy Castillard complained that philanthropy and humanitarian ideals favored the criminals and could not figure in any adequate system of social defense. "No more sentimentality!" he demanded. "No more false humanity and especially no more humanitarian posturing!"[102] Louis Puech, for his part, reviled the "gushing lyricism [of Lamartine and Hugo] . . . who have raised the art of saying everything to such an abstract level that the contingencies of this vulgar world disappear and are covered over, and, for those who follow and admire them, there remains only . . . a certain number of phrases that have passed into the state of dogma, absolute dogma, that one no longer has the right to dispute, even in an honest discussion."[103]

The antihumanitarian barrage was of such force and intensity that only a very small portion of abolitionist speakers had recourse to a moralistic discourse. Even Briand, the principal abolitionist debater, shunned "reasons of pity and humanity, reasons of sentiment, or of a philosophic nature," in favor of "arguments based on numbers, facts; I will examine the contingencies with you, the realities of the question."[104] Nearly abandoned altogether by Radical and other moderate Republicans, humanitarian ideals became, by default as it were, the sole preserve of the left. Only Jaurès, Willm, Allemane, and a few other leftists could be found employing the formulas of brotherly love, forgiveness, and human solidarity with the unfortunate. The winds of change had been reshaping the structure of political discourse and the parliamentary alliances that depended on them for several years prior

[100] See Charles Rearick, "Festivals in Modern France: The Experience of the Third Republic," *Journal of Contemporary History* 12 (1977) pp. 435-460.

[101] See the comments of Gabriel Faillot, Charles Benoist, and Louis de Folleville, *Journal officiel*, "Chambre des députés," July 3, November 4, December 7, 1908, pp. 1534, 2025, 2779.

[102] Castillard, *Journal officiel*, "Chambre des députés," November 11, 1908, p. 2209.

[103] Puech, *Journal officiel*, "Chambre des députés," November 11, 1908, p. 2210.

[104] Briand, *Journal officiel*, "Chambre des députés," November 11, 1908, p. 2210.

to 1908, but in the debate on capital punishment the nearly utter bankruptcy of Republican social idealism was openly revealed. The very subject matter of the debate made the evasions that had theretofore veiled the extent of that bankruptcy impossible. The visionary aspects of the eighteenth-century dream of human perfectibility had passed definitively into the hands of Jaurès and his friends for future safekeeping.

The practical effect of the mood of "realism" that permeated the debate was the nearly universal acceptance of a medical model of deviance. Speakers of all persuasions made linkages that were originally popularized in medical and criminological discourse; there were differences over the nature or possibility of the "cure" of the disease, but no dissenting voices challenged the model itself. In essence, all agreed that, the figures on first-degree murder notwithstanding, voluntary homicide figures *had risen* dramatically in the previous five years or so, as had assault and other crimes against persons. Abolitionist speakers themselves often referred to the authors of this genre of crime in the popular terminology, labeling them "impulsives," "apaches," "degenerates," or by their collective title, "bandits."[105]

This concession on the part of the abolitionists was part of their general strategy to separate first-degree murders, punishable by death, from varieties for which the penalty fell lower in the hierarchy of punishments. Accordingly, opponents of the guillotine sought to demonstrate that the authors of these violent crimes were created by a pathological environment in which alcohol was a particularly important factor in the spawning of criminals. Each speaker made the direct connection between an "unhealthy" environment and alcohol; each appropriated the standard clinical terminology that made of alcoholism a hereditary syndrome leading to degeneracy and its associated problems. Crimes committed by the victims of this syndrome, they argued, were of a special sort and deserved a unique classification.

For Joseph Reinach alcoholic degeneracy led directly to crime through "deadening the will, provoking 'abulia,' exposing the brain to irresistible impulses, so that moral responsibility vanishes and is no longer anything but a fiction."[106] The Socialist Albert Willm made the connection with recent urban growth and abandoned children quite clear. These "unfortunates" were left "without help or sustenance, without support, abandoned to all the hazards of the street, all the temptations

[105] See in particular the presentations of Joseph Reinach, Albert Willm, and Jean Jaurès, *Journal officiel*, "Chambre des députés," July 3, November 18, 1908, pp. 1536, 1543-1544, 2393-2395.
[106] Reinach, *Journal officiel*, "Chambre des députés," July 3, 1908, p. 1535.

of alcohol. And you know well the role, either directly, or as an atavism, alcoholism plays in the development of criminality."[107] Jaurès also emphasized the hereditary nature of the problem and drew conclusions that put the responsibilty on society itself. He worried that "a great number of children committed to a life of crime have been affected by the hereditary influence of alcohol. Until we have courageously struggled against this evil for which we are in part responsible, we have no right to make inebriates who are corrupted by the hereditary defect they carry in their veins bear themselves what is in effect a collective responsibility."[108]

Retentionists used much the same clinical terminology, made the same connections between alcohol, degeneracy, and apacheism, and characterized the motives of killers of this type as impulsive or gratuitous. There was, in other words, no dispute on this essential portion of the formula for violent crime. The retentionists revealed their differences with abolitionists in two ways. One was in their general failure to root the degeneracy syndrome in poverty and social disadvantages. A favorite strategy was to speak of "misery" and "alcoholism" as among "contributing causes" but to treat these as part of a range of "multiple causes" chief among which, after all, were the relaxation of repression and the regime of pardons. In the end, the retentionists put the emphasis not on causes but on the general rise of "cruelty and atrocity" in recent crimes.[109]

The other line of reasoning was presented by Maurice Barrès, a speaker not noted for his lack of frankness, who developed most clearly the argument lying at the heart of the retentionist outlook. Most retentionists shared his sentiments even if they did not endorse his vivid language. Barrès freely conceded the utter "determinism" of these kinds of violent crime, and urged his colleagues to help "combat the conditions that have prepared this atavism." Science gives us clear indications, he said, of what we must do to combat the "causes of degeneracy." "But when we are in the presence of an individual who is already infected, in the presence of this unfortunate being—unfortunate if we consider the social conditions in which he was formed,

---

[107] Willm, *Journal officiel*, "Chambre des députés," November 4, 1908, p. 2027. Together with prostitution and syphilis, he continued, these causes create "degenerates" who, "materially and morally are incapable of swimming against the current or reacting against unhealthy environments."

[108] Jaurès, *Journal officiel*, "Chambre des députés," November 18, 1908, pp. 2396-2397.

[109] de Folleville, *Journal officiel*, "Chambre des députés," December 7, 1908, p. 2779; see also Puech, ibid., November 4, 1908, p. 2041.

but miserable if we consider the sad crime he has committed—it is the interests of society that must inspire us and not the coddling of an antisocial being."[110]

Barrès then developed a theme not unfamiliar to the readers of his novels about "new" human types emerging from the masses to inject vitality and force into the life of overrefined civilization: "But apaches are not forces overflowing with life, beautiful barbarians who adorn the framework of our collective moral life: these are degenerates. Far from being oriented toward the future, they are burdened by hideous defects. Ordinarily, when we are in the presence of a criminal, we find a failed man, a man who falls beyond the pale, not a man who is yet to arrive at a state of humanity."[111]

Jaurès rose to his feet following this remark to say: "And these are Christians who say this: very well! It is odd to hear human failings called irremediable by our Christians of the right."[112] Barrès shrugged off the ironic catcalls that greeted his rejoinder that secular and sacred tasks were not always in harmony; he continued by saying that "for my part, I ask that one continue to get rid of these degraded beings, these degenerates, within the legal framework of the moment, not overlooking the testimony given us by competent men of science, if they should conclude that they deserve asylums rather than punishment."[113]

To this argument, and indeed to all arguments that held repression to be the only realistic response to crime, abolitionists replied with a comprehensive social and economic analysis. The Socialist speakers in particular, while conceding that alcoholism and degeneracy were the immediate causes of violent crime, hammered away at the theme that the long-term causes were effects of the social and economic inequalities of capitalism. Victor Déjéante emphasized the illnesses and bad nutrition rife among the working and popular classes. Marcel Sembat presented a sophisticated account of the psychological forces working on poor and uneducated men to display their manhood in emulation of the monstrous criminal antiheroes created by the bourgeois press. Unemployment and discrimination were the themes developed by Jean Allemane in his remarks about the criminogenic nature of capitalistic society, and Briand used statistics to demonstrate conclusively that violent crime was localized in the new industrial suburbs of the capital and other rapidly growing urban areas and was overwhelmingly at-

[110] Barrès, *Journal officiel*, "Chambre des députés," July 3, 1908, p. 1539.
[111] Ibid.
[112] Jaurès, *Journal officiel*, "Chambre des députés," July 3, 1908, p. 1539.
[113] Barrès, *Journal officiel*, "Chambre des députés," July 3, 1908, p. 1539.

tributable to young men out of work or with few permanent prospects.[114]

All these speakers emphasized the glaring class inequalities in the
distribution of justice. Countering an argument presented by Barrès
early in the debate that the poor were the chief beneficiaries of the
guillotine since they were most often the victims of violent crimes,
Allemane held that 80 percent of transported prisoners did not know
how to read or write and nearly the same percentage were the products
of broken homes. The wheels of justice ground the poor more pitilessly
than anyone else, especially those charged with serious crimes. When
the executioner harvested his grisly crop, said Allemane, it was chiefly
among the children of the poor: "Wherever one has never known
hunger, wherever one has not been terribly haunted by animal need,
one cannot grasp why one commits misdemeanors, and why, having
committed them, one goes on to commit more serious crimes."[115]

The Abbé Lemire and Jaurès both emphasized society's ultimate
responsibility for creating crime. How, asked Lemire, can one punish
with the full force of repression the man whose acts are dictated by
forces generated in society itself? It is, he argued, "as if the individual
was made for society and not society for the individual."[116] Jaurès
admitted that "these men" were "detestable" and "tainted," but he held
that "it is too simple to solve the problem with a blade, to lop a head
off into a basket and imagine that you have finished with the problem.
It is too easy to draw a line in this way between the guilty and the
innocent. There are chains of responsibility between all of us. . . . We
are all in a condition of solidarity with all men, even in crime."[117]

The left was asking, or so it must have seemed, for nothing less than
a massive financial effort to eliminate the economic and social roots of
criminality. This rather bold widening of the agenda of the debate
merely increased the anxiety of the center and right, since to acknowledge their "solidarity" with criminals as Jaurès had urged would have
meant the virtual acceptance of the entire Socialist program. It was
more in keeping with the retentionist's view of the proper social and
economic roles of the state to proclaim a different species of solidarity.
In the words of Louis de Folleville: "Our devotion to solidarity must

[114] See their respective remarks in *Journal officiel*, "Chambre des députés," November 11, November 4, December 7, and November 18, 1908, pp. 2207, 2043,
2787, and 2214-2215.
[115] Allemane, *Journal officiel*, "Chambre des députés," December 7, 1908, p. 2788.
[116] Abbé Lemire, *Journal officiel*, "Chambre des députés," November 18, 1908, p.
2400.
[117] Jaurès, *Journal officiel*, "Chambre des députés," November 18, 1908, p. 2397.

cease at the margins of crime." We must know how to "protect and defend society against incorrigible criminals who have broken their contract with it."[118]

It is a crucial part of the history of this great debate, however, that the idea of social defense, which had largely penological origins, had become a dominant metaphor in French political life and the ruling concept in the war against pathologies sapping the vital roots of the nation. The notion of social defense, once limited to the political lexicon of the nationalist right, enjoyed a wide currency in the 1908 debate, and was often linked explicitly with "national defense" or "national security," or joined to military metaphors that glorified collective struggles against alien invaders.[119]

It is also clear that most of the participants in the debate were conversant with the discourse of an organic medical model. Even abolitionist speakers, as we have seen, employed the pathological language of the clinic to explain the "resurgence" of crime; no one doubted the existence of degenerative alcoholism or questioned its relationship to crime, even if they differed over how best this threat might be met. Far from calming the fears of the retentionist majority, not to mention the anxieties of public opinion, the abolitionist's use of clinical descriptions of "irresponsible" killers probably provoked even higher levels of anxiety and worked against their ultimate aims. References to the population problem, to prostitution and tuberculosis, and to the dangers of infection to the "race" were made by speakers in both camps, thus bringing directly to the fore the grave concerns of an entire generation.[120]

The entire debate over capital punishment became, accordingly, a key test of the willingness and ability of the French national organism to defend itself against the pathologies threatening its existence. For the retentionist de Folleville, a society's mere existence gave it a right to defend itself by all means available.[121] Even Jaurès had suggested that if the Committee of Public Safety had not been loyal to its own abolitionist theories, it was because abolition could only be put into

[118] de Folleville, *Journal officiel*, "Chambre des députés," December 7, 1908, p. 2778.

[119] See the linkages made in the remarks of Faillot, Reinach, Labori, and de Folleville, *Journal officiel*, "Chambre des députés," July 3, November 4, December 7, 1908, pp. 1533, 1535, 2044, 2778.

[120] See, in addition to previously mentioned references of this nature, the remarks of Joseph Reinach and Victor Déjéante on race and population. *Journal officiel*, "Chambre des députés," July 3, November 11, 1908, pp. 1534-1535, 2207.

[121] de Folleville, *Journal officiel*, "Chambre des députés," December 7, 1908, p. 2778.

practice in "a society in a state of harmonious equilibrium which is not plagued by violence."[122] Another abolitionist, Louis Gérard-Varet, stated flatly that to abolish the supreme punishment, "one must have a people in a condition of moral health, equilibrium, and serenity."[123] But was France normal in 1908? Was there not excellent precedent, acknowledged here by the abolitionists themselves, for the suspension of Republican principles when the fatherland was in danger?

Gérard-Varet himself described the crisis of the public spirit in profoundly pathological language. All around us, he said, was "a flood of violent and troubling images and spellbinding emotions; a kind of collective neurasthenia seems to be guiding popular curiosity, not toward objects worthy of our interest, but toward the troubled and the obscure, gravitating around the melodramas that burden our public life, where the shadows of lies prowl cloaked in mysterious disguises. A derangement of the collective consciousness is developing which has awakened a taste for perverse and unhealthy emotions, and which is turning our minds and our consciences from sentiments of serenity and resolve."[124]

Other abolitionists characterized this public spirit in terms that recall the pathological models of crowd psychology introduced in the mid-1890s by LeBon, Tarde, and the Italian criminologists. Jean-Marie Magnaud spoke of the dangers of the "fickle and delirious crowd," and Briand warned the popular press that "when the crowd feels its security menaced it becomes unreasonable, imperious, ferocious." The "excited crowd," he warned, that today calls vociferously for the "blood of criminals," will tomorrow demand the opposite and turn against authority. It is easier today than ever before, Briand went on, to inflame public opinion. There is no peasant, however humble, who does not read his newspaper and feel his "security menaced" by the dramatization of gruesome blood crimes.[125] In calling for statesmanlike behavior, Briand made it quite clear that the Chamber should take the reins of leadership of this fickle and impulsive crowd out of the hands of the editors of the mass press and channel its morbid energy in more useful directions.[126]

[122] Jaurès, *Journal officiel*, "Chambre des députés," November 18, 1908, p. 2394.
[123] Gérard-Varet, *Journal officiel*, "Chambre des députés," December 7, 1908, p. 2777.
[124] Ibid.
[125] Magnaud, *Journal officiel*, "Chambre des députés," December 7, 1908, p. 2781; and Briand, ibid., November 11, 1908, pp. 2215-2216.
[126] The rhetoric expressed here about crowds is typical of the language of this era, and a further instance of the deep saturation of public discourse by the images

All speakers agreed that the Chamber had to provide some decisive leadership in the present condition of crisis. Political survival, if nothing else, demanded strong action. And here the retentionists had both expediency and the logic of the medical model on their side. The triumph of the humanitarian and sentimental theories of the abolitionists would be a grave blow to the nation in this hour, reasoned Jules Dansette. These ideas have as their source "a kind of unhealthy sentimentality which is, I dare say, to societies what neurasthenia is to individuals."[127] This condition of neurasthenia, which everyone regarded as the first fearful symptom of degeneration, expressed itself, in the words of Maurice Barrès, as a "moral feebleness," a "weakening of the will" that attaches to all doctrines, such as Tolstoy's, of nonresistance to evil.[128] In the face of clear symptoms of pathology, reasoned Barrès, spontaneous repugnance for evil or sickness ought to be taken as a sign of health, of willingness to resist the further spread of disease, and even as a sign of recovery. Retention, he argued with great force, was clear evidence that the softness that had brought virile nations to their knees would make no further headway in France.

When the Paris papers reported the news of the final vote on December 8, their tone was even more self-satisfied than usual. Though the outcome of the vote was not really in doubt after the November sessions, some dramatic events on the crime scene and an energetic press campaign had kept violent crime on the front burner. The Steinheil affair had taken a new turn at the end of November, and crime correspondents touched new lows in unrestrained speculation about the mental condition and motives of Marguerite Steinheil. Aided by a cooperative *juge d'instruction*, who fed the journalists a daily ration of tidbits, the newspapers announced in huge headlines each new fact that came to light, each new turn in the investigation. Thus, if the retention of capital punishment was "the will of the country," as *Le matin* proudly announced, it was also excellent theater, feeding the drama of the current *cause célèbre*.[129]

The certainty of retention once again made good copy out of psychiatry, and mental experts played their new role without a hitch. Interviewed in *L'intransigéant* Professor Berillon certified that Mar-

---

and terminology of medicine and social science. The crowd psychologists worried considerably about the "morbid" effects of the press in "suggesting" disorder to the "crowd." See Paul Aubry, *La contagion du meurtre*, 3d ed. (Paris, 1896) and my *The Origins of Crowd Psychology*.

[127] Dansette, *Journal officiel*, "Chambre des députés," November 11, 1908, p. 2217.
[128] Barrès, *Journal officiel*, "Chambre des députés," July 3, 1908, p. 1539.
[129] *Le matin*, December 9, 1908.

guerite Steinheil was certainly "a pervert, bereft of any moral sense," but that hers was that peculiar sort of "reasoning perversion" that made her responsible enough to be a candidate for the guillotine.[130] For the short run at any rate, medical experts had learned to utter the formulas that best satisfied the appetites of the nation. Even Fallières got the message to stop considering the moral responsibility of criminals and to "execute them on the basis of their responsibility to society."[131] At the end of the year the president refused to grant clemency in two particularly gruesome cases, and heads fell for the first time since 1905. Nothing could resist the cold new wind that seemed to sweep up everything in its path.

[130] "L'affaire," *L'intransigéant*, December 1, 1908.
[131] "Justice armée," *Le petit Marseillais*, December 10, 1908.

CHAPTER IX

Sport, Regeneration, and National Revival

In recent years some scholars have made an effort to challenge the received wisdom about the origins and extent of the so-called national revival. It had long been held that an upsurge of nationalist sentiment following the Tangiers crisis of 1905 swelled into a huge wave of sympathy for the army, for the "lost" provinces of Alsace-Lorraine, and for revenge against Germany. One of the earliest investigations of modern French nationalism, Carlton J. H. Hayes's *France, a Nation of Patriots* (1930) took as its premise the assumption that the French had survived the Great War intact because their traditional patriotism had "been pruned and trained in order to produce the perfect flower of supreme national loyalty."[1] Hayes examined the institutions and the cultural artifacts in which modern nationalist ideas were expressed, and found, not surprisingly, overwhelming evidence for a vigorous nationalism in government and bureaucracy, in voluntary organizations, in the press, in the literature, and in the textbooks used in public schools.[2] In 1959 Eugen Weber used sources of this sort to identify the dimensions of the prewar revival and to illustrate how it penetrated intellectual and political milieux after 1905.[3] In the same year that Weber's book appeared, Claude Digeon chronicled an extraordinary about-face of French intellectuals in their attitudes toward Germany, and wrote about the "intellectual nationalism" that swept through the community of French artists and thinkers after 1900 or so.[4]

Recent scholars have not doubted the existence of a nationalist revival. They have, however, questioned its influence and its role in leading the French to war. It has been denied, for instance, that the

[1] Carlton J. H. Hayes, *France, a Nation of Patriots* (New York: Octagon, 1974), p. 16. A reprint of the 1930 edition.

[2] See the lengthy digests of textbooks and periodicals, and the nationalist orientations in the press in Hayes's appendices. Ibid., pp. 343-370. Two of Hayes's contemporaries reached similar conclusions. See Carrol, *French Public Opinion and Foreign Affairs*; Hale, *Germany and the Diplomatic Revolution*.

[3] Weber, *The Nationalist Revival in France*.

[4] Digeon, *La crise allemande de la pensée française*, pp. 470-488.

French went to war with any specific war aims, including a collective desire to regain Alsace-Lorraine.[5] Recent students of the immediate prewar generation have also generally played down the universality of nationalist impulses in French youth, emphasizing the Parisian and the upper-middle-class nature of the phenomenon, of the difficulty of distinguishing nationalism from growing enthusiasm for radical right-wing politics.[6] Raoul Girardet has attempted to distinguish between two different nationalisms, an "old" one associated with the Jacobin left, and a "new" one springing from the integral nationalism of Maurice Barrès and his disciples. When the political elements peculiar to each tradition are subtracted, Girardet argues, we are left with a much more modest set of common ingredients—adoration of the military and its historic achievements—which does not appear to measure up to the notion that nationalism embodied some all-embracing *Weltanschauung*.[7] Girardet opposes the commonly made connection between nationalism and aggressive expansionism, asserting that the common heritage of French nationalism emphasized defensive warfare and security.[8]

The most ambitious revision of the thesis that a nationalistic revival prepared the French to fight a war of revenge against Germany has been made by Jean-Jacques Becker in his *1914: Comment les Français sont entrés dans la guerre* (1977). Becker uses a huge array of contemporary evidence to argue that the French went to war only when attacked, and in a spirit of resignation rather than enthusiasm. He presents a digest of electoral information to show that the Chamber elections of the spring of 1914 revealed much support for a reversion of the three-year military service law back to the former term of two years, concluding this to be a setback for nationalist aspirations. Becker also attempts to discredit the argument that a nationalist revival had been

[5] Douglas Johnson, "French War Aims and the Crisis of the Third Republic," in Barry Hunt and Adria Preston, eds., *War Aims and Strategic Policy in the Great War, 1914-1918* (Totowa, N.J.: Rowman and Littlefield, 1977), pp. 41-54.

[6] Robert Wohl discusses these issues in *The Generation of 1914* (Cambridge, Mass.: Harvard University Press, 1979), pp. 2-3, 17-18, 208-209; see also Paul Lachance, "The Nature and Function of Generational Discourse in France on the Eve of World War I," in Seymour Drescher, David Sabean, and Allan Sharlin, eds., *Political Symbolism in Modern Europe: Essays in Honor of George L. Mosse* (New Brunswick, N.J.: Transaction Books, 1982), pp. 239-255.

[7] Raoul Girardet, *Le nationalisme français, 1871-1914* (Paris: Colin, 1966), pp. 20-24; Jean-Pierre Azéma and Michel Winock make a case for a larger number of elements in common between the older "patriotism" and the newer "nationalism." *La IIIe République (1870-1940)* (Paris: Calmann-Lévy, 1976), pp. 182-186.

[8] Girardet, *Le nationalisme français*, p. 18.

in preparation since 1905; he maintains that the popularity of nationalist ideals did not extend much beyond an elite crust of writers, students, army officers, and bourgeois Parisians.[9]

Becker's portrait of the French as distinctly unchauvinistic in the summer of 1914 is convincing. But he offers little evidence for his assertion that the prewar nationalist revival was an insignificant phenomenon. He does not, for instance, directly confront the arguments presented by Philippe Bénéton, J. P. Azéma, and Michel Winock, or the important book of Eugen Weber;[10] Becker appears to regard high-spirited bellicosity as the supreme touchstone of nationalist sentiment. Thus the case for nationalism is only proven where a *desire* for war can be demonstrated; the *willingness* to go to war is not enough. In the end, Becker treats nationalism as though it must be the tail wagging the dog of the Great War. If it cannot be shown that the war was in some way the consequence of rising nationalist passions, then nationalism did not exist, or is unimportant enough to be dismissed as a minority phenomenon.

I wish to argue that Becker found less evidence for a movement of national revival than might be expected because he looked in the wrong places. He did not find widespread support for revenge on Germany or unanimity on the issue that war was a worthwhile risk for the return of the "lost provinces."[11] He found only deep respect for the army which was, after all, deeply rooted in French tradition and the monopoly of no party or group. But cannot a national revival take other forms? Can it not express itself in a language other than the traditional discourse of *revanche* and natural borders? And can a movement of national revival only reach its highest historical form as war, in a kind of historical teleology gone mad?

National revivals may take certain well defined material forms, such as military renewals or economic takeoffs, but they are essentially cultural movements. As such, national revivals are not obliged to express themselves in a particular fixed set of cultural symbols. They may take any form that allows them to fulfill the emotional needs and the collective pride of the movement's participants, and that satisfies the gen-

[9] Jean-Jacques Becker, *1914: Comment les Français sont entrés dans la guerre* (Paris: Presses de la fondation nationale des sciences politiques, 1977), pp. 18-52, 116-118, 575-580.

[10] So far as I can tell, Becker refers in his notes only to a brief essay by Weber, which appeared in 1958 in the *Revue d'histoire moderne et contemporaine*: "Le renouveau nationaliste en France et le glissement vers la droite (1905-1914)," 5 (1958), pp. 14-28. The evidence in *The Nationalist Revival* is not considered.

[11] J.-J. Becker, *1914*, pp. 40-45, 61-62.

eral aim of renewal or regeneration. In some ways an open clamor for a war of revenge with Germany would have been the least appropriate form for a French national revival to assume. The huge and ever-widening imbalance in population between France and Germany ensured battlefield ratios of notable disadvantage to the French. Thus, while such a position of relative inferiority did not foreclose a heroic resistance to German attack, it consigned an unprovoked war of revenge on the part of the French to the realm of the quixotic.

This is not to say that individuals and groups could not be found in the *avant-guerre* who urged such a course of action; all societies have endured chauvinists in their midst, and the French had their fair share. But, on the whole, the French chose to reaffirm their sense of collective pride in ways that strengthened them, perhaps even readied them for war, but that would not directly entail a military showdown with the German Empire. The central aim of the French national revival was perfectly articulated by the senator from the Meuse, Charles Humbert, who wrote in support of physical education that the aim of France must be "to augment the worth of men since we are no longer able, alas, to augment their number."[12]

Such strategies are bound to involve a certain amount of self-deception and to be partly compensatory in nature. They are likely, as a consequence, to favor "spiritual" over material factors and measure progress in terms of heightened states of mind or changed attitudes. John Bowditch, in an essay now many years old, traced the Bergsonian notion of *élan vital* and its popular manifestations to a "rationalization of weakness."[13] Douglas Johnson has also argued that the French high command chose to compensate for the weaknesses of firepower by praising the virtues of the "all-out offensive."[14] Such a point may also be made about the so-called youth movement. As Paul Lachance has written, "to those who blamed France's slide into decadence on the cowardice and lack of energy of the bourgeoisie, youth promised a recovery of self-confidence in the elite. . . . The young generation sig-

---

[12] Charles Humbert, "Pour la race: L'éducation physique obligatoire," *Le journal*, October 1, 1907.

[13] John Bowditch, "The Concept of Elan Vital: A Rationalization of Weakness," in Edward M. Earle, ed., *Modern France* (Princeton, N.J.: Princeton University Press, 1951), p. 33.

[14] Johnson, "French War Aims and the Crisis of the Third Republic," pp. 43-44. See also my chapter on the importance of "moral factors" and crowd psychology to the military theorists of offensive warfare prior to the Great War. *The Origins of Crowd Psychology*, pp. 123-153.

nified that France had fully recovered from the defeat of 1870 and could reassert itself as a power of the first rank."[15]

As Robert Wohl has shown, the concepts of generations and of generational revolts emerged at precisely this time in France; while they did describe, at least in part, the social reality of a new generation of youthful activism, they also played the role of wish-fulfilling myths for the older partisans of a national revival.[16] The "generation of 1914" was not an autonomous embodiment of a renewed national faith. It was nurtured in this faith by many in the older generation, who recited a litany of their own sins as a rallying cry for the youth they hoped might redeem them. The new nationalist youths, whose taste for action and spiritual commitment seemed to reverse the intellectualistic tendencies of their elders, were very much a product of their own times.

Between the coup of Tangiers in 1905 and that of Agadir in 1911, French political and intellectual opinion underwent a decided shift in the direction of support for military preparedness. If not exactly desirable, war seemed to many preferable to a constant state of tension between the two powers. The resurgence of the German threat inevitably encouraged many to reflect on the readiness and willingness of the French to defend themselves against aggression. The strikes and labor unrest of the era, coupled as they were with the proliferation of pacifist and antimilitarist propaganda, provoked the gravest concerns in the patriotic press and among intellectuals who had previously been well disposed toward the social and economic grievances of the working classes. This concern stimulated a vein of antisocialist and antipacifist discourse which drew upon the medical model of deviance and assimilated crime to internal disorder. In his review of the political and journalistic pronouncements of these years, Eugen Weber has noted the tendency to equate "strikers, hooligans, terrorists, revolutionaries and anarchists with anti-militarists, freemasons, socialists and anticlericals."[17] The right-wing press in particular lost no opportunity to confuse criminals and socialists: "lawbreakers were anarchists, anarchists were socialists . . . , all crimes could be connected with the more-than-regrettable spread of noxious doctrines."[18]

[15] Lachance, "The Nature and Function of Generational Discourse," p. 248.

[16] Wohl, *The Generation of 1914*, pp. 213-215; see also Philippe Bénéton, "La génération de 1912-1914; Image, mythe ou réalité," *Revue française de science politique* 21 (October 1971), pp. 981-1010; Phyllis Stock, "Students versus the University in Pre-World War Paris," *French Historical Studies* 7 (Spring 1971), pp. 83-110.

[17] Weber, *The Nationalist Revival in France*, p. 40.

[18] Ibid., p. 45. In the chain of relations, according to Weber, "apaches [were] to be equated with anarchists, then with socialists, and socialists [were] to be discredited

These connections led logically to concerns about the whole constellation of pathologies embedded in the medical model, stimulating, in turn, the most profound pessimism about the future of the fatherland. Typical of these gloomy assessments were the thoughts the Marquise Arconati-Visconti confided to Emile Combes in 1908. An extremely wealthy Frenchwoman, the marquise ran a brilliant salon in Paris before the war, catering to the progressive Republican left and various Sorbonne intellectuals. Dreyfusard (with most of her political protégés) before 1905, she had become disillusioned with the course of events after Tangiers: "And how many other sad perspectives confront us! The number of rebels and army deserters has tripled in ten years, and, in 1907, deaths in the population exceeded births. It's like the end of the Roman Empire: depopulation. The empty spaces are being filled by Belgians, Italians, Germans, Jews, or others. Tomorrow they will be filled by the yellow races. And, at the same time, we are working to destroy the French spirit itself by our so-called educational reforms and by letting literature, theater, and journalism be invaded by the most disgusting pornography."[19]

The worries that surfaced in 1907-1908 about the state of national health were clearly connected to the German menace, often in striking metaphors. A provincial editor in Nancy, complaining about the "degenerate" French race, pornography, and the rising rates of divorce and alcoholism, compared the population figures of France and Germany, concluding that "Germany will enter France like a thief in the night, only to find the master of the house on the point of killing himself."[20]

In the face of this deteriorating internal condition, one measure of national revival lay in a vigorous opposition to antimilitarism, strikes, and all other forms of deviance. There was a standard form for this discourse of opposition to internal disorder. One mourned the over-

by continual reference to their apache 'supporters' " p. 154. See Charles Maurras's linking of the excesses of anticlericalism, public violence, and "the reign of bandits, which the pardoning of Soleilland synthesizes and symbolizes." *L'action française*, June 2, 1908.

[19] Letter of the Marquise Marie Arconati-Visconti to Emile Combes, April 1908, quoted in Gérard Baal, "Un salon dreyfusard, des lendemains de l'Affaire à la grande guerre: La marquise Arconati-Visconti," *Revue d'histoire moderne et contemporaine* 28 (1981), p. 451. See, apropos of antisocialist rhetoric, the letter of Harduin of *Le matin* to the marquise, complaining of Jaurès and the "apaches of his party," no date, cited in ibid., p. 453.

[20] Maurice Dambrun, "Les vivants et les morts," *L'éclair de l'est*, July 11, 1908. See also Jacques Lux, "Nôtre suicide," *Revue politique et littéraire* 9, 5th ser. (June 13, 1908), pp. 767-768.

refinement and tenderness of modern society, occasionally attributing the weakness to the neurasthenic delicacy of hypercivilized urban culture.[21] Instances of self-blame for contributing to this state of affairs were common, but, as with the Republican administrator Henry Roujon, affirmations of a return to vigor were uttered in the same breath: "Ah, dear friend, I am in the process of doubting all the ideas of my youth. I believe that we have deceived ourselves cruelly; it is necessary to react at any price. If not, we will perish miserably."[22] Sympathizers with this point of view took hope from the harsh repression of strikers, from unwillingness to amnesty participants in civil disorder, and from a criminal justice that replaced the concern for individual liberties with a desire for social defense.[23] Examples of this sort of discourse could be endlessly multiplied, but it is more important to emphasize the nature of the connections between deviance, labor unrest, and anti-patriotism that joined to provoke, to borrow a phrase from Maurice Spronck, a stiffening of "the backbone of the French spirit."[24]

The discourse of national revival took other forms as well. Several writers have mentioned the importance of the public schools in maintaining the message of patriotism intact and innoculating the young against the "microbes" of pacifism and antimilitarism.[25] A recent study

[21] Guillaume Loubat, "La crise de la répression," *Revue politique et parlementaire* 68 (June 1911), pp. 234-237. Loubat was the general prosecutor at the Lyon Assizes Court.

[22] Letter of August 14, 1907, Henry Roujon to the Marquise Arconati-Visconti, quoted in Baal, "Un salon Dreyfusard," p. 451. See also the citation from Maurice Donnay's novel *Les Eclaireuses* (1913), which mourns a youthful conflation of antimilitarism, generosity to criminals, and free marriage. Quoted in Digeon, *La crise allemande de la pensée française*, p. 496n.

[23] See the account of the "new adversary" of revolutionary syndicalism in Paul Leroy-Beaulieu, "Le syndicalism—la confédération générale du travail: La théorie de la violence," *Revue des deux mondes* (August 1, 1908), pp. 481-515; Henri Joly also mixes crime, disorder, and culture criticism in "Le problème pénal au moment présent et la peine de mort," ibid. (January 1, 1909), pp. 173-204. See editorials by Lucien Leguillon, "Police et magistrature," *L'action française* (June 27, 1908); "Du poison ou du plomb," *La croix* (June 11, 1908); Arthur Huc, "Contre l'apachisme," *Dépêche de Toulouse* (July 10, 1908).

[24] Maurice Spronck, "La colonne vertébrale de l'esprit français," *La liberté* (July 8, 1908). Many newspapers took the numerous episodes of lynching attempts reported during 1908 to be evidence of a spontaneous recovery of the will to punish: Griff, "Justice sommaire," *Dépêche de Toulouse* (August 4, 1908); *Le réveil du nord* (June 27, 1908); *Phare de la Loire* (July 4, 1908); *Le petit journal* (November 18, 1908).

[25] Azéma and Winock, *La IIIᵉ République*, pp. 185-186, 205-211; Jacques Ozouf, "Le théme du patriotisme dans les manuels scolaires," *Le mouvement social* 45 (October 1964), pp. 25-29.

of the schoolbooks and teacher-training manuals of the Republic explores new ground by examining the linguistic *strategies* of the texts rather than compiling themes. Dominique Maingueneau did not concentrate on illuminating a "dominant ideology" in these texts, but sought to isolate particular significations that help explain certain aspects of the mentality of the period 1880-1914.[26]

Maingueneau found a widespread employment of binaries that depended in some way on the opposition of savage and civilized. History texts often characterized the evolution of modern French civilization as a veneer overlaying the "original sin" of Gaulish savagery.[27] This metaphor was invoked to condemn the violence of primitive man, but it was also used to celebrate the victory of self-discipline and civilization over the ancient Gaul lurking within all modern Frenchmen. Once established in this way, the "Gaulish paradigm" was applied in the textbooks, Maingueneau shows, to North Africans, criminals, vagabonds, bohemians, and the insane.[28] An important point for my later argument about the virtues of sport is Maingueneau's finding that the ancient Gaul was never celebrated for possessing reserves of energy and vitality allegedly lacking in overcivilized moderns, a view associated with the young Barrès under the sway of Nietzsche. Instead, the Gauls— and their metaphorical variations—were lazy and given to fatalism and inertia. They were indeed capable of great feats of strength and daring, but they could not harness their energies for "regular, monotonous work." They were perpetually "exhausted," victimized by bad habits, and incapable of repressing "unproductive" outbursts of anger and extreme emotions.[29]

The faculty that was repeatedly identified as responsible for these feats of self-discipline was the will. Jules Payot, who was rector of the Chambéry Academy and a school inspector, was the most prolific and influential proponent of the virtues of will power. Payot drew heavily on pathological psychology to describe the dangers of will sickness, laziness chief among them. In his *Cours de morale* (1904), written to be a handbook for teachers, Payot held that "we have personal worth so far as we have intensity and an enduring moral energy; whoever cannot

[26] For her method, Dominique Maingueneau, *Les livres d'école de la République, 1870-1914: Discours et idéologie* (Paris: Le Sycomore, 1979), pp. vii-xv.

[27] Ibid., pp. 51-65.

[28] Ibid., pp. 181-188, 199-224.

[29] Ibid., pp. 187-188, 199-203. Undisciplined laziness was regularly associated with thieves, the inhabitants of asylums and prisons, vagabonds, and workers in "low" trades, p. 212.

sustain persevering and coordinated efforts over a period of days, months, and years, will not count among the guides and heroes of humanity."[30] The "Gaulish willessness" of students was also a crucial element in pedagogical manuals. In Maingueneau's words, "the teacher is in effect invested with a sacred mission: he must root out the primitiveness and animality of the student to make him suitable to the rationality of the material world."[31] Indeed, the pedagogical theorist, par excellence, of the Third Republic, Emile Durkheim, was perfectly representative of these views. As he explained in his lectures on moral education about the pathological nature of a lack of self-regulation, "an inability to restrict one's self within determinate limits is a sign of disease—with respect to all forms of human conduct and, even more generally, for all kinds of biological behavior."[32] Individuals (and societies in "historical periods like ours") whose lives have no discipline experience the "malady of infinite aspiration" which disrupts the "complex equilibrium" on which life is based and draws upon our "limited reserve of vital energy," thereby producing "unhappiness and illness."[33]

Another rich vein of linguistic signifiers identified by Maingueneau relates to a medical discourse of hygiene versus infection. She found that the terms health, light, reason, and hygiene were regularly linked, and were found in opposition to alcohol and filth, which awakened the "obscure beast" in man, and invoked the "shadows" of urban decay, where "thieves and killers" lay in wait.[34] Maingueneau found a precise "homology between the body and the social body, between hygiene and political practice," whose aim was to maintain intact the "treasure of our energy."[35] Indeed, the relation between health and strength was explicitly identified. One of the teachers in G. Bruno's *Le tour de France par deux enfants*, the most popular text in the schools of the Third Republic, asks, "How could we neglect hygiene, the mother of strength?"[36] Maingueneau concludes her analysis with the observation that it was

---

[30] Quoted in ibid., p. 203 from p. 35 of *Cours de morale*, 6th ed. (Paris: Colin, 1908). See also Maingueneau, *Les livres d'école*, pp. 195-217. Among Payot's most important publications were *De la croyance* (Paris: Alcan, 1896); *L'éducation de la volonté* (Paris: Alcan, 1894). This volume reached over thirty editions by 1919.

[31] Maingueneau, *Les livres d'école*, p. 207.

[32] Emile Durkheim, *Moral Education: A Study in the Theory and Application of the Sociology of Education*, trans. Everett K. Wilson and Herman Schnurer (Glencoe, Ill.: Free Press, 1961), p. 38.

[33] Ibid., pp. 39-40.

[34] Maingueneau, *Les livres d'école*, pp. 291-299.

[35] Ibid., p. 295.

[36] Ibid., p. 236.

the scientists and the doctors who "incarnated the 'purified' religion, the purely rational morality of the future."[37]

Quite a lot has been written about the "revolt against reason" and the "idealistic revolt against science" as the intellectual hallmarks of the generations of the period 1890-1914. No doubt, many could be found who continued to exalt the Barrèsian *culte de moi* or Nietzschean antirationalism long after the turn of the century, after even Barrès himself had repudiated them as the posturings of his youth. But the "generation of 1914" was much more affected by a realistic and pragmatic mentality than is often conceded. It was not irrational to embrace the church, the army, and the nation, it was merely traditional. Henri Massis, Jacques Rivière, and other members of the new generation rejected their "past of neurasthenic dandyism" and, in the words of Maurice Barrès, "had surmounted nihilism as a healthy body overcomes a debilitating disease."[38] In adopting the language of hygiene, energy, and spiritual action, the prewar generation was simply bringing an important theme in the ideology of the positivist Republic to its logical fulfillment, a theme, moreover, that they had learned in their school texts. But they used it in a manner that made it pulse with the excitement of a great crusade and promised a regeneration of the French nation that would transform it in body and soul.[39] The self-discipline and persistent devotion to duty preached by the *jeunes gens d'aujourd'hui* helped prepare the ancient mission of public hygiene for its apotheosis into a component of national revival.

A last, related expression of national revival was the extraordinary explosion of sport and physical culture in the *fin de siècle*. During the thirty years or so before 1914, sporting activity attained a level of political significance it had never before reached in France. No doubt the simple availability of leisure time and the gradual spread of wealth made the spectacular twentieth-century growth of sport inevitable. But, in this era of concern about national health, sport took on a more profound meaning to many Frenchmen and Frenchwomen; the body became an ideological variable in the first burst of modern sportive nationalism.

[37] Ibid., p. 340.
[38] Quoted in Wohl, *The Generation of 1914*, p. 16.
[39] For a fine summary of the ideas and activities of this prewar generation see Roland N. Stromberg, *Redemption by War: The Intellectuals and 1914* (Lawrence: The Regents Press of Kansas, 1982), pp. 11-38. See also Wohl, *The Generation of 1914*; Edward Tannenbaum, *1900: The Generation before the Great War* (Garden City, N.Y.: Anchor, 1976); and Digeon, *La crise allemande de la pensée française*, pp. 451-533.

Eugen Weber has shown that sport had already begun to absorb a good part of the attention of the boat, car, and cycle set in the 1880s and 1890s in France.[40] Team sports such as football and rugby also put down firm roots in this period, while gymnastics clubs continued the growth that had begun around mid-century.[41] Tens of thousands of French men and women lent their encouragement to sport as spectators in the gala automobile and cycle races that were organized by Paris newspapers—the original media event—largely to enhance their circulation. The psychic community of sport was spread even more widely by the coverage given all sporting activities in the mass press; in those innocent days even the Socialist paper *L'humanité* failed to see the "alienation" inherent in mass spectator sports, and devoted at least as much space to sports as any of the great dailies.

France was also the homeland of Baron Pierre de Coubertin, whose indefatigable efforts in behalf of the restoration of the olympic games finally bore fruit in 1896.[42] The image that is presented to us of Coubertin by the great man's heirs in the olympic movement is of a gentleman sportsman rigorously internationalist in his views, and motivated by elevated ideals about the grand moral effects of sporting competition. Obtaining his organizational support from all social milieux, Coubertin's activities created a widespread interest in international sporting competition in France, which became the host nation of the games in 1900.

But the allure of sport in turn-of-the-century France was much more profound than might be concluded from merely counting the rising number of participants in sport and the even larger spectator public that followed their achievements. Certainly the aims of the sporting entrepreneurs and their political associates far exceeded the modest intentions of encouraging patriotism or contributing to the genteel amusement of the leisured classes. Indeed, many hoped that sport and fitness would stimulate a total moral and physical regeneration of the French race.

The organizational matrix that attempted to implement these hopeful views was formed by an alliance of professional public hygienists

[40] See, in general, the articles of Eugen Weber, "Gymnastics and Sports in Fin-de-Siècle France: Opium of the Classes?," *American Historical Review* 76 (February 1971), pp. 70-99; "Pierre de Coubertin and the Introduction of Organized Sport in France," *Journal of Contemporary History* 5 (1970), pp. 3-26.

[41] Marcel Spivak, "Le développement de l'éducation physique et du sport français de 1852 à 1914," *Revue d'histoire moderne et contemporaine* 24 (1977), pp. 28-48.

[42] See Weber, "Pierre de Coubertin," and Richard D. Mandell, *The First Modern Olympics* (Berkeley: University of California Press, 1976), pp. 49-94.

and psychiatrists, and moralists with a taste for the language of the clinic. Medical terminology was deeply embedded both in the discourse of sport and fitness and in the pronouncements of the purity crusaders who wholeheartedly believed in the healing properties of exercise. As we have seen, the French were concerned enough about the physical and moral condition of their national stock that by the end of the nineteenth century many of them had learned to think about the nation's relative decline in biological and medical terms. Of the means to national recovery inherent in the medical model, perhaps none was more appealing than that of physical culture.

As was true in virtually all areas penetrated by medical thinking, the primary conceptual link between the pathologies that tormented the French and the virtues of a sporting movement that might heal them was the idea of degeneration. On account of the Lamarckian conception of environmental influence associated with degeneracy, hygiene reformers did not need to succumb to despair, despite the grim diagnosis of the contemporary situation. The unhealthy environment which had worked its evil on human victims could be changed to regenerate the afflicted and shape the generations of the future. This supposition was indeed a premise of many of the medical and lay hygiene reformers who combatted depopulation, alcoholism, prostitution, and the organic diseases of the urban masses. Though less unified in format than these other single-issue groups, the physical culture and sports movement was to a great extent a response to the same hygienic concerns; its enthusiasts shared similar hopes that its program would breathe new life into a fatigued and sensual civilization.

A relatively new feature of the medical idea of degeneration made it possible for sport to assume the status of a therapeutic strategy for the masses. For those who had traveled too far down the road to degeneration, there was little hope of cure. Doctors held that the genetic material of these individuals—most of whom were from the lower orders—was hopelessly damaged, disqualifying them as future contributors to a healthy genotype. But most doctors believed that individuals in the *initial* stages of the syndrome might be responsive to rehabilitation. By the late 1880s clinicians had begun to identify a series of "nervous" and organic symptoms that they regarded, in practice, as signs of the onset of degeneracy. The most popular term for this disorder, as we have seen, was neurasthenia, the invention of the American physician George M. Beard.

The immediate source of the tics, sleeplessness, and general exhaustion typical of neurasthenia was the tendency of modern urban life to overtax the intellectual and emotional forces of modern men and women.[43] Some practitioners employed the economic metaphors of deficit and expenditure to express the seriousness of this debilitating weakness,[44] and nearly all medical observers agreed that the condition was worsened by tobacco, alcohol, excessive sexual activity, or other "intoxicants," which drew upon the more or less finite stores of human vitality.[45] Anson Rabinbach has convincingly analyzed the scientific and cultural origins of the late nineteenth-century obsession with fatigue: "Underlying the anxiety and hostility which surrounded fatigue is a utopian ideal of its supersession. The result would be not only a vast release of mankind's latent energies, a productivity without constraint, but a civilization resistant to moral decay and disorder."[46]

The illness struck primarily professionals, young adults, and over-worked students, that is, precisely those whom well-bred French men and women regarded as the future leaders of the nation. If these victims of "civilization" did not take the strongest measures in dealing with their debility, or if they exacerbated their problem by making "unhygienic" choices for marital partners, their fate would be the same as their compatriots from the popular classes.[47] If we recall the geo-political premise that originated the French obsession with degeneracy, one physician's metaphor seems particularly apt: "If the struggle for existence becomes more desperate, if the effects of this fatal weakening become more disastrous, and intellectual demands more murderous, one will see legions of the inept, the neurasthenics, and the degenerates grow along with those who will fall shattered by fatigue and exhausted

[43] Proust and Ballet, L'hygiène du neurasthénique, p. 10; Dr. Contet explained the onset of neurasthenia as an illness of the "highest degrees of civilization" in which "the illness attacks by preference the organs that function most actively." G. Contet, Pour lutter contre les maladies nerveuses (Paris: Baillière, 1903), pp. 6-12.

[44] See Charles Burlureaux, La lutte pour la santé: Essai de pathologie générale (Paris: Perrin, 1906), pp. 1-2.

[45] Proust and Ballet, L'hygiène du neurasthénique, pp. 10-24; Gilbert Ballet, Leçons de clinique médicale: Psychoses et affections nerveuses (Paris: Doin, 1897), pp. 145-170; Emile Laurent, La neurasthénie et son traitement (Paris: Maloine, 1895), pp. 5-7.

[46] Anson Rabinbach, "The Body without Fatigue: A Nineteenth-Century Utopia," in Drescher, Sabean and Sharlin, eds., Political Symbolism in Modern Europe, p. 45.

[47] The major writers on neurasthenia found that a large percentage of the cases they treated were a product of unfortunate heredity, and were sometimes accompanied by physical "stigmata" not unlike the more advanced cases of degeneracy. Likewise, neurasthenia that was stimulated in an otherwise healthy individual by grief, mental overwork, or "intoxicants" could be passed on, if only as a "tendency," to the offspring of the victim. Together with Proust and Ballet, L'hygiène du neurasthénique, see Bouveret, La neurasthénie; Levillain, La neurasthénie; Laurent, La neurasthénie et son traitement.

by their weakness, like the less robust soldiers that a great army leaves in its rear during its forced marches on the road to victory."[48]

Inescapable to the close observer of the turn-of-the-century hygiene movement is the great similarity between the technical literature on neurasthenia and psychotherapy and writings that focused on physical culture and sport. Thus clinicians such as Dr. Hubert Lavrand aimed their psychotherapeutic efforts at building new habits in will-damaged individuals. "Habit," he wrote, "is for the individual what heredity is for the race. It conserves, stores, fixes the acquisitions that man makes at each moment in order to save them as reserve capital."[49] Proust and Ballet even held out hope for hereditary degenerates by suggesting that one could create "artificial instincts capable of balancing off and even negating the hereditary ones, eventually substituting altogether acquired individual habits for those of innate ancestry."[50] For their part physical culture texts stressed the importance of regaining lost "equilibrium" in weakened individuals through therapeutic routines whose repetition would "leave a trace in the nervous system."[51] There can be little doubt here that the native Lamarckian theory that had been used to explain the grievous health of the French stock was also the key to its salvation.

The idea of inculcating new habits through repetition was part of a revival of interest in the rehabilitation of the mentally ill and enfeebled that swept French psychiatry in the late 1890s, reversing the hereditarian determinism that had prevailed for nearly twenty years. This therapeutic revival did not entail a break with the degenerational schemata that dominated French psychiatry, but was a relaxation of the presumption, initiated by Morel and underscored by Magnan, that degeneration was largely an irreversible process.[52] In mental medicine

[48] A. Mosso, "Etude sur Mesmer," *Revue scientifique*, 4th ser. 6 (August 29, 1896), p. 264.

[49] Hubert Lavrand, *Traitement de la volonté et psychothérapie* (Paris: Bloud, 1907), p. 13. Lavrand elsewhere expressed the new therapeutic optimism of the era in the statement: "Ideas, affective states, and acts form the rings of a closed chain: it is enough to act on one of the three groups for the others to follow." *Reéducation physique et psychique* (Paris: Bloud, 1909), pp. 64-65.

[50] Proust and Ballet, *L'hygiène du neurasthénique*, p. 128. See also Paul Dubois, *Les psychonévrosés et leur traitement moral* (Paris: Masson, 1906), pp. 20-29.

[51] Emile Laurent, *Précis d'éducation physique moderne* (Paris: Vigot frères, 1906), p. 52; see also Philippe Tissié, *L'exercice physique au point de vue thérapeutique* (Bordeaux: G. Gounouilhou, 1901), pp. 2-10.

[52] On the new orientation in degeneration theory see Georges Genil-Perrin, *Histoire des origines et de l'évolution de l'idée de dégénérescence en médecine mentale* (Paris: Leclerc, 1913).

a new interest in the treatment of idiocy and "degenerate" children surfaced, and new methods, or renovated traditional ones, were employed.[53]

Exercise or some regular physical regime was added to the traditional therapeutic stock in trade of "moral" treatment, drugs, massage, and hydro- or electrotherapy. However, because of the nature of the illness clinicians were attempting to treat, physical or sports activity had to be of a certain kind, lest it risk overturning the cumulative benefits of general therapy. Since the authors of most physical culture texts wrote with the same hygienic object in mind, their sporting preferences were remarkably similar to those favored by the clinicians.

The problem was to exercise and build up the strength of individuals who were by nature "*épuisé*" and incapable of sustained physical effort of any sort. Nearly all writers on physical hygiene warned against physical extremes with the same fervor they had always used to preach against moral ones. Philippe Tissié cited in this connection the example of a rabbit that died straightaway upon being injected with a small amount of the urine of Stéphane, the famous twenty-four-hour long-distance runner.[54] In many cases the search for proper forms of exercise was accompanied by stinging criticism of the entire educational system, which in general encouraged fiercely competitive intellectual achievement over "action" and "decisiveness," producing "only rhetoricians and dilettantes and so few men of character, will, and action."[55]

Many favored the system of "rational" gymnastics, imported from Sweden in the early nineteenth century, which relied largely on deliberate calisthenics and on the tonic effects of group or dual counterbalancing routines in which individuals could aid one another by providing light resistance to muscular effort. Proponents ridiculed the "violent gestures so dear to English brutality and American barbarism," and the "harsh and automatic movements cherished by German mil-

---

[53] See Pelicier and Thullier, "Pour une histoire de l'éducation des enfants idiots en France"; also E. Berillon, "Les applications de l'hypnotisme et l'éducation des enfants vicieux ou dégénérés," Ve *Congrès d'anthropologie criminelle*, pp. 302-308.

[54] Philippe Tissié, *La fatigue et l'entraînement physique* (Paris: Alcan, 1897), p. 37.

[55] Ibid., pp. 176-177. See also Proust and Ballet, *L'hygiène du neurasthénique*, pp. 130-143. In this connection, the criticism by Henri Massis and Alfred de Tarde of the suffocating and depersonalizing "scientific method" favored at the Sorbonne provides a direct link with the ideological aims of the physical culturists: "Nothing is more suspect to that doctrine of intellectual specialties than talent and genius; nothing is more foreign to it than the prestige bestowed on heroes, inventors, and artists, those who affirm the personality most completely and by whom the human condition is most perfected and ennobled." Henri Massis and Alfred de Tarde, *L'esprit de la nouvelle Sorbonne* (Paris: Mercure de France, 1911), p. 74.

itarists."[56] The "circus" technique of French gymnastics, which relied heavily on rings, bars, and other equipment, was also regarded with suspicion, since it appealed to the performing egos of gymnasts and in any event was inappropriate for the weak, the old, and women and children.[57] A fascinating struggle in France between the enthusiasts of these rival gymnastic styles continued until the war. Largely through the efforts of Georges Demëny, Philippe Tissié, and Professor Desbonnet, the most prominent sports impresarios of the period, the Swedish method made headway in military training, in the public schools, and as the "official" style of the important Union des sociétés de gymnastique de France.[58]

Other activities such as swimming, cycling, or horseback riding were also recommended, providing they were practiced in moderation and mastered in a gradual way that would permit the mutual reinforcement of willpower and the vital forces of the body. The "incomparable brutes" produced by obsessive athleticism and the vulgar worship of "record men" were far less valuable to the race than individuals exhibiting the less dramatic virtues of endurance, equilibrium, and tenacity.[59] This moderate approach did not, however, discourage physical culture hucksters from charging that "it is criminal to remain weak," and promising strength and joy to "neurasthéniques, épuisés, faibles et malingres."[60] Still, even the less utopian hygienists held out the hope of immediate physical rejuvenation, promising improvements in the birthrate if women submitted to rational and sensible exercise.[61] Some

[56] See Tissié, *L'exercise physique au point de vue thérapeutique*, pp. 2-12.

[57] Philippe Tissié, *L'évolution de l'éducation physique en France et en Belgique (1900-1910)* (Pau, 1911), pp. 3-4.

[58] Ibid., pp. 8-45; Georges Demëny, *Les bases scientifiques de l'éducation physique* (Paris: Alcan, 1902), pp. 1-6; Lieutenant Colonel Derue and Emile Laurent, *Manuel de gymnastique éducative et corrective* (Paris: Colin, 1902), pp. 3-5; Burlureaux, *La lutte pour la santé*, pp. 184-187.

[59] Laurent, *Précis d'éducation physique moderne*, pp. 2-3. See also Philippe Tissié's attack on "Ludomania" in *La fatigue*, p. 8. Other studies recommending this approach are Emile Bocquilion, *Etude expérimentale et comparée de l'action des différentes méthodes d'éducation-physique sur le développement corporel et le développement musculaire* (Paris, 1905); Henri Roger, *L'éducation physique dans la famille et à l'école* (Paris, 1902).

[60] Advertisement reprinted in Alain Ehrenberg, ed., *Aimez-vous les stades? Les origines historiques des politiques sportives en France (1870-1930)*, Recherches, no. 43 (April 1980), p. 55. In this connection, Professor Desbonnet, one of the more entrepreneurially oriented of the physical culturists, established a string of Ecoles de culture physique throughout France. See his handbook, written with Dr. Georges Rouhet, and advertised by Berger-Levrault as "necessary for the future of our country" and "the regeneration of the race." *L'art de créer le pur-sang humain* (Paris: Berger-Levrault, 1908).

[61] See Tissié, *La fatigue*, p. 312; Laurent, *Précis d'éducation physique moderne*, p. 133;

specialists took a slightly more eugenical line, recommending "sensible marriage" along with physical culture as the most effective strategy.[62]

Many of the medically oriented physical culture texts were themselves unambiguous about the important role exercise and sport must play in a French military and nationalist revival. No doubt the most important function these texts served, however, was to provide comfort and support for the nationalists who saw sport and youth as the foundation for both *revanche* and the rebuilding of France as a great power.[63] The Republican Victor Margueritte, founder of the pro–physical culture Ligue républicaine d'action nationale, expressed his fears about the low birthrates, alcoholism, and the "vital weakening" of French society. Sport, he argued, would treat the mind through the body and would stimulate a "cult of energy" that would "preserve the race and extend its strength."[64]

Similar language permeated the most celebrated prewar manifesto for sport, Paul Adam's *Le morale des sports* (1907). Adam defined sport as "any activities that coordinate a series of homogeneous and methodical physical actions whose aim is the increase of man's dexterity, courage, and power."[65] These organized activities would allow individuals to triumph over "weariness, indolence, neurasthenia, and boredom," and contribute to the "healing of our public illness."[66] He urged his readers to resist the "fashionable" habit of blaming all our "atavisms" on our ancestors; we may learn, he wrote, from our past

A. Desbonnet, *La force physique, culture rationelle* (Paris: Berger-Levrault, 1901), pp. 12-20.

[62] Laurent, *La neurasthénie et son traitement*, p. 59; E. Contet, *La régénération des familles et races tarées: Prophylaxie et hygiène thérapeutique de l'hérédité morbide* (Paris: Vigot frères, 1906). Also Schneider, "Toward the Improvement of the Human Race," pp. 270-277.

[63] See Emile Laurent's statements about sport, patriotism, and sang-froid and his comment that "I have seen many young men who did not hesitate to sacrifice their Sunday packet of cigarettes to be able to fire a few rounds at the firing range." *La neurasthénie et son traitement*, pp. 154-155, 157. Philippe Tissié praises the benefits of team sports, and ends his book on exhaustion with the exhortation: "Act, act, always act; such is the function of a healthy man and strong nations. More athletes, fewer aesthetes." *La fatigue*, p. 334. See, in general, the writings of Georges Demény and Professor Desbonnet. A summary of these hopes for the sporting movement may be found in Bernard Gillet, *Histoire du sport* 6th ed. (Paris: Presses Universitaires de France, 1980), pp. 84-88. See also Frederic Canonge, "L'éducation physique," *La grande revue* (September 25, 1908), pp. 236-259; J. L., "Le sport et la neurasthénie," *La presse*, July 7, 1908.

[64] Victor Margueritte, "L'éducation physique," *Dépêche de Toulouse*, November 9, 1908; *Le journal*, November 19, 1908.

[65] Paul Adam, *Le morale des sports* (Paris: Librarie Mondiale, 1907), p. 9.

[66] Ibid., p. 22.

326

errors and may gain new "acquired energy" through systematic reeducation. Adam was powerfully attracted to the James-Lange theory, a currently popular idea in physiological psychology, as a means of inculcating in would-be athletes the sort of conditional reflexes that would strengthen the power of the "will." Adam "paraphrased" William James in suggesting that "if we want to gain control of undesirable emotions (fear, anger) we must give ourselves over calmly to the 'exterior movements' corresponding to the interior dispositions that we prefer to cultivate."[67]

The genteel Baron Pierre de Coubertin, the most eminent representative of the sports revival in prewar France (and Europe), could scarcely be regarded as an expert in physiology or psychiatry, but his writings are occasionally remarkably explicit about the "hygienic" virtues of sport. He announced his aims in the *Essais de psychologie sportive* (1913): "I want to establish the correlation between psychology and physical movement and create a social therapeutic that will halt the universal neurosis of modern life. Sport is an incomparable psychic instrument, and a dynamic to which one can profitably appeal in the treatment of many psychoneuroses. For, very often, the psychoneuroses are distinguished by a kind of disappearance of the virile sensibility and there is nothing like sport to revive and maintain it. It is the art of virilizing bodies and souls."[68]

Since the disastrous defeat of 1870, there had been a firm connection between sport and patriotism. This bond was initially strongest within the Republican left. Paschal Grousset, an inheritor of this Jacobin tradition, agitated throughout the 1870s for a sporting revival, eventually founding the Ligue nationale de l'éducation physique (1888), the most effective sports lobby of the era.[69] By the 1880s, however, prominent right-wing nationalist groups such as the Ligue des patriotes, on the theory that democracies could no longer rely wholly on elite initiatives, had begun to agitate for mass participation in gymnastics and paramilitary sporting activities.[70] Though there are signs that these first organizational efforts recognized the generally healthy effects that these

[67] Ibid., pp. 119-120, 132-133.

[68] Pierre de Coubertin, *Essais de psychologie sportive* (Lausanne and Paris: Payot, 1913), p. 79.

[69] Weber, "Pierre de Coubertin," pp. 8-11.

[70] These developments are well covered in Pierre Chambat, "Les muscles de Marianne—Gymnastique et bataillons scolaires dans la France des années 1880," in Ehrenberg, ed., *Aimez-vous les stades?*, pp. 139-184. See also Zeev Sternhell, *La droite révolutionnaire, 1885-1914: Les origines françaises du fascisme* (Paris: Editions du Seuil, 1978), pp. 77-97.

activities would have for participants, the hygienic benefits were regarded as secondary to the purely *military* utility of having cadres of young men engage in training that readied them for possible future combat.

Only in the 1890s did the emphasis of the sporting movement change from the promotion of simple patriotism to "patriotic and sanitary concerns."[71] Medical figures gained a much more prominent place in promotional activities at this time, leading attacks on the military orientation of previous gymnastic and sporting activities, and arguing, as we have seen, in favor of exercise that would have the greatest possible benefits for the entire population.[72] The power and the importance of this largely medical appeal have been underestimated in much of the earlier scholarship on sport. In the midst of a deepening sense of anxiety about the biological (and therefore moral) health of the national stock, and faced with ever worsening population statistics and rising rates of social pathology, the French, not surprisingly, reacted favorably to a "hygienic" physical culture that promised some hope of national regeneration. The practically universal adoption of the clinical terminology and the assumptions of a medical model of cultural crisis is the best evidence that the foundations of a modern sportive nationalism were securely laid in prewar France.

The Republican left and the nationalist right felt equally at home with this hygienic discourse. It also held a certain appeal for all classes. Owing to the relatively new middle- and upper-class disease of neurasthenia, degenerative nervous diseases were no longer considered to be the exclusive province of the poor and the disinherited; and democratic diseases required, after all, democratic cures. This new conjunction of sport and nationalism also provided a potential basis for the exiles from the Republican political synthesis—Socialism and Catholicism—to rejoin the community of the nation as full participants. By 1908 Socialists and Catholics were actively engaged in the business of promoting health and vigor through their own sporting organizations.[73]

As I have argued was the case with the other expressions of national revival examined here, sportive nationalism was a profoundly com-

[71] Weber, "Gymnastics and Sports in Fin-de-Siècle France, p. 87.
[72] See Spivak, "Le développement de l'éducation physique," pp. 40-44.
[73] See Alain Ehrenberg, "Note sur le sport rouge," in Ehrenberg, ed., *Aimez-vous les stades?*, pp. 75-82. For the Catholic youth movement, Bernard Dubreuil, "La naissance du sport catholique," ibid., pp. 221-252. The most prominent hygienist in the Catholic camp was Antonin Eymieu. See his *Le gouvernement de soi-même: Essai de psychologie pratique* (Paris: Perrin, 1906).

pensatory movement. It took the place of an unrealizable military revenge on Germany, while helping to convince the French that they
had not fallen into an irremediable moral and physical decadence. The
role that sportive discourse played in the national revival is well illustrated by an editorial that appeared in the Republican *Progrès de Lyon*
in the summer of 1908: "The formidable gymnastic to which France
has been condemned for the last thirty-eight years has not been without
excellent effects on her health, her richness, and her strength. It has
kept at the ready wills once prepared to capitulate. . . . It has shaped
highly disciplined and robust men. It has promoted the talented and
built dikes against egoism."[74]

The sport and physical culture movement was manifestly a variation
of the same medical model of deviance and social pathology that provoked the other discourses of national revival I have discussed. It had
causes more profound than a simple collective desire for national health.
The meaning of regenerational discourse lay buried in the latent con-
nective tissues of words and things, mobilizing a logic and a terminology
that dovetailed it smoothly with the national pathologies it was meant
to heal. The real significance of these various modes of revival lies in
the rationalizations invoked in their behalf and the precise anxieties
they expressed.

It is difficult to escape the conclusion that by the end of the first
decade of the twentieth century there existed, at several levels of *men-
talité*, the conviction that the nation was grievously ill, suffering from
a syndrome that wrenched it out of its "normal" path of development.
This illness attacked the minds and bodies of French men and women
and could be made to explain plausibly the relative failings of the
fatherland since the defeat of 1870. This great syndrome of degenerative decline was first articulated by the doctors, psychiatrists, and
other health professionals whose scientific training and bourgeois
professional outlook encouraged the creation of a hygienic model with
cultural as well as organic dimensions. In a nation deeply worried about
its relative vitality, doctors found their medical knowledge selling at a
premium and their social prestige greater than at any other time in
the previous century. They were encouraged, as we have seen, to suggest cures for this illness in the same biological discourse in which the
symptomatology of the natural pathology had been originally constructed.

[74] "L'énergie nationale," *Le progrès de Lyon*, July 8, 1908.

CHAPTER X

Conclusion: Comparative Reflections on Great Britain and Germany

Though the French may have been unique in Europe for the sheer obsessiveness with which they investigated deviance and linked it to national decline, such concerns were not uncommon elsewhere. Throughout Europe in the late nineteenth century, there was an unprecedented preoccupation with crime statistics, with the numbers and forms of insanity, and with the appearance of apparently novel forms of sexual behavior. Much of this concern was quite simply a reflection of the moral outlook of the "respectable" middle classes, whose high regard for continence and self-discipline encouraged a suspicion of unregulated or unrestrained social behavior.[1] Thus, one can explain the proliferation of temperance movements and purity crusades as, to some extent, a natural extension of the ethos of bourgeois private morality into the domain of social action.

But by the late 1880s, in an era of active imperialism and growing national antagonisms, the typically moral outlook of mid-century took different forms. First, as happened in France, a medical and biological discourse of social deviance gradually gained widespread hearing outside the professional community and became an integral part of the language of everyday political and popular culture. A work of cultural criticism such as Max Nordau's *Degeneration* (1892), in other respects an old-fashioned liberal attack on modernism and antirationalism, formulated its distinctions from the perspective of modern mental medicine. Nordau's principal targets were literary and intellectual figures, but madness, alcoholism, suicide, and crime were also symptoms of the "sickness of the age," which he took to be exhaustion and enervation of the will.[2] In Nordau's work, and in that of many of his contempo-

[1] Cominos, "Late Victorian Sexual Respectability and the Social System," pp. 18-48, 216-250.

[2] P. M. Baldwin, "Liberalism, Nationalism and Degeneration: The Case of Max Nordau," *Central European History* 13 (June 1908), pp. 105-106; see also George L. Mosse, "Max Nordau and His *Degeneration*," introduction to *Degeneration* (New York: Fertig, 1968), pp. xv-xxiv.

raries, "the physical horizon of the body was identified with the moral horizon of the species, the moral infirmity of the subject was proportional to the debilitating effects of fatigue."[3]

In view of the supremely grim prospects for cure that dominated medical diagnostics in much of this era, the hegemony of a medical model of deviance guaranteed that contemporaries would have regular doses of cultural pessimism administered by doctors and hygiene specialists. The Austrian psychiatrist Richard von Krafft-Ebing, whose monumental *Psychopathia Sexualis* (1886) was a stupefying catalogue of contemporary sexual aberration, warned sententiously that

> episodes of moral decay always coincide with the progression of effeminancy, lewdness and luxuriance of the nations. These phenomena can only be ascribed to the higher and more stringent demands which circumstances make upon the nervous system. Exaggerated tension of the nervous system stimulates sensuality, leads the individual as well as the masses to excesses, and undermines the very foundations of society, and the morality and purity of family life. The material and moral ruin of the community is readily brought about by debauchery, adultery and luxury. . . . In such periods of civic and moral decline the most monstrous excesses of sexual life may be observed, which, however, can always be traced to psychopathological or neuropathological conditions of the nation involved.[4]

Krafft-Ebing's analysis illustrates another of the forms assumed by fin-de-siècle discourse on deviance: the identification of biological pathologies as "cause-symptoms" in the decline of nation-states. Ruminations of this sort—endemic, as we have seen, to France—became widespread elsewhere, particularly in those places where citizens had cause to suspect that their nation had reached its apogee on the world-historical stage. One might choose any number of European countries, or the United States, to demonstrate this point, but Great Britain and Germany provide especially good examples of this phenomenon because both were indisputably in the first rank of world powers in 1900.

In Great Britain concern about degeneration of the race originated in Victorian criticism of the demoralizing squalor of urban life. As Gareth Stedman Jones has shown in *Outcast London*, the metropolis, once seen as a place of creative opportunity, upward mobility, and only transitory impoverishment, after 1870 was regarded as the breeding ground of a subhuman class of permanently pauperized beings known

---

[3] Rabinbach, "The Body without Fatigue," p. 44.

[4] Richard von Krafft-Ebing, *Psychopathia Sexualis: A Medico-Forensic Study*, translated from the Latin by Dr. Harry E. Wedeck (New York: G. P. Putnam's Sons, 1965), pp. 34-35.

as the "residuum." What Jones calls "the theory of urban degeneration" replaced the outmoded notion that poverty and its attendant evils were a product of rampant lower-class hedonism.[5] This theory closely resembled the conception of degeneracy held by French writers in its assertion that drink, idleness, and improvidence were symptoms *and* causes of a syndrome of poverty whose locus was the pathological ecology of the urban slum. The varieties of social theory of which "urban degeneration" was a part flowered during the crisis in classical political economy that followed the unexpected economic downturn of the late 1870s and early 1880s. The liberal economics of Alfred Marshall and the scientific poverty surveys of the Booths and others were reflections of an effort to incorporate more "realistic" information into social science knowledge in the interests of accurate policy making.[6]

Concern about the "residuum" remained moderate until around 1900, when the reverses of the Boer War concentrated public attention on the fitness of British recruits. The fear that the British Empire was ebbing from its high tide under the old queen provoked an uproar in public opinion, forcing the government to assemble an official Committee on Physical Deterioration to take testimony on the issue from military and medical experts. The committee delivered a soothing report in 1904, playing down the danger of permanent damage, but, as Samuel Hynes has pointed out, far from stilling anxieties, the report was generally taken as proof of the seriousness of the biological situation, and the word "deterioration" was used interchangeably with "degeneracy" and "decadence."[7] The smoldering worries of the 1880s and 1890s burst into a nationwide debate on the sources of imperial greatness. Suggestions were aired about segregating the "residuum," and a decade-long crusade began that sought to regenerate the "national efficiency" of the Victorian era.[8]

The belief that biological deterioration lay at the root of the problem lent special force to medical expertise and contributed to the popularity

[5] Gareth Stedman Jones, *Outcast London: A Study in the Relationship between Classes in Victorian Society* (Oxford: Clarendon Press, 1971), pp. 127-131, 281-289.

[6] Ibid., pp. 6-16, 127-155; see also, for developments in social and economic theory, Reba N. Soffer, *Ethics and Society in England: The Revolution in the Social Sciences, 1870-1914* (Berkeley: University of California Press, 1977), pp. 65-88, 165-213; and Stefan Collini, *Liberalism and Sociology: L. T. Hobhouse and Political Argument in England, 1880-1914* (Cambridge: Cambridge University Press, 1975).

[7] Samuel Hynes, *The Edwardian Turn of Mind* (Princeton, N.J.: Princeton University Press, 1968), pp. 22-24; also G. M. Searle, *Eugenics and Politics in Britain, 1900-1914* (Leyden: Noordhoff, 1976), pp. 20-33.

[8] Jones, *Outcast London*, pp. 330-336; see in general G. M. Searle, *The Quest for National Efficiency, 1899-1914* (Oxford: Oxford University Press, 1971).

of eugenical organizations and publications. The core of the eugenist argument was the notion that there was a grievous "fertility differential" between the prosperous and healthy, who limited their births, and the diseased and destitute masses of the poor, who bred like rabbits. Owing to the improvident generosity of modern welfare, many more of the allegedly defective offspring of the poor now survived to reproduce more of their own kind, replacing, in the words of Karl Pearson, the "survival of the fittest" with the "survival of the most fertile."[9]

This obsession with national decadence led in several directions. First, and most obviously, it provoked a concern about the birthrate. Fertility, which had reached a peak in 1876 of 36.3 births per thousand, declined rapidly thereafter, standing in 1914 at only 24, a drop of 33 percent.[10] These figures raised the familiar questions about the "will" to reproduce, and about the likelihood of "race suicide" in the formerly prolific British stock, leading to the formation of a National Birth Rate Commission in 1913. Second, with the encouragement of the growing eugenist movement, Britons were reminded of the growing legions of the insane, the mentally defective, and criminals and warned that prompt eugenical measures were needed to safeguard the vitality and fitness of the people at large.[11] Both the foregoing worries fed the anxieties of military and civilian officials about the soundness of the British recruit. Richard Soloway has shown that despite the inconclusive nature of the statistical studies on this issue they invariably attracted widespread attention up to the war and into the period of conscription after 1916.[12]

Finally, the whole question of biological decline simply encouraged the wildest sorts of comparisons between the British situation and that of rival nations. The Germans, of course, with whom the British were engaged in a naval race, headed the list of relatively more healthy adversaries.[13] The gloomy "invasion" literature discussed by Hynes was one of the consequences of these reflections; the British troops in these novels were often pictured as unprepared and physically inferior to their opponents.[14] More significant is the clear possibility that the link-

---

[9] Karl Pearson, "Reproductive Selection," in *The Chances of Death and Other Studies in Evolution* (London: Edward Arnold, 1897), p. 102.

[10] These figures are from Richard Soloway, "Counting the Degenerates: The Statistics of Race Deterioration in Edwardian England," *Journal of Contemporary History* 17 (1982), p. 153.

[11] Hynes, *The Edwardian Turn of Mind*, pp. 15-33.

[12] Soloway, "Counting the Degenerates," pp. 140-143, 159-160. See J. M. Winter, "Military Fitness and Civilian Health in Britain during the First World War," *Journal of Contemporary History* 15 (1980), pp. 211-244.

[13] Soloway, "Counting the Degenerates," pp. 143, 147.

[14] Hynes, *The Edwardian Turn of Mind*, pp. 34-53.

age of race decline to the idea of national survival lessened public sympathy for the unfortunate individuals who were its putative manifestations. To take the treatment of prostitutes as an example, the number of prosecutions of brothels between 1885 and 1895 averaged fourteen times that of the preceding ten-year period, and arrests of individual streetwalkers grew in tandem. The old conflict between medical and "purity" crusaders against prostitution was resolved by their joint resolution to strive equally for the chastity favored by the moralists and the surveillance and eugenical proposals of the doctors. Out of this coalition, writes Judith Walkowitz, "the social-hygiene movement of the early twentieth century was born."[15]

Doubts about the health of the population continued into the war. In a speech Lloyd George made in September 1918 about the million men rejected from service owing to disability, he said: "I solemnly warn my countrymen, that you cannot maintain an A-1 Empire with a C-3 population."[16] With the war won, most fears were dispelled by the fact of victory itself.[17] It is perhaps more troubling to consider that, for many observers, the sheer willingness to go to war in 1914 may have been the best proof of the unsuspected reserves of strength in modern men. Thus the exultant tone in 1915 of the prewar Jeremiah of decline, Max Nordau: "[Mankind] now has hoards of energy such that earlier ages have never seen their like; it has of this most precious of all goods so much that it can and does wantonly waste it. Even the most arid and wizened pedant . . . is forced to acknowledge with sparkling eyes that we live in a proud age of human greatness."[18] Might some Europeans have welcomed war as a chance to resolve their own nagging fears of biological decline?

By the 1890s psychiatrists, forensic experts, and jurists in imperial Germany had forged the same links between degeneracy, madness, and crime as their counterparts in France.[19] However, until near the end of the century, as had been the case elsewhere in Europe, the

---

[15] Judith Walkowitz, *Prostitution and Victorian Society: Women, Class, and the State* (Cambridge: Cambridge University Press, 1980), pp. 252-255; See Walkowitz's remarks on the "hydra-headed assault" of the purity campaign against "nonmarital, nonproductive sexuality." "Male Vice and Feminist Virtue: Feminism and the Politics of Prostitution in Nineteenth-Century Britain," *History Workshop* 13 (Spring 1982), p. 89.

[16] Quoted in J. M. Winter, "Military Fitness and Civilian Health," p. 212.

[17] Soloway, "Counting the Degenerates," pp. 159-160.

[18] Quoted in Baldwin, "Liberalism, Nationalism and Degeneration," p. 119.

[19] For these connections in German criminal anthropology see Knut Engelhardt, *Psychoanalyse des Strafenden Gesellschaft* (Frankfurt am Main: Haag und Herchen, 1976).

occasions for medical intervention in the sphere of public life were few; doctors confined their actions largely to the private sphere, and the state respected the zone of personal and family autonomy required by liberal political values. By the 1880s, however, this essentially laissez faire attitude had begun to lose favor. Rising public concern about the demographic situation, crime, prostitution, and pornography, and the dramatic appearance of forms of "abnormal" sexuality encouraged a higher level of state regulation of private life and a more important civic function for medical professionals.

To a certain extent the assumption by the state of the power to enforce "respectable" behavior was a natural outgrowth of the close historical alliance between nationalism and liberalism.[20] The right of the national community to set standards governing collective survival overrode, in the outlook of German liberalism, the claims of private interests. Liberal nationalism freed individuals from *Stand* and *Land*, but it subordinated them, in exchange, to the nation. Thus, under certain circumstances, particularly in regard to sexual matters, the liberal outlook could slide "into the tracks of the older conservative *Weltanschauung*, and then its own momentum carried it further along the road to state intervention."[21]

Though German marriage fertility was much higher than in France, or even Great Britain, the birthrates of the 1850s and the 1860s had begun to decline, provoking discussion about geopolitical consequences around the turn of the century. At about the same time Germany had begun to feel the constraints of the Bismarckian system in the form of disappearing diplomatic options. Encirclement, the great fear of Bismarck and his successors, seemed a genuine likelihood by 1904: Algeciras signaled Germany's diplomatic isolation, and it became evident that the British Admiralty would not allow the high seas fleet, on which the kaiser and his advisers had staked Germany's claim to hegemony, to achieve parity with His Majesty's Navy.

When these difficulties are added to the ominous rise in social pathologies stimulated by Germany's rapid urbanization and industrialization at the end of the century, one can appreciate the speculations that linked pornography, prostitution, and abnormal sexuality to the falling birthrate. Gary Stark has shown how doctors attempted to demonstrate the contributions of pornographic literature to madness, sex-

[20] George L. Mosse, "Nationalism and Respectability: Normal and Abnormal Sexuality in the Nineteenth Century," *Journal of Contemporary History* 17 (1982), pp. 227-233.

[21] Isabel Hull, "Reflections on 'Nationalism and Respectability,' " *Journal of Contemporary History* 17 (1982), p. 256.

ual perversions, and the ebb of the breeding instincts.[22] Prosecutions for trading erotic materials rose dramatically following the passage of new restrictive legislation at the turn of the century.[23] Prostitution also aroused public alarm at this time. As was the case in England and France, the state cooperated willingly with doctors and purity crusaders struggling against the rising tide of venereal disease.[24] The essentially biological discourse that rationalized these developments was powerful enough after the turn of the century to convince German feminist leaders to renounce their liberal support of abortion and to replace their wholly political demands for suffrage with the argument that they deserved to vote because they bore and bred the nation's soldiers.[25]

The most dramatic evidence for the ubiquity of a medical model of national decline in Germany does not come from the sinister underworld of urban slums, however, but from a series of homosexual scandals that touched the highest summits of the Reich itself. Moved by the conviction that the foreign policy of the Reich was in the grip of a sinister pro-Entente cabal, the liberal journalist Maximilian Harden exposed a number of the kaiser's personal entourage as homosexuals, thus provoking a series of scandalous trials between 1907 and 1909. Harden had previously opposed the magnetic personal influence Philipp Eulenberg appeared to have on Kaiser Wilhelm; some partial revelations in 1902 forced Eulenburg from the embassy in Vienna and into a premature retirement. But Eulenburg's partial rehabilitation led Harden to reveal all he knew about Eulenburg's relations with other members of the kaiser's intimate inner circle, and with a few individuals from the lower orders whom he induced to testify in court.[26]

Harden's motives were political, but it was not accidental, as Isabel Hull has argued, that the grounds he chose were sexual:

> By doing so he was reflecting a dominant theme in current political discourse. Much of the language of compensatory bellicosity was in fact sexual. The virtues of strength, military preparedness, courage, hardness, aggression, vitality, comradeship, productivity, and so forth were all virtues associated with masculinity. Even [Hofmarschall Rob-

[22] Gary D. Stark, "Pornography, Society and the Law in Imperial Germany," *Central European History* 14 (September 1981), pp. 210-212.

[23] Ibid., pp. 216-221.

[24] Richard J. Evans, "Prostitution, State, and Society in Imperial Germany," *Past and Present* 70 (1976), pp. 106-129.

[25] Richard J. Evans, *The Feminist Movement in Germany, 1894-1933* (London and Beverly Hills: Sage, 1976), pp. 158-170.

[26] Isabel V. Hull, *The Entourage of Kaiser Wilhelm II, 1888-1918* (Cambridge: Cambridge University Press, 1982), pp. 109-145.

ert von] Zedlitz-Trutzschler, whose views on these matters were much more sensible than many of his contemporaries, betrayed the same prejudices when he took refuge from his pessimism only in the growing population figures, which, he thought, reflected the "strength" of the people. Thus to seize on the question of Eulenburg's masculinity was to touch a raw metaphoric nerve with the hot iron of actual sexual scandal.[27]

As "a symbol for all that ailed Germany," Eulenburg, Kuno von Moltke, and the others exposed in this affair were made the sacrificial lambs to assuage the pessimism and pervasive self-doubt of Germany's ruling elite. The links between decadence, homosexuality, and effeminacy were so strong that the political cartoons of the period regularly connected them, delighting especially in the irony of homosexuals dressed in military garb.[28]

One effect of the scandal was to promote a wave of homophobia of such dimensions that unmarried officers felt obliged to marry to head off suspicion, while purges from the ranks reached an all-time high. But the most significant effect may have been the influence that the exposures had on the aristocracy itself. Partly as compensation for the doubts raised about homosexual influence, the kaiser and some of his military-political entourage projected an image of "military manliness" that made diplomacy and politics "suspect as manifestations of indecision or weakness" and favored "vigorous and bellicose policies."[29] This attitude applied most especially to men who, like the emperor himself, feared they did not measure up to the masculine ideal. Hull discusses the extraordinary obsession with the officers' honor code, the "rigidity of social expectations and the all-pervading repression" that prevailed in the noble ethos at the end of the century. It may have been, she speculates, that preventive war was the only means of relieving the unbearable tension created within the aristocracy between the required standard of soldierly masculinity and the dishonored luxury of homoerotic friendships.[30]

In the long run it may prove that there are as many differences as similarities in the meaning of a medical model of deviance for the citizens of Britain, France, and Germany. Yet it seems that such a model

[27] Ibid., p. 133.
[28] There are several excellent examples of these themes in the collection assembled by James D. Steakley in "Iconography of a Scandal: Political Cartoons of the Eulenburg Affair," *Studies in Visual Communication* 9 (March 1983), pp. 20-51.
[29] Hull, *The Entourage of Kaiser Wilhelm II*, p. 296.
[30] Ibid., pp. 297, 300-304.

responded to certain general needs. The idea of biological degeneration summed up for late nineteenth-century Europeans the terrible human costs of modernization. It explained the alleged rise in urban crime and violence, madness, alcoholism, and sexual perversion and presented, in a medical discourse, the reasons for their stubborn intractability. The medical model also served as the vehicle for the expression of class and national anxieties about exhaustion and decline. But if it suggested new cures for national degeneracy such as sport, it also stimulated, as compensations for perceived weaknesses, the more traditional responses of military preparedness and nationalism.

The medical idea of degeneration did not long survive the end of World War I. This was in part attributable to the progress of modern genetics, which seriously discredited the neo-Larmarckian inheritance theory that explained the onset of degenerative syndromes. But it may also have taken the sacrifice of millions of dead and wounded to prove to Europeans that they had the will and the means to overcome the terrible harbingers of illness. While it still retained its vitality, however, this mixture of anxieties and curative processes signaled that twentieth-century Europeans stood at the threshold of a peculiarly modern form of political consciousness that had as its ultimate object "materials for the instruction of a new man, a eugenics rising to its climax in a propaedeutics of the masses."[31]

In his brilliant novel of *fin-de-siècle* Vienna, *The Man without Qualities*, Robert Musil has Ulrich, his hero of indeterminate character, display a grim fascination with the fate of Moosbrugger, an unstable carpenter on trial for his life for cutting a young girl to ribbons with a blade:

> It is not advisable to feel oneself akin to a notorious lunatic; nor did Ulrich do so. But why did one medical authority declare that Moosbrugger was a lunatic, and the other that he was not? Where had the reporters got their nimble expertness in describing the work of his knife? And by what qualities did Moosbrugger cause the excitement and gooseflesh that for half of the two million people living in this city amounted to practically as much as a family quarrel or a broken-off engagement? . . . "Grand Guignol!" he held against himself. To admire the gruesome or the taboo in the permissible form of dreams and neuroses seemed to him thoroughly appropriate to this age of middle-class mentality.[32]

[31] Lion Murard and Patrick Zylberman, "La cité eugénique," *L'haleine des faubourgs, Recherches* no. 29 (December 1977), pp. 424-425.

[32] Robert Musil, *The Man without Qualities*, vol. 1, trans. Eithne Wilkins and Ernst Kaiser (New York: G. P. Putnam's Sons, 1980), p. 139.

It is clear from this and other episodes in the novel that Musil believes crime, madness, and sexual peculiarities to have been objects of unusually intense interest in this period of Europe's history. I have examined some of the sources of this interest in pre–World War French culture, but it may be that the most convincing sort of treatment of this extraordinary phenomenon is beyond the craft of the historian and lies in the hands of artists of the rank of Dostoevsky and Musil. The historian can show how deviance came to assume an important symbolic role in assessments of civic health and national destiny, and can chart, and even partially explain, the rise of the biological and medical metaphors in which such discussions were conducted. But formal history lacks the tools, and historians the skills, to reconstruct the obsessive power that madness and deviance exercised over the men and women of this era. We know intuitively that the story of a murder generated a profound emotional resonance in those who reported and read about it and especially in those who judged the crime or who treated or punished the criminal, but we can only hint in a clumsy and imperfect way at the range of thoughts and feelings experienced by contemporaries. The nuances of these responses are lost in the historical analysis of what are essentially psychological events. In the end, perhaps, we must be content with Musil's decidedly matter-of-fact rendering of Ulrich's final statement on the Moosbrugger case, a description at once thoroughly wise and terribly unsatifying: " 'And now I will explain to you,' Ulrich added smilingly, 'why one can, of course, feel all sorts of things for Moosbrugger, but can't, all the same, do anything. In the last resort all these cases are like a loose end of a thread hanging out, and if one pulls at it, the whole tightly knit fabric of society begins to come undone.' "[33]

[33] Ibid., p. 312.

BIBLIOGRAPHY

This bibliography is not meant to be a comprehensive list of all the sources used in this study. I have chosen, for instance, to list only the titles of the nineteenth and early twentieth-century periodicals, and have eliminated some of the less useful contemporary books. On the other hand, I have included virtually all the modern secondary literature, much of which is quite recent, for the convenience of readers. I realize that a division between "contemporary" and "modern secondary" literature is necessarily an artificial one, but it may have some utility for readers with different interests. In all cases the most complete account of the sources must be found in the notes.

MANUSCRIPT SOURCES

Archives nationales. Henri Joly, F^{17} 21007.
Fonds Lacassagne. Ln5.5174. Bibliothèque municipale de Lyon.

COLLECTIONS

Garçon, Emile, ed. *Code pénal annoté.* 2d ed. by Marcel Rousselet, Maurice Patin, and Jacques Acel. 3 vols. Paris, 1952-1959.
Mueller, Gerhard O. W., ed. *The French Penal Code.* Translated by Gerhard O. W. Mueller and Jean F. Moreau. London, 1960

GOVERNMENT DOCUMENTS

Conseil supérieur de l'assistance publique. Fascs. 50, 52. Paris, 1899.
———. Fasc. 83. Paris, 1901.
———. Fasc. 92. Paris, 1902.
Direction de la statistique générale et de la documentation. *Compte générale de l'administration de la justice criminelle. Annuaire statistique.* Paris.
Journal officiel de la République française. Débats parlementaires, Chambre des députés.
———. Débats parlementaires, Sénat.

BIBLIOGRAPHY

Procès-verbaux of Congresses

Actes du premier congrès international d'anthropologie criminelle. Rome, 1885.
Actes du deuxième congrès d'anthropologie criminelle. Paris, 1889.
Actes du troisième congrès d'anthropologie criminelle. Brussels, 1893.
Congrès international d'anthropologie criminelle. Geneva, 1897.
Vᵉ Congrès international d'anthropologie criminelle. Amsterdam, 1901.

Premier congrès national du patronage des libérés. Paris, 1894.
Deuxième congrès national du patronage des libérés. Lyon, 1895.
Troisième congrès national du patronage des libérés. Bordeaux, 1896.
Quatrième congrès national du patronage des libérés. Lille, 1898.

Newspapers

L'action française
La croix
Dépêche de Toulouse
Echo de Paris
L'echo du nord
L'éclair
L'éclair de l'est
Le Figaro
Le Gaulois
La gazette des tribuneaux
L'humanité
L'intransigéant
Le journal
Journal de débats
La justice
La lanterne
La liberté

Lyon république
Le matin
La patrie
La petite gironde
Le petit journal
Le petit Marseillais
Le petit Parisien
Le petit Provençal
Phare de la Loire
La presse
Le progrès de Lyon
La réforme de Paris
La République française
Le réveil du Nord
Le siècle
Le soleil
Le temps

Periodicals

L'alcool
Annales de démographie internationale
Annales d'hygiène publique et de médecine légale
Annales médico-psychologiques
L'année psychologique
L'année sociologique
Archives de l'anthropologie criminelle et des sciences pénales
Archivio di psichiatria, scienze penali ed antropologia criminale

Bulletin de la Société d'anthropologie de Paris
Bulletin de la Société de médecine légale
Bulletin de la Société générale des prisons
Bulletin de l'union internationale de droit pénal
Etudes religieuses, philosophiques et littéraires
Gazette des hôpitaux
La grande revue
Le grand journal
Journal de la Société de statistique de Paris
Journal de psychologie
Lectures pour tous
Mercure de France
La nouvelle revue
La réforme sociale
Revue d'anthropologie
Revue de l'hypnotisme et de psychologie physiologique
Revue de Lille
Revue de médecine légale
Revue de médecine légale, psychiatrique et d'anthropologie criminelle
Revue de Paris
Revue de psychiatrie
Revue de science criminelle et de droit pénal comparé
Revue des cours et conférences
Revue des cours scientifiques
Revue des deux mondes
Revue des idées
Revue des sciences criminelles
Revue du mois
Revue judiciaire
Revue latine
Revue philanthropique
Revue philosophique
Revue politique et littéraire
Revue politique et parlementaire
Revue scientifique
Séances et travaux de l'Académie des sciences morales et politiques

CONTEMPORARY BOOKS

Abbo, Albert. *Les crimes des foules.* Marseille, 1910.
Adam, Paul. *Les disciplines de la France.* Paris, 1908.
————. *Le morale des sports.* Paris, 1907.

BIBLIOGRAPHY

Aubry, Paul. *La contagion du meurtre.* 3d ed. Paris, 1896.

Ballet, Gilbert. *L'expertise médico-légale et la question de la responsabilité.* Geneva, 1907.

Ballet, Gilbert, et al. *Traité de pathologie mentale.* Paris, 1903.

Bérard, Alexandre. *La transportation des récidivistes et les colonies françaises.* Lyon, 1885.

Bertheau, Charles. *De la transportation des récidivistes incorrigibles.* Paris, 1882.

Bertillon, Jacques. *La dépopulation de la France, ses conséquences, ses causes, mésures à prendre pour la combattre.* Paris, 1911.

Boilley, P. *Les trois socialismes, anarchisme, collectivisme, réformisme.* Paris, 1895.

Bonger, Willem A. *Criminality and Economic Conditions.* Translated by Henry P. Horton. New York, 1967.

Bonneville de Marsangy, Arnould. *De la récidive.* Paris, 1844.

Boue, Pierre. *Vagabondage et mendicité.* Pithiviers, 1908.

Bouveret, Léon. *La neurasthénie.* 2d ed. Paris, 1891.

Bureau, Paul. *La restriction volontaire de la natalité et la défense nationale.* Paris, 1913.

Burlureaux, Charles. *La lutte pour la santé: Essai de pathologie générale.* Paris, 1906.

Cahen, Georges. *L'autre guerre: Essais d'assistance et de prévoyance sociale (1905-1920).* Paris, 1920.

Cazalis, Henry. *Science et marriage.* Paris, 1900.

Chauteau, Fernand. *Vagabondage et mendicité: Les plaies sociales.* Paris, 1907.

Colin, Henry. *Les aliénés vicieux dans les asiles.* Paris, 1900.

Collet, Georges. *Sur les évasions des aliénés.* Lyon, 1907.

Contet, E. *Pour lutter contre les maladies nerveuses.* Paris, 1903.

———. *La régénération des familles et races tarées: Prophylaxie et hygiène thérapeutique de l'hérédité morbide.* Paris, 1906.

Corre, Armand. *L'ethnographie criminelle.* Paris, 1894.

Coubertin, Pierre de. *Essais de psychologie sportive.* Lausanne and Paris, 1913.

Coutagne, Henry. *La folie au point de vue judiciaire et administratif.* Lyon, 1889.

———. *Précis de médecine légale.* Paris, 1896.

Coutance, Amedée. *La lutte pour l'existence.* Paris, 1882.

Crocq, Jean. *L'état mental des anarchistes.* Paris, 1894.

Cruppi, Jean. *La cour d'assises.* Paris, 1898.

Dallemagne, Jules. *Les théories de la criminalité.* Paris, 1896.

Daniel, André. *L'année politique 1883.* Paris, 1884.

Darnand, Emile. *Vagabonds et mendiants: Etude de droit pénal.* Paris, 1876.

Debierre, Charles-Marie. *Le crâne des criminels.* Lyon, 1895.

Deherme, Georges. *Croître ou disparaître.* Paris, 1910.

Demëny, Georges. *Les bases scientifiques de l'éducation physique.* Paris, 1902.

Derue, Lieutenant Colonel and Laurent, Emile. *Manuel de gymnastique éducative et corrective.* Paris, 1902.

Desbonnet, A. *La force physique, culture rationelle.* Paris, 1901.

Desportes, Fernand. *La récidive: Examen du projet de loi sur la relégation des récidivistes.* Paris, 1885.

Dubois, Paul. *Les psychonévrosés et leur traitement moral.* Paris, 1906.

Dumans, T. *De la récidive.* Caen, 1877.

Duprat, G. L. *Les causes sociales de la folie.* Paris, 1900.

DuPuy, Hubert. *Vagabondage et mendicité.* Paris, 1891.

Durkheim, Emile. *Leçons de sociologie: Physique des moeurs et du droit.* Paris, 1950.

———. *Moral Education: A Study in the Theory and Application of the Sociology of Education.* Translated by Everett K. Wilson and Herman Schnurer. Glencoe, Ill., 1961.

———. *The Rules of Sociological Method.* 8th ed. Translated by Sarah A. Solovay and John H. Mueller. Glencoe, Ill., 1938.

———. *Suicide: A Study in Sociology.* Translated by John H. Spaulding and George Simpson. Glencoe, Ill., 1951.

Esmein, A. *A History of Continental Criminal Procedure: With Special Reference to France.* Translated by John Simpson. Boston, 1913.

Esquirol, Etienne. *De la lypémanie ou mélancolie.* Presented by P. Fédida and J. Postel. Toulouse, 1977.

———. *Des maladies mentales.* Vol. 1. Paris, 1838.

Eymieu, Antonin. *Le gouvernement de soi-même: Essai de psychologie pratique.* Paris, 1906.

Fauconnet, Paul. *La responsabilité: Etude de sociologie.* Paris, 1919.

Féré, Charles. *Dégénérescence et criminalité.* Paris, 1888.

———. *Les épileptiques et les épilepsies.* Paris, 1890.

Fontanille, Raphael. *Aliénation mentale et criminalité: Historique expertise médico-légale. Internement.* Grenoble, 1902.

Fouillée, Alfred. *L'idée moderne de droit.* 2d ed. Paris, 1923.

———. *Psychologie du peuple français.* Paris, 1898.

———. *La science sociale contemporaine.* 6th ed. Paris, 1922.

Fournier, Alfred. *Danger social de la syphilis.* Paris, 1905.

———. *La Ligue contre la syphilis.* Paris, 1904.

———. *Les stigmates distrophiques de l'hérédosyphilis.* Paris, 1898.

Francotte, Xavier. *L'anthropologie criminelle.* Paris, 1891.

Gendron, E. *Alcoolisme héréditaire.* Paris, 1880.

BIBLIOGRAPHY

Genil-Perrin, Georges. *Histoire des origines et de l'évolution de l'idée de dégénérescence en médecine mentale.* Paris, 1913.

Grasset, Joseph. *Demi-fous et demi-responsables.* Paris, 1907.

Guillot, Adolphe. *Les prisons de Paris et les prisonniers.* Paris, 1889.

Hélie, Jean. *Le vagabondage des mineurs.* Mayenne, 1899.

Homberg, Théodore. *Etudes sur le vagabondage.* Paris, 1880.

Jacoby, Paul. *Etude sur les sélections chez l'homme.* 2d ed. Paris, 1905.

Joly, Henri. *Le crime—étude sociale.* Paris, 1888.

———. *La France criminelle.* Paris, 1889.

Krafft-Ebing, Richard von. *Psychopathia Sexualis: A Medico-Forensic Study.* Translated by Dr. Harry E. Wedeck. New York, 1965.

Lacassagne, Alexandre. *Peine de mort et criminalité: L'accroissement de la criminalité et l'application de la peine capitale.* Paris, 1908.

———. *Précis de médecine légale.* Paris, 1906.

———. *Les tatouages—étude anthropologique et médico-légale.* Paris, 1881.

———. *Des transformations du droit pénal et le progrès de la médecine légale de 1810 à 1912.* Lyon, 1913.

Lacassagne, Alexandre and Thoinot, Louis. *Le vade-mecum du médecin-expert.* 3d ed. Paris, 1911.

Lagrésille, Alfred. *Vagabondage et de la transportation.* Nancy, 1881.

Laurent, Emile. *L'année criminelle (1889-1890).* Paris, 1891.

———. *L'anthropologie criminelle et les nouvelles théories du crime.* 2d ed. Paris, 1893.

———. *Le criminel aux points de vue anthropologique, psychologique et social.* Paris, 1908.

———. *La neurasthénie et son traitement.* Paris, 1895.

———. *Précis d'éducation physique moderne.* Paris, 1906.

Lavrand, Hubert. *Traitement de la volonté et psychothérapie.* Paris, 1907.

LeBon Gustave. *La psychologie des foules.* Paris, 1895.

Le Dantec, Félix. *Science et conscience.* Paris, 1908.

LeGrain, Paul-Maurice. *Dégénérescence sociale et alcoolisme.* Paris, 1895.

Le Grand du Saulle, Henri, et al. *Traité de médecine légale de jurisprudence médicale, et de toxicologie.* Paris, 1886.

LeLorraine, E. *De l'aliéné au point de vue de la responsabilité pénale.* Paris, 1882.

LeRoux, Charles. *Le vagabondage et mendicité à Paris.* Paris, 1907.

Leroy-Beaulieu, Paul. *La question de la population.* Paris, 1911.

Levillain, Fernand. *La neurasthénie.* Paris, 1891.

Lombroso, Cesare. *L'homme criminel.* Paris, 1887.

Lombroso, Cesare and Laschi, R. *Le crime politique et les révolutions.* Paris, 1892.

Lombroso-Ferrero, Gina. *Criminal Man According to the Classification of Cesare Lombroso.* New York, 1911.

Macé, Gaston. *Le gibier de Saint-Lazare.* Paris, 1888.

Magitot, Emile. *Lettres de Rome.* Havre, 1894.

Magnan, Valentin and LeGrain, Paul Maurice. *Les dégénérés.* Paris, 1895.

Mairet, Albert. *Le régime des aliénés: Révision de la loi de 1838.* Paris, 1914.

————. *La responsabilité: Etude psycho-physiologique.* Paris, 1907.

Marie, A. and Meunier, Raymond. *Les vagabonds.* Paris, 1908.

Masoin, Paul. *Alcoolisme et criminalité.* Paris, 1891.

Massis, Henri and de Tarde, Alfred. *L'esprit de la nouvelle Sorbonne.* Paris, 1911.

Mathé, L. *La responsabilité atténuée.* Paris, 1911.

Maurel, E. *De la dépopulation en France.* Paris, 1896.

Michaux, Hubert. *Etude sur la question des peines.* Paris, 1872.

Morache, Georges. *La responsabilité.* Paris, 1906.

Nass, Lucien, and Witkowsky, A. J. *Le nu au théâtre.* Paris, 1909.

Pagnier, Armand. *Du vagabondage et des vagabonds.* Paris, 1906.

Picard, Roger. *La philosophie sociale de Renouvier.* Paris, 1908.

Prévost-Paradol, Lucien. *La France nouvelle.* Paris, 1868.

Proal, Louis. *Crime et la peine.* Paris, 1892.

————. *La criminalité politique.* Paris, 1898.

Proust, Adrien and Ballet, Gilbert. *L'hygiène du neurasthénique.* Paris, 1897.

Raux, Emile, *Nos jeunes détenus: Etude sur l'enfance coupable.* Lyon and Paris, 1890.

Reinach, Joseph. *Les récidivistes.* Paris, 1882.

————. *La vie politique de Léon Gambetta.* Paris, 1917.

Ribot, Théodule. *Les maladies de la volonté.* Paris, 1884.

Rouhet, Georges and Desbonnet, A. *L'art de créer le pur-sang humain.* Paris, 1908.

Ryckère, Raymond de. *La servante criminelle: Etude de criminologie professionelle.* Paris, 1908.

Saleilles, Raymond. *L'individualisation de la peine.* Paris, 1898.

Salomon, L. *L'alcool et la dépopulation de la France.* Paris, n.d.

Sévin-Desplaces, Louis. *Récidivistes et patronage des libérés.* Paris, 1882.

Sighele, Scipio. *La foule criminelle.* 2d French ed. Paris, 1901.

Steinheil, Marguerite. *My Memoirs.* London, 1912.

Tarnowsky, Pauline. *Les femmes homicides.* Paris, 1908.

Testut, Eugène. *Les vagabonds mineurs.* Paris, 1908.

Thulié, Henri. *La lutte contre la dégénérescence et la criminalité.* 2d ed. Paris, 1912.

BIBLIOGRAPHY

Tissié, Philippe. *L'évolution de l'éducation physique en France et en Belgique (1900-1910)*. Pau, 1911.

———. *L'exercise physique au point de vue thérapeutique*. Bordeaux, 1901.

———. *La fatigue et l'entraînement physique*. Paris, 1897.

Troismaux, Edgard. *Les procès célèbres de l'année 1904-1905*. Paris, 1905.

Vibert, Charles. *Précis de médecine légale*. 7th ed. Paris, 1908.

Vidal, Georges. *Cours de droit criminel et de science pénitentiaire*. 2d ed. Paris, 1902.

———. *Principes fondamentaux de la pénalité dans les systèmes les plus modernes*. Paris, 1890.

Vuillermet, L. *Le suicide d'un race*. Paris, 1911.

Modern Secondary Sources

Abbatiateci, A., et al. *Crimes et criminalité en France sous l'ancien régime*. Paris, 1971.

Albert, Pierre, et al., eds. *Histoire générale de la presse française*. Vol. 3. Paris, 1967.

Anderson, Malcolm. *Conservative Politics in France*. London, 1974.

Anderson, Robert D. *France 1870-1914: Politics and Society*. London, 1977.

Armengaud, André. *Les Français et Malthus*. Paris, 1975.

———. *La population française au XIXᵉ siècle*. Paris, 1971.

Azéma, Jean Pierre and Winock, Michel. *La IIIᵉ République (1870-1940)*. Paris, 1976.

Baal, Gérard. "Un salon dreyfusard, des lendemains de l'Affaire à la grande guerre: La marquise Arconati–Visconti." *Revue d'histoire moderne et contemporaine* 28 (1981): 433-463.

Baldwin, P. M. "Liberalism, Naturalism and Degeneration: The Case of Max Nordau." *Central European History* 13 (June 1980): 99-120.

Barral, Pierre. *Les fondateurs de la IIIᵉ République*. Paris, 1968.

Barrows, Susanna. "After the Commune: Alcoholism, Temperance, and Literature in the Early Third Republic." In John Merriman, ed., *Consciousness and Class Experience in Nineteenth-Century Europe*. (New York, 1979).

———. *Distorting Mirrors: Visions of the Crowd in Late Nineteenth-Century France*. New Haven, 1981.

Baruk, Henri. *La psychiatrie française de Pinel à nos jours*. Paris, 1967.

Bastié, Jean. *La croissance de la banlieue parisienne*. Paris, 1964.

Becker, George. *The Mad Genius Controversy: A Study in the Sociology of Deviance*. London and Beverly Hills, 1978.

Becker, Howard S. *Outsiders: Studies in the Sociology of Deviance.* New York, 1973.

Becker, Jean-Jacques. *1914: Comment les Français sont entrés dans la guerre.* Paris, 1977.

Bender, Donald. "The Development of French Anthropology." *Journal of the History of the Behavioral Sciences* 1 (April 1965): 139-151.

Bénéton, Philippe. "La génération de 1912-1914: Image, mythe, ou réalité." *Revue française de science politique* 21 (October 1971): 981-1010.

Bensman, Joseph and Lilienfeld, Robert. *Craft and Consciousness: Occupational Technique and the Development of World Images.* New York, 1973.

Bertocci, Phillip. *Jules Simon: Republican Anti-Clericalism and Cultural Politics in France, 1848-1886.* Columbia, Mo., 1978.

Besnard, Philippe. "Durkheim et les femmes, ou le suicide inachevé." *Revue française de sociologie* 14 (September 1973): 37-60.

Black, D. *The Behavior of Law.* New York, 1976.

Bléandonu, Gerard and Le Gaufey, Guy. "The Creation of the Insane Asylums of Auxerre and Paris." In Robert Forster and Orest Ranum, eds., *Deviants and the Abandoned in French Society.* Translated by Elborg Forster and Patricia Ranum. Baltimore, 1978.

Bonnefous, Edouard. *Histoire politique de la troisième République 1906-1914.* Vol. 3. Paris, 1956.

Borel, Jacques. *Du concept de dégénérescence à la notion d'alcoolisme dans la médecine contemporaine: Les campagnes antialcoolismes de 1865 à 1965.* Montpellier, 1968.

Bowditch, John. "The Concept of Elan Vital: A Rationalization of Weakness." In Edward M. Earle, ed., *Modern France.* Princeton, N.J., 1951.

Bury, J.P.T. *Gambetta and the Making of the Third Republic.* London, 1973.

Candeloro, Giorgio. *Storia dell'Italia moderna: Lo sviluppo del capitalismo e del movimento operaio.* Vol. 6. Milan, 1970.

Canguilhem, Georges. *Le normal et le pathologique.* 3d ed. Paris, 1975.

Cannavo, A. "Le référendum du 'Petit Parisien' sur la peine de mort." Paris, n.d.

Carrol, E. Malcolm. *French Public Opinion and Foreign Affairs, 1870-1914.* New York, 1931.

Carroll, Denis and Pinatel, Jean, et al. *Les Sciences sociales dans l'enseignement.* Vol. 7 *Criminologie.* Paris, 1956.

Carter, A. E. *The Idea of Decadence in French Literature, 1830-1900.* Toronto, 1958.

BIBLIOGRAPHY

Castel, Robert. *L'ordre psychiatrique: L'âge d'or d'aliénisme.* Paris, 1976.

Charles, Raymond. *Histoire du droit pénal.* 3d ed. Paris, 1969.

Chastenet, Jacques. *La France de M. Fallières.* Paris, 1949.

———. *Histoire de la troisième République: Jours inquiets et jours sanglants.* Vol. 4. Paris, 1957.

Chen, Yak-Yon. *Etudes statistiques sur la criminalité en France de 1855 à 1930.* Paris, 1937.

Chevalier, Louis. *Laboring Classes and Dangerous Classes in Paris during the First Half of the Nineteenth Century.* Translated by Frank Jellinek. New York, 1973.

Clark, Terry N., ed. *Gabriel Tarde: On Communications and Social Influence.* Chicago, 1969.

Cobb, Richard. *A Second Identity: Essays on France and French History.* London, 1969.

Coleman, William. "Health and Hygiene in the Encyclopédie: A Medical Doctrine for the Bourgeoisie." *Journal of the History of Medicine and Allied Sciences* 29 (1974): 399-421.

Collini, Stefan. *Liberalism and Sociology: L. T. Hobhouse and Political Argument in England, 1880-1914.* Cambridge, 1975.

Cominos, Peter. "Late Victorian Sexual Respectability and the Social System." *International Review of Social History* 8 (1963): 18-48, 216-250.

Conry, Yvette. *L'introduction du Darwinisme en France au XIXe siècle.* Paris, 1974.

Cooper, David. *The Lesson of the Scaffold.* London, 1974.

Corbin, Alain. *Les Filles de noce: Misère sexuelle et prostitution aux 19e et 20e siècles.* Paris, 1978.

———. "Le péril vénérien au début du siècle: Prophylaxie sanitaire et prophylaxie morale." *L'haleine des faubourgs. Recherches.* No. 29 (December 1977): 245-283.

Coser, Lewis, ed. *The Sociology of Georg Simmel.* New York, 1950.

Coury, Charles. *L'enseignement de la médecine en France.* Paris, 1968.

Croce, Benedetto. *A History of Italy: 1871-1915.* Translated by Cecilia M. Ady. New York, 1963.

Curtis, L. Perry, Jr. *Apes and Angels: The Irishman in Victorian Caricature.* Washington D.C., 1971.

David, René. *French Law: Its Structure, Sources, and Methodology.* Translated by Michael Kindred. Baton Rouge, 1972.

Deyon, Pierre. *Le temps des prisons: Essai sur l'histoire de la délinquance et les origines du système pénitentiaire.* Lille, 1975.

Digeon, Claude. *La crise allemande de la pensée française, 1870-1914.* Paris, 1959.

Donovan, James M. "Justice Unblind: The Juries and the Criminal Classes in France, 1825-1914," *Journal of Social History* 19 (Fall 1981): 89-108.

Donzelot, Jacques. *The Policing of Families*. Translated by Robert Hurley. New York, 1979.

Douglas, Jack D. *The Social Meaning of Suicide*. Princeton, N.J., 1967.

Dupeux, Georges. *French Society 1789-1970*. Translated by Peter Wait. London, 1976.

Duprat, Catherine. "Punir et guérir: En 1819, la prison des philanthropes." In Michelle Perrot, ed., *L'Impossible prison*. Paris, 1980.

Ehrenberg, Alain, ed. *Aimez-vous les stades? Les origines historiques des politiques sportives en France (1870-1930)*. Recherches. No. 34 (April 1980).

Elwitt, Sanford. *The Making of the Third Republic: Class and Politics in France, 1868-1884*. Baton Rouge, 1975.

Engelhardt, Knut. *Psychoanalyse des Strafenden Gesellschaft*. Frankfurt am Main, 1976.

Ericson, Richard V. *Criminal Reactions: The Labelling Perspective*. Lexington, Mass., 1975.

Erikson, Kai. *Wayward Puritans: A Study in the Sociology of Deviance*. New York, 1966.

Evans, Richard J. *The Feminist Movement in Germany, 1894-1933*. London and Beverly Hills, 1976.

———. "Prostitution, State, and Society in Imperial Germany." *Past and Present* 70 (1976): 106-129.

Farmer, Paul. *France Reviews Its Revolutionary Origins: Social Politics and Historical Opinion in the Third Republic*. New York, 1963.

Foucault, Michel. *The Birth of the Clinic: An Archaeology of Medical Perception*. Translated by A. M. Sheridan Smith. New York, 1975.

———. *Discipline and Punish: The Birth of the Prison*. Translated by Alan Sheridan. New York, 1977.

———. *The History of Sexuality*. Vol. 1. Translated by Robert Hurley. New York, 1980.

———, ed. *I, Pierre Rivière, Having Slaughtered My Mother, My Sister, and My Brother*. Translated by Frank Jellinek. New York, 1975.

———. *Madness and Civilization: A History of Insanity in the Age of Reason*. Translated by Richard Howard. New York, 1973.

———. *Mental Illness and Psychology*. Translated by Alan Sheridan. New York, 1976.

———. *Power/Knowledge: Selected Interviews and Other Writings, 1972-1977*. Edited by Colin Gordon. Translated by Colin Gordon, Leo Marshall, John Mepham, and Kate Soper. New York, 1980.

BIBLIOGRAPHY

Friedmann, Georges, ed. *Villes et campagnes.* Paris, n.d.
Gaillac, Henri. *Les maisons de correction, 1830-1945.* Paris, 1971.
Gaudemet, Yves-Henri. *Les juristes et la vie politique de la IIIe République.* Paris, 1970.
Geisert, M. *Le système criminaliste de Tarde.* Paris, 1935.
Giddens, Anthony. *Studies in Social and Political Theory.* London, 1977.
Gillet, Bernard. *Histoire du sport.* 6th ed. Paris, 1980.
Girardet, Raoul. *Le nationalisme français, 1871-1914.* Paris, 1966.
Goguel, François. *La politique des partis dans la IIIe République.* 3d ed. Paris, 1958.
Goldstein, Jan. "The Hysteria Diagnosis and the Politics of Anticlericalism in Late Nineteenth-Century France." *Journal of Modern History* 54 (June 1982): 209-239.
Gonjo, Yves. "Le Plan Freycinet, 1878-1882: Un aspect de la 'grande dépression économique' en France." *Revue historique* (July-September 1972): 49-79.
Gould, Stephen Jay. *The Mismeasure of Man.* New York, 1981.
Gove, Walter R. *The Labelling of Deviance: Evaluating a Perspective.* London and Beverly Hills, 1975.
Greenberg, David F., ed. *Corrections and Punishment.* Sage Criminal Justice System Annuals, Vol. 8. London and Beverly Hills, 1977.
Guilleminault, Gilbert, ed. *La belle époque.* Paris, 1958.
Guirol, Pierre. "Présentation, problèmes d'histoire de la presse." *Revue d'histoire moderne et contemporaine* 18 (1971): 481-488.
Gurr, Ted Robert. *Rogues, Rebels, and Reformers: A Political History of Urban Crime and Conflict.* London and Beverly Hills, 1976.
Gurr, Ted Robert; Grabosky, Peter N.; and Hula, Richard C. *The Politics of Crime and Conflict: A Comparative History of Four Cities.* London and Beverly Hills, 1977.
Halbwachs, Maurice. *The Causes of Suicide.* Translated by Harold Goldblatt. New York, 1979.
Hale, Oron J. *Germany and the Diplomatic Revolution: A Study in Diplomacy and the Press.* Philadelphia, 1931.
Harrison, Brian. *Drink and the Victorians: The Temperance Question in England, 1815-1872.* Pittsburgh, 1971.
Hartman, Mary. *Victorian Murderesses: A True History of Thirteen Respectable French and English Women Accused of Unspeakable Crimes.* New York, 1977.
Hayes, Carlton J. H. *France, a Nation of Patriots.* New York, 1930.
Hayward, J.E.S. "The Official Philosophy of the French Third Republic: Léon Bourgeois and Solidarism." *International Review of Social History* 6 (1961): 20-32.

Heider, Fritz. *The Psychology of Interpersonal Relations.* New York, 1958.

Henriques, H. R. "The Rise and Decline of the Separate System of Prison Discipline." *Past and Present* 54 (1972): 61-93.

Heppenstall, Rayner. *Little Patterns of French Crime.* London, 1969.

Hildreth, Martha. "The Foundations of the Modern Medical System in France: Physicians, Public Health Advocates, and the Medical Legislation of 1892 and 1893." Department of History, University of California, Riverside, 1980.

Huber, Michel. *La population de la France pendant la guerre.* Paris, n.d.

Hufton, Olwen. *The Poor of Eighteenth-Century France, 1750-1789.* Oxford, 1974.

Hull, Isabel V. *The Entourage of Kaiser Wilhelm II, 1888-1918.* Cambridge, 1982.

———. "Reflections on 'Nationalism and Respectability.' " *Journal of Contemporary History* 17 (1982): 247-268.

Hutton, Patrick H. "The History of Mentalities: The New Map of Cultural History." *History and Theory* 20 (October 1981): 237-259.

Hynes, Samuel. *The Edwardian Turn of Mind.* Princeton, N.J., 1968.

Ignatieff, Michael. *A Just Measure of Pain: The Penitentiary in the Industrial Revolution, 1750-1850.* New York, 1978.

Imbert, Jean and Levasseur, Georges. *Le pouvoir, les juges, et les bourreaux.* Paris, 1972.

Ingraham, Barton L. *Political Crime in Europe: A Comparative Study of France, Germany, and England.* Berkeley, 1979.

Jacquemet, Gérard. "Médecine et 'maladies populaires' dans le Paris de la fin de XIXᵉ siècle." *L'haleine des faubourgs. Recherches.* No. 29 (December 1977): 349-364.

Jameson, Frederic. *The Prison-House of Language: A Critical Account of Structuralism and Russian Formalism.* Princeton, N.J., 1972.

Jeffrey, Clarence Ray. "The Historical Development of Criminology." In Hermann Mannheim, ed., *Pioneers in Criminology.* 2d ed. Montclair, N.J., 1972.

Johnson, Douglas. "French War Aims and the Crisis of the Third Republic." In Barry Hunt and Adria Preston, eds., *War Aims and Strategic Policy in the Great War, 1914-1918.* Totowa, N.J., 1977.

Jones, Edward E., et al. eds. *Attribution: Perceiving the Causes of Behavior.* Morristown, N.J., 1972.

Jones, Gareth Stedman. *Outcast London: A Study in the Relationship between Classes in Victorian Society.* Oxford, 1971.

Julliard, Jacques. *Clemenceau, briseur des grèves.* Paris, 1965.

Kayser, Jacques. *Les grandes batailles du radicalisme, 1820-1901.* Paris, 1962.

BIBLIOGRAPHY

Lachance, Paul. "The Nature and Function of Generational Discourse in France on the Eve of World War I." In Seymour Drescher, David Sabean, and Allan Sharlin, eds., *Political Symbolism in Modern Europe: Essays in Honor of George L. Mosse*. New Brunswick, N.J., 1982.

Laingui, André and Lebigre, Arlette. *Histoire du droit pénal*. Paris, 1979.

Lalouette, Jacqueline. "Discours bourgeois sur les débits de boisson aux alentours de 1900." *L'haleine des faubourgs. Recherches*. No. 29 (December 1977): 315-347.

Lamarche-Vadel, Gaëtane, and Preli, Georges. *L'asile. Recherches*. No. 31 (February 1978).

Landes, David. *The Unbound Prometheus: Technological Change, 1750 to the Present*. Cambridge, 1969.

Lanteri-Laura, Georges. *Lecture des perversions: Histoire de leur appropriation médicale*. Paris, 1979.

Larguier, Jean. *Le droit pénal*. 3d ed. Paris, 1969.

Lauderdale, Pat, ed. *A Political Analysis of Deviance*. Minneapolis, 1980.

Léauté, Jacques. *Criminologie et science pénitentiaire*. Paris, 1972.

Legrand, L. *L'influence du positivisme dans l'oeuvre scolaire de Jules Ferry*. Paris, 1961.

Léonard, Jacques. *La France médicale: Médecins et malades au XIXᵉ siècle*. Paris, 1978.

———. "L'historien et le philosophe: A propos de *Surveiller et punir*." In Michelle Perrot, ed., *L'impossible prison*. Paris, 1980.

———. *La médecine entre les savoirs et les pouvoirs: Histoire intellectuelle et politique de la médecine française au XIXᵉ siècle*. Paris, 1982.

———. *La vie quotidienne du médecin de province au XIXᵉ siècle*. Paris, 1977.

Levasseur, Georges, and Doucet, Jean-Paul. *Le droit pénal appliqué*. Paris, n.d.

Locke, Robert. *French Legitimists and the Politics of Moral Order in the Early Third Republic*. Princeton, N.J., 1974.

Lodhi, Abdul, and Tilly, Charles. "Urbanization, Crime, and Collective Violence in Nineteenth-Century France." *American Journal of Sociology* 79 (September 1973): 296-318.

Loubère, Leo A. *Radicalism in Mediterranean France: Its Rise and Decline, 1848-1914*. Albany, N.Y., 1977.

Lukes, Steven. *Emile Durkheim: His Life and Work*. London, 1973.

McHale, Vincent E., and Johnson, Eric A. "Urbanization, Industrialization and Crime in Imperial Germany." *Social Science History* 1 (Fall 1976): 45-78, and (Winter 1977): 210-247.

Machelon, Jean-Pierre. *La République contre les libertés? Les restrictions aux libertés publiques de 1879 à 1914.* Paris, 1976.

Maingueneau, Dominique. *Les livres d'école de la République, 1870-1914: Discours et idéologie.* Paris, 1979.

Maitron, Jean. *Ravachol et les anarchistes.* Paris, 1964.

Mandell, Richard D. *The First Modern Olympics.* Berkeley, 1976.

Mannheim, Hermann. *Group Problems in Crime and Punishment.* London, 1955.

————, ed. *Pioneers in Criminology.* 2d ed. Montclair, N.J., 1972.

Marrus, Michael R. "Social Drinking in the Belle Epoque." *Journal of Social History* 7 (1974): 115-141.

Martin, Ben F. *Count Albert de Mun, Paladin of the Third Republic.* Chapel Hill, 1978.

Mayeur, Jean-Marie. *Les débuts de la IIIe République, 1871-1898.* Paris, 1973.

Megill, Alan. "Foucault, Structuralism, and the Ends of History." *Journal of Modern History* 91 (September 1979): 451-503.

Merton, Robert and Nisbet, Robert A. *Contemporary Social Problems.* New York, 1966.

Mitchell, Allan. *The German Influence in France after 1870.* Chapel Hill, 1981.

Mitchell, Harvey. "Rationality and Control in French Eighteenth-Century Medical Views of the Peasantry." *Comparative Studies in Society and History* 21 (January 1979): 82-112.

Monnerville, Gaston. *Clemenceau.* Paris, 1968.

Mosse, George L. "Max Nordau and His *Degeneration.*" Introduction to *Degeneration.* New York, 1968.

————. "Nationalism and Respectability: Normal and Abnormal Sexuality in the Nineteenth Century." *Journal of Contemporary History* 17 (1982): 221-246.

Musil, Robert. *The Man without Qualities.* Vol. I. Translated by Eithne Wilkins and Ernst Kaiser. New York, 1980.

Nguyen, Victor. "Situation des études maurrasiennes: Contribution à l'histoire de la presse et des mentalités." *Revue d'histoire moderne et contemporaine* 18 (1971): 503-538.

Nye, Robert A. "Crime in Modern Societies: Some Research Strategies for Historians." *Journal of Social History* 11 (1978): 492-507.

————. "Degeneration and the Medical Model of Cultural Crisis in the French *Belle Epoque.*" In Seymour Drescher, David Sabean, and Allan Sharlin, eds., *Political Symbolism in Modern Europe.* New Brunswick, N.J., 1982.

————. "Degeneration, Neurasthenia and the Culture of Sport in *Belle*

Epoque France." *Journal of Contemporary History* 17 (January 1982): 51-68.

——. "Heredity or Milieu: The Foundations of Modern European Criminological Theory." *Isis* 67 (September 1976): 335-355.

——. "Heredity, Pathology, and Psychoneuroses in Durkheim's Early Work." *Knowledge and Society* 4 (1982): 103-142

——. *The Origins of Crowd Psychology: Gustave LeBon and the Crisis of Mass Democracy in the Third Republic.* London and Beverly Hills, 1975.

O'Brien, Patricia. *The Promise of Punishment: Prisons in Nineteenth-Century France.* Princeton, N.J., 1981.

Paul, Harry. *The Sorcerer's Apprentice.* Gainesville, Fla., 1972.

Pelicier, Yves, and Thullier, Guy. "Pour une histoire de l'éducation des enfants idiots en France (1830-1914)." *Revue historique* 261 (January-March 1979): 99-130.

Perrot, Michelle. "Dans la France de la belle époque, les 'Apaches,' premières bandes des jeunes." In *Les marginaux et les exclus dans l'histoire.* Paris, 1979.

——. "Délinquance et système pénitentiaire en France au XIXᵉ siècle." *Annales: Economies, sociétés, civilisations* 30 (1975): 67-91.

——. "La fin des vagabonds." *L'histoire* 3 (July-August 1978): 23-33.

——, ed. *L'impossible prison: Recherches sur le système pénitentiaire au XIXᵉ siècle.* Paris, 1980.

——. *Les ouvriers en grève: France, 1871-1890.* 2 vols. Paris, 1974.

Peter, J.-P. "Un enquête de la Société royale de médecine (1774-1794): Malades et maladies à la fin du XVIIIᵉ siècle." *Annales: Economies, sociétés, civilisations* 22 (1967): 711-751.

Petit, Jacques. "Folie, langage, pouvoirs en Maine-et-Loire." *Revue d'histoire moderne et contemporaine* 27 (1980): 529-564.

Ponty, Janine. "La presse quotidienne et l'affaire Dreyfus en 1898-1899: Essai de typologie." *Revue d'histoire moderne et contemporaine* 21 (1974): 193-220.

Pope, Whitney. *Durkheim's Suicide: A Classic Analyzed.* Chicago, 1979.

Prost, Antoine, and Rosenzweig, Christian. "Measurement of Attitude Changes among the Members of the French Chamber of Deputies, 1882-1884." In William O. Aydelotte, ed., *The History of Parliamentary Behavior.* Princeton, N.J., 1977.

Quetel, Claude. "L'asile d'aliénés en 1900." *L'histoire* 7 (December 1978): 25-34.

Quinney, Richard. *The Social Reality of Crime.* Boston, 1970.

Rabinbach, Anson. "The Body without Fatigue: A Nineteenth-Century Utopia." In Seymour Drescher, David Sabean, and Allan Sharlin, eds., *Political Symbolism in Modern Europe*. New Brunswick, N.J., 1982.

Radzinowicz, Leon. *Ideology and Crime*. New York, 1966.

———. *In Search of Criminology*. Cambridge, Mass., 1962.

Radzinowicz, Leon, and Hood, Roger. "Incapacitating the Habitual Criminal: The English Experience." *Michigan Law Review* 78 (August 1980): 1305-1389.

Rearick, Charles. "Festivals in Modern France: The Experience of the Third Republic." *Journal of Contemporary History* 12 (1977): 435-460.

Rébérioux, Madeleine. *La République radicale, 1898-1914*. Paris, 1975.

Ridley, F. F. *Revolutionary Syndicalism in France*. Cambridge, 1973.

Ronsin, Francis. *La grève des ventres: Propagande néo-malthusienne et baisse de la natalité française (XIX-XX siècles)*. Paris, 1980.

Roth, Robert. *Pratiques pénitentiaires et théorie sociale: L'exemple de la prison de Genève (1825-1862)*. Geneva, 1981.

Royer, Jean-Pierre. *La société judiciaire depuis le XVIIIᵉ siècle*. Paris, 1979.

Ruggiero, Guido. *Violence in Early Renaissance Venice*. New Brunswick, N.J., 1980.

Sagarin, Edward, ed. *Deviance and Social Change*. London and Beverly Hills, 1977.

Savey-Casard, Paul. *La peine de mort*. Geneva, 1968.

Schnapper, Bernard. "La correction paternelle et le mouvement des idées au dix-neuvième siècle (1789-1935)." *Revue historique* 263 (April-June 1980): 320-349.

Schneider, William. "Toward the Improvement of the Human Race: The History of Eugenics in France." *Journal of Modern History* 54 (June 1982): 268-291.

Scott, John A. *Republican Ideas and the Liberal Tradition in France*. New York, 1966.

Scott, Robert A. and Douglas, Jack D., eds. *Theoretical Perspectives on Deviance*. New York, 1973.

Scull, Andrew. "Humanitarianism or Control? Some Observations on the Historiography of Anglo-American Psychiatry." *Rice University Studies* 67 (Winter 1981): 21-41.

———, ed. *Madhouses, Mad-Doctors, and Madmen. The Social History of Psychiatry in the Victorian Era*. Philadelphia, 1981.

———. *Museums of Madness: The Social Organization of Insanity in Nineteenth-Century England*. London, 1979.

Searle, G. M. *Eugenics and Politics in Britain, 1900-1914*. Leyden, 1976.

Sérieux, Paul. *Valentin Magnan: Sa vie et son oeuvre*. Paris, 1921.

BIBLIOGRAPHY

Smith, Roger. *Trial by Medicine: Insanity and Responsibility in Victorian Trials.* Edinburgh, 1981.

Soffer, Reba N. *Ethics and Society in England: The Revolution in the Social Sciences, 1870-1914.* Berkeley, 1977.

Soloway, Richard. "Counting the Degenerates: The Statistics of Race Deterioration in Edwardian England." *Journal of Contemporary History* 17 (1982): 137-164.

Sorlin, Pierre. *La société française, 1840-1914.* Paris, 1969.

———. *Waldeck-Rousseau.* Paris, 1966.

Spengler, Joseph J. *France Faces Depopulation.* Durham, N.C., 1938.

Spivak, Marcel. "Le développement de l'éducation physique et du sport français de 1892 à 1914." *Revue d'histoire moderne et contemporaine* 24 (1977): 28-48.

Stark, Gary D. "Pornography, Society and the Law in Imperial Germany." *Central European History* 14 (September 1981): 200-229.

Staum, Martin S. *Cabanis: Enlightenment and Medical Philosophy in the French Revolution.* Princeton, N.J., 1980.

Steakley, James D. "Iconography of a Scandal: Political Cartoons of the Eulenburg Affair." *Studies in Visual Communication* (March 1983).

Stearns, Peter. *Lives of Labor: Work in a Maturing Industrial Society.* New York, 1975.

Sternhell, Zeev. *La droite révolutionnaire, 1885-1914: Les origines françaises du fascisme.* Paris, 1978.

Stock, Phyllis. "Students versus the University in Pre-World War Paris." *French Historical Studies* 7 (Spring 1971): 83-110.

Stromberg, Roland N. *Redemption by War: The Intellectuals and 1914.* Lawrence, Kans., 1982.

Sussman, George D. "The Glut of Doctors in Nineteenth-Century France." *Comparative Studies in Society and History* 19 (July 1977): 287-304.

Swain, Gladys. *Le sujet de la folie: Naissance de la psychiatrie.* Toulouse, 1977.

Swart, Koenraad. *The Sense of Decadence in Nineteenth-Century France.* The Hague, 1964.

Sykes, Gresham M. "The Rise of Critical Criminology." *Journal of Criminal Law and Criminology* 65 (June 1974): 209-213.

Szabo, Denis. *Crimes et villes.* Paris, 1960.

Szasz, Thomas. *The Manufacture of Madness.* New York, 1970.

———. *The Myth of Mental Illness.* New York, 1961.

Tannenbaum, Edward. *1900: The Generation before the Great War.* Garden City, N.Y., 1976.

Taylor, Ian; Young, Jack; and Walton, Paul. *The New Criminology: For a Social Theory of Deviance.* London, 1973.

Teeters, Negley H. *New Horizons in Criminology.* 2d ed. New York, 1951.

Thompson, Edward P. *Whigs and Hunters: The Origin of the Black Act.* New York, 1975.

Tilly, Charles, and Shorter, Edward. *Strikes in France, 1830-1968.* Cambridge, 1974.

Tobias, John Jacob. *Crime and Industrial Society in the Nineteenth Century.* London, 1972.

Vaux de Foletier, François. *Les bohémiens en France au XIXᵉ siècle.* Paris, 1981.

Vexliard, Alex. "La disparition du vagabondage comme fleau social universal." *Revue de l'Institut de sociologie* 36 (1963): 53-80.

Voget, Fred W. "Progress, Science, History and Evolution in Anthropology." *Journal of the History of the Behavioral Sciences* 3 (April 1967): 132-155.

Vold, George B. *Theoretical Criminology.* New York, 1958.

Waldberg, Patrick. *Eros in la Belle Epoque.* Translated by Helen R. Lane. New York, 1969.

Walkowitz, Judith. *Prostitution and Victorian Society: Women, Class, and the State.* Cambridge, 1980.

Watson, D. R. "The Nationalist Movement in Paris, 1900-1906." In David Shapiro, ed. *The Right in France, 1890-1919.* Saint Antony's Papers, no. 13. Carbondale, Ill., 1962.

Weber, Eugen. "Gymnastics and Sports in Fin-de-Siècle France: Opium of the Classes?" *American Historical Review* 76 (February 1971): 70-99.

———. *The Nationalist Revival in France, 1905-1914.* Berkeley, 1959.

———. *Peasants into Frenchmen: The Modernization of Rural France, 1870-1914.* Stanford, Calif., 1977.

———. "Pierre de Coubertin and the Introduction of Organized Sport in France." *Journal of Contemporary History* 5 (1970): 3-26.

Weisz, George. "The Politics of Medical Professionalization in France, 1845-1848." *Journal of Social History* 12 (1978): 1-30.

———. "Reform and Conflict in French Medical Education, 1870-1914." In George Weisz and Robert Fox, eds., *The Organization of Science and Technology in France, 1808-1914.* Cambridge, 1980.

Williams, Roger L. *Manners and Murders in the World of Louis-Napoleon.* Seattle, 1976.

Winter, J. M. "Military Fitness and Civilian Health in Britain during the First World War." *Journal of Contemporary History* 15 (1980): 211-244.

BIBLIOGRAPHY

Wohl, Robert. *The Generation of 1914*. Cambridge, Mass., 1979.
Wright, Gordon. *Between the Guillotine and Liberty: Two Centuries of the Crime Problem in France*. New York, 1983.
Wrigley, E. A., ed. *Nineteenth-Century Society: Essays in the Use of Quantitative Methods for the Study of Social Data*. Cambridge, 1972.
Zehr, Howard. *Crime and the Development of Modern Society: Patterns of Criminality in Nineteenth-Century Germany and France*. London, 1976.
Zeldin, Theodore. *France, 1848-1945*. 2 vols. Oxford, 1973, 1977.

INDEX

Adam, Paul, 226n, 326-27
Agadir Crisis, 314
Ajam, Pierre, 276, 294
Alain (Emile Chartier), 266
Albanel, Louis, 175
alcoholism: and crime, 215, 224-25, 235, 238, 240-42, 244-47, 298, 302-304, 306; and degeneration theory, 123, 143, 149, 152, 154, 158, 166, 235, 240, 245, 262, 302-304, 306, 321-22; and insanity, 123, 235, 238, 242, 245-47; statistics, 135-36
Allain-Targé, François, 52, 88, 91, 94
Allemane, Jean, 297, 301, 304-305
Alliance démocratique, 187-88
Alliance nationale pour l'accroissement de la population française, 167
anarchism, 178-81, 314
anti-semitism, 298-99
Apaches: and crime, 181, 201-202, 207-11, 215-19, 222-23, 226n, 290, 294, 302, 304; image in popular culture, 197-98, 201-202, 207-11; social and ecomomic origins, 199-201
Arconati-Visconti, Marquise, 315
asylums: law of 1838, 29-33, 227-28, 232, 234, 236-37, 247; *placement d'office*, 32, 229, 233, 238; *placement volontaire*, 32-33; private asylums, 30, 232, 238; public asylums, 30-34, 229, 232, 242-44
autopsies, 287-88

Ballet, Gilbert, 148-49, 251, 260, 323
Barrès, Maurice, 280-81, 298-99, 303-305, 308, 311, 317, 319
Barthélémy, Toussaint, 161
Beard, George M., 148, 321
Beaumont, Gustave, 35-36
Beccaria, Cesare, 34, 217n
Benedikt, Moritz, 106
Benoist, Charles, 220

Bentham, Jeremy, 35
Béranger, René, 61, 91, 93, 165, 174, 202, 216n
Bergeron, Jules, 155
Bernard, Claude, 43, 47, 122
Berr, Henri, 250-51
Berry, Georges, 279, 282-84, 294, 299
Bert, Paul, 68, 300
Bertheau, Charles, 73
Bertillon, Jacques, 167
Bigot, V., 64
Blanche, Esprit-Sylvestre, 77
bloc des gauches, 186-87
Blondel, Charles, 251
Boer War, 332
Bonaparte, Louis-Napoleon, 36
Bonaparte, Napoleon, 25, 27
Bonapartism, 52, 88, 138
Bonger, Willem, 131
Bourget, Paul, 253
Bourneville, D. M., 230, 235-36
Briand, Aristide, 268, 284-87, 292-93, 300-301, 307
Briand, Marcel, 234, 236
Brieux, Eugène, 162
Brisson, Henri, 88, 90, 298-99
Broca, Paul, 65-66, 108, 111, 122
Brouardel, Paul, 106, 108, 125, 252-53
Buimard, Achille, 256
Buisson, Ferdinand, 300

Canguilhem, Georges, 13n, 47, 121n
capital punishment: and anxieties about national decline, 181, 306-309; and the criminologists, 220-26; debates in the Chamber of Deputies, 277-307; debates in Penitentiary Society, 214-20, 282; and deterrence, 215-19, 280-95; in Europe, 281-82, 285-86; and judicial error, 288-90; legislative proposals to abolish, 188, 267, 276-77, 297; press opinion,

361

Library of Congress Cataloging in Publication Data

Nye, Robert A.
Crime, madness & politics in modern France.

Bibliography: p.   Includes index.

1. Public opinion—France—History—19th century.
2. Deviant behavior—Public opinion—History—19th century.
3. Physicians—France—Attitudes—History—19th century.
4. Degeneration—Public opinion—History—19th century.
5. France—Politics and government—1870-1940.
6. Criminal justice, Administration of—France—
History—19th century. I. Title. II. Title: Crime, madness, and
politics in modern France.
HN440.P8N94 1984   302.5'42'0944   83-43087
ISBN 0-691-05414-2